CW01162682

# The Middle-Income Trap in Central and Eastern Europe

New Perspectives on Central and Eastern European Studies

Published in association with the Herder Institute for Historical Research on East Central Europe, Marburg, Germany

**Series Editors**
Peter Haslinger, Director
Heidi Hein-Kircher, Head of the Department Academic Forum

Decades after the political changes that accompanied the fall of the Soviet Union, Eastern Europe remains one of the most misunderstood parts of the world. With a special focus on the Baltic states, Poland, the Czech Republic, Slovakia and Hungary, New Perspectives on Central and Eastern European Studies investigates the historical and social forces that have shaped the region, from ethnicity and religion to imperial legacies and national conflicts. Each volume in the series explores these and many other topics to contribute to a better understanding of contemporary Central and Eastern Europe today.

**Volume 4**
*The Middle-Income Trap in Central and Eastern Europe: Causes, Consequences and Strategies in Post-Communist Countries*
Edited by Yaman Kouli and Uwe Müller

**Volume 3**
*The World beyond the West: Perspectives from Eastern Europe*
Edited by Mariusz Kałczewiak and Magdalena Kozłowska

**Volume 2**
*Heritage under Socialism: Preservation in Eastern and Central Europe, 1945–1991*
Edited by Eszter Gantner, Corinne Geering and Paul Vickers

**Volume 1**
*Rampart Nations: Bulwark Myths of East European Multiconfessional Societies in the Age of Nationalism*
Edited by Liliya Berezhnaya and Heidi Hein-Kircher

# The Middle-Income Trap in Central and Eastern Europe

*Causes, Consequences and Strategies
in Post-Communist Countries*

Edited by
Yaman Kouli and Uwe Müller

berghahn
NEW YORK • OXFORD
www.berghahnbooks.com

First published in 2024 by
Berghahn Books
www.berghahnbooks.com

© 2024 Yaman Kouli and Uwe Müller

All rights reserved. Except for the quotation of short passages
for the purposes of criticism and review, no part of this book
may be reproduced in any form or by any means, electronic or
mechanical, including photocopying, recording, or any information
storage and retrieval system now known or to be invented,
without written permission of the publisher.

**Library of Congress Cataloging-in-Publication Data**

A C.I.P. cataloging record is available from the Library of Congress
Library of Congress Cataloging in Publication Control Number: 2023043243

**British Library Cataloguing in Publication Data**

A catalogue record for this book is available from the British Library

ISBN 978-1-80539-181-4 hardback
ISBN 978-1-80539-395-5 epub
ISBN 978-1-80539-182-1 web pdf

https://doi.org/10.3167/9781805391814

# Contents

| | |
|---|---|
| List of Illustrations | vii |
| Preface | xi |
| Abbreviations | xii |

**Introduction.** Transformation of the Transformation? The Middle-Income Trap and the Search for a New Development Strategy in the Post-Communist States of Central and Eastern Europe ............................................. 1
*Yaman Kouli and Uwe Müller*

## Part I. Historical Legacies

**Chapter 1.** Poland's Communist Heritage and Its Impact on Post-1990 Economic Development ............................................. 25
*Yaman Kouli*

**Chapter 2.** Institutional Development and Growth as Outputs of Early Transition Policies ............................................. 54
*Tal Kadayer*

## Part II. Development Strategies on the Economic, Entrepreneurial and Individual Level

**Chapter 3.** The Middle-Income Trap and Its Narrow Escape Hatches: Dependent Development and FDI-Led Growth in Romania ............................................. 97
*Cornel Ban and Zoltán Mihály*

**Chapter 4.** Between Domestic Entrepreneurship and Global Technology Chains: Upgrading Paths of Two Large IT Firms from Poland ............................................. 122
*Grzegorz Lechowski*

**Chapter 5.** The Value of Return Migration: The Case of Bulgaria ............................................. 143
*Birgit Glorius*

## Part III. The Impact of European Integration

**Chapter 6.** The Winners and Losers of Economic Openness: Eastern Europe's Growth Path Post-1989 — 169
*Kiril Kossev*

**Chapter 7.** Developmentalist Illusion? EU Cohesion Policy, Dependent Development and the State in East Central Europe — 204
*Daniel Šitera*

**Chapter 8.** East-Central Europe: The Eternal Periphery of the EU? — 231
*Christian Schweiger*

**Chapter 9.** Cohesion Policy for Escaping the Middle-Income Trap — 254
*Andrea Filippetti and Raffaele Spallone*

**Conclusion and Outlook** — 281
*Uwe Müller*

Index — 287

# Illustrations

## Figures

| | | |
|---|---|---|
| **Figure 1.1.** | GDP per capita (in 2011 US$). | 29 |
| **Figure 1.2.** | Relative share of overall industrial production. | 31 |
| **Figure 1.3.** | Employment share 1958–87. | 31 |
| **Figure 1.4.** | Equipment investments (1950 = 100). | 34 |
| **Figure 1.5.** | Gross capital formation per GDP (in percent). | 34 |
| **Figure 1.6.** | Gross capital stock of Poland, Hungary and Czechoslovakia (1950 = 100). | 35 |
| **Figure 1.7.** | NUTS1 Divisions of Poland, since 2018. | 37 |
| **Figure 1.8.** | Human capital stock (per person, 1945–2010). | 43 |
| **Figure 2.1.** | Corporate restructuring and GDP per capita (1990 value = 100). | 69 |
| **Figure 2.2.** | Competition enhancement and GDP per capita (1990 value = 100). | 76 |
| **Figure 3.1.** | Percentage growth in GDP (PPP-adjusted) 1990–2018 in selected regions. | 100 |
| **Figure 3.2.** | Percentage growth in GDP (PPP) 1990–2018. | 101 |
| **Figure 6.1.** | GDP growth rates across Eastern Europe and the former Soviet Union as compared to the industrialized Western market economies (GDP per capita growth, annual percentage, 1998–2019). | 175 |
| **Figure 6.2.** | GDP levels across Eastern Europe and the former Soviet Union as compared to the industrialized Western market economies (GDP per capita, constant 2010 US dollars, 1990–2019). | 178 |

**Figure 6.3.** Labour productivity across Eastern Europe and the former Soviet Union in comparison to the industrialized Western market economies (GDP per person employed, US dollars, constant prices, constant PPP, base year 2015). 179

**Figure 6.4.** Economic Complexity Index (index of trade of complex products, 1995–2018). 184

**Figure 6.5.** Labour productivity across cities in selected Eastern European countries (GDP per person employed, millions of USD, constant prices, constant PPP, base year 2015). 188

**Figure 6.6.** Economic activity by type of region, urban or rural (regional GDP, USD per head, constant prices, constant PPP, base year 2015). 191

**Figure 7.1.** Comparison of FDI net inflows and ESIF inflows into ECE, 2005–20 (as percentage of GDP). 207

**Figure 7.2.** Share of ESIF in the General Government Investment, 2008–20 (by percent). 217

**Figure 8.1.** Unemployment annual data by sex and age (1992–2020). 233

**Figure 8.2.** Purchasing power adjusted GDP per capita. 237

**Figure 8.3.** Gross wages and salaries per employee in 1,000 PPS in 2000 and 2017. 239

**Figure 8.4.** Persons at risk of poverty or social exclusion by degree of urbanisation – EU 2020 strategy. 239

**Figure 8.5.** Attitudes towards economic and monetary union. 245

## Tables

**Table 0.1.** Patents per 1 million inhabitants. 5

**Table 1.1.** Relative production efficiency per worker (total = 100). 33

**Table 1.2.** GDP per capita in Poland's NUTS1-regions (Poland = 100). 36

**Table 1.3.** Industrial production per worker (Poland = 100). 38

**Table 1.4.** Educational attainment for total population (1935–2010). — 44

**Table 2.1.** Privatization and enterprise restructuring policies 1989–95. — 65

**Table 2.2.** Competition enhancement policies 1989–95. — 67

**Table 2.3.** Enterprise restructuring policies and governance institutional indices. — 70

**Table 2.4.** Enterprise restructuring policies and economic freedom institutional indices. — 71

**Table 2.5.** Enterprise restructuring policies and private sector data 1991–98. — 73

**Table 2.6.** Enterprise restructuring policies and GDP growth 1990–95. — 74

**Table 2.7.** Competition transition policies and WGI Institutional indices. — 77

**Table 2.8.** Bankruptcy enforcement and legal framework ranking. — 78

**Table 2.9.** Competition transition policies and EFW institutional indices. — 79

**Table 2.10.** Competition transition policies and private sector data 1991–98. — 80

**Table 2.11.** Competition transition policies and GDP growth 1990–95. — 80

**Table 4.1.** Basic data on the two case-study firms (from company reports). — 124

**Table 4.2.** Sources of historical online data (1990–2017). — 138

**Table 5.1.** Key characteristics of the interviewed migrants. — 149

**Table 6.1.** GDP growth rates across Eastern Europe and the former Soviet Union as compared to the industrialized Western market economies (GDP per capita growth, average annual percentage, 1998–2019). — 176

**Table 6.2.** Patterns of economic openness and integration into the globalized market economy post-1989. 181

**Table 6.3.** Economic complexity index (index of trade of complex products, selected years). 185

**Table 6.4.** Patterns of development within regions and societies as a result of openness in and integration into the globalized market economy post-1989. 187

**Table 6.5.** Labour utilization, capital regions versus the average for the country (percent of total employment of population). 192

**Table 6.6.** Income inequality and poverty across Eastern Europe, various indicators. 195

**Table 6.7.** Regional well-being, various indicators, for Czech Republic, Poland and Slovak Republic in 2014. 197

**Table 7.1.** North-West, South and East according to the GDP per capita in PPS, 2000–18 (index: EU = 100, 4- to 5-year averages). 213

**Table 9.1.** R&D and innovation allocation in former objective 1 regions, percentage of total ERDF and cohesion funds. 270

**Table 9.2.** R&D and innovation allocation in less developed regions of CEE countries, percentage of total ERDF and cohesion funds. 271

# Preface

In all former socialist states of Central and Eastern Europe, there is a more or less intensive, public debate about the problem of the so-called middle-income trap. As a rule, the existence (or at least, in the near future, the danger) of this "trap" is recognized. While the causes for this trap are discussed, in the centre of the debate lies the question: what might be the best strategy to escape this trap? Initially, the problem appeared to be a matter of state economic policy. But the behaviour towards social and regional divergences, the design and implementation of education, research and migration policies are also affected by the middle-income trap. And, of course, in a market-based economic order "politics" of the national governments *and* the European Union can 'only' create framework conditions and – in some cases – support the development of knowledge-based industries. Finally, significant contributions to overcoming the middle-income trap must be made by companies.

The first aim of the book' editors was to define the problem of the middle-income trap on the basis of a review of the post-socialist transformation process and to analyse it in relation to its effects in different countries of the region. We attached importance to the participation of political scientists, geographers and economic historians in addition to economists. While all the chapters look at a longer period of study, they cannot include most recent developments. However, the problem of the middle-income trap has persisted in the region under study until today. Indeed it may even have worsened. The Conclusion discusses some recent trends that have emerged in the wake of the Covid-19 pandemic and that are emerging as a result of the Russian attack on Ukraine.

In addition to the editors and the authors, other institutions and people have also contributed to the creation of this book. The German Herder Research Council, the Leibniz ScienceCampus 'Eastern Europe – Global Area' (EEGA) and the Leibniz-Institute for the History and Culture of Eastern Europe (both based in Leipzig) supported the scientific exchange between the authors and assumed expenses for the linguistic editing as well as the printing of the figures. We would like to express our gratitude towards these institutions. Many thanks also go to Deniz Bozkurt-Pekar for linguistic editing and to Iryna Svistunova, Jenny Appel and Darina Stoytcheva for technical assistance. Finally, we would like to thank Berghahn Books for accepting this volume into their publishing programme and for the cooperative collaboration.

# Abbreviations

| | |
|---|---|
| AGH | Akademia Górniczo-Hutnicza |
| ANIS | Asociaţia Patronală a Industriei de Software şi Servicii (Software Services Industry Employer Association) |
| BNR | Banca Naţională a României (National Bank of Romania) |
| BPH | Bank Przemysłowo-Handlowy |
| CEE | Central and East Europe |
| CEE7 | Bulgaria, the Czech Republic, Hungary, Poland, Romania, Slovakia and Slovenia |
| CEEC | Central and Eastern European Countries |
| CEO | Chief Executive Officer |
| CIS | Commonwealth of Independent States |
| CMEA | Council for Mutual Economic Assistance |
| CNR | Institute for the Study of Regionalism, Federalism and Self-Government of the National Research Council of Italy |
| COMECON | The Council for Mutual Economic Assistance |
| CSF | Community Support Framework |
| DME | Dependent Market Economy |
| EA | EEA Agreement |
| EBRD | European Bank for Reconstruction and Development |
| ECB | European Central Bank |
| ECE | East Central Europe |
| ECE-8 | Czech Republic, Estonia, Hungary, Latvia, Lithuania, Poland, Slovakia and Slovenia |
| ECU | European Currency Union |
| EEA | European Economic Area |
| EEGA | Leibniz ScienceCampus 'Eastern Europe – Global Area' |
| EFSF | European Financial Stability Facility |
| EFW | Economic Freedom of the World |

| | |
|---|---|
| EI | Enterprise Investors |
| EIT | Enterprise Information Technology |
| EIU | Economist Intelligence Unit |
| ERDF | European Research and Development Fund |
| ERP | Enterprise Resource Planning |
| ESM | European Stability Mechanism |
| EU | European Union |
| EU-12 | EU member states between 1986 and 1995: Germany, France, Italy, the Netherlands, Belgium, Luxembourg, Denmark, Ireland, United Kingdom, Greece, Spain and Portugal |
| EU-15 | EU member states in 1995: Germany, France, Italy, the Netherlands, Belgium, Luxembourg, Denmark, Ireland, United Kingdom, Greece, Spain, Portugal, Austria, Finland and Sweden |
| FDI | Foreign Direct Investment |
| FTA | Free Trade Agreement |
| GDP | Gross Domestic Product |
| GEC | Global Economic Crisis |
| GLOBSEC | Global Security Forum |
| ICL | International Computers Limited |
| ICRG | International Country Risk Guide |
| ICT | Information and Communication Technology |
| IMF | International Monetary Fund |
| IPO | Initial Public Offering |
| IT | Information Technology |
| ITC | Information Technology and Computing |
| KGHM | Kombinat Górniczo-Hutniczy Miedzi |
| MEBO | Management and Employee Buy Out |
| MIT | Massachusetts Institute of Technology |
| MNC | Multinational Corporation |
| n.a. | not available |
| NASDAQ | National Association of Securities Dealers Automated Quotations |

| | |
|---|---|
| NGO | Non-Governmental Organization |
| NHS | National Health Service |
| NIS | National Innovation Systems |
| NPL | Non-Performing Loans |
| NSFR | National Strategic Reference Framework |
| NUTS | The Nomenclature of Territorial Units for Statistics |
| OECD | Organization for Economic Co-operation and Development |
| PA | Partnership Agreement |
| PiS | Prawo i Sprawidliewość (Polish Law and Justice Party) |
| PKO BP | Powszechna Kasa Oszczędności Bank Polski |
| PLN | Polish złoty (currency unit) |
| PPP | Purchasing Power Parity |
| PPS | Purchasing Power Standard |
| PZU | Powszechny Zakład Ubezpieczeń |
| R&D | Research and Development |
| RIS | Regional Innovation Systems |
| RTD | Research and Technological Development |
| S3 | Smart Specialisation Strategies |
| SEE | South East Europe |
| SGP | Stability and Growth Pact |
| SME | Small and Medium-sized Enterprises |
| TFP | Total Factor Productivity |
| TFUE | Treaty on the Functioning of the European Union |
| TNE | Transnational Enterprises |
| TPSA | Telekomunikacja Polska SA |
| UN | United Nations |
| US | United States (of America) |
| USD | United States Dollar |
| V4 | Visegrád 4 (Czech Republic, Hungary, Poland and Slovakia) |
| WGI | World Governance Indicators |
| WSE | Warsaw Stock Exchange |
| ZUS | Zakład Ubezpieczeń Społecznych (Social Insurance Institution) |

INTRODUCTION
# Transformation of the Transformation?
*The Middle-Income Trap and the Search for a New Development Strategy in the Post-Communist States of Central and Eastern Europe*

Yaman Kouli and Uwe Müller

For centuries, the European continent has been characterized by the uneven level of socioeconomic development in its subregions (see Broadberry and Malinowski 2020, 23; Kopsidis and Schulze 2020, 42). At least since the industrialisation in the nineteenth century, the West has been a constantly present point of reference as the more modern part of the continent for the economic and political elites of Eastern Europe. In the twentieth century, various attempts were made in the East to catch up with the West, for example, through economic nationalism and import substitution in the interwar period or even through the installation of a completely new economic system, that is, the socialist planned economy (Janos 2000). It was largely the fact that the party and state leaders had not succeeded in achieving the economic efficiency and material standard of living of the states of Western Europe which caused the collapse of communism as a political system in 1989 in Central and Eastern European states. After an initially and often rather painful transformation process to a market economy system in the early 1990s (Kollmorgen 2019), many national economies of Central and Eastern Europe finally found the chance to catch up with the West.

From a historical perspective, the overall framework conditions for the catching-up process were exceptionally favourable. This was especially true for the East Central European (the so-called Visegrád) and Baltic states (Orłowski 2020, 15). The individual opportunities for advancement as well as the high acceptance of the Western model of democracy and market economy in these countries led to a spirit of optimism in large segments of the population. In countries such as Hungary and Poland, attempts at market-economy reforms had already taken place during the communist era and could be taken up during the transition period once again (Pula 2018, 67–90). In general, the communist economic system had left behind an outdated, partly dilapidated capital stock in industry and infrastructure,[1] but the level of human capital was high both in terms of general school education and training of skilled workers and engineers.

The external framework conditions were also generally favourable. The Eastern European economies opened up to the influx of capital from Western Europe, the US and Asia, the latter of which was looking for profitable yet safe investment opportunities. In contrast to the interwar period, which was characterized by crisis and economic nationalism (Szlajfer 2012), the integration of the Eastern European transformation states into the world economy, especially into the European Union, was actively supported by Western states, because it corresponded with Western economic and political interests. Aiming at preparing the accession of the Central and Eastern European states, the European Union's cohesion policy ensured compliance with standards important from the European Union's point of view and thus simultaneously promoted the reform process in the Central and Eastern European countries (Berend 2009).

Economic growth and structural change in the countries were driven to a very high degree by foreign direct investment (FDI). A large amount of the goods produced in the new enterprises were in turn exported to Western Europe (Pula 2018, 108–41; Orłowski 2020, 21–22). This flow of capital and goods was also chiefly facilitated by association agreements with the EU and by accession to the EU (Kossev and Tompson 2020). This situation without a doubt also meant that Central and Eastern Europe once again took on a semiperipheral position in the European and global economies, as they often had in history (Morys 2020). Nonetheless, taking the growth of economic output as a yardstick for convergence to Western levels of development, one can observe a massive process of convergence taking place in Central and Eastern Europe, especially between 1995 and 2008 (Galgóczi and Drahokoupil 2017, 8), which incidentally also applies to indicators reflecting the standard of living, such as life expectancy.

The economic and financial crisis of 2008/09 affected the states in Central and Eastern Europe to varying degrees (ibid., 8). Although all countries returned to a growth course in the 2010s, admittedly with the exception of Romania, growth rates did not reach the level of the precrisis years (Orłowski 2020, 23–24). Therefore, the financial crisis of 2008 'marked a breaking point in the growth and development model of Central and Eastern European ... middle-income economies'. Galgóczi and Drahokoupil are convinced that the 'CEE middle-income economies need to refine the future role of FDI and at the same time explore other growth engines in order to continue the process of convergence with the high-income countries' (Galgóczi and Drahokoupil 2017, 7). After 2008, the number of newly created jobs declined significantly, as did the amount of FDI that flowed into Central and Eastern Europe, as well as Greece and Portugal (Hunya 2015, 58). Still, the decline in FDI was not catastrophic; it was even minor in parts, depending on the economic branch (ibid., 44).

Compared to some southern European countries, the EU member states from Central and Eastern Europe were considered relatively stable economies. Nevertheless, the discussions on the economic development in the countries themselves gained an increasingly critical tenor. The fact that globalisation and economic growth has produced not only winners but also losers was for a long time a significant debate subject.[2] It was assumed that innovative and modern economies would sooner or later develop, from which the majority of the working-age population would automatically benefit. This expectation was in stark contrast to the employment history of a specific group of the workforce that had been forced to make personal sacrifices as a result of an economic policy from which they hardly benefited for several decades. Low national debts, increased productivity per capita and falling unemployment figures were therefore juxtaposed against a perceived increase of precarious employment opportunities, lower wages and the latent risk of job losses as a result of the structural change. The increasing critique of these growing insecurities was for a long time underestimated in the Western 'core' of the European Union, whose attention was directed mainly at the Euro and the fiscal crises in some Southern European countries, the Brexit process, the growing external challenges from rising China and the often unpredictable United States in the Trump era (Szabo and Laguna 2021, 49–52). The critique addressed some problems accompanying the transformation process almost from the beginning, such as the growing regional inequality within the countries – that is, the divergence between the capital regions and centres of FDI on the one hand and rural peripheries on the other – and the increasing social inequality, in particular the polarization of the wage distribution (Gorzelak and Smętkowski 2020; Tyrowicz and Szewczyk 2020, 144–47).

Summing up, FDI-led economic growth on the one hand and integration in the Single European Market on the other, even though inseparable, had contradictory effects. Theoretically, one might make a good case in arguing that economic integration caused the problems that we tackle in this book. Were it not for international competition, there would not be a situation where countries try to attract buyers and investors by being cheap. The countries did have to pay a price for international economic integration.

What was new in this discussion is the identification of a 'middle-income trap'. An already existing or looming 'middle-income trap' is increasingly cited as a central argument for the need to stop relying primarily on a growth model based on FDI. 'The dependence on foreign investments and poor endogenous potential for innovation that have not been overcome in the course of transformation are considered as the main weaknesses of the CEE economies, which can remain stuck in the "middle income trap"' (Gorzelak 2020, 1–2). This argument is combined with a call for a change in the position of Central and Eastern European economies in international supply chains and a critique of EU structural policies. The fight against the 'middle-income trap' plays a central role in the economic policy programmes of the Central European governments and even becomes explicit in the Polish case,[3] showing the awareness of countries about the challenge.

The most obvious way out of this state of low innovation is hardly surprising: the countries must unlock new productivity reserves through innovations. Yet the trap mentioned earlier makes it hard to achieve and creates several problems. The Central and Eastern European countries are confronted by contradictory economic incentives. While there is no fail-safe way to create innovation-based economic growth, several influential levers are certainly well-known: investing in academic education, research and development, and a vocational training system. Yet, these measures are associated with higher government spending and whilst Germany invests 3.1 percent of its GDP into research and development, Hungary invests only 1.5 percent and Poland only 1.2 percent (2018 figures).[4] Consequently, higher state investments could require higher taxes. However, by increasing taxes, the countries catching up in economic terms would risk becoming less attractive to investors that continue to appreciate the comparatively low wage and employment costs.

The number of patents granted is one of the most meaningful indicators of the innovative capacity of an economy. While other production factors like the amount of human capital are extremely hard to quantify, patents can be counted easily. However, they still have shortcomings. There are inventions that cannot be patented, or cannot be patented in every country because of legal differences. Moreover, not every patent is equally profitable. The number of patents does therefore not allow a precise assessment of the innovativeness of a country. That is not to say that measuring patent-output is not of value (see Streb 2016, 449). Yet it is also important to consider that a service-based economy depends less on patents than an industry-based one does. This explains the difference between the UK on the one hand and Germany, Belgium or France on the other. Nevertheless, Table 0.1 shows that the ability to develop innovations was unevenly distributed among the EU regions. It most certainly reflects the different economic structures on

**Table 0.1.** Patents per 1 million inhabitants.

|  | 2012 | 2013 | 2014 | 2015 | 2016 | 2017 | 2018 | 2019 | 2020 | 2021 |
|---|---|---|---|---|---|---|---|---|---|---|
| France | 74 | 75 | 71 | 82 | 106 | 110 | 128 | 131 | 124 | 100 |
| Germany | 166 | 167 | 162 | 174 | 228 | 228 | 251 | 255 | 241 | 199 |
| Italy | 38 | 39 | 37 | 41 | 53 | 51 | 57 | 62 | 64 | 54 |
| Belgium | 101 | 101 | 100 | 121 | 156 | 171 | 195 | 198 | 199 | 167 |
| Netherlands | 102 | 112 | 101 | 118 | 164 | 187 | 220 | 250 | 228 | 168 |
| Denmark | 101 | 109 | 106 | 123 | 181 | 187 | 197 | 226 | 218 | 196 |
| United Kingdom | 32 | 32 | 32 | 32 | 45 | 47 | 58 | 62 | 60 | 48 |
| Ireland | 42 | 41 | 55 | 58 | 82 | 92 | 104 | 109 | 123 | 104 |
| Greece | 3 | 3 | 2 | 2 | 4 | 3 | 4 | 5 | 8 | 6 |
| Portugal | 3 | 2 | 2 | 4 | 6 | 7 | 9 | 11 | 12 | 11 |
| Spain | 9 | 8 | 10 | 11 | 16 | 17 | 21 | 20 | 19 | 17 |
| Finland | 124 | 123 | 116 | 136 | 197 | 224 | 280 | 294 | 283 | 220 |
| Austria | 95 | 99 | 105 | 121 | 157 | 167 | 188 | 188 | 197 | 149 |
| Sweden | 166 | 187 | 177 | 199 | 270 | 290 | 349 | 375 | 346 | 279 |
| Hungary | 4 | 5 | 4 | 4 | 6 | 6 | 7 | 8 | 8 | 5 |
| Estonia | 4 | 7 | 6 | 7 | 8 | 14 | 16 | 12 | 15 | 9 |
| Lithuania | 2 | 2 | 3 | 4 | 6 | 7 | 5 | 8 | 6 | 7 |
| Latvia | 3 | 2 | 6 | 4 | 8 | 7 | 6 | 3 | 3 | 10 |
| Poland | 2 | 2 | 3 | 4 | 5 | 6 | 6 | 6 | 7 | 6 |
| Slovenia | 18 | 25 | 25 | 32 | 39 | 45 | 37 | 35 | 45 | 37 |
| Slovakia | 2 | 1 | 2 | 2 | 3 | 3 | 5 | 6 | 3 | 6 |
| Czech Republic | 5 | 6 | 6 | 7 | 9 | 12 | 12 | 16 | 14 | 13 |
| Bulgaria | 1 | 1 | 1 | 1 | 2 | 3 | 3 | 2 | 3 | 3 |
| Romania | 0 | 0 | 0 | 0 | 1 | 1 | 0 | 1 | 1 | 1 |
| Croatia | 3 | 2 | 2 | 1 | 1 | 1 | 1 | 3 | 2 | 2 |

Source: European Patent Office (EPO), Eurostat, for the population of the UK in 2021 https://databank.worldbank.org/source/population-estimates-and-projections.

these countries. Nonetheless, the table clarifies the imbalances among the European countries. The EU members in Southern Europe (Greece, Portugal and also Spain) stand out as countries that 'produce' relatively few patents, even though Italy performs well in the peer group. Specifically striking is the case of the new member states. They show a low performance. Among them, only Slovenia stands out. At the same time, even countries that are praised for their economic policy – namely Poland – have much room for improvement. It is also striking that the number of patents does not grow in some of the new member states. In Poland, Slovenia and in the Czech Republic, there is growth, yet only on a low level. In the remaining countries, the number of patents stagnates.

Nominally, the advantages of a more innovation-driven economy are obvious. First – this has been indicated by works focusing on economic geography, for example – knowledge-based companies are less mobile than companies relying largely on semi-skilled labour. This reduces the risk of such companies choosing the exit option and deciding to shift to a 'cheaper' country with little effort. Second, a better qualified workforce is usually associated with higher wages and therefore with an increase in domestic demand, which can be a stabilising element. Third, the existence of such companies can at least mitigate the emigration of qualified workers, a chance that cannot be underestimated. For example, between 1990 and 2015, Poland has witnessed a yearly emigration of between 18,000 and 47,000 people.[5]

This book starts from the diagnosis that the concept of the 'middle-income trap' is used in many ways in the (economic) policy debate while rarely critically questioned. In the following, we explain the basic assumptions about the concept and examine its empirical evidence for Central and Eastern Europe. It becomes clear that the evaluation of the FDI-driven growth model requires an economic-historical view of the transformation process. For an adequate analysis of the successes and side effects of this growth model, it is necessary to include non-economic perspectives, too. In this book, authors with diverse disciplinary backgrounds review different parts of the transformation of societies and economies in Central and Eastern Europe. What unites the authors within this book are their common interests in the analysis of the manner of socioeconomic transformation, the question of the relevance and possible impact of the middle-income trap and finally the search for ways to escape this trap. They consider an economy based more heavily on knowledge and modern technologies as the way out of the middle-income trap. In many contributions, the European Union plays an important role, which is sometimes seen as part of the problem but should also be part of the solution.

## Which Kind of Middle-Income Trap?

When journalists and scholars mention the middle-income trap, there appears to be two profoundly different perspectives on it and hence two different versions of the phenomenon. The first is based on the purely macroeconomic perspective which models economic growth as the pure result of input factors. The better the availability of these input factors, the higher growth per capita. Consequently, the aim is to compute the threshold that marks the middle-income trap. Eichengreen, Park and Shin arrive at the conclusion that there are two figures of per capita GDP that mark a threshold – 11,000 and 15,000 US$ (2005) – even though they add that they 'continue to find considerable dispersion in the per capita incomes at which slowdowns (of GDP per capita growth rates, Y.K./U.M.) occur' (Eichengreen, Park and Shin 2013). From this point of view, the middle income is defined by a certain level of economic production per capita which seems to be hard to pass through. Some experts do not even consider this threshold to be a huge obstacle. With regard to Poland, Piątkowski forecasts that Poland will grow through the critical phase (Piątkowski 2018).

There is, however, a second perspective on the middle-income trap. It focusses more on the necessary conditions that come with FDI. Due to the lack of innovative power, these emerging countries attract FDI by low costs. This concerns the revenues themselves, which are significantly lower in the emerging countries than they are in the EU15 (Galgóczi and Drahokoupil 2017, 9). These countries also keep costs low by limiting labour expenditures. A glance at the social protection expenditure figures between 2003 and 2013 confirms this assumption: in 2018, Poland's welfare spending amounted to 19.2 percent of GDP; the Czech Republic spent 17.9 percent, Estonia, 16.1 percent – to name but three examples, in comparison to Germany's 28.4 percent and France's 31.4 percent).[6] In this case, the notion 'trap' does not refer exclusively to production levels but rather to the economic and social policy that comes with the necessity to remain attractive for FDI. The more labour and welfare expenditures increase, the less attractive the countries are for foreign investors. In this respect, the FDI-driven growth model slows down the growth not only of individual incomes but also of societal wealth. On the other hand, as long as salaries and welfare spending remain on a low level, the national market cannot grow. In this case, producing for exports remains top priority. As low prices for export goods improve their competitiveness, export-driven production is an incentive to freeze labour costs and intervene once there is a risk of a significant increase. There is also another mechanism which is a direct consequence of the fact that FDI tends to flow where the prices are low and the potential returns-on-investment are higher. It is always possible for any country to be even cheaper than others, which may draw FDI away from countries that hitherto profited from capital net-inflows. Even though it is impossible to know if and when that threat is imminent, it is still a powerful incentive to keep labour costs low. This might explain why the 'social model

Europe' is not particularly attractive to these governments, as it would require them to increase welfare expenditures.

Some authors argue that there is an issue that further complicates the question of how countries can free themselves from the trap, as correct timing is both extremely important and almost impossible. Theoretically, there is little argument that investment in highly qualified personnel is key to reach sustainable growth. Moreover, these investments have to be made while FDI-driven growth is still successful and generates growth. Yet there is no guarantee that investments in human capital will remain in the country to be harvested. 'As things are now, the CEEC R&D sectors are close to extinction, with the more creative personnel leaving for the United States or Western Europe, while production, banking and trade are firmly in foreign hands – as it used to be the case over a couple of recent centuries' (Podkaminer 2013, 41). This quote is from nine years ago. Since then, the economic growth has not deteriorated. Yet, the overall argument remains valid, for highly qualified people, especially within the European Union, are always free to leave their country for an economically more attractive job abroad. Theoretically, this can also go the other way around, as it is similarly possible to attract highly qualified people from abroad and profit from their human capital.

In short, although higher prices for labour and labour quality are in the interest of a country, the incentives to prevent these from happening are still powerful and 'trap' the economy at its current state. Therefore, the distinction of the two different kinds of traps are not merely academic; it is at the heart of economic policy. Ideally, countries are able to attract FDI *and* to successfully develop an economy that is able to nurture self-sustaining, intensive growth based on innovations. If the middle-income trap were merely a productivity-threshold that countries had to leave behind, it would be possible to achieve both. Social scientists, however, insist that the economies that attract FDI are profoundly different from more innovation-based ones.[7]

Authors who disagree argue that FDI actually can induce knowledge transfer. Theoretically, if the transfer of knowledge solved *the* main issue that FDI caused, it would indeed be possible to exploit the comparative advantage of low prices and develop an innovative economy at the same time (Szabo and Laguna 2021, 48–49). Some authors describe this as a paradox, as trade and foreign investments make technology transfer actually possible (Gomułka 2016, 22). The more firms invest in human capital, the better they are able to absorb new technologies via technology transfer (Chiacchio, Gradeva and Lopez-Garcia 2018, 23–24). Hence they arrive at a conclusion similar to that which Borensztein, Gregorio and Lee published twenty years earlier. Borensztein and his colleagues argue that 'FDI is in fact an important vehicle for the transfer of technology' and that 'there is a strong complementary effect between FDI and human capital' (Borensztein, Gregorio and Lee 1998, 117). At this point, however, this expectation turns into a circular reasoning. To attract FDI, costs have to remain low. Yet, for FDI to induce technology improvements – and therefore the foundations of long-term growth – it is imperative to invest in human capital. This puts any government in an even more serious dilemma.

## Common Diagnosis, Different Therapies

From a researcher's standpoint, the question is how things turned out 'in reality'. Evidently, the answer depends not only on the reviewed case but also on the point of view. The contributions in this volume are written by authors with different disciplinary backgrounds and with diverging perspectives, who also evaluate certain developments differently. As the editors, we see this as an advantage since a single volume can provide only interim results of an ongoing discussion.

However, the divergent results are sometimes related to the fact that the authors examine different levels: the spectrum of foci in the chapters in this volume ranges from the relationship of Central and Eastern European countries and economies with the EU and the world market (Daniel Šitera, Cornel Ban and Zoltán Mihály, Kiril Kossev, Christian Schweiger), to national policies (Šitera, Birgit Glorius, Tal Kadayer, Yaman Kouli), to regional levels (Andrea Filippetti and Raffaele Spallone, Kossev), as well as individual sectors (Ban and Mihály) and companies (Grzegorz Lechowski).

Despite different disciplinary backgrounds and levels of investigation, there are four common diagnoses.

*First*, there is a consensus that a catching-up process has taken place, but its continuation is at serious risk with the middle-income trap playing a central role. Most authors emphasize the extraordinarily dynamic economic development of the states of Central and Eastern Europe in the last twenty-five years, especially between 1998 and 2008. After the drop in economic output between 1990 and 1993, the CEE7 (Bulgaria, the Czech Republic, Hungary, Poland, Romania, Slovakia and Slovenia) enjoyed five years of growth of about 3 percent in average. During the following decade (1998–2008), the average growth amounted to almost 5 percent (Voskoboynikov 2020, 392). However, the outcome of this catching-up process varies greatly among the individual countries. Among the Central and Eastern European EU members, the difference in the pace of growth was the greatest between Poland and Bulgaria. The GDP per capita of Poland, measured in PPS, increased from 78 percent of the Bulgarian level in 1989 to 136 percent in 2017 (Orłowski 2020, 11–12). However, this was also a result of the low starting level on the Polish side, which was caused by the deep recession in the country during the 1980s (see Kouli, Chapter 1) and by the fact that Poland was the only country in Europe that did not experience a decline in social product during the financial crisis of 2008/09 (Barczyk, Breziński and von Delhaes 2012).

Even Daniel Šitera, who is generally critical of the development of the last decades, admits that 'most of the ECE states have experienced socio-economic catch-up', especially 'Czechia, Hungary, Poland, and Slovakia are categorized as ranging from "less" to "moderately developed" economies'. But the author criticizes that they were 'falling behind the "highly developed" club in the EU' and 'remaining in this never-ending catch-up game'. According to Šitera's interpretation, the problem of the middle-income trap, at least in the case of East-Central Europe, is that while there is a possibility of moving up from 'less to moderately developed', a 'highly developed' level is unattainable (Chapter 7 in the book). The decisive criterion for evaluating a catching-up process should therefore not be the growth rates of an economy but its structural change.

Indeed, in order to explain the phenomenon of the middle-income trap, one needs to analyse not only the growth rates but also the changes in structures, which leads to the question of the structural effects of the FDI-based growth model. It must first be emphasized that FDI significantly slowed down the inevitable deindustrialisation of Central and Eastern Europe after the collapse of communism (see Ban and Mihály, Chapter 3). The countries in Central and Eastern Europe had experienced at least forty years of a socialist planned economy. Especially in the first two decades after the war, the socialist economies had been able to realize relatively high and extensive economic growth through the development of heavy industry. In the 1970s and especially in the 1980s, however, a glaring weakness in innovation became apparent. In addition, a growing share of the national product was used for consumption and social policy in order to maintain political stability. This happened at the expense of investment, leaving the physical capital in an extremely poor condition in 1990 (Vonyó and Markevich 2020; see also Kouli, Chapter 1, on the Polish case).

Therefore, all former socialist states were dependent on the urgent import of technology and capital from the West. After the collapse of an economic system tending towards autarky and the dissolution of the CMEA, access to new export markets was also necessary. Integration into European value chains and access to the EU internal market were thus essential prerequisites for the catching-up process of the Central and Eastern European economies. At least for the Polish case, we know that the FDI had a positive impact on labour productivity and thereby also on the competitiveness of the manufacturing sector on the world market – in the vast majority of industries (Weresa 2008).

The contributions by Cornel Ban and Zoltán Mihály and Kiril Kossev offer comparisons between countries as well as groups of countries (East-Central Europe/Visegrád, South-Eastern Europe, the Baltic States as [potential] EU members, South-Eastern Europe outside the EU/Western Balkans, Ukraine and other post-Soviet states). These comparisons show that the degree of openness of the economies and their geographical and cultural proximity to Western Europe correlated positively with economic development at least until 2008. Ban and Mihály emphasize that the rise of East Asia has been primarily at the expense of Latin America and the non-EU Eastern European states, while East-Central Europe has nonetheless rather improved its position in the world economy. Tal Kadayer, on the other hand, points to the close connection between the course set in the early period of transformation, the extent of FDI and economic growth. For example, countries that relied less on management buyout and issuing of vouchers during privatisation and more on the direct sale of former state property were particularly attractive for FDI (see also Kossev, Chapter 6). The same applies to the liberalisation of wages: 'wage liberalization is crucial for increasing productivity, as productivity and compensation are tightly correlated. Wage is strongly connected to competitiveness and productivity. Countries that maintained high control of wages prevented the private sector's share in the economy from increasing' (Kadayer, Chapter 2, p. 78).

However, the phenomenon of the middle-income trap draws attention to the fact that the liberalisation of wages cannot permanently guarantee the competitiveness of an economy. In the first phase of transformation, which Kadayer focuses on, the pace of change might have been more important for medium-term success than the often cumbersome attempts of the state to regulate this change. In the present, by contrast, overcoming the middle-income trap is obviously only possible through active state intervention. This argument is supported by the analyses of the situation in Central and Eastern Europe presented in this book as well as by examples of success, such as South Korea and Taiwan (Wade 2018).

From our point of view, neither an orientation towards a normative free-market model nor a blanket criticism of 'neoliberalism' is helpful. What is decisive is the classification of an issue in the respective historical context. This also applies to the legacy of the communist period, which differed between the individual countries within the 'Eastern bloc' more than one would expect. Kadayer points out that relatively good initial conditions favoured the active promotion of transformation. Yaman Kouli discusses this question with a focus on Poland. He shows in his contribution that even though the transformation is supposed to have profoundly reshaped the national economies, they are still to a large extent shaped by their heritage. Poland's industrial capital was in a bad state compared to Czechoslovakia and Hungary. Ironically, there is good reason to assume that it was this low starting position of Poland that played a key role in its high growth rates. Yet these rates, by 2019, did not let Poland overtake the GDP per capita of the Czech Republic or Hungary. The expectation that the middle-income trap will not hinder Poland from becoming a high-income economy may therefore be premature.

The *second* basic consensus among our authors is that the FDI-based growth model has reached (or will soon reach) its limits in Central and Eastern Europe and these economies have fallen (or will soon fall) into a middle-income trap. Some authors even tend to believe that the concept of the middle-income trap indicates that the neoliberal reform policies and the past waves of foreign investment in the post-communist Central Europe have created massive barriers to further growth by stabilizing the national economies on the path of development driven by low wages (see especially Šitera, Chapter 7; as well as Myant 2018; Gorzelak 2020, 3).

Other negative side effects of the growth model developed during the transformation phase are also becoming increasingly clear. First and foremost among these are the growing regional and social disparities, as presented in Chapter 6 by Kossev. From an economic-historical perspective, it is true that such disparities are to some extent unavoidable in fundamental processes of structural change (Williamson 1996). However, the hopes that FDI would bring about transfers of modern technologies, the involvement of suppliers from the region (spread effects) and an increase in human capital have not been sufficiently fulfilled. Kossev concludes:

> The region must tackle the underlying inefficiencies of unbalanced growth and newly created inequalities and must seek to reinvigorate its economic institutions. This means devising a new growth model that is mindful of regional disparities, can find an economic place for those that have been left behind by the early transition, and provides an incentive to keep institutional modernization reform going. This will assist the Central and Eastern European countries to avoid falling into the middle-income trap and experiencing a long-term economic stagnation. (Chapter 6, p. 171)

However, there are also other assessments with regard to the connection between the FDI growth model and the middle-income trap. While Cornel Ban and Zoltán Mihály acknowledge the danger of the middle-income trap in Romania's case, they also point to the potentials of the current growth strategy. In their view, the main obstacle is inadequate state action. Grzegorz Lechowski points out that larger countries such as Poland and Romania have a smaller share of foreign companies in the national product and are also less dependent on exports. He analyses the domestically driven industrial dynamics in post-communist Central Europe and questions the general validity of the thesis of its failure in a dual economy. Evidence of this hypothesis is provided by two Polish IT companies which were founded in the 1990s, then adapted Western technologies to answer to the needs of Polish customers, and are now becoming multinationals in their own right. Decisive for this success has been the growing demand for IT systems, the increasing specialisation in the IT industry, as well as positive framework conditions in Poland, such as the existence of relevantly trained university graduates, a national banking system and the Warsaw Stock Exchange.

*Third*, many contributions also study the role of the EU, be it in the implementation of the FDI-based growth model, in the path into the middle-income trap or in developing possible strategies leading out of this trap.

Overall, it must first be emphasized that the process of preparing the new member states for admission to the European Union has made an important contribution to the formation of institutions that strengthen the principles of democracy, market economy and the rule of law (see Schweiger, Chapter 8). Šitera criticizes, however, that in its behaviour towards the (potential) new member states, the European Union from the beginning pursued an economic policy strategy that primarily benefited the old (Western) member states. This strategy consisted of actively supporting the FDI model, which turned Central and Eastern Europe into an extended workbench of Western European corporations. For this reason, the Visegrád states in particular have developed into 'dependent market economies' (Nölke and Vliegenthart 2009). This 'division of labour' was seen as an instrument to preserve the EU's competitiveness in global competition. The economies of Central and Eastern Europe were given the task of holding their own against competition from Asia, primarily through low manufacturing costs, while the Western European economies were able to concentrate on improving their technological competitiveness. A particularly problematic result was concentrated in areas with low labour costs. Moreover, the EU continued this strategy even after the 2008 crisis. This can be seen, for example, in the criticism of the allegedly excessive wage increases in Romania in 2017 and 2018 by the World Bank and the European Bank for Reconstruction and Development. As Ban and Mihály argue, these wage increases were still below productivity growth and therefore quite justified in economic terms.

Schweiger illustrates that the peripheralisation of the Central and Eastern European countries within the framework of the European Union went beyond assigning them the role of an extended workbench with correspondingly low wages. The social spending of the new member states, too, generally remained below the EU average. This enabled the Eastern European states to attract foreign investors through low non-wage labour costs. In addition, low social spending facilitated the consolidation of state budgets, which was essential for admission to the EU, and especially in some cases (Slovenia, Slovakia, Baltic states) also for participation in the Euro area. Lower wages, poorer social security, the restrictions on the free movement of workers from the states that joined the union in 2004 and 2007, which were in place for several years, as well as the unequal treatment vis-à-vis southern European states in the Euro crisis reinforced the impression of many citizens of the new member states that they were seen as second-class Europeans.

According to Šitera, for the EU to implement the 'dual' economic policy strategy to increase global competitiveness its most important instrument was the so-called cohesion policy. This may seem surprising at first glance, as the main task of cohesion policy was actually to compensate for the disadvantages caused by the internal market (see Filippetti and Spallone, Chapter 9). However, Šitera claims that the infrastructure investments made under cohesion policy have mainly favoured FDI. At the same time, the core of the EU has de facto bought the consent of the new EU member states with the lure of cohesion policy. This naturally raises the question of the extent to which cohesion policy has also promoted the other parts of the national economy.

Andrea Filippetti and Raffaele Spallone point out that the middle-income trap can also be observed at the regional level, often allowing for a more precise identification of its structural causes. In its cohesion policy, the European Union has for more than two decades given greater priority to the promotion of regions, on the one hand, and to increasing expenditure on research and development, on the other. Nevertheless, many European regions, especially in Southern Europe and Eastern Europe, currently have 'middle-income status'. Filippetti and Spallone attribute this fact to the relative easiness of implementing regional redistribution through Keynesian policies in a Fordist economy in comparison to the implementation of cohesion policies in knowledge economies. The production factor 'knowledge' is obviously much less mobile than one would expect despite the increasing availability of digital networks.

*Fourth*, nevertheless, the expansion of digitalisation and the shift to knowledge-based industries are considered the most important strategy towards more balanced growth and getting out of the middle-income trap (Kossev, Chapter 6). But how can this structural change be initiated and enforced?

The geographers Filippetti and Spallone see two approaches that should ideally complement each other: the promotion of individual agglomerations, such as technology parks, by the respective headquarters and a consistent decentralisation that relies on regional diversity giving birth to different forms of knowledge-based economies.

In contrast, more state-driven and 'developmentalist' industrial policies have dominated in Central and Eastern Europe for some years. In this context, the political scientist Šitera speaks of nationalist development strategies that determine economic policy above all in Hungary, Poland and to some extent also in the Czech Republic (Scheiring 2020; Smiecinska 2021). Shifting the focus of support from a few multinational to many medium-size enterprises would certainly be suitable for bringing the development levels of these two elements of an overly dual economic structure closer together. Šitera doubts, however, whether nationalist strategies can lead the countries out of their semiperipheral positions in the global economy and peripheral positions in the EU. Above all, it is quite questionable whether the structural problems that led to the middle-income trap can actually be solved in this way. He argues that especially illiberal democracies fail to offer good conditions for managing the shift of the engine of economic growth from industry to human-capital-intensive services, as economic freedom plays a much greater role in bringing about this second great structural change than what was the case for industrialisation (Winiecki 2016). Technology upgrading is a shift to higher value-added products and production stages through increasing specialization; instead of national isolation, it requires greater international integration (Gereffi 1999). The key to a significant strengthening of the knowledge economy, according to all authors, lies in an expansion of activities in the field of research and development by both the EU and the nation states as well as by private companies and – even more important – in the transfer of new technologies into economic application (see also Radosevic, Yoruk and Yoruk 2020). Almost all authors emphasize that the countries of Central and Eastern Europe spend too little on research and development compared to other EU countries.

Despite these deficits, there is apparently the possibility in individual cases to escape the middle-income trap. Lechowski points out that there have been development opportunities for innovative companies on the national market in Poland long before the turn to etatist strategies. In the long term, however, the prospects of such companies depend on successful specialisation and their own orientation towards international markets. Therefore, economic nationalist concepts tend to be counterproductive. Ban and Mihály also point out that there are some niches at the sectoral level that can circumvent the middle-income trap. Structural changes at the national economic level, however, would fail mainly due to the inefficient policies of the state and the neglect of research and development. The Romanian state subsidizes individual sectors through tax privileges, but ultimately only a small part of the economy benefits from this. More important, however, would be investments in innovation, health, and education by the state, whereby the optimal use of European funding programmes is of central importance.

A major obstacle to the strengthening of knowledge-based industries that is often overlooked by economists is the lack of adequately qualified labour. While a very small portion of the workforce are well trained, many highly qualified and skilled workers and university graduates leave Central and Eastern European countries and emigrate to the West. The middle-income trap also plays a role in this because low wages are still the most important motive in the decision to emigrate. In her chapter on Bulgaria, which has been hit by the problem particularly hard, Birgit Glorius points to a way of reducing the shortage of well-educated labour forces. Thirty to 50 percent of Bulgarians who emigrate to Western Europe are willing to return home under certain circumstances. Social and emotional motives often play a major role here – in contrast to emigration. Potentially returning migrants are thus quite willing to accept a loss of salary under certain conditions. These include, among other things, the possibility of becoming self-employed in the knowledge economy. The state should encourage return migration – something that has been almost non-existent up to now. More importantly, the state and administrative structures should be more open and flexible than in the 'established' West, while still preventing corruption.

Glorius thus directs attention to the actors who might be able to overcome the middle-income trap not only for themselves but ultimately also for their country. This is not necessarily about being at the forefront of technology. The success stories described in various contributions (Lechowski, Chapter 4; Ban and Mihály, Chapter 3) show that the strengthening of science and research and the implementation of modern technologies in companies and, finally, the openness of markets are the most important preconditions in order to escape the middle-income trap. National and European economic and technology policy should focus on achieving these conditions.

## Conclusion

Since the 1990s, the Central European countries have greatly profited from economic growth. They were able to capitalize on their comparative advantage of lower costs, close proximity to the highly developed Western European states, and relatively well-developed human capital. Consequently, they have successfully attracted FDI, the social and economic improvements of which have been undeniable. This strategy of FDI-driven growth, however, needs to be revised in the near future. The question the new EU member-states currently have to tackle pertains to the nature of the changes to be employed now. Even though it is unclear whether FDI-driven growth can still offer some potential, the general impression is that its end is near. The majority of publications indicate that the development of a more innovative economy and therefore higher investments in research and development and human capital as well as an increase of wages and social expenditures are key for future economic growth. These steps, however, are evidently incompatible with a low-cost strategy usually associated with FDI-fuelled growth.

As the contributors to this volume demonstrate, the problems linked with the middle-income trap depend on the specific perspective and the respective object of investigation. The overall successful economic development of the new member states should not cloud the fact that each of them has developed very differently. The general picture becomes even more complex once the analysis focusses on specific countries, economic branches or regions. Escaping the middle-income trap appears to be much more complicated and cannot be reduced to a matter of economic growth. The new economic policies need to be accompanied by modified social policies and strategies to increase the national human-capital stock.

There are good reasons to assume that the main challenges that will come with this change of strategy are not economic but political ones. Although not at the centre of this book, the argument that the current appeal of illiberal policies may be one of the results of a social policy that exists mainly to keep costs low is still worth mentioning. Relatively low labour costs even for well-educated labour can provide economic reasons to attract FDI. Yet, in the long run, they increase dissatisfaction among the population. The role of good and well-paying jobs for social cohesion is obvious. Yet creating such jobs is a long-term project. In this situation, populists with illiberal economic policies might appear attractive, which would explain the popularity of the democracy-backlash in many Eastern and Central European countries. Maybe, this is the irony of the middle-income trap. It has helped populists reach political power, even though the solutions they propose – for instance, shutting off the national market and fighting immigration – are insufficient to deal with the problem. Thus, the (economic) middle-income trap has brought about a political trap.

The contributions to this edited volume lay bare that to better understand current developments in Central and Eastern Europe, it is essential to also understand the impact of the middle-income trap.

**Yaman Kouli** wrote his dissertation at the Chemnitz Technical University and worked there as a research assistant from 2011 to 2018. From 2012 to 2013, he was also an A.SK-fellow at the Berlin Social Science Center. In 2018 and 2019, he was a visiting scientist at the UMR Sirice 8138 in Paris, funded via a scholarship from the Alexander von Humboldt Foundation. From October 2019, he has worked as a research assistant at the Heinrich-Heine-University in Düsseldorf. His fields of expertise are Poland's economic history during the twentieth century, the knowledge-based economy and European economic integration before 1914.

**Uwe Müller** earned a PhD in economic history at the Humboldt University in Berlin. He has done research and taught at the Humboldt University, the European University Viadrina in Frankfurt (Oder) and the Saarland University in Saarbrücken. Since 2011 he is a senior researcher at the GWZO Leibniz Institute for the History and Culture of Eastern Europe. His research interests include the economic history of Eastern Europe from the middle of the nineteenth century to the present day with a special focus on the integration of this region in the European and world economy.

## Notes

1. As has recently been shown, the state of the infrastructure and the capital stock differed widely among the Central and Eastern European states (Vonyó and Klein 2019; Vonyó 2017); see Kouli's contribution (Chapter 1) in this volume.
2. As presented in the renowned book by Joseph Stiglitz (Stiglitz 2003).
3. The 2017 Polish 'Plan for Responsible Growth' (Plan na rzecz Odpowiedzialnego Rozwoju, retrieved 30 April 2021 from https://www.gov.pl/web/fundusze-regiony/plan-na-rzecz-odpowiedzialnego-rozwoju) was directed explicitly against the middle-income trap. One key step of the plan against the trap was to raise investments in 'Research and Development' to a level of 2 percent of national GDP.
4. Gross domestic spending on R&D, retrieved 16 May 2021 from https://data.oecd.org/rd/gross-domestic-spending-on-r-d.htm.
5. Source: Główny Urząd Statystyczny, Struktura Ludności, retrieved 10 March 2021 from https://stat.gov.pl/obszary-tematyczne/ludnosc/ludnosc/struktura-ludnosci,16,1.html. More information on the socioeconomic status of the emigrants is not available.
6. Expenditure on social protection benefits, 2018, retrieved 16 May 2021 from https://ec.europa.eu/eurostat/statistics-explained/index.php?title=Social_protection_statistics_-_social_benefits.
7. Although not in the centre of this publication, there is also a political side to this argument. While countries may usually not complain against considerable investments by big companies, they are nonetheless undeniably reluctant to always pay the price. As Galgóczi and Drahokoupil emphasize, it has come to a distinction be-

tween 'good' and 'bad' FDI. Especially the idea that big foreign companies come to CEE to profit from the attractive market only to later repatriate economic surpluses made Poland and Hungary introduce taxes in order to fight this strategy (Galgóczi and Drahokoupil 2017, 11). There are also additional incentives to reduce the dependence on FDI. The volatility of FDI-inflows is a problem in and of itself, as the dependency on FDI is high and every reduction has direct effects on the production levels.

## References

Barczyk, Ryszard, Horst Breziński and Karl von Delhaes. 2012. *Consequences of World Economic Crisis for Poland and Central East Europe*. Poznań: Wydawn. Uniw. Ekonomicznego.

Berend, Ivan T. 2009. *From the Soviet Bloc to the European Union: The Economic and Social Transformation of Central and Eastern Europe since 1973*. Cambridge: Cambridge University Press.

Borensztein, Eduardo, Jose d. Gregorio and Jong-Wha Lee. 1998. 'How Does Foreign Direct Investment Affect Economic Growth?' *Journal of International Economics* 45: 115–35.

Broadberry, Stephen, and Mikołaj Malinowski. 2020. 'Living Standards in the Very Long Run: The Place of Central, Eastern and South-Eastern Europe in the Divergence Debate'. In *The Economic History of Central, East and South-East Europe: 1800 to the Present*, edited by Matthias Morys, 13–36. London: Routledge.

Chiacchio, Francesco, Katerina Gradeva and Paloma Lopez-Garcia. 2018. 'The Post-Crisis TFP Growth Slowdown in CEE Countries: Exploring the Role of Global Value Chains'. ECB Working Paper No. 2143. Retrieved 2 May 2021 from https://papers.ssrn.com/sol3/Delivery.cfm/SSRN_ID3161312_code485639.pdf?abstractid=3161312&mirid=1.

Eichengreen, Barry, Donghyun Park and Kwanho Shin. 2013. 'Growth Slowdowns Redux: New Evidence on the Middle-Income Trap'. NBER Working Paper No. 18673. Retrieved 12 May 2021 from http://www.nber.org/papers/w18673.

Galgóczi, Béla, and Jan Drahokoupil. 2017. 'Abandoning the FDI-based Economic Model Driven by Low Wages'. In *Condemned to Be Left Behind? Can Central and Eastern Europe Emerge from Its Low-Wage Model?* edited by Béla Galgóczi and Jan Drahokoupil, 7–24. Brussels: ETUI aisbl.

Gereffi, Gary. 1999. 'International Trade and Industrial Upgrading in the Apparel Commodity Chain'. *Journal of International Economics* 48(1): 37–70.

Gomułka, Stanisław. 2016. 'Poland's Economic and Social Transformation 1989–2014 and Contemporary Challenges'. *Central Bank Review* 16: 19–23.

Gorzelak, Grzegorz. 2020. 'Introduction'. In *Social and Economic Development in Central and Eastern Europe: Stability and Change after 1990*, edited by Grzegorz Gorzelak, 1–8. London: Routledge.

Gorzelak, Grzegorz, and Maciej Smętkowski. 2020. 'Regional Dynamics and Structural Changes in Central and Eastern European Countries'. In *Social and Economic Development in Central and Eastern Europe: Stability and Change after 1990*, edited by Grzegorz Gorzelak, 207–24. London: Routledge.

Hunya, Gábor. 2015. 'Mapping Flows and Patterns of Foreign Direct Investment in Central and Eastern Europe, Greece and Portugal During the Crisis'. In *Foreign Investment in Eastern and Southern Europe after 2008: Still a Lever of Growth?* edited by Bela Galgoczi, Jan Drahokoupil and Magdalena Bernaciak, 37–69. Brussels: ETUI aisbl.

Janos, Andrew C. 2000. *East Central Europe in the Modern World: The Politics of the Borderlands from Pre- to Postcommunism*. Stanford: Stanford University Press.

Kollmorgen, Raj. 2019. 'Post-socialist Transformations in the Twentieth and Twenty-first Centuries'. In *The Handbook of Political, Social, and Economic Transformation*, edited by Wolfgang Merkel, Raj Kollmorgen and Hans-Jürgen Wagener, 348–65. Oxford: Oxford University Press.

Kopsidis, Michael, and Max-Stephan Schulze. 2020. 'Economic Growth and Sectoral Developments, 1800–1914'. In *The Economic History of Central, East and South-East Europe: 1800 to the Present*, edited by Matthias Morys, 39–68. London: Routledge.

Kossev, Kiril, and William Tompson. 2020. 'Political and Economic Integration with the Western Economies Since 1989'. In *The Economic History of Central, East and South-East Europe: 1800 to the Present*, edited by Matthias Morys, 434–67. London: Routledge.

Morys, Matthias, ed. 2020. *The Economic History of Central, East and South-East Europe: 1800 to the Present*. London: Routledge.

Myant, Martin. 2018. 'Dependent Capitalism and the Middle-Income Trap in Europe Na East Central Europe'. *International Journal of Management and Economics* 54(4): 291–303.

Nölke, Andreas, and Arjan Vliegenthart. 2009. 'Enlarging the Varieties of Capitalism: The Emergence of Dependent Market Economies in East Central Europe'. *World Politics* 61(4): 670–702.

Orłowski, Witold M. 2020. 'Trajectories of the Economic Transition in Central and Eastern Europe'. In *Social and Economic Development in Central and Eastern Europe: Stability and Change after 1990*, edited by Grzegorz Gorzelak, 11–34. London: Routledge.

Piątkowski, Marcin. 2018. *Europe's Growth Champion: Insights from the Economic Rise of Poland*. Oxford: Oxford University Press.

Podkaminer, Leon. 2013. 'Development Patterns of Central and East European Countries (in the Course of Transition and following EU Accession)'. Retrieved 23 April 2021 from https://wiiw.ac.at/development-patterns-of-central-and-east-european-countries-in-the-course-of-transition-and-following-eu-accession--dlp-2985.pdf.

Pula, Besnik. 2018. *Globalization under and after Socialism*. Stanford: Stanford University Press.

Radosevic, Slavo, Deniz E. Yoruk and Esin Yoruk. 2020. 'Technology Upgrading and Growth in Central and Eastern Europe'. In *Social and Economic Development in Central and Eastern Europe: Stability and Change after 1990*, edited by Grzegorz Gorzelak, 178–204. London: Routledge.

Scheiring, Gábor. 2020. *The Retreat of Liberal Democracy, Authoritarian Capitalism and the Accumulative State in Hungary*. Cham: Springer.

Smiecinska, Nadia. 2021. 'Crisis of Neoliberalism and the Rise of Authoritarianism in Poland: How a "Good Change" Is Turning Poland into a Neo-Authoritarian State'.

In *The Global Rise of Authoritarianism in the 21st Century: Crisis of Neoliberal Globalization and the Nationalist Response*, edited by Berch Berberoglu, 251–74. New York: Routledge.
Stiglitz, Joseph E. 2003. *Globalization and Its Discontents*. 1st ed. New York: W.W. Norton.
Streb, Jochen. 2016. 'The Cliometric Study of Innovations'. In *Handbook of Cliometrics*, edited by Claude Diebolt and Michael Haupert, 447–68. Berlin: Springer References.
Szabo, Septimiu, and Jorge D. Laguna. 2021. 'FDI as Force of Convergence in the CESEE Countries'. In *Does EU Membership Facilitate Convergence? The Experience of the EU's Eastern Enlargement – Volume II: Channels of Interaction*, edited by Michael Landesmann and István P. Székely, 37–66. Cham: Palgrave Macmillan.
Szlajfer, Henryk. 2012. *Economic Nationalism and Globalization: Lessons from Latin America and Central Europe*. Leiden: Brill.
Tyrowicz, Joanna, and Peter Szewczyk. 2020. 'Labour Markets'. In *Social and Economic Development in Central and Eastern Europe: Stability and Change after 1990*, edited by Grzegorz Gorzelak, 133–50. London: Routledge.
Vonyó, Tamás. 2017. 'War and Socialism: Why Eastern Europe Fell behind between 1950 and 1989'. *The Economic History Review* 70(1): 248–74.
Vonyó, Tamás, and Alexander Klein. 2019. 'Why Did Socialist Economies Fail? The Role of Factor Inputs Reconsidered'. *The Economic History Review* 72(1): 317–45.
Vonyó, Tamás, and Andrei Markevich. 2020. 'Economic Growth and Structural Developments, 1945–1989'. In *The Economic History of Central, East and South-East Europe: 1800 to the Present*, edited by Matthias Morys, 277–302. London: Routledge.
Voskoboynikov, Ilya. 2020. 'Economic Growth and Sectoral Developments During the Transition Period, 1990–2008'. In *The Economic History of Central, East and South-East Europe: 1800 to the Present*, edited by Matthias Morys, 383–412. London: Routledge.
Wade, Robert H. 2018. 'The Developmental State: Dead or Alive?' *Development and Change* 49(2): 518–46.
Weresa, Marzenna Anna. 2008. 'Foreign Direct Investment and the Competitiveness of Polish Manufacturing'. In *Reinventing Poland: Economic and Political Transformation and Evolving National Identity*, edited by Martin Myant and Terry Cox, 33–46. London: Routledge.
Williamson, Jeffrey G. 1996. 'Globalization, Convergence, and History'. *The Journal of Economic History* 56(2): 277–306.
Winiecki, Jan. 2016. *Shortcut or Piecemeal: Economic Development Strategies and Structural Change*. Budapest: CEU Press.

# PART I

# Historical Legacies

CHAPTER 1

# Poland's Communist Heritage and Its Impact on Post-1990 Economic Development

Yaman Kouli

### Introduction

From an economic point of view, Poland has been the economic role model of all transformation countries. A recent publication even awards the country with the unofficial title 'Europe's Growth Champion' (Piątkowski 2018). Poland is the only country that came through the financial crisis of 2009 without a single year of recession. The country's GDP-growth rates are remarkable. According to the economic forecast for Poland by the European commission, Poland would have profited from growth rates beyond 3 percent in 2021 and 2022, were it not for the pandemic. Other economic indicators also correspond with a healthy economy. Gross public debt is below 60 percent. Unemployment remains at a very low level.[1] Given the macroeconomic indicators, Poland's position as an economic role model seems well deserved. The fact that Poland was by far the biggest among the ten countries (Cyprus, the Czech Republic, Estonia, Hungary, Latvia, Lithuania, Malta, Poland, Slovakia and Slovenia) that became European Union members in 2004, in what remains to this date the largest expansion in the history of the EU, most certainly contributed to the great attention that the country drew.

Despite this impressive growth, there are some developments that potentially spoil the view. It is crucial to bear in mind that an important reason for the impressive growth is the country's low starting point. In 1991, the Polish GDP per capita amounted to only 57 percent of the GDP per capita of the Czech Republic.[2] By 2019, Poland came close (73 percent) to the Czech level without actually catching up.[3] Paradoxically, one could as well argue that the reason for Poland's economic success since the 1990s was its poor performance during communism which was dismal even in comparison to the country's communist peers. In this line of reasoning, Poland's economic weight was based on its sheer size. Most certainly, the large domestic market – more than 38 million inhabitants[4] – was also helpful in attracting FDI. On the other hand, a low starting point alone does not explain high economic growth. If a low starting point (in comparison to other countries) alone sufficed, it would automatically come to a convergence in the long run, no matter what the individual circumstances might be. Unfortunately, it is not that easy. Economic divergence is still an unresolved issue even in the European Union, despite the high level of economic integration.[5] Moreover, integration can also lead to more divergence, as Filippetti and Spallone show in their contribution (Chapter 9).

This points to another problem linked to the Polish development. While economists tend to emphasize the positive developments, social scientists often focus on the negative aspects. It is not hard to find challenges that have persisted during the last thirty years and have their roots in communism. One striking example concerns emigration. From 1960 on, more people left Poland than immigrated to the country. 2016 – probably because of the Brexit – was the first year where this trend turned around.[6] This brain drain most certainly took its toll on the national economy.

Understanding the development perspectives of Central European countries is one goal of this edited volume. With this aim in mind, I take the classic path of a historian in this chapter and tackle the question from where the Polish industry came. What were the starting conditions in Poland after the fall of the Iron Curtain? Did these conditions constitute a burden against or the material basis for the post-1990 development? By taking this macroeconomic perspective, I explicitly decide against an institutional analysis, even though it plays a prominent role in research. In doing so, I do not want to belittle the role of effective institutions and informal rules for economic success, as did Lawrence and Sznajder-Lee, who consider Poland's success unique and the result of a successful usage of state-ownership (King and Sznajder 2006). Yet by looking at the economic development using quantifiable data, we look at the factual outcome and call into question Poland's position as an undisputed role model.

In this chapter, I focus on three questions. The first question concerns the state of the Polish industrial capital by the end of the 1980s: was there relatively highly developed yet insufficiently managed industrial capital during communism? If this was the case, Poland would have been able to unleash high economic growth once the chains of communism were taken off. The second question pertains to the regional distribution of GDP and economic development, namely the gap between the Polish East and West. Were more than forty years of communist economic policy sufficient to equalize regional differences in production levels? Or did they persist, despite all attempts to level the economic playing field. Economic polarization on a national level is a common theme in Europe: Italy (Northern Italy vs. Mezzogiorno), Germany (former vs. newly formed German states) or France (Paris region vs. the rest of the country) are only three examples. Though not at the centre of this chapter, it is safe to assume that regional income distribution plays a crucial role for vote behaviour and thus for Poland's economic policy. The third and last question relates to human capital development. A main argument by Piątkowski is that the modernization of the Polish society – and the Polish institutions – between 1945 and 1989 also laid the foundations for an educational system from which post-1990 Poland immensely profited through the high level of human capital created by this system which became the basis of high GDP growth after 1990. Whether this conclusion is justified constitutes the second of the three central questions of this chapter.

After a brief overview of Poland's economic growth-development during communism, the chapter dedicates a section to each of these three questions. These are followed by a conclusion.

## Poland's Economic Performance During Communism

For a comprehensive evaluation of Poland's economic development during the transformation, one should ask how Poland performed and developed during the communist regime. Or more precisely: When and why did communist Poland fall behind in comparison even to its local peers? The link between the communist and transformation periods has not always been self-evident. For a long time, publications that dealt with the economies of the Central European countries made a clear distinction between the communist period and the transformation era. Although the publications are numerous, most of these focus on the transformation period[7] and blame the general inefficiencies linked to communist economies when it comes to the pre-1990 era. During the last two decades, however, the picture that authors draw from the communist economies has become more and more comprehensive. There have been substantial contributions to research that gives a much clearer view of the economies in the communist area. Although these works have not changed the picture entirely, they have made it possible to understand the individual differences among the Eastern Bloc countries better. One assessment has been that the seemingly causal link between economic inefficiencies and the downfall of communism did in fact not exist: 'One fact should be acknowledged: the fundamental problems of the command economy cannot explain the rapid and sudden collapse of socialism, and thus the role of politics and exogenous factors cannot be easily ignored' (Markevich and Vonyó 2020, 320).

This does not mean that communism as the main culprit for the pre-1990 economic problems is off the hook. The most popular and perhaps also the most intuitive argument remains that communism is simply not an economy good at maintaining – or more precisely rewarding – efficiency. This fact holds true. As centrally planned economies are primarily focused on economic output, the argument goes that such economies do not provide much incentive to use resources efficiently. Quite the contrary. For instance, factory leaders had an incentive to overestimate the amount of resources that they needed annually, as production growth was the major goal of industrial production.[8] Another rather old argument points in a similar direction. The absence of a functioning market[9] led to a situation where market prices (that is, prices that customers were willing to pay) were not worked out freely on the market. Preferences of the customers had thus no impact on the production.

However, although these descriptions are plausible, they remain on a general level. Thus, while they explain the general underperformance of communist economies, they are insufficient to clarify the differences between these economies. As Figure 1.1 clarifies, Poland's GDP per capita was below that of Hungary and much lower than that of the Czech Republic. This was especially the case in the late-1970s and the 1980s.[10] Moreover, the descriptions often appear to fall into a teleological trap, for they give the impression of constant failure. From this perspective, the events of 1989 and 1990 appear to be an inevitable consequence of the economic downfall.[11] Meanwhile, one must not forget that observers during the 1970s and 1980s did not have the impression that collapse was imminent. Recent research emphasizes that although growth was not that impressive from today's perspective, it is crucial to realize that 'never prior to 1945 had this region increased its productive potential and standards of living so fast as in the post-war era' (Vonyó and Markevich 2020, 277). Indeed, during the 1950s and 1960s, Central European countries including Poland were able to profit from extensive economic growth. At first sight, the development on both sides of the Iron Curtain seemed to share some similarities. Yet, already then, the technological gap was large. As Berend puts it, the GDP growth in the eastern half of Europe was 'based on technology that was obsolete even then' (Berend 2009, 20). Therefore, even the extensive growth path did not live up to its potential. Tamás Vonyó and Andrei Markevich admit that 'these were the decades when Eastern European economies did not only fail to realize their catch-up potential but noticeably fell behind Western nations' (Vonyó and Markevich 2020, 281). Therefore, Central and Eastern Europe had already lost the Cold War economically by the time the economic crisis hit during the first half of the 1970s.

Nevertheless, there were obvious differences between the countries, which cannot be uncovered by references to the world economy alone. As a consequence of these differences, the individual performance of the communist economies has returned to the centre of some analyses, since having a better understanding of their development and foundations seems to be a good strategy for developing a better understanding also of their post-1989 performance. The magnitude of these differences is shown in Figure 1.1, which illustrates GDP growth in Poland since the Second World War in comparison to that of Czech Republic and Hungary. Figure 1.1 reveals the uniqueness of Poland's development. Compared to the 1950s, Poland's GDP grew in sync with that of Hungary until the 1970s. During the 1970s, Poland fell significantly behind. The Czech Republic was already at a much higher level than Poland. Moreover, while Hungary continued to grow during the subsequent years, Poland's GDP per capita dropped substantially. According to these figures, Poland had virtually zero growth between 1974 and the end of the 1980s. Although the country started at a higher level than Hungary in 1950, it dropped to the last place by the end of the communist era and became the lowest performer in East Central Europe. In the end, the country started low and stayed on that level.

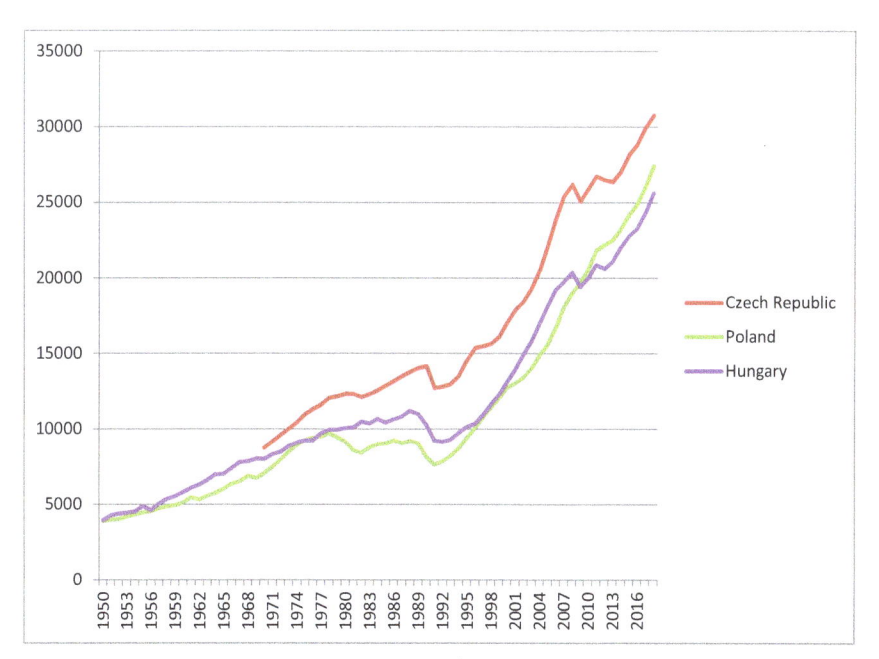

**Figure 1.1.** GDP per capita (in 2011 US$). Source: Data taken from the Maddison Project Database, 2020. Retrieved 6 December 2022 from https://www.rug.nl/ggdc/historicaldevelopment/maddison/releases/maddison-project-database-2020. Created by the author.

## Poland's Communist Industry

It goes without saying that there is a close link between the development of the Polish industry and economic performance. Although the link is not causal, researchers have devoted much effort to shed more light on the industry itself. A group among such researchers focuses on material developments including investment levels (that is, the accumulation of capital) and thus the quality of the available machines and buildings. A 2015 publication by Karpiński et al. seeks to directly link the development during communism to that in the 1990s and draws an interesting conclusion. The authors address the question of which kind of factories were most exploitable during the post-1990 transformation. Their general aim is to show that Poland's industrial capital was relatively well developed. Eventually, they argue that the factories that were constructed during communism were economically much more valuable than those that were constructed before 1938. It was only due to a hasty privatization that Poland became no more than merely the workbench of the world. To support their argument, the authors study the Polish companies and ask whether these companies were built during or before the communist period. They make rather harsh accusations. Accordingly, the one thing communism got right was the improvement of industrial machines, buildings and infrastructure. Based on their analysis had there been a concise industrial strategy, deindustrialization in Poland during the transition could have been avoided. The knowledge-based companies especially should have been protected better. With more effective negotiators, so the authors say, the whole situation might have played out entirely differently and Poland could have developed and maintained a much more modern economy (Karpiński et al. 2015).

However, one should not take this conclusion at face value. A similar argument has also been made in the case of Germany, suggesting that the country sold the industrial capital way too quickly. This legend of botched privatization that did more harm than good and was also destabilized by corruption still persists in Germany (Böick 2018). Moreover, the Polish companies constructed after 1950 were also much younger than those built during the interwar period. This simple fact might also explain their relatively higher popularity compared to the older ones. Whatever the case, the book shows that Polish economists more actively tried to link the pre- and the post-1990 periods.

The following figures illustrate the changes among Poland's industrial branches more closely. Figure 1.2 shows the relative share of the industrial branches of overall industrial production, while Figure 1.3 demonstrates the matching relative employment share. In general, a look at industrial production reveals that there were several industries that underwent

POLAND'S COMMUNIST HERITAGE AND ITS IMPACT    31

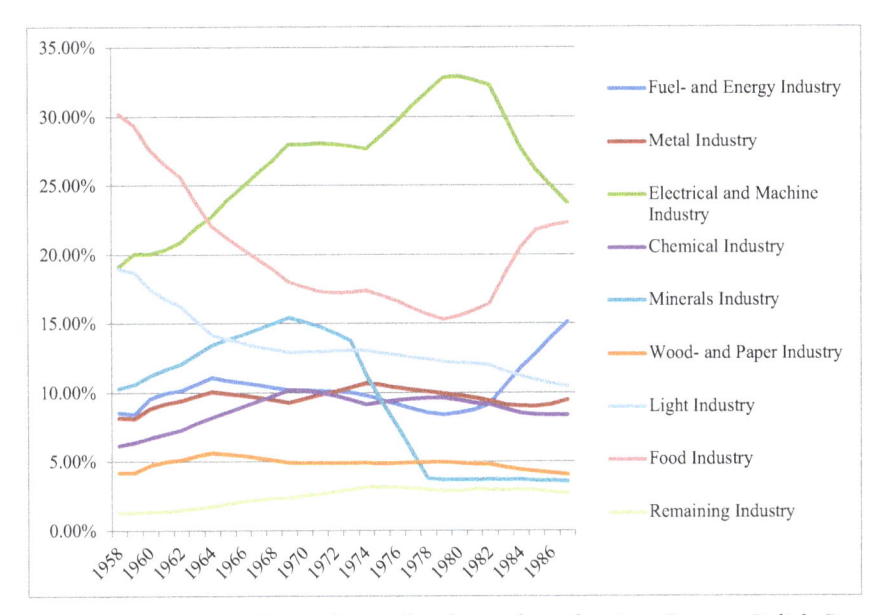

**Figure 1.2.** Relative share of overall industrial production. Source: Polish Statistical Office, statistical yearbooks of Poland, Warsaw, years 1958–90. Created by the author.

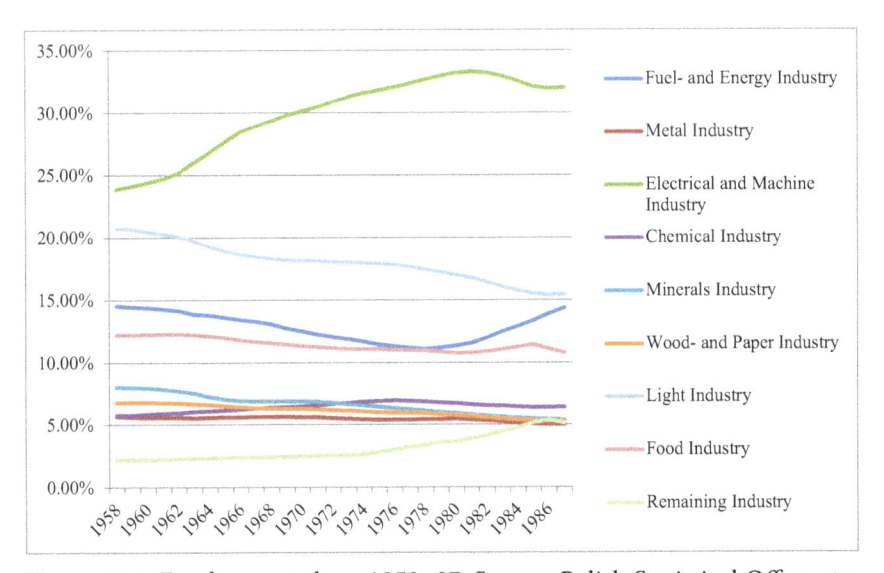

**Figure 1.3.** Employment share 1958–87. Source: Polish Statistical Office, statistical yearbooks of Poland, Warsaw, years 1958–90. Created by the author.

abrupt changes. This is true for the minerals industry, which dropped during the 1970s, compared to a steady development for the metal industry, the chemical industry, the wood and paper industry and also the remaining industrial branches. The fuel and energy industry appears to have grown in importance, especially during the 1980s. Most striking is the relationship of the food industry and the electrical and machine industry, as relative growth of one industry was matched by a decline of the other and vice versa. Meanwhile, the share of employed workers did not change abruptly in any case. This might be expected, as labour markets do indeed change incrementally and it is reasonable to assume that centrally planned economies tend to slow down this process even more. In the metal industry, chemical industry, minerals industry, wood and paper industry and food industry, the shares of employed people were relatively stable. Light industry showed a steady decline, meanwhile fuel and energy industry remained on their relatively high level, despite the downward curve during the 1970s. Electrical and machine industry as well as the remaining industries showed an upward development. Despite this relative stability, production levels were – at least in some cases – a lot more unstable. Minerals industry decreased sharply during the 1970s, as did the food industry.

With the availability of production and employment figures, however, one could also ask how the efficiency growth among the different industrial branches developed over time. For Table 1.1, I have used the deflated production levels per worker. Clearly, the interpretability of these data is limited. A mere calculation of the increase of productivity levels is not possible, as the available figures do not cover changes in the factor-intensity.[12] It is thus entirely possible that the increase of productivity per worker is not the result of more effective workers but rather of the extensive use of material factor inputs. To deal with this challenge, I have looked at the relative increase, thus the increase (or decrease) in comparison to other branches rather than the absolute productivity increase. That way, I could assess which industrial branches contributed more to overall production and which lagged behind.

What do the computed figures show? Unsurprisingly, the fuel and energy industry, which includes coal production, was the clear leader. Metal industry, wood and paper industry as well as the chemical industry remained relatively stable. Light industry, food industry and minerals industry on the other hand fell behind. Finally, electrical and machine industry remained on average. Given the high relative share of overall industrial production that the fuel and energy industry claimed, these figures confirm the overweight of this particular industrial branch, which continued to cause problems long after 1990 (Kouli 2016).

**Table 1.1.** Relative production efficiency per worker (total = 100).

| | Fuel- and Energy Industry | Metal Industry | Electrical and Machine Industry | Chemical Industry | Minerals Industry | Wood- and Paper Industry | Light Industry | Food Industry | Remaining Industry |
|---|---|---|---|---|---|---|---|---|---|
| 1958 | 100 | 100 | 100 | 100 | 100 | 100 | 100 | 100 | 100 |
| 1960 | 141 | 129 | 100 | 116 | 123 | 139 | 82 | 79 | 115 |
| 1965 | 135 | 118 | 110 | 139 | 165 | 134 | 80 | 68 | 173 |
| 1970 | 146 | 136 | 104 | 128 | 150 | 134 | 82 | 65 | 213 |
| 1975 | 135 | 133 | 119 | 131 | 48 | 135 | 78 | 59 | 153 |
| 1980 | 135 | 120 | 115 | 125 | 52 | 137 | 80 | 65 | 149 |
| 1985 | 178 | 130 | 92 | 124 | 50 | 125 | 77 | 81 | 88 |
| 1987 | 173 | 142 | 98 | 126 | 52 | 130 | 74 | 76 | 107 |

Source: Polish Statistical Office, Statistical yearbooks of Poland, Warsaw, years 1958–90.

*Note:* The calculations are based on figures of employment and deflationed production levels.

As Figure 1.1 shows, Poland's starting point at the beginning of the 1990s was low. The country lost sight of its peers during the 1970s and 1980s. Therefore, the question is how it did come to this. Evidently, there is not a single culprit but several that can be blamed. One of these is the level of investments, even though this may seem contradictory. In Polish historiography, the first half of the 1950s is considered an era during which the Central Committee directed most investments into heavy industry at the expense of the consumer industry.[13] A closer look on the investments changes this picture.

Although one cannot argue that there is a direct causality between capital stock and GDP production levels, the link between the two is a close one. Looking at the growth rates of Poland's general investments rates in equipment (Figure 1.4), one can get the impression that Poland had acceptable investment rates, at least not lower than its peers. Especially during the 1970s, Poland seems to have increased its yearly investments. Especially during the last fifteen years of communism, nominal investment rates decreased until the collapse of the Communist regimes in 1990. Although the Polish decrease appears to have been the sharpest, the trends in Hungary and Czechoslovakia were similar.

Nominal investment ratios may explain national stories, as, for instance the emphasis on heavy-industry investments during the early 1950s. Yet, they are only of limited explanatory value, as they merely show how they developed in comparison to the 1950s. To make the figures internationally

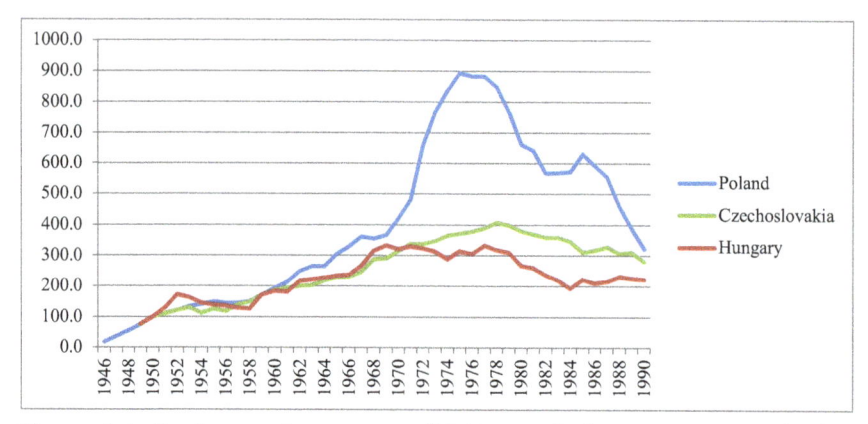

**Figure 1.4.** Equipment investments (1950 = 100). Source: Vonyó and Klein (2019), Appendix. Created by the author.

comparable, Tamás Vonyó and Alexander Klein have calculated the investment ratios per GDP in percent (see Figure 1.5). That way, the nominal investments figures appear in a different perspective. While investment levels seem to be on a similar level during the 1950s and 1960s according to Figure 1.4, Poland's actual efforts paled in comparison, especially to Hungary and Czechoslovakia. The only time period during which Poland

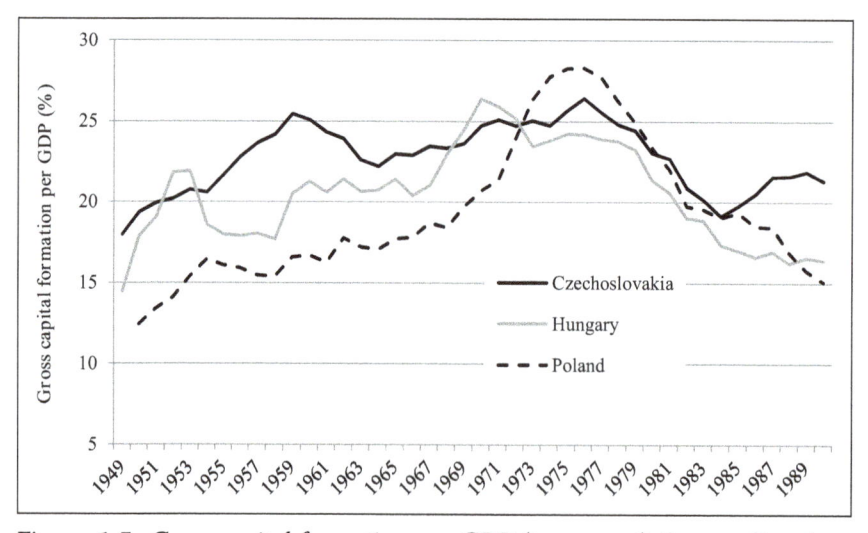

**Figure 1.5.** Gross capital formation per GDP (in percent). Source: Based on Vonyó and Klein (2019, 330), data kindly provided by the authors.

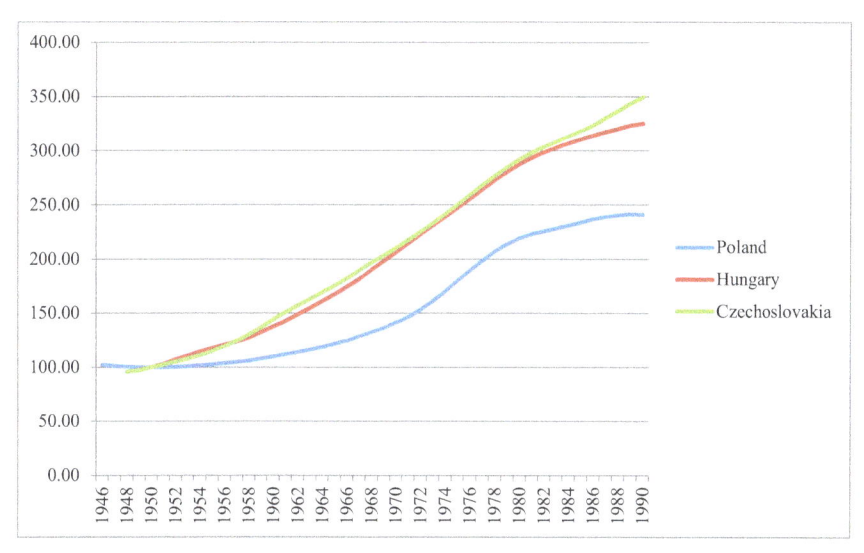

**Figure 1.6.** Gross capital stock of Poland, Hungary and Czechoslovakia (1950 = 100). Source: Vonyó and Klein (2019), Appendix. Created by the author.

was able to catch up was the 1970s. Yet, given the fact that Poland's GDP per capita was much lower during the 1970s, the growth rates indicated in Figure 1.3 can partly be qualified as a side-effect of this drop in national production levels. While investment levels increased in Poland by a factor of 2.4 (in comparison to 1950), they did so by a factor of 3.2 in Czechoslovakia and 3.5 in Hungary.

The calculations of the industrial capital in Poland – as well as in other countries – are an important factor in the debate on how Poland profited from its industrial basis after 1990. Karpiński and his colleagues' main premise is that there were better ways to profit from Poland's industry during the transformation (Karpiński et al. 2015). Yet, given the level of investments during the communist era, it is doubtful whether that expectation was ever realistic. Arguing that post-communist Poland should have profited from a renewed industrial capital stock, one has to assume that the economic value was at least in the range of that of its neighbouring countries. The recalculated investment figures show, however, that this was not the case. Vonyó and Klein's article indicates that the quality of the Polish industrial capital stock never justified the expectation that smart negotiators and a coherent industrial strategy might have prevented Poland's deindustrialization after 1990. Poland's industrial capital was in a poor state even in comparison to its regional peers.

## Regional Industrial Development

In the previous section, it was insinuated that Poland suffered from a deindustrialization because of insufficient investments. In the following, I will turn this question around and ask if communism led to equal living conditions in all Polish regions? Or did differences in productivity levels persist? The assumption is that if the general distribution of regions with higher productivity remained (close to) unchanged, this would mean that even communist economic policy would not have been able to completely reset production in Poland.

Clearly, there are regional differences. Among the seven Polish NUTS2 macroregions, the individual levels of productivity are quite diverse. Table 1.2 illustrates the GDP per capita level during the last decade in relation to the Polish average. The figures show that the region around the capital Warsaw (*województwo mazowieckie*) is the clear leader with GDP per capita levels being at least fifty-six index points higher than in every other Polish region. Second place – once again measured by GDP per capita levels – goes to the South-Western macroregion, which is mostly Lower Silesia. At the same time, those are the only two regions that perform above the national average. The pattern the figures show is not surprising. In virtually

**Table 1.2.** GDP per capita in Poland's NUTS1-regions (Poland = 100).

|  | 2009 | 2010 | 2011 | 2012 | 2013 | 2014 | 2015 | 2016 | 2017 | 2018 |
|---|---|---|---|---|---|---|---|---|---|---|
| Poland | 100 | 100 | 100 | 100 | 100 | 100 | 100 | 100 | 100 | 100 |
| Southern Macroregion (PL2) | 99 | 99 | 100 | 99 | 98 | 98 | 98 | 98 | 99 | 99 |
| North-Western Macroregion (PL4) | 98 | 96 | 95 | 96 | 97 | 97 | 98 | 98 | 98 | 96 |
| South-Western Macroregion (PL5) | 102 | 105 | 106 | 105 | 104 | 104 | 104 | 103 | 102 | 105 |
| Northern Macroregion (PL6) | 87 | 85 | 85 | 85 | 85 | 84 | 85 | 85 | 87 | 85 |
| Central Macroregion (PL7) | 87 | 87 | 87 | 87 | 86 | 87 | 86 | 86 | 87 | 87 |
| Eastern Macroregion (PL8) | 71 | 70 | 71 | 70 | 71 | 71 | 70 | 70 | 71 | 70 |
| Macroregion Masovian Voivodeship (PL9) | 156 | 159 | 159 | 159 | 160 | 160 | 160 | 160 | 156 | 159 |

Source: Calculations based on Eurostat.

all European countries the regions around the capital cities takes up the first place. The differences among the economic regions are also still well within expectations (Rosés and Wolf 2019). What makes Poland stand out is the geographical tendency. Leaving the capital area aside, there is a clear increase in GDP per capita levels from east to west. Theoretically, this confirms the assumption that a relatively higher appreciation for and accumulation of human capital leads to higher productivity levels (per person).[14]

The figures illustrate the level of dispersion. Intuitively, there was always good reason to acknowledge the role of the booming western cities like Wrocław, Szczecin or Gdańsk for the economic development of Poland. The structure of the data reveals a clear pattern: the closer a region is to the east, the higher the production levels per capita. The eastern territories, namely South-Western and the North-Western macroregions, perform very well, while the Central and the Eastern macroregions as well as the northern region clearly fall behind. The question is whether this pattern already characterized Poland during the communist era or whether it emerged afterwards.

Tackling the same issue for the communist Poland is much more complicated. Data on the regional development of Poland are not easy to retrieve.

**Figure 1.7.** NUTS1 Divisions of Poland, since 2018. Source: Wikimedia Commons, author: Aotearoa, modified by Periwinklewrinkles, CC-BY-3.0.

**Table 1.3.** Industrial production per worker (Poland = 100).

| | 1970 | 1974 | 1975 | 1976 | 1977 | 1978 | 1979 | 1980 | 1981 | 1982 | 1983 | 1984 | 1985 | 1986 | 1987 |
|---|---|---|---|---|---|---|---|---|---|---|---|---|---|---|---|
| Poland | 100 | 100 | 100 | 100 | 100 | 100 | 100 | 100 | 100 | 100 | 100 | 100 | 100 | 100 | 100 |
| Southern Macroregion / Południowy(PL2) | 102 | 100 | 99 | 98 | 99 | 99 | 98 | 96 | 95 | 94 | 95 | 96 | 97 | 98 | 100 |
| North-Western Macroregion / Północno-Zachodni (PL4) | 104 | 104 | 103 | 105 | 104 | 105 | 105 | 105 | 107 | 104 | 103 | 102 | 103 | 98 | 98 |
| South-Western Macroregion / Południowo-Zachodni (PL5) | 101 | 102 | 103 | 103 | 103 | 103 | 104 | 100 | 103 | 102 | 100 | 101 | 100 | 102 | 101 |
| Northern Macroregion / Północny (PL6) | 103 | 106 | 105 | 105 | 104 | 104 | 103 | 104 | 107 | 107 | 100 | 101 | 99 | 100 | 101 |
| Central Macroregion / Centralny (PL7) | 83 | 81 | 80 | 82 | 83 | 83 | 83 | 84 | 83 | 83 | 80 | 82 | 85 | 85 | 84 |
| Eastern Macroregion / Wschodni (PL8) | 105 | 96 | 97 | 95 | 95 | 94 | 95 | 100 | 100 | 101 | 99 | 97 | 95 | 94 | 92 |
| Macroregion Masovian Voivodeship / Województwo Mazowieckie (PL9) | 100 | 111 | 112 | 113 | 113 | 114 | 115 | 116 | 115 | 116 | 129 | 127 | 126 | 126 | 124 |

Source: Calculations based on Eurostat (figures for the years 1971–1973 unavailable). See also explanations in the text.

So far, I have consulted several publications that contain calculations on the macro-economy of Poland. Finding information on the regional and sectorial development, however, proves to be more challenging. Perhaps the biggest reason for this is that the absence of a market which made it extremely complicated, if not impossible, to compute a regional GDP, as reliable information on local prices, salaries and inflation levels are beyond reach.[15] Hence, there seems to be no reliable method to calculate regional development in pre-1990 Poland.

Therefore, I have used a workaround for this chapter. Although there are numerous limitations, the Polish statistical yearbooks are still among the most consulted and reliable sources. However, it must be emphasized that while this is mostly true for the data that cover production figures that measure production via physical units, the reliability is much more contested, when it comes to loans and prices. My solution to this challenge is to employ the production-figures in a different way. I calculate the figures available on a regional – thus voivodeship – basis. The statistical yearbooks contain information on the sum of the paid loans as well as the number of the active workers. The quotient of both can be used to compute the efficiency of every worker for every voivodeship. Theoretically, this still leaves us at the mercy of the planners in the ministries that calculated salaries and prices. Yet, it still is a credible assumption that planners tried to push industrial branches that they considered more productive.

To achieve a certain level of comparability, I have matched regions according to the NUTS2-structure and the voivodeships as they were between 1979 and 1998.[16] This way, it is possible to link the development since the 1970s with the one described in Table 1.2, although it is imperative to keep in mind that the figures do not pertain to regional GDP but to production levels per worker measured by non-market prices. Table 1.3 contains the results of these calculations. The figures unveil a pattern that shows similarities to what has been observed for the decade prior to 2018. The region around Warsaw was the economically strongest and the clear leader when it came to productivity. The Southern (PL2), North-Western (PL4) and the South-Western Macroregion (PL5), on the other hand, were close to the Polish average. In all three cases, they were close to one hundred. Another similarity is that the Central and the Eastern Macroregions were behind, although the Eastern Macroregion did not lag as much in the 1980s as it would thirty years later. The main difference emerges in the position of the Northern Macroregion. In post-1970 Poland, productivity levels were always slightly above average. After 2009, however, the Northern Macroregion clearly remained behind. One explanation for this may lay in the lost significance of the shipyards, which played a huge role in communist Poland, not only in Poland but in all of Europe.

For research on the long-term development of Poland during the transition, this is an interesting finding. This reveals that when it comes to productivity, the regional pattern persisted despite the tremendous political and economic changes that took place between the 1970s and 1980s on the one hand, and the decade before 2018 on the other. This might also explain the regional differences in Poland's elections in 2020, where the pro-European presidential candidate Rafał Trzaskowski was much more successful not only in the urban areas but also in the western regions of Poland. But this is a question for another study.[17]

## Bad at Marketing Innovations, but Good at Producing Human Capital?

In the previous sections it was mentioned that communist economies were not good at knowledge-based production. This argument is partly a variant of the aforementioned assertion that centrally planned economies do not provide any incentive to improve efficiency. Yet, it goes a step further. In markets, successful companies with certain products or services cause other companies to follow in their footsteps and profit from the newly found demand. Ideally, this leads to competition among companies via prices and better quality. The absence of substantial consumer-feedback was one of the reasons why it did not come to a refinement of products in communist economies (Crafts and Toniolo 2010, 323). Vonyó also confirms that this argument is more than just a prejudice. In a factor-analysis, he shows that improvement in education did not have any significant effect on economic production or efficiency levels (Vonyó 2017, 263).[18]

Technically, however, this does not say much on a country's ability to produce human capital itself. To do so, one needs to go beyond a mere comparison of input and output and look at the qualitative aspects of the Polish economic performance. A major advocate of this approach is Piątkowski. He argues that even though communism was an economic disaster, institutional changes that it brought to Poland laid the foundations of Poland's economic success. For instance, Piątkowski points to the compelling function in educating the Polish population (Piątkowski 2018, 103).

The discussion of the effect of human capital as economic input and the ability to get closer to a knowledge-based economy is tightly linked with the subject of modernization. In this context, Piątkowski is an especially ardent supporter of the argument that communism was crucial in modernising the Polish society. According to him, school participation and university level education increased, as agricultural employment decreased in favour of employment in the industry. The destruction of feudalist structures – he uses the expression 'feudalism' – laid the foundations of an inclusive society with a high social mobility. Social inequality was therefore reduced dramatically (Piątkowski 2018, 94–107). Scholars in Poland are often much less enthusiastic. In 2010, Polish historians addressed the question of whether communist Poland witnessed 'modernization or botched modernization' only to find virtually no evidence for successful modernization (Chumiński 2010). This perspective has hardly changed. In 2013, the Polish political scientist Wojciech Musiał wrote a dissertation studying modernization by focussing on government policies between 1918 and 2004 and suggested that the communist era was the only period during which there was no modernization in Poland whatsoever (Musiał 2013).

Scholars usually focus on 'intended' modernization-attempts. However, there also is good reason take a look at unintended modernization. Given the Polish success during the transformation, it appears reasonable to tackle this question by examining the state of Poland's immaterial capital at the end of the 1980s, especially given the fact that the Polish industrial basis itself does not appear to have been a key factor for Poland's economic growth during the transformation. Yet one could expect that human capital development was the more decisive factor. In general, it is hard to overstate the role education plays for the economy, as the availability of well-educated workers is crucial for long-term economic growth. But the discussion goes beyond economy. Improving the education system was also part of the general plan to modernize the Polish society (Musiał 2013, 181, 184). In most Central and Eastern European societies, education was seen as an important task for governments. The question thus is whether Poland was successful at educating its population and accumulating human capital and hence laying the foundations of its subsequent economic success.

There are several ways to address this question. One popular strategy is to assess the share of people active in agriculture. The underlying assumption is that people working in agriculture would be more efficient if they worked in industry or the service sector. Therefore, the lower the share of the work force active in the primary sector, the higher the chance for economic success, higher productivity and growth. Consequently, efficient agriculture is key for reaching a certain level of modernity. This logic also affected Poland's policy, as agrarian overpopulation was one of the challenges that the country wanted to deal with right after 1945. Although there is no monocausal link between the aforementioned arguments, the share of people that live on agricultural production is with good reason considered a reliable estimator to assess the level of modernity of an economy.

Still during the first half of the twentieth century, agriculture played an important role in the Central European countries, especially compared to Western Europe. Poland was no exception to this. In 1950, an astounding 57 percent of the Polish population still worked in agriculture (Houpt, Lains and Schön 2010, 335). This is especially surprising once the fact that Poland lost its eastern territories to Russia is taken into consideration. These so-called *kresy* were in general less efficient than the rest of Poland and had a large agricultural sector (Kouli 2020). During the following decades, the share of people working in agriculture declined. Until 1975, this figure dropped down to 30 percent. In 2000, it amounted to 18.8 percent. On the one hand, this represents a considerable improvement. On the other hand, it is still much higher than the shares of agricultural workforce in the Czech Republic (5.1 percent) or Hungary (6.5 percent). That is, although Poland was able to take significant steps towards an economy that depended on agriculture much less than it did before or during the communist era, the country's development was not exceptionally good. This holds true even though Poland managed to substantially reduce the labour productivity-gap between agricultural and non-agricultural sectors (Houpt, Lains and Schön 2010, 335–36). Moreover, regional distribution of agricultural production indicates that contribution to GDP production is unequally distributed among the Polish regions. As data from the Polish Statistical Office for the year 2007 indicate, the share of the population depending on agriculture was much higher in the eastern regions (Central Statistical Office 2009, 14).[19]

Even given all this information, the question remains valid: how successful was Poland at increasing its human capital? If the increase of the work force in the industry is an important element of economic development, the quality of this work force should be taken into account as well. Education and training are an essential part of human capital (Goldin 2016). Therefore, many researchers focus on the analysis of school education to assess human capital better, as I will also do in the next section.

Human capital is not easy to measure. One of the few reliable ways to do it is via proxy. Figure 1.7 is based on the database by Robert Barro and Jong-Wha Lee.[20] The list shows the educational attainment for five-year-cohorts from the 1950s to the year 1990. Next to Poland, Czechoslovakia and Hungary, I have also included Germany (before 1990: West Germany) in the list. As it can be seen clearly, Poland started as the country with the lowest attainment. By 1990, Poland overtook Hungary and Germany and became second only to the Czech Republic. However, these figures should not be taken at face value, because educational and vocational systems vary considerably and hence a comparison of 'human capital stocks' – as the authors call them – can be tricky.

As previously mentioned, Piątkowski argues that the Polish tertiary educational system's ability to provide the labour market with a sufficient number of well-qualified people for the needs of the new economy was an important factor in Poland's remarkable post-1990 success. This was, in fact, a crucial part of Poland's success, which has for the most part led to the expectation that the new members of the European Union would be able to start catching up to the EU average: Western quality at much lower prices.

Jong-Wha Lee and Hanol Lee have constructed a data set of historical enrolment ratios. Based on these data, they have calculated the national human capital stocks of numerous countries from 1870 to 2010 (Lee and Lee 2016, 147). Yet, the calculation of this stock is entirely based on enrolment ratios. It is thus important to emphasize that the figures that indicate the human capital levels do not have physical units. It is more realistic to construe them as relative ones.

To strengthen the argument, Table 1.4 contains raw information on educational attainment. These figures can be consulted to compare the different levels of school attendance. According to Piątkowski, school attendance was essential for Poland's economic success, which was due to how the country successfully opened the national society and widely improved its educational system. Notwithstanding, it is also crucial to bear in mind that during the entire period in question, the individual capital stock (per person) was below the corresponding figures for Hungary and the Czech Republic. However, this was also the case in West Germany especially during the 1970s and 1980s. This clarifies why this comparison should be treated carefully. It also challenges the assumption that the level of production of human capital was exceptionally high in Poland. Even in comparison to its local peers, this is an unlikely conclusion.

The interpretation of Table 1.4 points in the same direction. Piątkowski argues that the rate of secondary schooling as well as the level of university

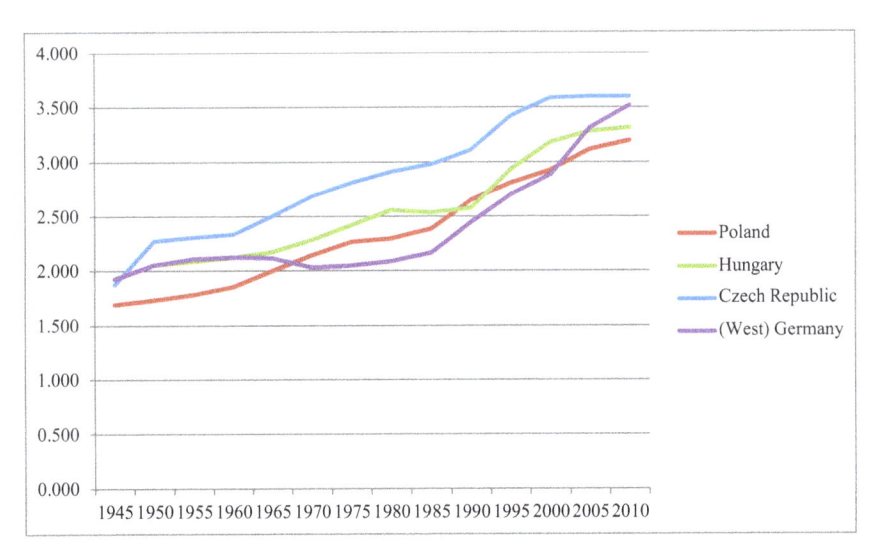

**Figure 1.8.** Human capital stock (per person, 1945–2010). Source: based on the database issued by Robert Barro and Jong-Wha Lee, Educational Attainment Dataset. Retrieved 24 February 2021 from www.barrolee.com. Created by the author.

**Table 1.4.** Educational attainment for total population (1935–2010).

| Country | Year | Age Group | No Schooling | Primary Total | Primary Completed | Secondary Total | Secondary Completed | Tertiary Total | Tertiary Completed | Avg. Years of Total Schooling | Avg. Years of Primary Schooling | Avg. Years of Secondary Schooling | Avg. Years of Tertiary Schooling |
|---|---|---|---|---|---|---|---|---|---|---|---|---|---|
| | | | | | | (% of population aged 15–24) | | | | | | | |
| Czech Republic | 1935 | 15–24 | 10.3 | 81.4 | 26.7 | 8.3 | 3.1 | 0.1 | 0.0 | 5.31 | 4.99 | 0.31 | 0.00 |
| | 1950 | 15–24 | 0.3 | 86.4 | 60.0 | 11.1 | 5.8 | 2.2 | 0.8 | 8.27 | 7.79 | 0.43 | 0.06 |
| | 1970 | 15–24 | 0.2 | 57.4 | 45.5 | 41.7 | 28.5 | 0.7 | 0.2 | 9.90 | 8.45 | 1.43 | 0.02 |
| | 1980 | 15–24 | 0.3 | 45.9 | 38.2 | 52.7 | 36.3 | 1.1 | 0.4 | 10.48 | 8.63 | 1.82 | 0.03 |
| | 1985 | 15–24 | 1.5 | 48.5 | 41.3 | 40.9 | 32.4 | 9.2 | 3.1 | 10.62 | 8.54 | 1.83 | 0.25 |
| | 1990 | 15–24 | 0.5 | 40.9 | 35.5 | 56.3 | 37.8 | 2.4 | 0.8 | 10.76 | 8.72 | 1.98 | 0.06 |
| | 2010 | 15–24 | 0.2 | 5.0 | 4.6 | 90.7 | 49.6 | 4.2 | 1.4 | 10.61 | 6.56 | 3.95 | 0.11 |
| Hungary | 1935 | 15–24 | 36.5 | 58.1 | 39.9 | 4.2 | 1.3 | 1.4 | 0.4 | 4.57 | 4.37 | 0.17 | 0.04 |
| | 1950 | 15–24 | 1.6 | 87.6 | 75.6 | 8.2 | 1.3 | 2.6 | 1.5 | 7.77 | 7.40 | 0.29 | 0.08 |
| | 1970 | 15–24 | 0.7 | 65.3 | 62.0 | 29.8 | 11.2 | 4.2 | 2.8 | 8.94 | 7.81 | 0.99 | 0.14 |
| | 1980 | 15–24 | 0.6 | 29.8 | 27.7 | 63.8 | 29.2 | 5.7 | 4.6 | 10.17 | 7.87 | 2.09 | 0.21 |
| | 1985 | 15–24 | 0.7 | 40.7 | 38.1 | 51.7 | 23.9 | 6.9 | 4.9 | 9.87 | 7.84 | 1.79 | 0.24 |
| | 1990 | 15–24 | 0.7 | 49.5 | 45.5 | 47.4 | 27.0 | 2.4 | 1.7 | 9.45 | 7.79 | 1.58 | 0.08 |
| | 2010 | 15–24 | 0.3 | 2.7 | 2.6 | 93.0 | 44.8 | 4.0 | 2.0 | 10.12 | 6.02 | 3.98 | 0.12 |

| Country | Year | Age Group | | No Schooling | Highest level attained | | | | | | | Avg. Years of Total Schooling | Avg. Years of Primary Schooling | Avg. Years of Secondary Schooling | Avg. Years of Tertiary Schooling |
|---|---|---|---|---|---|---|---|---|---|---|---|---|---|---|---|
| | | | | | Primary | | Secondary | | | Tertiary | | | | | |
| | | | | | Total | Completed | Total | Completed | | Total | Completed | | | | |
| | | | | | (% of population aged 15–24) | | | | | | | | | | |
| Poland | 1935 | 15 | 24 | 19.9 | 60.2 | 22.4 | 19.4 | 6.0 | | 0.6 | 0.2 | 4.84 | 4.29 | 0.53 | 0.02 |
| | 1950 | 15 | 24 | 2.1 | 67.3 | 29.5 | 28.2 | 7.6 | | 2.4 | 0.9 | 6.40 | 5.53 | 0.81 | 0.07 |
| | 1970 | 15 | 24 | 0.2 | 56.9 | 49.7 | 39.1 | 24.1 | | 3.8 | 1.4 | 8.25 | 6.73 | 1.41 | 0.10 |
| | 1980 | 15 | 24 | 0.2 | 41.9 | 39.5 | 57.1 | 8.7 | | 0.8 | 0.3 | 8.71 | 7.34 | 1.35 | 0.02 |
| | 1985 | 15 | 24 | 0.5 | 41.0 | 38.5 | 53.8 | 7.0 | | 4.7 | 1.8 | 9.39 | 7.86 | 1.40 | 0.13 |
| | 1990 | 15 | 24 | 0.2 | 48.8 | 47.3 | 50.3 | 39.4 | | 0.5 | 0.2 | 9.74 | 7.91 | 1.81 | 0.01 |
| | 2010 | 15 | 24 | 0.1 | 11.7 | 11.6 | 80.9 | 47.7 | | 7.3 | 2.8 | 10.26 | 7.07 | 2.99 | 0.20 |

Source: Lee and Lee Long-Run Education Dataset. Retrieved 16 September 2022 from https://barrolee.github.io/BarroLeeDataSet/DataLeeLee.html.

enrolment increased significantly, particularly in comparison to the interwar period (Piątkowski 2018, 89, 103). While this may be true, the insinuation that Poland exceeded its regional peers can hardly be confirmed by the facts, as the average years of tertiary schooling confirms. The growth in all three countries is impressive. Yet, it seems implausible to deduce that Poland's development was exceptional.[21] During and after the communist era, Poland performed just as well as its peers, which may be notable but not sufficient to explain Poland's development as 'Europe's growth champion'.

There are, however, two factors that affected human capital development and were unique to Poland. The first concerns the Polish economy during the 1980s. As indicated by Figure 1.1, Poland's GDP suffered a substantial drop during the 1980s. Paradoxically, it was during this period that the roots of the plant called post-1990 economic growth began to develop. In the shadows of an economic crisis, the share of private companies increased. This development was reflected by the changes in overall production (excluding agriculture), where the share increased from 4 percent in 1980 to 6.8 percent in 1987. Employment share followed accordingly and grew from 3.5 percent to 6.2 percent during the same period (Grala 2005, 264–65). Therefore, the first steps of the Polish market economy developed after 1990 had already been taken before 1990s, and by 1990 some entrepreneurs already knew how to run a private company.

The second exclusively Polish issue relates to the long-term effects of migration after 1945. The Polish people who left the eastern Polish borderlands – the so-called *kresy* – during the expulsion came from a mostly rural area dominated by agriculture. According to a recent publication, this situation had a contradictory effect. On the one hand, literacy in this region was below the Polish average. Only 57.6 percent of the population in the eastern borderlands were literate, while this figure was 63.9 percent in Central Poland. On the other hand, Polish nationals with ancestors that originated from the *kresy* (that is, they had been expulsed) had significantly more human capital in 2015. While the average secondary school attainment rate in Poland amounted to 49.55 percent, the figure for those with *kresy* ancestors was much higher: 62.4 percent (Becker et al. 2020, 1433). The observation itself is not surprising: People who experienced migration observed that material possession – real estate, money, jewellery, etc. – did not last forever; the only thing that could not be taken away was knowledge (Oz 2005, 172; quoted in Becker et al. 2020, 1430–31). It is also a reasonable assumption that a certified education was the only way to succeed in a society dominated by autochthons. As the authors demonstrate with reference to the migration of two million Poles that took place mostly in 1945, there are good reasons to support this assumption. It has recently also been shown that the descendants of families had to leave everything behind when they left the *kresy* during and after the end of the Second World War. This impacted their attitude towards material possessions and human capital accumulation. Generations later, the effects of this lessons could still be traced in the behaviour of their descendants (Becker et al. 2020).[22]

## Conclusion

Let us, at this point, return to the question insinuated in the title: what was Poland's communist heritage? Were there positive aspects to communism that at least laid the foundations for Poland's economic success?

A look at the industry shows that the idea that communist economic policy laid the foundations for subsequent economic growth that ultimately served as a 'ladder' towards higher production levels appears implausible. Investments were low and the attempts to substantially improve the industrial basis was unsatisfying even in comparison to the country's local peers, namely, Czechoslovakia and Hungary. This was also true for the production levels. As a consequence, Poland's starting position in 1990 was remarkably bad. At the end of the 1980s, the Polish capital stock was insufficient. Per capita GDP was 40 percent lower than the GDP in Czechoslovakia and more than 20 percent lower than in Hungary.

This assessment has clear consequences for the debate. From a purely economic point of view, the general concept of a post-communist economic transformation that could have been stabilized via more social measures that also protected certain industries has always been arguable. With regard to Poland and based on the poor state of the country's industry, it appears justified to refute the assumptions that some industries in Poland could have been saved.

All that does not belittle Poland's current position. Among the East European countries, Poland is a special case. When the ten new countries joined the European Union in 2004, more than half of the new EU-citizens were Polish nationals. Consequently, more than 45 percent of the GDP of the new member states came from Poland alone. At the same time, Poland's nominal GDP per capita was undercut only by Slovakia in 2004. Even today, Poland's GDP per capita is still (2021) about one third lower than that of the Czech Republic.[23] It is important to consider this fact when assessing Poland's success story. However, there is also good news. Poland's society has become less dependent on agricultural workplaces. Human capital has developed and continues to develop positively.

Yet, a comparison to other transition-countries once again reveals that Poland has not performed exceptionally well. There is no reason for great enthusiasm. The dependence on agriculture remains comparatively high in

Poland. This is one of the reasons for the deep cleavage between urban and rural regions, against which Poland's changing governments still struggle to find a solution. The high inequality in Poland shows a regional pattern. As both regional productivity levels in the last fifty years and local election trends show, the structural differences between the Polish East and West are considerable. These differences existed already during the communist era and have persisted until today. The methods used in this chapter to measure these differences are very different, so they cannot be employed to make reliable assumptions on how regional equalities changed quantitatively. The regional differences in productivity are not specific to the Polish case, as virtually no European country is a stranger to high disparities in GDP per capita (Rosés and Wolf 2019). Yet, it is noticeable that even an egalitarian communist regime that claimed to align differently developed regions via a system of central investment planning was unable to erase the differences.

There is yet another communist 'heritage'. Almost 55 percent of Poland's energy consumption is based on coal. During the 2015 electoral campaign, the leading candidate of the Polish Law and Justice Party (PiS) Beata Szydło emphasized the role of mines for her family, as well as for social cohesion and Polish culture.[24] Poland's reluctance to be an active protagonist of the European energy transition can also be explained by the country's social affinity to coal. One could even argue that Poland is a victim of the 'curse of natural resources' (Kouli 2016).

As Sitera's chapter in this book shows, it was evidently reasonable to follow an FDI-driven strategy in order to generate economic growth. While Poland was successful in doing so, foreign companies hardly contributed to the establishment of Polish knowledge-based production. Too often, Poland served as a workbench. And even for that, Poland's industry required significant investments, as the post-communist industrial capital was of no help. If anything, it deepened the middle-income trap that Poland is in. Therefore, a new strategy is required in order to escape the middle-income trap and create more innovative and knowledge-based economic branches. Currently, Poland's situation is not exceptionally good, its GDP per capita still remains relatively low. The pandemic did not profoundly change this picture, and only time will tell whether Poland will catch up.

This does not mean that there is no hope. On the contrary, there are industries in which Poland is exceptionally successful. A widely known example is the video-game industry. Poland's flagship is undoubtedly the CD Project group with a current market capitalization of almost 6 billion Euros.[25] From 2013 to 2019, the company generated an average revenue of over 110 million US dollars,[26] with 'The Witcher 3' (2015) and 'Cyperpunk 2077' (2020) being their most popular games. Techland (Dying Light),

Playway, 11 Bit Studios and other companies are the several Polish companies with international success.[27] Lechowski (Chapter 4) also argues that the software industry might be key to reaching an innovation-driven path of growth. There is thus good reason to believe that Poland has a decent chance to escape the middle-income trap, although it will certainly take a lot of effort.

**Yaman Kouli** wrote his dissertation at the Chemnitz Technical University and worked there as a research assistant from 2011 to 2018. From 2012 to 2013, he was also an A.SK-fellow at the Berlin Social Science Center. In 2018 and 2019, he was a visiting scientist at the UMR Sirice 8138 in Paris, funded via a scholarship from the Alexander von Humboldt Foundation. From October 2019, he has worked as a research assistant at the Heinrich-Heine-University in Düsseldorf. His fields of expertise are Poland's economic history during the twentieth century, the knowledge-based economy and European economic integration before 1914.

## Notes

1. The figures are based on calculations for the European Commission, retrieved 23 November 2020 from https://ec.europa.eu/info/business-economy-euro/economic-performance-and-forecasts/economic-performance-country/poland/economic-forecast-poland_en; for the unemployment rate in Poland, retrieved 9 September 2022 from https://stat.gov.pl/en/topics/labour-market/registered-unemployment/unemployment-rate-1990-2022,3,1.html.
2. For reasons of comparability, I have used the calculated GDP data for the Czech Republic. For the source of the data, see endnote 3.
3. Figures for 1991: Poland 9.218 US$ (in 2011 US$), Czech Republic 16.409 US$ (in 2011 US$). See, Maddison Project Database, retrieved 24 August 2020 from https://www.rug.nl/ggdc/historicaldevelopment/maddison/releases/maddison-project-database-2018?lang=en. Figures for 2019: Poland 15,592.2 US$, Czech Republic 23,101.8 US$. See: World Bank Database, retrieved 23 November 2020 from https://data.worldbank.org/indicator/NY.GDP.PCAP.CD?locations=PL-GR-PT-DE-EU.
4. Source: Główny Urząd Statystyczny, Struktura Ludności, retrieved 10 March 2021 from https://stat.gov.pl/obszary-tematyczne/ludnosc/ludnosc/struktura-ludnosci,16,1.html.
5. See for instance Dauderstädt (2014).
6. Source: Główny Urząd Statystyczny, Struktura Ludności, retrieved 10 March 2021 from https://stat.gov.pl/obszary-tematyczne/ludnosc/ludnosc/struktura-ludnosci,16,1.html.
7. Among the more recent publications are Galgóczi and Drahoupil (2017), Cernat (2006) and Heydemann and Vodička (2017).

8. With regard to the 1950s, see Kaliński and Landau (2003, 236).
9. This does not include the black market. Factory leaders often had access to an unofficial market that could provide companies with the necessary equipment and materials to enhance production. In this particular case, the black market served as a stabilising factor of the production system. The distribution of petrol is a telling example; see Kochanowski (2013, 303–21).
10. The same is true for the economic development during the economic transformation. As mentioned in the introduction, the spread between the growth rates during the 1990s as well as absolute GDP per capita was noticeable, and it appears self-evident to assume a connection between the communist economy and the individual success rates after 1990.
11. The title of Albrecht Ritschl's paper 'An Exercise in Futility' is a telling example (Ritschl 1995).
12. Klein and Vonyó calculated investment levels on a macroeconomic level. It is thus not possible to specify which industrial branches came to have higher levels of investment. See Vonyó and Klein (2019), Figure 4.
13. See Tokarski (1999). Sources did not allow the authors to isolate the Czech Republic.
14. To prove this assumption, it would be necessary to compare the income levels of those who have ancestors that originated from the *kresy* with those who do not. Yet the available data do not allow to measure individual incomes and compare them to those who do not have a family history of emigration. The calculations are based on Eurostat (retrieved 18 December 2020 from https://ec.europa.eu/eurostat/statistics-explained/index.php?title=GDP_at_regional_level#Regional_gross_domestic_product_.28GDP.29). Source for map of statistical regions, Wikipedia, retrieved 10 December 2020 from https://en.wikipedia.org/wiki/NUTS_statistical_regions_of_Poland#/media/File:POLSKA_NUTS1_2018.png.
15. Theoretically, it is possible to put together a list of all industrial products and services that were 'fabricated'. By adding their assumed market value, it is possible to estimate regional GDP. This, for instance, is the strategy Jaap Sleifer pursues in his dissertation. (See Sleifer 2006.)
16. To do so, I have anachronistically linked the voivodeships from before 1998 to the NUTS2-regions. South-Eastern Macroregion/ Macroregion Południowy (PL2): Voivodeships Częstochowskie, Katowickie, Krakowskie, Bielskie, Nowosadeckie and Tarnowskie; North-Western Macroregion and Macroregion Północno-Zachodni (PL4): Voivodeships Szczecińskie, Koszalińskie, Gorzowskie, Pilskie, Zielonogórskie, Poznańskie, Leszczyńskie, Konińskie and Kaliskie; South-Western Macroregion/Macroregion Południowo-Zachodni (PL5): Voivodeships Jeloniogórskie, Legnickie, Wrocławskie, Wałbrzyskie and Opolskie; Northern Macroregion/ Macroregion Północny (PL6): Viovodeships Słupskie, Bydgoskie, Gdańskie, Elblaskie, Toruńskie, Włocławskie, Olsztyńskie and Suwalskie (50 percent); Central Macroregion/Macroregion Centralny (PL7): Voivodeships Sieradzkie, Łódzkie, Skierniewickie, Piotrkowskie and Kieleckie; Eastern Macroregion/Macroregion Wschodni (PL8): Voivodeships Suwalskie (50 percent), Łomżyńskie, Białostockie, Bialskopodlaskie, Lubelskie, Chełmskie, Tarnobrzeski, Zamojskie, Rzeszowskie, Krośnieńskie and Przemyskie; Macroregion Masovian Voivodeship/Macroregion Województwo Mazowieckie (PL9): Voivodeships Płockie, Ciechanowskie, Warszawskie stołeczne, Ostrołęckie, Radomskie and Siedleckie. Note that, for the

17. Voivodeship Suwalski which was placed exactly on the border of two regions (PL6 and PL8), I have decided the best solution is to assign half of the voivodeship to each region.
17. For regional results see 'The Election of the President of the Republic of Poland, 28th June 2020', retrieved 4 January 2021 from https://prezydent20200628.pkw.gov.pl/prezydent20200628/en/wyniki/1/pl.
18. It is also necessary to point out that in an earlier article, Tamás Vonyó came to another conclusion. In his article on the Hungarian development after the Second World War, he pointed out that the country's relative success was among other factors based on human capital production (Vonyó 2010).
19. Regional contribution to GDP production will be examined in a later chapter.
20. See Barro-Lee Educational Attainment Dataset, retrieved 24 February 2021 from www.barrolee.com.
21. It is also important to emphasize that the figures provided by the Barro Lee database show great fluctuations along the years and within one timeline. It is thus doubtful whether the figures can be taken at face value.
22. Becker et al. did not ask whether there was a link between the positive attitude towards human capital of the descendants of the displaced Poles and their individual economic success. This still is a matter of future research.
23. Website of the World Bank, GDP per capita, retrieved 10 November 2022 from https://data.worldbank.org/indicator/NY.GDP.PCAP.CD?locations=CZ.
24. Beata Szydło during a PiS party-convention, 20 June 2015, retrieved 5 January 2021 from https://www.youtube.com/watch?v=q-Jr_MLE5CQ.
25. See https://www.onvista.de/aktien/CD-PROJEKT-Aktie-PLOPTTC00011, retrieved 23 February 2021.
26. The figures are based on 'Annual revenue generated by CD Projekt Group worldwide from 2013 to 2019', retrieved 23 February 2021 from https://www.statista.com/statistics/523934/cd-projekt-annual-revenue/.
27. See 'Revenue and net profit of selected major game developer companies in Poland between 2019 and 2020', retrieved 23 February 2021 from https://www.statista.com/statistics/1046009/poland-revenue-of-game-developers/.

## References

Becker, Sascha O., Irena Grosfeld, Pauline Grosjean, Nico Voigtländer and Ekaterina Zhuravskaya. 2020. 'Forced Migration and Human Capital: Evidence from Post-WWII Population Transfers'. *American Economic Review* 110(5): 1430–63. https://doi.org/10.1257/aer.20181518.

Berend, Ivan T. 2009. *From the Soviet Bloc to the European Union: The Economic and Social Transformation of Central and Eastern Europe Since 1973*. Cambridge: Cambridge University Press. https://doi.org/10.1017/CBO9780511806995.

Böick, Marcus. 2018. *Die Treuhand: Idee – Praxis – Erfahrung 1990–1994*. Göttingen: Wallstein Verlag.

Central Statistical Office. 2009. *Regions of Poland*. Warsaw: Zakład Wydawnictw Statystycznych. Retrieved 15 January 2020 from https://stat.gov.pl/cps/rde/xbcr/gus/regiony_polski_2009.pdf.

Cernat, Lucian. 2006. *Europeanization, Varieties of Capitalism and Economic Performance in Central and Eastern Europe*. Basingstoke: Palgrave Macmillan.
Chumiński, Jędrzej, ed. 2010. *Modernizacja czy pozorna modernizacja. Społeczno-ekonomiczny bilans PRL 1944–1989*. Wroclaw: Wydawnictwo Gajt.
Crafts, Nicholas, and Gianni Toniolo. 2010. 'Aggregate Growth, 1945–2005'. In *The Cambridge Economic History of Modern Europe, Volume 2: 1870 to the Present*, edited by Stephen N. Broadberry and Kevin H. O'Rourke, 296–332. New York: Cambridge University Press.
Dauderstädt, Michael. 2014. *Convergence in Crisis: European Integration in Jeopardy*. Internationale Policy Analysis. Berlin: Friedrich-Ebert-Stiftung.
Galgóczi, Béla, and Jan Drahokoupil, eds. 2017. *Condemned to Be Left Behind? Can Central and Eastern Europe Emerge from Its Low-Wage Model?* Brussels: ETUI aisbl.
Goldin, Claudia. 2016. 'Human Capital'. In *Handbook of Cliometrics*, edited by Claude Diebolt and Michael Haupert, 55–86. Berlin: Springer References.
Grala, Dariusz T. 2005. *Reformy gospodarcze w PRL, 1982–1989: Próba uratowania socjalizmu* [Economic reforms in the People's Republic of Poland, 1982–1989: An attempt to save socialism]. W krainie PRL. Warsaw: Wydawnictwo TRIO.
Heydemann, Günther, and Karel Vodička, eds. 2017. *From Eastern Bloc to European Union: Comparative Processes of Transformation since 1990*. Studies in Contemporary European History Volume 22. New York: Berghahn Books.
Houpt, Stefan, Pedro Lains and Lennart Schön. 2010. 'Sectoral Developments, 1945–2000'. In *The Cambridge Economic History of Modern Europe. Volume 2: 1870 to the Present*, edited by Stephen N. Broadberry and Kevin H. O'Rourke, 333–59. New York: Cambridge University Press.
Kaliński, Janusz, and Zbigniew Landau. 2003. *Gospodarka Polski w XX wieku*. 2nd edition. Warsaw: Polskie Wydawnictwo Ekonomiczne.
Karpiński, Andrzej, et al. 2015. *Od uprzemysłowienia w PRL do deindustrializacji kraju* [From industrialisation in communist Poland to the deindustrialisation of the country]. Warsaw: Muza SA.
King, Lawrence P., and Aleksandra Sznajder. 2006. 'The State-Led Transition to Liberal Capitalism: Neoliberal, Organizational, World-Systems, and Social Structural Explanations of Poland's Economic Success'. *American Journal of Sociology* 112(3): 751–801.
Kochanowski, Jerzy. 2013. *Jenseits der Planwirtschaft: Der Schwarzmarkt in Polen 1944–1989* [Beyond the Planned Economy: The Black Market in Poland 1944–1989]. Moderne Europäische Geschichte 7. Göttingen: Wallstein Verlag.
Kouli, Yaman. 2016. 'Klątwa surowcowa – Węgiel w Polsce w XX wieku' [The Raw material Curse – Coal in Poland in the 20th Century]. In *Od regaliów po dobro narodowe: Ochrona i wykorzystanie zasobów środowiska naturalnego na ziemiach polskich – aspekt historyczny (Wrocławskie Spotkania z Historią Gospodarczą, spotkanie XI)* [From regalia to national asset: Protection and use of environmental resources on Polish lands – a historical aspect (Wrocław Meetings with Economic History, meeting XI)], edited by Tomasz Głowiński and Marek Zawadka, 81–88. Wrocław: Wydawnictwo Gajt.
———. 2020. 'Ein guter Deal? Vorschlag für eine makroökonomische Berechnung der wirtschaftlichen Folgen der Westverschiebung Polens' [A Good Deal? A Proposal

for a Macroeconomic calculation of the Economic Consequences of the Westward Shift of Poland]. *Jahrbücher für Geschichte Osteuropas* 68(1): 27–42.
Lee, Jong-Wha, and Hanol Lee. 2016. 'Human Capital in the Long Run'. *Journal of Development Economics* 122: 147–69.
Markevich, Andrei, and Tamás Vonyó. 2020. 'Economic Policy under State Socialism, 1945–1989'. In *The Economic History of Central, East and South-East Europe: 1800 to the Present*, edited by Matthias Morys, 307–27. London: Routledge.
Musiał, Wojciech. 2013. *Modernizacja Polski: Polityki rządowe w latach 1918–2004* [Modernization of Poland: Government Policies in the Years 1918–2004]. Monografie Fundacji na Rzecz Nauki Polskiej. Toruń: Fundacja na Rzecz Nauki Polskiej.
Oz, Amos. 2005. *A Tale of Love and Darkness*. New York: Vintage Books.
Piątkowski, Marcin. 2018. *Europe's Growth Champion: Insights from the Economic Rise of Poland*. Oxford: Oxford University Press.
Ritschl, Albrecht. 1995. 'An Exercise in Futility: East German Economic Growth and Decline, 1945–1989'. In *Economic Growth in Europe since 1945*, edited by Nicholas Crafts and Gianni Toniolo, 498–540. Cambridge: Cambridge University Press.
Rosés, Joan R., and Nikolaus Wolf. 2019. *The Economic Development of Europe's Regions: A Quantitative History Since 1900*. Routledge Explorations in Economic History 82. London: Routledge.
Sleifer, Jaap. 2006. *Planning Ahead and Falling Behind: The East German Economy in Comparison with West Germany 1936–2002*. Jahrbuch für Wirtschaftsgeschichte. Beihefte 8. Berlin: De Gruyter.
Tokarski, Peter. 1999. *Die Wahl wirtschaftspolitischer Strategien in Polen nach dem Zweiten Weltkrieg bis 1959* [The Choice of Economic Policy Strategies in Poland after the Second World War until 1959]. Materialien und Studien zur Ostmitteleuropa-Forschung 4. Marburg: Herder-Institut.
Vonyó, Tamás. 2010. 'Socialist Industrialisation or Post-War Reconstruction? Understanding Hungarian Economic Growth 1949–1967'. *The Journal of European Economic History* 39(2): 253–300.
———. 2017. 'War and Socialism: Why Eastern Europe Fell Behind Between 1950 and 1989'. *The Economic History Review* 70(1): 248–74.
Vonyó, Tamás, and Alexander Klein. 2019. 'Why did Socialist Economies Fail? The Role of Factor Inputs Reconsidered'. *The Economic History Review* 72(1): 317–45.
Vonyó, Tamás, and Andrei Markevich. 2020. 'Economic Growth and Structural Developments, 1945–1989'. In *The Economic History of Central, East and South-East Europe: 1800 to the Present*, edited by Matthias Morys, 281–306. London: Routledge.

CHAPTER 2
# Institutional Development and Growth as Outputs of Early Transition Policies

Tal Kadayer

## Introduction

Since the beginning of the twentieth century, empirical work of growth literature has been aimed at explaining divergences in growth rates. While previous growth models explain income-per-capita variation by measuring accumulation of factors of production[1] or exogenous characteristics,[2] the evolution of growth literature has shifted the discussion towards the importance of institutions as determinants of economic growth and catalysts for this divergence.[3] Many indices were created in order to link different institutions to economic outcome and measure their influence on growth.[4] Only one set of indices, that is, the European Bank for Reconstruction and Development's (EBRD) transition indices, aims at measuring the transition process. Yet this set does not measure, rank or link transitional policies to the progress of market institutions. It is the premise of this chapter to establish this missing link.

The variance between the income levels of countries is especially visible once developing and post-communist countries are compared, in the latter of which economies either skyrocketed or descended during their transition period. The divergence in post-communist countries growth rate can be traced back to the early days of transition and were most prominent during the first decade after the beginning of the transition (1989–2000).

Income levels, as defined by the World Bank, vary from low income for Tajikistan up to high income for nine Central and Eastern European (CEE) countries. At first glance, it is tempting to argue that geographical factors rather than transitional ones are responsible for this divergence.[5] Although it is reasonable to say that geographical factors (mainly proximity to the developed West European countries) as to initial condition (mainly macroeconomic distortions and unfamiliarity with market processes) played a role in the outcome of transition, especially for trade and FDI, institutional change is a stronger determinant for a country's income level (see de Melo et al. 2001; Hall and Jones 1999). Both the costs of reforms (e.g., higher unemployment and inflation, lower consumption) and their outcomes (e.g., increase in productivity and GDP, sectoral changes) depend on country-specific characteristics.[6] However, these costs cannot be avoided or mitigated by delaying implementation of market reforms, which should thus not be a dominant policy (see Fries and Taci 2002; de Melo et al. 2001).

Research in transition and growth literature has not sufficiently contributed to the enhancement of knowledge on the impact of pro-market policies as a promoter of institutional development and growth in post-communist countries in the early 1990s. This shortage of knowledge was most prominent during the crucial period of 1989–96, when stabilization programs were implemented. This gap in transitional literature arises from three reasons: (1) some studies base their cross-country analysis on a small, homogeneous and not representative sample size (usually only CEE), which is likely to be affected by European Union (EU) membership;[7] (2) some studies examine a narrow aspect of transitional policy in cross-country comparison using the EBRD indices, which were not created for this purpose and are relatively unspecific (see for example, Fries and Taci 2002; de Melo et al. 2001); (3) some studies include all transitional countries in their sample but use institutional indices assembled after 1996, a time when a large part of transition policies had already been implemented. Thus, such studies cannot observe the development originating from these policies.[8] Additionally, cross-country studies of growth literature that focus on developing countries typically omit the post-communist countries, arguing that these countries lacked institutions to measure economic data.[9]

The shortage of indices to measure transition and the missing data from post-communist countries in existing institutional indices, such as the World Governance Index (WGI), make existing cross-country statistical analyses of the post-communist countries unfeasible. For this reason, this chapter takes an untraditional approach of qualitative analysis, in which transition policies in early periods are linked to institutional development in later periods.

In this chapter, this connection is established by using a new index for transition policies (see 'Measurements of Transition Policies', below). The new index covers the early transition policies of corporate restructuring and competition enhancement in all post-communist countries (1990–95). By including three separate types of transition policies in the 'enterprise restructuring index' and five types in the 'competitive enhancement index', this chapter avoids relying on the EBRD's equivalent indices of enterprise restructuring and competition. Measuring the policies during the early transition period and for all post-communist countries, it provides a more representative connection between transition policies, institutional development, productivity and growth.

The debate about which transition reform approach is superior – Gradual or Big Bang (sometimes referred to as Shock Therapy) – has been explored in the transition literature. Its origin emanates from the time inconsistency nature of transition, in which socioeconomic costs are predominant in early transition while the benefits from the reforms arrive in a later period. This timing discrepancy creates ex post and ex ante obstacles for the politic system. Both approaches agree that pro-market reforms are generally positive, but they differ regarding the optimal scope and implementation speed and whether reforms should be tailor made to capture the unique characteristics of each country.[10] The author's approach presented in this chapter is pro-liberal and assumes that the Big Bang transition strategy is superior.[11] The ranking of transition indicators reflects this view. According to the Big Bang strategy, fast and widescale transition measures should be taken early in the transition period, rather than later, and at a slow, gradual pace. The Big Bang approach advocates for economic freedom,[12] and is presumed to be better, because implementing the opposing gradual approach encompasses a risk for public backlash against market reforms due to high social costs. Such backlash can lead to partial implementation of reforms or even transition reversal.[13] In the existence of such risk for reverse transition, the importance of fast implementation rises, thus a point in favour for the Big Bang approach. Another factor that mitigates the risk for social backlash is politic stability and non-populist regimes.[14] Given that the EU – which is an impartial organization that is unconstrained by internal national politics – imposed pro-market policies on countries that wished to join it, and the fact that these are the most successful transitional countries, is testimony for the benefits of pro-market reforms and is support for the methodology used in this chapter. The drawback of constructing indicators in light of the Big Bang approach is that it disregards the adverse effects of it.[15] The supporters of the Gradual approach over Shock Therapy point out that (A) the Big Bang approach failed to achieve its goals in Latin America's transitional countries and had negative social impact with lasting implications,[16] and (B) tailor-made institutional reform programs achieve better results than a 'once size fits all' program.[17]

The contrasting GDP growth trend between countries that implemented the two opposing transition approaches will be explored in an upcoming paper. Preliminary results of comparing transition plans using scale, timing and velocity as explanatory variables for GDP per capita growth show validity to the advantages and disadvantages associated to both approaches. The results favour the Big Bang approach for time periods over six years in regard to promoting growth. On the one hand, the Gradual approach is supported by the findings that periods of intense reforms lead to GDP per capita decline in the short run – up to 15.7 percent decrease for the first three years, and high velocity reforms have a low explanatory value for determine GDP growth. On the other hand, the Big Bang approach is supported by the findings that a country which implemented significant institutional reforms in the first time interval of transition (1990–92) increased its total GDP per capita by 4.36 percent after nine years. Most prominently, for every one year earlier implementation of significant market reforms, a country raises its GDP per capita by 1.26 percent on average, which advocates implementing the Big Bang approach as early as possible. It appears that countries presented better post-transition growth due to the timing effect. The fact that the Big Bang approach drives countries to implement large-scale reforms in a short period of time encouraged their policy makers to reform more institutions, which is associated with better growth. The reforms of these institutions were absent in the low-growth countries and can explain much of the cross-country GDP variation. The indices used in this chapter are therefore tailored to detect these superior institutional reforms.

This chapter establishes that bad governance and market institutions inherited from the communist era, which were not transformed correctly in early transition stages (e.g., due to politic pressure to delay restructuring or mitigate social and economic costs), hindered several transitional countries in their development and pushed them to the bottom of the middle-income trap. Among the countries that predominantly failed to implement appropriate market economy policies are Bulgaria, the Kyrgyz Republic, Moldova, Romania, Tajikistan, Turkmenistan, Ukraine and Uzbekistan. Countries that implemented a high level of transitional policies – namely Albania, the Czech Republic, Estonia, Hungary, Latvia, Lithuania, Poland, Slovakia and Slovenia – established better market institutions which, assisted by the privatization and restructuring process, increased competitiveness and productivity, provided a higher level of employment and improved resource allocation.

For the purpose of establishing the link between the growth of the market institutions and early transition policies and development, I have examined the policy measures taken by twenty-five post-communist countries in early transition periods (1989–1995), where no explicit detailed indicator exists. The policy measures are separated into two general aspects of transitional policies: enterprise restructuring and competitiveness enhancement. I have divided each broad aspect of transition into several subcategories and ranked these as high, medium and weak with respect to the level of the specific transition policy implemented. Later, I have linked each sub-policy to institutional development indices typically used in empirical growth literature, namely the WGI and Economic Freedom of the World (EFW) indices. In addition, I have connected each sub-policy to GDP growth by examining its correlation to productivity and private sector development, which are known growth catalysts.

There are several drawbacks in using this approach. First, the index is designed as liberal and measures the level of pro-market actions. In general, it categorizes market deregulation policies as 'high' and state interference as 'weak'. It does not measure the social costs of more intense liberalization policies such as pension erosion, unemployment increases or economic inequality increase. Not discounting for social costs, the study overstates the positive outcomes of the pro-market policies and disregards their imperfections. Secondly, the index does not take into consideration country-specific factors that may influence the policy implementation. Country-specific factors such as market size, labour market size, level of education, natural resources and, most notably, the proximity to the EU free-market area can influence the chosen transitional policy. The existence of natural resources, for instance, has proven to be a positive attraction for international investors who become involved in the privatization process.[18] This higher attractiveness for foreign direct investment (FDI) made the direct sales privatization method more feasible. This study reveals that direct sales is a superior privatization method and thus countries with natural resources had theoretically easier access to better transition policies. Due to the omission of country-specific characteristics and the variance of social costs between countries in the index, one should be cautious when drawing policy implications regarding the optimal way for choosing and implementing transition policies.[19] Thirdly, this approach highlights the connection between the transition policies and institutional development. It does not presume to explain why or how policies improve institutions.

Additionally, this approach creates connection between different time frames – transition policies in the early period (1990–95) and institutional development in later stages. The asynchronous nature of the data resulting from the insufficiency of data regarding institutional development in most Commonwealth of Independent States (CIS) countries and some CEE countries before 1996 prevents the use of panel data analysis to determine the nature of relation between transition measures and institutional development. However, the data that the chapter presents regarding productivity and private sector changes with respect to intense transition policies illustrates that the relation between transition measures and high ranking of institutional indices is indeed a causality. This statement is supported by the comparison of institutional changes in transitional countries with respect to the benchmark of developing countries. As reviewed below, institutions such as government effectiveness, regulatory quality, rule of law and control of corruption are all determinants of higher efficiency, productivity and GDP. Thus, if high levels of productivity and GDP are observed in countries that implemented intensive transition policies and the correlation between pro-market policies and institutional development is high, it can be concluded that such policies lead to institutional development. As a result, the chapter adopts the terminology of causation when describing the relation between policy and institution accompanied by strong empirical evidence. It uses terminology of correlation, when describing results that seem circumstantial.

For most subcategory policies, I observe a gap in the ranking of institutional indices between countries that implemented different levels of transition by the mid-1990s. Moreover, all subcategories are positively associated with GDP growth during 1990–95. The gap in institutional indices as to the gap in GDP typically remains constant, even when countries in the medium and weak policy groups pick up the pace of transition.[20] This indicates the persistence of transition policies and the importance of the 'first move effect' in preventing policy reversal. The initial growth gap created due to institutional differences emanating from transitional policies remained constant in the following decades, leading to the growth variance observed today.

The rest of this chapter is organized as follows: overview of the empirical literature documenting the relationship between institutions and growth, description of the methodology used to rank the transitional policy measures, linking of different transition policies to the development of institutions, discussion and conclusion.

## Institutions as Determinant of Growth Variance

One of the most renowned advocates of institutions is North (1990), who describes institutions as constraints that dictate social interaction. He divides these constraints into three major categories: informal constraints such as culture and ideology, formal constraints such as laws and constitution, and the enforcement of constraints such as state enforcement organs and the judiciary system. These constraints and the interactions between them create a country's institutional framework. According to North (1990), some institutions increase efficiency, while others decrease it. The following definition helps to capture the characteristics of institutions as they are examined in this chapter: 'Some ways of organizing societies encourage people to innovate, to take risks, to save for the future, to find better ways of doing things, to learn and educate themselves, solve problems of collective action and provide public goods. Others do not' (Acemoglu, Johnson and Robinson 2005, 397).

Governance explanatory institutions typically used in growth literature include voice and accountability, quality of bureaucracy, civil liberties, property rights and rule-based governance, government effectiveness, law and order, tradition, political instability and violence, political rights, regulatory burden and rule of law.[21] Politics governance institutions influence the economy in different ways. For instance, an efficient judicial system that can enforce contracts improves trust and therefore private entrepreneurship. A high level of property rights legislation and enforcement encourages investment and technological development via patent and investment in human capital. In contrast, bad governance institutions reduce investment and productivity due to inefficient resource allocation and decrease production accumulation factors. For example, excessive bureaucracy hinders innovation and investment in human capital and technology (Meon and Weill 2005).

## The Origin of Cross-Country Institution Variance

There are four main theories explaining differences in institutions across countries.[22] The trajectory of growth divergence observed in the world could be best explained by the Social Conflict theory according to which economic and political institutions are determined by the group or coalition of groups that holds the political power rather than the society as a whole. As a result, economic institutions may be preserved even if they are inefficient, as long as they are strong enough to maintain power.[23]

Following the premise of this theory, radical change cannot come from within the system, as this would hurt the source of power for those who hold it. Accordingly, it is not surprising that it was in the CEE countries – among all the transitional countries – where more radical institutional changes have occurred as an exogenous power such as EU membership steered towards larger change in the CEE.

## Institutional Variance in Empirical Growth Literature

Cross-country studies prove that differences in the quality of institutions are among the most important causes for economic growth differences across countries. Growth literature which links policy and governance institutions to economic growth focuses on the encouragement (or respectively the discouragement) for engaging in a productive activity due to good (or bad) institutions. Empirical growth literature generally agrees that economic and political-freedom-related institutions contribute to growth due to the increase of productivity factors and the rate of their accumulation. The creators of the WGI indices present empirical evidence that improving governance, as measured by these six indicators, leads to better economic development outcomes including higher income per capita, higher literacy ratio and lower infant mortality rate (Kaufmann, Kraay and Zoido-Lobaton 1999).

In this chapter, I review post-reform institutional changes using the following WGI and EFW indices:

1. 'Government Effectiveness' (also referred as 'Quality of Bureaucracy') measures the perception of the state by the people, consequently its credibility and the ability to successfully implement significant policies. The index includes the perception of the quality of public services provision and bureaucracy concerning independence of state services from political pressure and the credibility of government. The credibility of state is highly important for inducing investment and encouraging compliance of the people and companies in times of transition.[24]
2. 'Regulatory Quality' (also referred as 'Regulatory Burden' or 'Red Tape') includes excessive bureaucracy and regulation of unfriendly market policies, such as protectionism, foreign exchange restrictions or limitation on foreigners. A low rank on this index signals the existence of non-efficiency related parameters in the determination of government policies or the allocation of public goods and lack of prudential clarity. This leads to distortion of investment, trade, capital investment and spill overs of foreign technology into the country, resulting in reduced competitiveness, inefficient resource allocation, reduced productivity and, consequently, lower growth.[25]
3. 'Rule of Law' measures a state's ability to provide autonomous legal environment, citizens abidance of the law and contract enforcement. Low credibility of a state's judicial system in officiating business disputes restricts economic activity, undermines the proper operation of the market's exchange system and hinders growth. Kraay and Zoido-Lobaton considers this institution as a strong determinant of growth, a result also supported by Barro who suggests that a high level of rule of law stimulates growth (Kaufmann, Kraay and Zoido-Lobaton 1999; Barro 2003). Meon and Weill suggest that the rule of law is the second most important determinant of efficiency, as it as-

sists in accumulation of factors of production and positively affects proper use of resources (Meon and Weill 2005).

4. 'Control of Corruption' (also referred as 'Graft') measures both the corruption or bribery and the perception of these. Kaufmann, Kraay and Zoido-Lobaton (1999) reveal that one standard deviation improvement in this index raises the GDP per capita by 250 percent. Shleifer and Vishny (1993) argue that corruption decreases economic growth by slowing development down and discouraging investment, constituting a significant impediment especially for developing countries. Corruption is costly for economic development because it increases the cost of entrepreneurship. As a result of corruption, the level of entrepreneurship descends. This result corresponds with the findings of other scholars who argue that corruption influences efficiency (Meon and Weill 2005).

5. 'Government size' measures the aggregate interference of the state in the economy. This index includes government consumption ratio, transfers and subsidies as a percentage of GDP, and state ownership of assets. Vijayaraghavan and Ward (2001) examines the effects of the size of government on growth. They conclude that government size measured as the share of government consumption out of total consumption is among the most influential institutions for growth (Vijayaraghavan and Ward 2001). Large size of government distorts capital accumulation and allocation, consequently leading to lower productivity and growth. Barro finds government size to be inversely related to economic growth across countries (Barro 1991, 2003).

6. 'Labour market regulations' measures wage control, minimum wage, layoff regulations, centralized collective bargaining and unions' participation in the decision-making process. Labour market regulations reduce the economic freedom of both employers and employees.[26] Such policies are implemented to reduce social costs and provide political support but also reduce the elasticity of the labour market and may lead to lower productivity and employment in the private sector.[27]

## Measurements of Transition Policies

In this section, the methodology used for the ranking of the transitional policy measures taken by twenty-five post-communist countries is elaborated upon. Here, transitional policies are separated into two main categories: privatization and enterprise restructuring policies (Part 1) and competitiveness-related policies (Part 2). The information used to compose the ranking of the transition policies in this section originate from the EBRD transition reports in 1994–96, 1998 and 2001. Below, the governance-related transition policies implemented between 1989 and 1995 are reviewed.

As mentioned above, the index is designed in a pro-market fashion and aims at measuring transition policies. The guiding line for the analysis is that the higher trade potential in some countries should not have discouraged others from pursuing market actions and enjoying the associated advantages. The EU prodigy is therefore not reflected in the ratings below. This approach is also supported by other studies. De Melo and her colleagues explore the relation between initial condition, economic stabilization and the liberalization process. They show that unfavourable initial conditions, such as in the CIS countries, discourage policy reforms but do not diminish their effectiveness once they are implemented (de Melo et al. 2001). Carstensen and Toubal (2004) explore the relation between transition policies and FDI flows. They reveal that the CEE countries were more successful in attracting FDI partly due to their relatively higher market potential. However, the level of transition (proxy by the share of the private sector in GDP) and corporate governance (proxy by the type of privatization) played a major role in determining FDI flows, while labour costs played no role. The two southeastern European countries (Bulgaria and Romania) were less successful in attracting FDI due to slow transition process and inferior corporate governance (Carstensen and Toubal 2004).

## *Enterprise-Restructuring Transitional Policies*

The transition instruments and policies included under enterprise restructuring are necessary for creating and developing both the supply and the demand in a new market economy. The transitional measure policies are highly correlated with a variety of country development and institutional indices. Privatization is the main instrument for transition restructuring,[28] while enterprise restructuring constitutes a complementary tool.

Enterprise restructuring is the adaptation of existing enterprises from state-economy to market-economy. From the single-enterprise perspective, it includes operational and financial restructuring. The operational restructuring includes adjustment of labour and capital input in addition to the volume and composition of output. It requires a strong and capable management and ownership that can discipline or replace existing management. The financial restructuring includes dealing with non-performing loans (NPL), strengthening of corporate financial discipline and reorganization of the balance sheet. From the state perspective, enterprise restructuring includes hardening enterprises' budget constrains by cutting subsidies and creating favourable credit conditions.

During the first years of transition, several enterprise restructuring policies were implemented. The transition policies differed greatly in terms of the scope of privatization and restructuring, the speed of implementation, the share of the remaining enterprise ownership by the state and the responsible organ for implementing the policies. The EBRD defined two general strategies[29] for privatization and enterprise restructuring that emerged in the transitional countries. The first strategy was early mass privatization, leaving the operational and financial restructuring to the new owners. This strategy established private ownership using massive voucher distribution and management and employee's ownership (MEBO), leaving management structure as it was. The second strategy included financial restructuring by the state prior to privatization in order to attract quality ownership that can implement successful operational restructuring. The choice between the two strategies was a trade-off between the speed of transition and its quality. It had implications regarding the quality of corporate governance, the structure of ownership, the resolution of the debt overhang and the enterprise's financial discipline. I take the general division of the EBRD and separate it into several policies, that is relation to privatization, restructuring and corporate competition. Table 2.1 presents the subcategories for enterprise-related transitional policies, while the Table 2.2 shows the subcategorization of competition enhancement.

1. Privatization method policy measures the primary and secondary privatization method. (a) Vouchers: distribution of ownership to the public by using investment coupons at a symbolic price. (b) Direct sales: ownership distribution for outside investors, domestic or foreign, usually via tender and sometimes conditioned by presenting operational restructuring plan. (c) Management and employee buyouts or liquidations (MEBO).
Management and employee buyouts or liquidations (MEBO):
2. Operational restructure policy indicates the responsible organ for the operational restructure of enterprises including operational reform and improved management structure. The operational restructuring consists of adjusting the scope and composition of production to the market demand and allocating labour and capital to meet corporate (rather than state) objectives. The indicator distinguishes the dominance of state-ownership and state-control (such as production quotas and the state order system) over mostly privatized companies.
3. Corporate financial discipline policy measures enterprise budget constraint, credit allocation via house banks,[30] extra budgetary vehicles and direct state subsidies. These constraints can be weak, medium or high. In the last case, there are no direct state subsidies whatsoever.

**Table 2.1.** Privatization and enterprise restructuring policies 1989–95.

| Income Level | Country | Privatization Method | Operational Restructure Responsibility | Corporate Financial Discipline |
|---|---|---|---|---|
| Upper middle | Albania | MEBOs Vouchers | State | High |
| Upper middle | Armenia | Direct sales MEBOs | State | Weak |
| Upper middle | Azerbaijan | Direct sales Vouchers | State | Weak |
| Upper middle | Belarus | MEBOs Vouchers | State | Weak |
| Upper middle | Bulgaria | Direct sales Vouchers | State | NA |
| High | Croatia | MEBOs Vouchers | Private | NA |
| High | Czech Republic | Vouchers Direct sales | Private | High |
| High | Estonia | Direct sales Vouchers | Private | NA |
| Upper middle | Macedonia | MEBOs Direct sales | State | Medium |
| Upper middle | Georgia | Vouchers Direct sales | State | Weak |
| High | Hungary | Direct sales MEBOs | private | High |
| Upper middle | Kazakhstan | Direct sales Vouchers | State | Weak |
| Lower middle | Kyrgyzstan | Vouchers MEBOs | private | Weak |
| High | Latvia | Direct sales Vouchers | State | High |
| High | Lithuania | Vouchers Direct sales | Private | Medium |
| Lower middle | Moldova | Vouchers Direct sales | State | NA |
| High | Poland | Direct sales MEBOs | Private | High |
| Upper middle | Romania | MEBOs Direct sales | State | Weak |

(*continued*)

Table 2.1. *continued*

| Income Level | Country | Privatization Method | Operational Restructure Responsibility | Corporate Financial Discipline |
|---|---|---|---|---|
| Upper middle | Russia | Vouchers<br>Direct sales | private | Weak |
| High | Slovakia | Direct sales<br>Vouchers | Private | High |
| High | Slovenia | MEBOs<br>Vouchers | Private | Medium |
| Low | Tajikistan | MEBOs<br>Direct sales | State | Weak |
| Upper middle | Turkmenistan | MEBOs<br>Direct sales | State | Weak |
| Lower middle | Ukraine | Vouchers<br>MEBOs | State | Weak |
| Lower middle | Uzbekistan | MEBOs<br>Direct sales | State | Weak |

Source: self-computing, EBRD transition reports 1994–96, Appendix.

## *Competition Enhancing Transitional Policies*

One of the main disadvantages of the communist era was inefficient resource allocation due to state steering. Industrial production based on non-market targets (such as employment targets or allocation of production according to regional political power) and discouraging incentives for research and investment hindered productivity. In addition, the state-controlled trade and exchange rate served to hide the countries' true level of competitiveness.

Adjustment to market economy required the state to establish market institutions, reduce its interference and strengthen competitivity in order to stabilize the economy. This included the legislation and enforcement of bankruptcy to dissolve unviable businesses in order to improve resource allocation, controlling of monopolies and breaking-up of large conglomerates in order to enhance productivity, investment and competitiveness, controlling of excessive wages in the public sector and allowing for emerging private sector in order to offer higher wages to attract labour; reduction of price control – particularly of input price control – to ensure that businesses operated based on their true profitability level.

These actions resulted in economic gains due to better resource allocation, incentivized investment and higher productivity but had social costs in the form of unemployment and wage reduction.

Table 2.2 presents the competition enhancing policy measures implemented by the transitional countries during the early years of transition.

**Table 2.2.** Competition enhancement policies 1989–95.

| Income Level | Country | Wage Liberal- ization | Price Liberal- ization | Bankruptcy Enforcement | Monopoly & Large Conglom- erates Control | Compe- tition Office |
|---|---|---|---|---|---|---|
| Upper middle | Albania | Medium | Medium | Weak | Medium | Yes |
| Upper middle | Armenia | Weak | Medium | Weak | Weak | Yes |
| Upper middle | Azerbaijan | Weak | Medium | Weak | Weak | Yes |
| Upper middle | Belarus | Medium | Weak | Weak | Medium | No |
| Upper middle | Bulgaria | Medium | High | Weak | High | Yes |
| High | Croatia | Medium | High | Weak | Weak | Yes |
| High | Czech Republic | High | High | High | Medium | Yes |
| High | Estonia | High | High | High | Weak | Yes |
| Upper middle | Macedonia | NA | Medium | Weak | Weak | No |
| Upper middle | Georgia | Weak | High | Weak | Weak | Yes |
| High | Hungary | High | High | High | Medium | Yes |
| Upper middle | Kazakhstan | Weak | Medium | Weak | Weak | Yes |
| Lower middle | Kyrgyzstan | Weak | High | Weak | Medium | No |
| High | Latvia | High | High | Weak | Weak | Yes |
| High | Lithuania | High | High | Weak | Medium | Yes |
| Lower middle | Moldova | Weak | Medium | Weak | Medium | No |
| High | Poland | High | High | High | High | Yes |
| Upper middle | Romania | Weak | High | Weak | Weak | Yes |
| Upper middle | Russia | Weak | Medium | Medium | Weak | Yes |
| High | Slovakia | High | High | High | Medium | Yes |
| High | Slovenia | Medium | High | Medium | High | Yes |
| Low | Tajikistan | Weak | Weak | Weak | Weak | Yes |
| Upper middle | Turkmenistan | Weak | Weak | Weak | Weak | No |
| Lower middle | Ukraine | Weak | Weak | Weak | Weak | Yes |
| Lower middle | Uzbekistan | Weak | Medium | Weak | Weak | Yes |

Source: self-computing, EBRD transition reports 1994–96, Appendix.

1. Wage liberalization policy measures the existence of restrictions or substantial taxes over the ability of private enterprises to adjust the average wage upwards.[31] This policy measure examines the relation between the public-wage adjustments and the increase of private wages in order to see if private companies are *de facto* independent in offering wages. In addition, the policy examines the existence of collective bargaining in the labour market. Wage liberalization policy

can be weak, medium or high. To be rated high, there must be complete absence of labour-market regulation and wage laws (e.g., a wage ceiling).
2. Price liberalization policy measures the existence of market price distortion policies and state control over retail prices, such as subsidies, price ceiling and control over monopolistic prices. This definition of price liberalization emphasizes the existence of price restrictions emanating from market control of monopolies. Therefore, I define price liberalization more as a price competition policy in which the high policy group follows world market prices that reflect production costs, while the weak policy group relies on the state to steer prices. For price liberalization policy to be high, more than 90 percent of retail products must follow market prices.
3. Bankruptcy enforcement policy calculates the existence and operation of a bankruptcy enforcement mechanism. The more effective the mechanism, the higher the ranking. In order to be ranked high, a country must provide debtors with an option to force bankruptcy procedures in case of lingering debt.
4. Monopoly and large conglomerates control policy refers to the actions taken to dismantle monopolies and large conglomerates and to enhance the competitiveness of enterprises in order to decentralize the market. To be qualified as high, this policy must lead to the dissolution of most monopolies.
5. Competition office examines whether a competition or anti-monopoly office existed separately from any ministry until 1998. This policy instrument was reported by the EBRD but did not measure the quality of the office's operation. This serves as a supplementary measure to the monopoly and large conglomerates control policy.

## Transition Policies and the Development of Institutions

This part links the policy measures as previously defined to the institutional governance indices WGI and EFW. Most policy measures included here have a very high correlation with GDP growth and EU membership. In this part of the chapter, remarkable trends of institution development are highlighted in the light of transition policies. Transitional policies are highly correlated with institutional parameters and indices. High, medium and weak ranks in transitional policies explain much of the institutional gap observed between countries since 1995. Based on the large body of institutional growth literature, it can safely be argued that the differences in institution ranking indices explain some[32] of the large divergence in growth, as can be seen in Figures 2.1 and 2.2.[33]

## The Relation between Enterprise Restructuring Transitional Policies, Institutional Development and Growth

The transitional policies included in this part diverge significantly between countries and periods. Some policies obstructed the development of market institutions, which is reflected in low institutional rank in a variety of governance indices. Impediments for restructuring included high state ownership, which delayed operational restructuring, soft budget constraints, direct subsidies, and credit, which prevented efficient resource allocation and dissolved unviable firms.

Figure 2.1 illustrates the relation between corporate restructuring policies and economic growth, represented by the GDP per capita trend. In order to emphasize the divergence of GDP trend that originates from policy differences rather than initial wealth, the figure takes all policy groups from the same level, although the initial level of GDP varied between groups. The focus during the interpretation of the figure should therefore be on the GDP trend of the different groups in relation to the starting point. The GDP trend reflects the productivity trend presented in Table 2.5. Countries in the high-policy group[34] increased their initial GDP per capita by fifty percent by the time that early transition policies were implemented (1995–96). Countries in the medium-policy group[35] had larger GDP deficit during the first years of transition. Their domestic product returned to its original level by 1995 and growth rate increased to the level of the high-policy group by the mid-2000s. Countries in the weak-policy group[36]

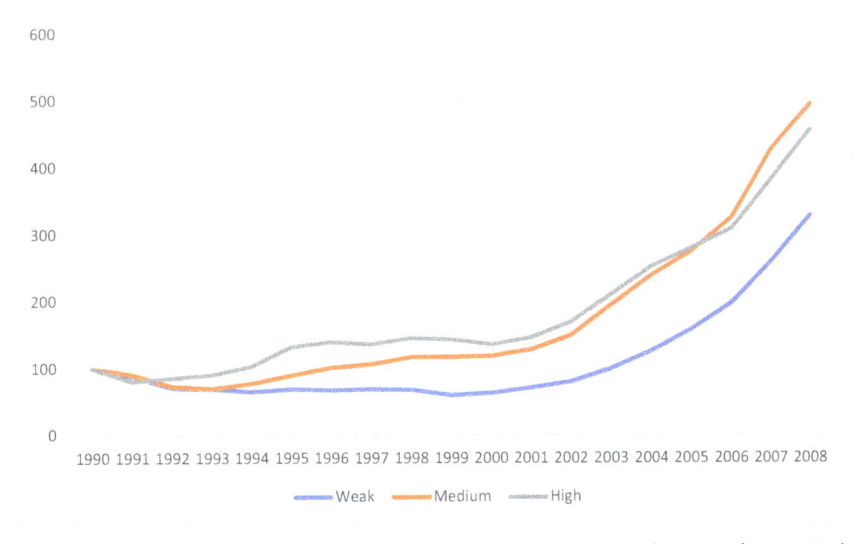

**Figure 2.1.** Corporate restructuring and GDP per capita (1990 value = 100). Source: self-computing, United Nations database. Created by the author.

suffered from thirty percent contraction in their GDP per capita by 1995, their domestic product returned to its original level by 2003. The gap between the growth levels of policies group was never closed.

Tables 2.3 and 2.4 present how transitional policies affected institutional change. Improvement in the indices of government effectiveness, regulatory quality, control of corruption, government size and labour market are highly correlated with enterprise-related transitional measures, thus the implementation of transitional policies that focus on enterprise restructuring established better market institutions. The tables present the institutional ranking of developing and developed countries during the time of

Table 2.3. Enterprise restructuring policies and governance institutional indices.

| Transitional policy | Policy groups | Government Effectiveness 1996 | 2002 | 2008 | Regulatory quality 1996 | 2002 | 2008 | Control of corruption 1996 | 2002 | 2008 |
|---|---|---|---|---|---|---|---|---|---|---|
| Privatization method | MEBOs Vouchers | (0.02) | (0.05) | 0.07 | (0.16) | (0.14) | 0.06 | (0.19) | (0.14) | (0.06) |
| | MEBOs Direct sales | (0.94) | (0.92) | (0.74) | (1.00) | (0.97) | (0.74) | (0.90) | (0.94) | (0.82) |
| | Direct sales MEBOs | 0.39 | 0.49 | 0.34 | 0.43 | 0.71 | 0.79 | 0.30 | 0.08 | 0.08 |
| | Direct sales Vouchers | (0.06) | 0.05 | 0.22 | 0.18 | 0.40 | 0.59 | (0.41) | (0.28) | (0.13) |
| | Voucher Direct sales | (0.03) | (0.03) | 0.16 | 0.13 | 0.17 | 0.44 | (0.38) | (0.51) | (0.27) |
| | Voucher MEBOs | (0.53) | (0.62) | (0.75) | (0.36) | (0.35) | (0.44) | (1.05) | (1.02) | (1.03) |
| Operational restructure responsibility | State | (0.61) | (0.61) | (0.49) | (0.61) | (0.55) | (0.24) | (0.83) | (0.85) | (0.65) |
| | Private | 0.39 | 0.48 | 0.54 | 0.58 | 0.75 | 0.74 | 0.16 | 0.14 | 0.14 |
| Corporate financial discipline | Weak | (0.73) | (0.77) | (0.65) | (0.81) | (0.77) | (0.52) | (1.00) | (0.99) | (0.89) |
| | Medium | 0.26 | 0.32 | 0.59 | 0.61 | 0.59 | 0.73 | 0.31 | 0.07 | 0.31 |
| | High | 0.40 | 0.52 | 0.54 | 0.62 | 0.82 | 0.91 | 0.20 | 0.08 | 0.22 |
| Transitional countries average | | (0.21) | (0.18) | (0.07) | (0.13) | (0.03) | 0.15 | (0.43) | (0.45) | (0.33) |
| Developing countries average | | (0.42) | (0.41) | (0.44) | (0.39) | (0.42) | (0.45) | (0.37) | (0.39) | (0.40) |
| Developed countries average | | 1.41 | 1.52 | 1.41 | 1.32 | 1.28 | 1.41 | 1.47 | 1.53 | 1.41 |

Source: self-computing, World Bank database.

INSTITUTIONAL DEVELOPMENT AND GROWTH 71

Table 2.4. Enterprise restructuring policies and economic freedom institutional indices.

| Transitional policy | Policy groups | State assets[i] | | | | | Transfer and subsidies | | | | | Labour market regulation[ii] | | | |
|---|---|---|---|---|---|---|---|---|---|---|---|---|---|---|---|
| | | 1990 | 1995 | 2000 | 2005 | 2010 | 1995 | 2000 | 2005 | 2010 | 1990 | 1995 | 2000 | 2005 |
| Operational restructure responsibility | State | 3.20 | 4.79 | 5.88 | 6.35 | 6.73 | 6.44 | 6.47 | 7.20 | 6.74 | 2.92 | 3.74 | 6.40 | 6.97 |
| | Private | 3.99 | 6.22 | 7.29 | 7.32 | 7.81 | 5.18 | 5.22 | 5.88 | 5.33 | 2.76 | 5.13 | 6.50 | 7.15 |
| Corporate financial discipline | Weak | 3.43 | 4.45 | 5.02 | 5.42 | 5.83 | 7.03 | 6.50 | 7.43 | 7.23 | | | | |
| | Medium | 2.98 | 6.01 | 7.19 | 7.75 | 8.74 | 4.20 | 5.47 | 5.91 | 4.65 | | | | |
| | High | 4.21 | 6.62 | 8.30 | 8.34 | 8.49 | 5.17 | 5.41 | 6.22 | 5.31 | | | | |
| Transitional countries average | | 3.54 | 5.44 | 6.49 | 6.77 | 7.20 | 5.60 | 5.72 | 6.57 | 6.10 | 2.83 | 4.63 | 6.46 | 7.05 |
| Developing countries average | | 5.23 | 6.07 | 6.50 | 6.54 | 6.42 | 8.71 | 8.73 | 8.84 | 8.75 | 5.22 | 5.66 | 5.58 | 6.00 |
| Developed countries average | | 8.31 | 8.49 | 8.61 | 8.82 | 8.60 | 5.13 | 5.28 | 5.18 | 4.60 | 6.08 | 6.03 | 6.10 | 7.29 |

Source: self-computing, EFW database.

Notes:
i. State assets measure the government's control over capital and serve as a proxy for government's size.
ii. Labour market regulations is an indicator including hiring and firing regulation, minimum wage and centralized collective bargaining.

transition in order to provide a benchmark[37] for the success of transition. The transitional countries are categorized as 'developing countries' by the UN, therefore comparing them to similar countries can shed light on their institutional development in respect to transition policies. Such a comparison is insightful, given the lack of institutional data of transitional countries in the pre-transition era. This comparison is significant, because the apparent change in the transitional countries institutional ranking, while the developing and developed countries ranking stagnated, shows that this institutional development is indeed related to the transition policies. The more efficient policies achieved institutional rankings superior to the developing countries' benchmark, but still fall short in comparison to the developed countries' benchmark. The less efficient policies receive institutional rankings which are lower than the developing countries' benchmark.

Tables 2.5 and 2.6 present the outcomes of strengthening market institutions. The correlation of enterprise restructuring policies with GDP growth is very high due to improvement of labour productivity and development of the private sector.

*Privatization Method Policies*

Privatization was the most important and common restructuring transitional tool. Different methods of privatization lead to different outcomes in establishing quality enterprise governance, productivity and the integration of privatized companies in market economy (Table 2.4). Direct sale was the most useful privatization method for achieving the development objectives in transition countries, which included reduction of state intervention, achieving economic stabilization, as well as employment and productivity enhancement. Implementing the MEBOs as a secondary privatization policy was the best complementary policy. The countries that choose privatization via direct sales strengthened their governance institutions as implied by the strong positive rank in the WGI indices of government effectiveness, regulatory quality and control of corruption, while MEBOs and voucher are associated with lower institutional rank (Table 2.3). It is notable that by 1996 countries in the direct-sales groups have significantly higher institutional ranking than the developing countries' benchmark. In comparison, the voucher with MEBOs and MEBOs with direct-sales policy groups received a lower institutional ranking than the developing countries.

The institutional development of direct sales was translated into growth via higher integration into a market economy. It contributed most to the labour transition from the public to the private sector[38] and enabled large reduction of state subsidies as well (Table 2.5). Early subsidy reduction was

**Table 2.5.** Enterprise restructuring policies and private sector data 1991–98.

| Transitional policy | Policy groups | Number of countries | Share in GDP 1995[i] | Share in labour 1998[ii] | Avg. subsidy 1992[iii] | Avg. subsidy 1998 | Labour productivity[iv] 1992 | 1995 | 1998 |
|---|---|---|---|---|---|---|---|---|---|
| Privatization method | MEBOs Vouchers | 4 | 41.2 | 50.3 | 5.8 | 2.5 | (2.7) | (8.3) | 34.7 |
| | MEBOs Direct sales | 5 | 33.0 | 59.5 | 9.9 | 1.0 | (11.3) | (10.3) | (8.4) |
| | Direct sales MEBOs | 3 | 55.0 | 75.2 | 6.6 | 1.9 | (8.3) | 27.5 | 64.0 |
| | Direct sales Vouchers | 6 | 46.7 | 63.9 | 3.6 | 1.7 | (4.3) | (20.1) | (9.5) |
| | Vouchers Direct sales | 5 | 50.0 | 30.5 | 6.9 | 4.1 | (10.2) | (15.8) | 3.6 |
| | Vouchers MEBOs | 2 | 42.5 | 76.0 | 15.4 | 2.5 | (12.7) | (39.7) | (9.2) |
| Operational restructure responsibility | State | 15 | 36.3 | 57.5 | 8.6 | 1.7 | (14.9) | (18.8) | (5.9) |
| | Private | 10 | 56.5 | 68.4 | 3.2 | 2.9 | (4.6) | 4.8 | 32.5 |
| Corporate financial discipline | Weak | 12 | 32.9 | 53.9 | 9.9 | 2.1 | (15.7) | (27.3) | (10.7) |
| | Medium-High[v] | 9 | 58.9 | 71.5 | 3.9 | 2.5 | (2.6) | 15.1 | 38.3 |

Source: self-computing, EBRD 2001.

*Notes*:

i. Private sector share in GDP (percent) includes income generated by the activity of private registered companies as well as by private entities engaged in informal activity.

ii. Private sector share in labour (percent) includes employment in private registered companies, as well as in private entities engaged in informal activity (when reliable information is available). This average should be taken into consideration with some caution, because not all countries reported the share of private sector.

iii. The average budgetary transfers (GDP percent) to enterprises and households, excluding social transfers.

iv. Labour productivity is calculated as the ratio of industrial production to industrial employment and presented as accumulative productivity since 1991.

v. Due to sporadic data, the medium-policy group was added to the high-policy group.

important to distinguish between viable and nonviable firms and encouraged productivity. Indeed, the most contributing methods of privatization to productivity were direct sales as primary and MEBOs as secondary.[39] These results imply that distributing ownership to employees or the public may not be the optimal way to enhance private sector integration into a market economy and it is better to rely on outsiders that may induce management turnover and thus foster product market restructuring.[40]

**Table 2.6.** Enterprise restructuring policies and GDP growth 1990–95.

| Transitional policy | Policy Groups | Avg. GDP 1990 | Avg. GDP 1995 | Correlation with initial GDP level[i] | Correlation with GDP growth[ii] | Correlation with EU membership |
|---|---|---|---|---|---|---|
| Operational responsibility | State | 1,490 | 1,028 | 0.57 | 0.56 | 0.52 |
|  | Private | 3,572 | 4,113 |  |  |  |
| Corporate financial discipline | Weak | 1,411 | 919 | 0.38 | 0.72 | 0.72 |
|  | Medium | 4,719 | 4,963 |  |  |  |
|  | High | 2,777 | 3,428 |  |  |  |

Source: self-computing, United Nations database.

*Notes*:
i. Correlation between the transitional policy and GDP in 1990.
ii. Correlation between the transitional policy and GDP growth between 1990–95.

## *Operational Restructure Policy*

Operational restructure responsibility is another important way to measure state intervention in light of privatization and enterprise restructure policies. Transferring operational restructure responsibility to new (private) ownership strengthened governance institutions and encouraged enterprise restructuring, which led to an increase in productivity and integration into a market economy.

Countries that choose to entrust operational restructuring to private owners strengthened their governance institutions, as indicated by the positive and growing trend of the private group in the ranking of the WGI institutional indices government effectiveness and regulatory quality between 1996 and 2002, while the state responsibility group had a negative ranking (Table 2.3).[41] The private-policy group had significantly higher institutional rankings than the developing countries' benchmarks by 1996, while the state-policy group had below benchmark ratings. The institutional gap between the groups remained constant until 2008, even as the state-policy group's index ranking increased. Thus, it seems that early advantages of this transitional policy lingered. Control of corruption index also favoured the private-policy group, which suggests that state involvement in the operational restructuring process comes with the negative effects attributed to corruption.[42]

Table 2.4 presents the policy groups' correlation with several economic-freedom institutional indices. The private-policy group is positively correlated with government size (proxy by state assets) and labour market regulation indices. This group encouraged larger institutional development by 1995 in comparison to the state-policy group, after starting from a similar rank in 1990. By doing so, the private-policy group passed the developing countries' institutional benchmark while the state group stayed behind. Thus, countries with private operational restructuring created more liberal labour market regulation (Botero et al. 2004) and had less state control over capital, which enabled them to integrate market operation easier. Private operational restructuring led to higher corporate integration into a market economy, as the private sector share in GDP and productivity increased substantially by 1995 for the private-policy group (Table 2.5).[43]

These developments explain the strong correlation with GDP growth presented in Table 2.6. Although the difference in institutional ranking between the groups mitigated by the mid-2000s, as the countries in the state policy group advanced with transition, the productivity and growth effects due to early transition policies continued.

Surprisingly, the private policy group is negatively correlated with subsidies (Tables 2.4 and 2.5). This trend is likely because operating under private ownership reduced the pressure for the state to provide subsidies in early transition, while public pressure created a partial setback in policy in late transition. At the same time, the state policy group was under social pressure to maintain subsidies in the early 1990s, which were cut sharply due to the deteriorating economic situation later in the decade.

### *Corporate Financial Discipline Policy*

Corporate financial discipline seems to be the transitional policy that contributes to GDP growth the highest. A higher level of corporate financial discipline induces the development of governance institutions, as indices of regulatory quality and control of corruption and state assets ranked significantly higher for the high-policy group (Tables 2.3 and 2.4). The gap in the indices ranking persisted throughout the 1990s and 2000s. By the year 1995 the high-policy group outranked the developing countries' benchmark and achieved almost the developed countries' benchmark ranking in some indices by 2000–2002.

Imposing strict corporate financial discipline was an important, low budgetary burden in the early phases. The state lowered its intervention by cutting credit to unviable firms, therefore improving resource allocation, which resulted in higher productivity.[44] This view is confirmed by the contrasting trend of productivity of the medium-high and weak-policy groups between 1991 and 1998 (Table 2.5). While the productivity of the medium-high-policy group increased by 38 percent between 1991 and 1998, the productivity of the weak-policy group declined by 10 percent. The increase of productivity due to better resource allocation is responsible for corporate financial discipline to be the highest contributor to growth among the transitional policies (Table 2.6).

## The Relation between Competition Enhancing Transitional Policies, Institutional Development and Growth

Although a competition office was established in all but five transitional countries during the early 1990s, the corresponding policies were implemented gradually and sporadically. Wage liberalization and bankruptcy enforcement policies were key factors in promoting competitiveness and functioned as the main catalysts for the development of the private sector by diverting resources from the public sector.

Figure 2.2 illustrates the relation between competitiveness-enhancing policies and growth. In order to emphasize the divergence of GDP trend that originate from policy differences rather than initial wealth, the figure initiate all policy groups from the same level, although the initial level of GDP varied between groups. The focus during the interpretation of the figure should therefore be on the GDP trend of the different groups in re-

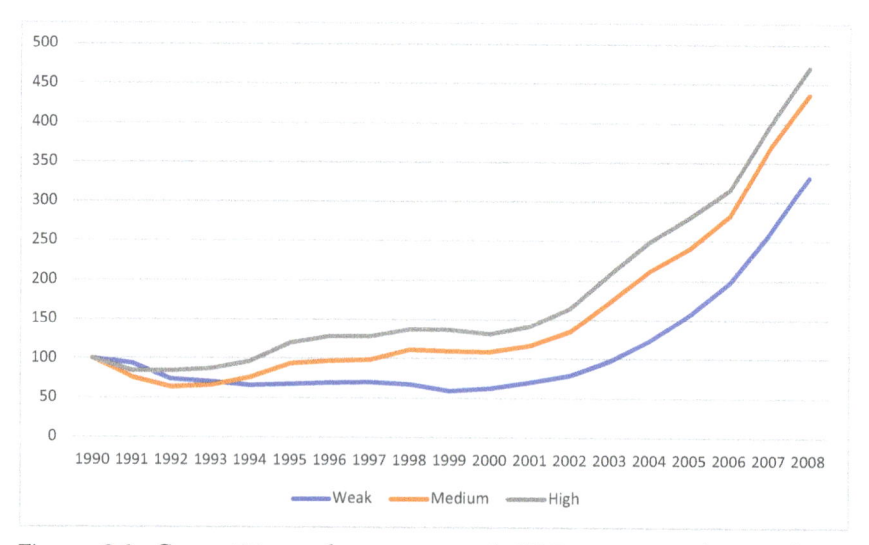

**Figure 2.2.** Competition enhancement and GDP per capita (1990 value = 100). Source: self-computing, United Nations database. Created by the author.

lation to the starting point. The growth trend of the policy group reflecting the divergence of their productivity is presented in Table 2.10. Countries in the high-policy[45] group recovered their GDP level by 1994 and had a positive growth rate thereafter. Countries in the medium-policy[46] group had a larger GDP deficit and their growth rate stagnated until the early 2000s. Countries in the weak-policy[47] group suffered from 50 percent contraction in their GDP per capita by the late 1990s, which reflects their productivity deterioration.

Tables 2.7, 2.8 and 2.9 clarify how competition transitional policies affected institutional change. Improvement of the indices of government effectiveness, regulatory quality, legal system, government size and labour market are highly correlated with competition transitional measures. Thus, implementing transitional policies that focus on competition enhancement succeeded in establishing better market institutions.

Tables 2.10 and 2.11 present the outcomes of strengthening market institutions. The correlation of competition policies with GDP growth is positive for all subcategories due to productivity increase and better resource allocation in the economy.

Table 2.7. Competition transition policies and WGI Institutional indices.

| Transitional policy | Policy groups | Government effectiveness 1996 | 2002 | 2008 | Regulatory quality 1996 | 2002 | 2008 |
|---|---|---|---|---|---|---|---|
| Wage liberalization | Weak |  |  |  | (0.72) | (0.68) | (0.44) |
|  | Medium |  |  |  | (0.17) | 0.00 | 0.19 |
|  | High |  |  |  | 0.93 | 1.08 | 1.12 |
| Price liberalization | Weak | (0.90) | (1.05) | (1.08) | (1.10) | (1.32) | (1.22) |
|  | Medium | (0.68) | (0.63) | (0.47) | (0.61) | (0.49) | (0.24) |
|  | High | 0.30 | 0.37 | 0.48 | 0.46 | 0.65 | 0.82 |
| Monopoly & large conglomerates control | Weak | (0.54) | (0.45) | (0.30) | (0.61) | (0.51) | (0.23) |
|  | Medium | 0.16 | 0.14 | 0.15 | 0.33 | 0.41 | 0.49 |
|  | High | 0.51 | 0.56 | 0.54 | 0.54 | 0.74 | 0.79 |
| Competition agency | Yes | (0.55) | (0.81) | (0.82) | (0.64) | (0.83) | (0.71) |
|  | No | (0.12) | (0.02) | 0.11 | (0.01) | 0.17 | 0.37 |
| Transitional countries average |  | (0.21) | (0.18) | (0.07) | (0.13) | (0.03) | 0.15 |
| Developed countries average |  | 1.41 | 1.52 | 1.41 | 1.32 | 1.28 | 1.41 |
| Developing countries average |  | (0.42) | (0.41) | (0.44) | (0.39) | (0.42) | (0.45) |

Source: self-computing, World Bank database.

**Table 2.8.** Bankruptcy enforcement and legal framework ranking.

| Transitional policy | Policy groups | Rule of law 1996 | 2002 | 2008 | Legal system 1995 | 2000 | 2005 | 2010 |
|---|---|---|---|---|---|---|---|---|
| Bankruptcy enforcement | Weak | (0.69) | (0.67) | (0.51) | 5.95 | 6.19 | 5.27 | 5.43 |
| | Medium | 0.14 | 0.07 | 0.03 | 5.93 | 5.77 | 5.54 | 5.57 |
| | High | 0.55 | 0.71 | 0.91 | 6.94 | 6.46 | 6.40 | 6.31 |
| Transitional countries average | | (0.35) | (0.33) | (0.20) | 6.30 | 6.20 | 5.57 | 5.64 |
| Developed countries average | | 1.46 | 1.39 | 1.45 | 8.55 | 8.37 | 7.96 | 7.65 |
| Developing countries average | | (0.35) | (0.38) | (0.41) | 4.83 | 4.62 | 4.43 | 4.55 |

Source: self-computing, WGI and EFW databases.

## *Wage Liberalization Policy*

Wage liberalization is highly significant for the successful transition of corporates into the market economy, as the correlation of the policy group with institutional development shows. Countries in the high-policy group are associated with strong and superior regulatory quality (Table 2.7) and better labour market regulation (Table 2.9). After ranking similarly low in 1990, a gap in the institutional ranking opened between the different policy groups in the labour market regulation index. While the ranking of the high- and medium-policy groups almost reached the benchmark of developing countries by 1995, the ranking of the weak-policy group lagged behind. This divergence explains the large correlation between productivity and GDP growth.

Wage liberalization is crucial for increasing productivity, as productivity and compensation are tightly correlated. Wage is strongly connected to competitiveness and productivity. Countries that maintained high control of wages prevented the private sector's share in the economy from increasing. Table 2.10 shows this connection via the increased share of the private sector in employment in the high policy countries. Wage liberalization allowed private companies to offer higher salaries, enabled the private sector to attract workers (70 percent of workforce in 1998) and incentivized the workers to be more productive (12 percent productivity increase by 1995). In comparison, the weak policy group prevented private businesses from incentivizing workers, which led to a deterioration of productivity.[48]

Table 2.11 presents the effects of wage liberalization on growth resulting from productivity increase and sectoral changes. A high positive correlation between wage liberalization and GDP growth can be observed in 1995. This correlation is significantly higher than the correlation between

**Table 2.9.** Competition transition policies and EFW institutional indices.

| Transitional policy | Policy groups | State assets 1990 | 1995 | 2000 | 2005 | 2010 | Transfer and subsidies 1995 | 2000 | 2005 | 2010 | Labour market regulation 1990 | 1995 | 2000 | 2005 | 2010 |
|---|---|---|---|---|---|---|---|---|---|---|---|---|---|---|---|
| Bankruptcy enforcement | Weak | 3.21 | 4.77 | 6.02 | 6.38 | 6.97 | 6.50 | 6.30 | 7.13 | 6.64 | | | | | |
| | Medium | 4.51 | 6.36 | 6.36 | 6.32 | 6.48 | 4.49 | 5.29 | 5.56 | 4.45 | | | | | |
| | High | 3.86 | 7.24 | 8.51 | 8.67 | 8.66 | 4.80 | 4.96 | 5.41 | 5.12 | | | | | |
| Wage liberalization | Weak | | | | | | 7.03 | 6.50 | 7.33 | 7.12 | NA | 3.21 | 5.78 | 6.87 | 6.96 |
| | Medium | | | | | | 5.36 | 5.57 | 5.93 | 5.41 | 3.14 | 4.87 | 6.59 | 6.85 | 7.06 |
| | High | | | | | | 5.29 | 5.37 | 5.94 | 5.23 | 3.35 | 5.10 | 6.78 | 7.38 | 7.51 |
| Price liberalization | Weak | NA | 3.29 | 3.49 | 3.73 | 4.53 | NA | 6.26 | 3.98 | 6.67 | | | | | |
| | Medium | 3.21 | 5.21 | 5.98 | 6.26 | 6.44 | 7.87 | 7.15 | 7.75 | 6.93 | | | | | |
| | High | 3.67 | 5.89 | 7.46 | 7.75 | 8.23 | 5.15 | 5.28 | 6.14 | 5.56 | | | | | |
| Monopoly & large conglomerates control | Weak | 3.12 | 5.29 | 6.03 | 6.51 | 6.94 | 6.29 | 6.08 | 6.88 | 6.51 | | | | | |
| | Medium | 3.63 | 5.35 | 6.80 | 6.86 | 7.39 | 6.18 | 5.84 | 6.83 | 6.00 | | | | | |
| | High | 4.37 | 6.19 | 7.51 | 7.55 | 7.69 | 3.72 | 4.78 | 4.88 | 4.83 | | | | | |
| Transitional countries average | | 3.54 | 5.20 | 6.49 | 6.77 | 7.20 | 5.60 | 5.72 | 6.57 | 6.10 | 2.83 | 4.63 | 6.46 | 7.05 | 7.21 |
| Developed countries average | | 8.31 | 8.49 | 8.61 | 8.82 | 8.60 | 5.13 | 5.28 | 5.18 | 4.60 | 6.08 | 6.03 | 6.10 | 7.29 | 7.58 |
| Developing countries average | | 5.23 | 6.07 | 6.50 | 6.54 | 6.42 | 8.71 | 8.73 | 8.84 | 8.75 | 5.22 | 5.66 | 5.58 | 6.00 | 6.30 |

Source: self-computing, EFW database.

**Table 2.10.** Competition transition policies and private sector data 1991–98.

| Transitional policy | Policy groups | Number of countries | Share in GDP 1995 | Share in labour 1998 | Avg. subsidy 1992 | Avg. subsidy 1998 | Labour productivity 1992 | Labour productivity 1995 | Labour productivity 1998 |
|---|---|---|---|---|---|---|---|---|---|
| Wage liberalization | Weak | 12 | 35.4 | 63.2 | 10.0 | 1.7 | (17.0) | (27.4) | (14.9) |
| | Medium | 5 | 43.0 | 53.0 | 4.9 | 2.4 | 0.8 | 6.1 | 31.6 |
| | High | 7 | 62.1 | 69.7 | 2.9 | 3.1 | (5.4) | 12.4 | 38.8 |
| Price liberalization | Weak | 4 | 25 | 36.7 | 11.0 | 2.6 | (10.3) | (28.8) | (14.9) |
| | Medium | 8 | 40 | 69.2 | 8.5 | 1.2 | (17.6) | (19.3) | (3.9) |
| | High | 13 | 53.1 | 66.8 | 4.7 | 2.6 | (7.1) | 2.75 | 25.2 |
| Bankruptcy enforcement | Weak | 18 | 38.3 | 59.2 | 7.4 | 1.7 | (15.1) | (19.59) | (3.48) |
| | Medium-High | 7 | 60.0 | 70.1 | 3.6 | 3.4 | 1.0 | 16.9 | 42.8 |
| Monopoly & large con-glomerates control | Weak | 15 | 41 | 59.8 | 7.7 | 1.6 | (17.3) | (24.1) | (11.3) |
| | Medium-High | 10 | 49.5 | 64.3 | 4.5 | 3.1 | 1.2 | 12.8 | 40.6 |
| Competition agency | Yes | 20 | 48.0 | 60.1 | 5.2 | 1.7 | (9.9) | (4.3) | 13.6 |
| | No | 5 | 30.0 | 46.2 | 5.3 | 2.5 | (14.2) | (29) | (7.1) |

Source: self-computing, EBRD 2001.

**Table 2.11.** Competition transition policies and GDP growth 1990–95.

| Transitional policy | Policy groups | Avg. GDP 1990 | Avg. GDP 1995 | Correlation with initial GDP level | Correlation with GDP growth | Correlation with EU membership |
|---|---|---|---|---|---|---|
| Wage liberalization | Weak | 1,327 | 835 | | | |
| | Medium | 3,484 | 3,888 | 0.46 | 0.59 | 0.78 |
| | High | 3,196 | 3,533 | | | |
| Price liberalization | Weak | 1,276 | 784 | | | |
| | Medium | 1,482 | 1,115 | 0.46 | 0.43 | 0.72 |
| | High | 3,162 | 3,422 | | | |
| Bankruptcy enforcement | Weak | 1,623 | 1,247 | | | |
| | Medium | 6,449 | 6,688 | 0.47 | 0.65 | 0.52 |
| | High | 3,194 | 4,145 | | | |
| Monopoly control | Weak | 1,993 | 1,630 | | | |
| | Medium | 2,187 | 2,339 | 0.36 | 0.49 | 0.38 |
| | High | 4,370 | 5,367 | | | |
| Competition office | No | 1,322 | 1,006 | 0.28 | 0.23 | 0.28 |
| | Yes | 2,573 | 2,576 | | | |

Source: self-computing, United Nations database.

the policy and initial GDP. These results imply a causality between wage liberalization and growth and show that high level of this transition policy stimulate competitiveness.

## Price Liberalization

Table 2.7 presents the relation of price liberalization policy to the institutional indices of regulatory quality and government effectiveness. Countries which implemented high price liberalization policies are affiliated with higher regulatory quality and larger state credibility from 1996 on. The rankings are well above the developing countries' benchmark. This trend was amplified during the following decade, probably due to the high-policy group's tendency to maintain reforms while the weak- and medium-policy groups withdrew from implementing transition policies. Table 2.9 presents no correlation between price liberalization and transfers and subsidies, but a robust positive correlation with the index of state assets. Based on this observation, it can be argued that high state intervention (i.e., weak-policy level) is likely to encourage market price distortions.

Encouraging price competitiveness rather than controlling monopolistic prices encouraged product market restructuring. This explains the high-policy group's positive productivity in 1995, while the medium- and weak-policy groups suffered from a double-digit industrial productivity decrease (Table 2.10).[49] Table 2.11 illustrates positive correlation between price liberalization policy and GDP growth, although it is the lowest among the correlations of transition policies and growth in early transition. These results imply that price competitiveness contributes relatively little to growth.

## Bankruptcy Enforcement Policy

Strong bankruptcy enforcement is a supplementary policy to improve corporate governance. It eliminated unviable firms and improved resource allocation between the private and public sector. Countries with high bankruptcy policy improved their legal framework and contained state interference. The high-policy group ranked significantly better than the developing countries' benchmark in legal market indices (Table 2.8). By the mid-1990s, a large difference in the institutional rank emerged between the policy groups. This gap widened in the next decade, as countries with high bankruptcy policy strengthened their rule of law, while countries with weak bankruptcy policy stagnated. A similar trend is observed in the legal system indicator. Enforcing losing companies to dissolve reduces the state interference in the economy, as the majority of losing companies are state-owned. This explains the high correlation between the policy group and the state assets index presented in Table 2.9. After starting from a similar ranking point in 1990, the high- and medium policy-groups advanced to a level above the benchmark of developing countries while the weak-policy group stagnated. The high-policy rating improved further and reached the developed countries' benchmark in 2000. That is, bankruptcy enforcement not only strengthens law-related institutions but also diminishes state interference.

Enforcing unviable enterprises to dissolve releases resources and prevents debt overhang from growing and clouding the financial system. This process explains the higher productivity, private sector's size, and the private sector's contribution to generating GDP in the high-policy countries (Table 2.10). The increase of productivity explains the strong growth trend in the high-policy group during the first (1990–95) and second (1995–2000) transition periods, during which the medium- and-weak groups stagnated (Table 2.11). These results imply a causality between bankruptcy enforcement and growth.

## Competition Office Policy

The EBRD reviewed whether an independent competition office or an anti-monopoly office exists in the transition countries. Such an office was assumed to contribute to enterprise restructuring processes. Countries that established a competition office indeed have a higher share of the labour force and of GDP, while they pay less subsidies. Unsurprisingly, countries with a competition office enjoyed a 13.6 percent increase of productivity, while countries without it suffered from a 7.1 percent decrease until 1998 (Table 2.10). However, while many countries establish an anti-monopoly office, it did little to improve market institutions, dismantle monopolies and promote competitiveness. This can be seen in the low correlation of the policy with the WGI governance indicators (Table 2.7) and growth (Table 2.11). It is therefore more appropriate to examine the decentralization of markets using the final measure for competitiveness enhancement.

## Competition and Anti-Monopoly Policy

Anti-monopoly policy and dissolving of large conglomerates were gradually pursued in the transitional countries. This policy is highly correlated with institutional development, as the rating of the different policy groups in the governance indices of government effectiveness, regulatory quality and state assets show (Tables 2.7 and 2.9). The rankings of the low-policy group were below the benchmark of developing countries until the early 2000s, which implies that excessive government interference and unfriendly market policies hindered productivity and growth.[50] The improvements of the weak-policy group in the institutional indices after 1996, during which the developing countries' benchmark stagnated, point to a relation of causality between the transition policy and institutions.

Indeed, productivity trends show that the medium-high policy groups had a positive productivity in the early 1990s that grew steadily, while the weak-policy group had a negative and fluctuated productivity all through the decade (Table 2.10).[51] The rise in productivity of the medium-high groups lead to higher GDP increase (Table 2.11). These results imply that monopoly control has a positive impact on growth.

## Discussion and Concluding Remarks

This chapter has provided empirical evidence that transitional measurements taken by post-communist countries led to institutional development and growth. Early-transition policies established strong market institutions in most of the CEE countries and Albania, while the delay in the implementation of transition policies hindered economic stabilization and growth in most CIS countries, Bulgaria, Macedonia and Romania. Countries that pursued fast transition raised their productivity level due to better resource allocation. The slow transitional countries, on the other hand, imposed anti-market policies that eroded productivity, investment and growth. The institutional development that originated in transitional policies is especially apparent when different policy groups are compared to the benchmark of developing countries. While the benchmark remained fairly constant for most institutions, the ranking of high-policy transitional countries showed significant improvement throughout the 1990s. The weak-policy transitional countries implemented pro-market transition policies in the early 2000s, which led to a similar institutional change throughout the 2000s. Even as the slow countries picked up the pace of transition, the initial growth gap remained constant in the following decades, leading to the growth variance observed today.

The institutional gap between transitional countries that has been observed since 1995 and can also be seen as 'first-move advantage' remained persistent in most policies during the following decade. Transitional policy measures explain the existence of contradicting growth and productivity trends between groups in the second half of the 1990s as well as the convergence trend throughout the early 2000s. Initial conditions seem to have played a role in determining the transition process. The positive correlations between initial wealth (i.e., GDP in 1990) and transitional measures indicate that richer countries were more prone to implement transitional policies, while the poorer countries struggled with the need for transition. Discouraged by their low initial conditions, the CIS countries delayed necessary adjustments, which eventually worsened their economic condition.[52]

The correlation between EU membership and a high level of transition policies is very strong. This raises the questions whether EU membership is responsible for the growth trend, and if so, how. Was it a consequence of trade increase (i.e., economics of scales) or of fostering institutional change that encouraged productivity? The analysis of institutional indices above shows a firm connection between high policy measures, institutional development and productivity increase, whereas being a part of the European Economic Area (EEA) helped CEE countries to build strong market institutions and restricted protectionism.[53] Abolishing state protectionism strengthened corporate financial discipline and assisted in dissolving monopolies. The EA contained international guidelines imposing compliance of the domestic governments to a higher level of governance and preventing them from retracting market policies.[54] The harmonization of legislative framework and institutional provisions to the Western Europe level forced the transitional countries to implement a higher level of institutional governance, compelled the state to a higher level of accountability and lowered protectionism and state interference in economically based decisions. For example, assuring a higher level of governance assisted in attracting foreign investors to purchase local enterprises. In this sense, the direct sales privatization method was more feasible in the case of an EU membership prodigy. The EU played a role in supporting the transition process by increasing the competitiveness not only via trade but also as a result of institutional harmonization.[55]

A key factor policy in promoting privatization and restructuring was the choice of primary privatization method. Early mass privatization, usually via a voucher program was pursued in several countries with different degrees of success. Direct sales have emerged as the most efficient method, with MEBOs as the second and voucher privatization the third. MEBOs – without a strong independent management – was an inferior method, only slightly better than ownership distribution via voucher program. The relative success of the direct sales method is likely because it aimed at attracting domestic and foreign investors, which assisted the promotion of operational restructuring and strengthening of corporate governance. Vouchers appear to be the least successful privatization method, probably because dispersed ownership of the public did not bring additional knowledge or other advantages that enhance corporate governance or productivity.[56]

State ownership and intervention are associated with lower level of governance and more bureaucracy, as the high correlations between the transitional policies operational restructure responsibility, corporate financial discipline and dissolving of large conglomerates with governance indicators present. Competitiveness-enhancing transition policies were crucial for building strong market institutions, dissolving unviable firms and transferring resources from state control to the private sector. These actions improved governance and market institutions from the benchmark below that of the developing countries to one above by the mid-to-late 1990s. The positive effects of the transition policies on institutions and productivity were persistent throughout the 1990s and explain much of the growth variation during the era. Wage liberalizing and bankruptcy enforcement were more effective policies, while price liberalization and competition were less effective in encouraging growth.

**Tal Kadayer** is a PhD student in political economy at the European University Viadrina and a former financial analyst for consulting companies and the European Investment Bank. His research focuses on identifying and understanding successful transition policies to a market economy in East European and Eurasia countries. His topics of research include economic and political integration in the EU, including the European sovereign debt crisis and the Unification and Separation of nations in the European Union.

## Notes

1. For a review of early economic growth models, see Renelt (1991).
2. Typical explanatory exogenous factors included geography and climate. Acemoglu, Johnson and Robinson refute these theories by using property right institutions as the unobserved variable to explain the correlation between geography and growth (Acemoglu, Johnson and Robinson 2001).
3. For the most influential studies in providing empirical cross-country comparisons that link institutions to economic development, investment and growth, see Barro (1991), Mauro (1995), Knack and Keefer (1995), Kaufmann, Kraay and Zoido-Lobaton (1999), and Acemoglu, Johnson and Robinson (2005).
4. International indices that provide cross-country comparison include the World Governance Index (WGI) of the World Bank, the Political Freedom Index of the Freedom House, the Economic freedom of the world (EFW) of the Fraser institute and the International Country Risk Guide indices (ICRG) of PRS group.
5. According to the World Bank's ten-year transition report, the CEE countries had positive GDP growth in the decade that followed the transition, while all the CIS had a negative real GDP growth for the same time period.
6. For a discussion about the relation between transitional policies and economic outcome as a product of country specific characteristics see Armstrong and Sappington (2006).
7. For studies that focus solely on CEE countries see Gray (1996), Holland and Pain (1998) and Carstensen and Toubal (2004).

8. For example, the World Governance Indicators (WGI), which is often used in institution growth literature, provides sporadic information starting 1996. Also see Kaufmann, Kraay and Zoido-Lobaton (1999), and Buterin, Škare and Buterin (2017).
9. For instance, Ulubasoglu and Doucouliagos exclude transitional countries from their database, finding them not fitting to a model based on economic and freedom indicators (Ulubasoglu and Doucouliagos 2004). Barro examines the influence of a socialist economic system in relation to growth but excludes the eastern European countries (Barro 1991). Some other scholars exclude transitional countries from their database due to lack of economic data of pre-transitional periods (see for example, Mauro [1995], Ali and Crain [2001], Rodrik [2000], Easterly [2001] and Vijayaraghavan and Ward [2001]).
10. For further discussion on the speed of transition, see Tommasi and Velasco (1996) and Hellman (1998).
11. For the advantages associated with the Shock Therapy transition strategy, see Gates, Milgrom and Roberts (1996); Mondino, Sturzenegger and Tommasi (1996); Auernheimer and George (1997); de Melo et al. (2001).
12. For further discussion on the benefits associated with economic freedom see Barro (1991); Ali and Crain (2001); Ulubasoglu and Doucouliagos (2004).
13. For further discussion regarding partial implementation of reforms in light of the gradual approach see Murphy, Shleifer and Vishny (1992); Martinelli and Tommasi (1993); Mondino, Sturzenegger and Tommasi (1996); Hellman (1998).
14. The credibility of the regime and the stability of the political system play a major role in the success of implementing pro-market reforms. See Qimiao and Schaffer (1994); Roland (1994); Haggard (1991).
15. For the shortcomings of the BIg Bang transition strategy, see Dewatripont and Roland (1992); Laban and Sturzenegger (1994); Roland (1994); Gavin (1996).
16. See Stiglitz and Pike (2004); Birdsall and de la Torre (2001).
17. See Yergin, Stanislav and Bothwell (1998); Meon and Weill (2005); Roy and Tisdell (1998).
18. For more information about the role of country-specific factors in determine privatization and corporate governance, see Gray (1996).
19. Rodrik particularly points to this problem (Rodrik 2000).
20. It is noteworthy that although the institutional indices gap remains significant, institutional indices of slow transition countries improve when they pick up transition, which gives further evidence for the causality between policies and institutions.
21. Notable studies that examine institutions as a determinant of growth include: Barro (1991, 2003); Shleifer and Vishny (1993); Knack and Keefer (1995); Mauro (1995); Kaufmann, Kraay and Zoido-Lobaton (1999); Rodrik (2000); Vijayaraghavan and Ward (2001); Meon and Weill (2005); Ulubasoglu and Doucouliagos (2004); Acemoglu, Johnson and Robinson (2005).
22. For a review of the origin for cross-country institution variance, see Acemoglu, Johnson and Robinson (2005).
23. This theory is supported by Rio and Lores, who have developed a model showing that the distribution of political and economic power plays a role in determining policies (Rio and Lores 2017).
24. See Kaufmann, Kraay and Zoido-Lobaton (1999); Meon and Weill (2005) and Djankov at el. (2003) for more detail.

25. See for instance Kaufmann, Kraay and Zoido-Lobaton (1999) and Mauro (1995).
26. Studying the labour market flexibility in transitional countries in light of labour institutional change, Cazes argues that wage setting institutions and labour market policies are associated with higher unemployment rates (Cazes 2002).
27. Private sector companies that provide monetary incentive attract more able workers, resulting in an increase of the average output per worker. This monetary incentive effect is explored in Paarsch and Shearer (2000); Lazear (2000); Shearer (2004).
28. D'souza and Megginson study privatization in both developing and developed countries and argue that privatization improves corporate operating outcomes such as profitability, output, operating efficiency while reducing financial leverage ratios (D'souza and Megginson 1999).
29. For example, the EBRD categorizes Czechoslovakia and Russia in the same category in this broad definition, ignoring the policy differences between the two countries and the transitional success of the Czech Republic and Slovakia, while Russia was lagging behind. For more information, see EBRD (1994).
30. Many pre-transition banks were owned by the enterprises to which they provided services (house banks), creating a poor relation between credit allocation and credit reception. As a result, the banking sector was not independent and allocated credit based on political rather than economic and financial guidelines.
31. Although wage liberalization (or wage regulation) is extensively reported under the enterprise restructure and liberalization sections in the yearly transitional reports (1994–2001), it was not included in the EBRD's indices of liberalization, privatization or competitiveness.
32. The other determinants of growth are country-specific and initial conditions, which are not covered in this chapter.
33. This view is supported by de Melo and her colleagues who suggest that economic liberalization is the most important factor in determining differences in growth, as well as Djankov, McLiesh and Ramalho who argue that improving business regulations in developing countries increases average annual growth (de Melo et al. 2001; Djankov, McLiesh and Ramalho 2006).
34. Countries ranked high if operational restructuring was entrusted to the private ownership and financial discipline was rated high.
35. Countries ranked medium if operational restructuring occurred under private ownership and financial discipline was rated medium, or if operational restructuring occurred under state ownership and financial discipline was rated high.
36. Countries ranked weak if operational restructuring occurred under state ownership and financial discipline was rated either weak or medium.
37. Developed countries' benchmark refers to the average of the G7 countries, while developing countries' benchmark includes the average of 144 countries that are defined as developing by the UN, excluding the twenty-five economies in transition reviewed in this chapter.
38. The correlation of privatization ownership with labour intensity corresponds with the findings in Bilsen and Konings (1998) and Dewenter and Malatesta (2001).
39. Holland and Pain claim cash sales to be a superior privatization method for attracting FDI, while Djankov and Murrell associate cash sales with operational restructuring. FDI and operational restructuring are both known catalysts for productivity enhancement (Holland and Pain 1998; Djankov and Murrell 2000).

40. For instance, Djankov and Murrell show that private-concentrated ownership increases management turnover, which is then associated with improved enterprise performance (Djankov and Murrell 2000). Frydman and his colleagues confirm that privatization to outsider owners has superior results over MEBOs privatization in terms of revenues, labour and cost reduction (Frydman et al. 1999).
41. The connection between public ownership and regulatory quality is explored by Edwards and Waverman, who find out that governments interfere in regulatory policies in favour of companies in which they are invested (Edwards and Waverman 2006).
42. This inference is in line with Shleifer and Vishny's model, which shows that operational restructuring is more likely to occur when bribery is costly and political gains are low, both attributing characteristics of countries that preferred to entrust operational restructuring to private ownership (Shleifer and Vishny 1994).
43. The relation between operational restructuring responsibility and productivity is discussed by Djankov and Murrell, who find out that private ownership encourages productivity via higher product market restructuring, as well as by Dewenter and Malatesta, who argue that government-owned firms are inferior in terms of profitability, leverage and labour intensity. Shleifer and Vishny argue that unviable state ownership firms delay operational restructuring, exchanging political support for monetary gains (Djankov and Murrell 2000; Dewenter and Malatesta 2001; Shleifer and Vishny 1994).
44. This conclusion is also supported by Konings and De Loecker, who show that soft budget constraint to state firms prevents the transfer of resources to the private sector and thus reduces the total factor productivity (TFP) (Konings and De Loecker 2006). Djankov and Murrell also arrives at the conclusion that hardening an enterprise's budget constraints increases its chances for implementing restructuring, thus increasing productivity (Djankov and Murrell 2000).
45. Countries have been ranked high if at least two of the four subcategories ranked high and the rest rated medium.
46. Countries have been ranked medium if maximum one subcategory ranked weak while the others are medium.
47. Countries have been ranked weak if at least two of four subcategories are ranked weak and the rest are medium at most.
48. These results are supported by Cazes, as well as Botero and his collages, who show that heavier labour regulation is associated with lower labour force participation and higher unemployment (Cazes 2002; Botero et al. 2004). In contrast, Gavin suggests that rapid market reforms cause the private sector to unduly react, creating excessively high unemployment compared to the market optimum (Gavin 1996).
49. The apparent productivity divergence supports the studies by Murphy, Shleifer and Vishny; Gates, Milgrom and Roberts; and Armstrong and Sappington. The former two studies demonstrate that partial price liberalization leads to disruption of the traditional supply chain production of state companies and resulting in decrease of productivity and total output (Murphy, Shleifer and Vishny 1992; Gates, Milgrom and Roberts 1996). The latter illustrates that restricting pricing flexibility and allowing below cost pricing hinder the development of long-term industry competition,

while allowing prices to reflect operating costs fosters industry competition (Armstrong and Sappington 2006).
50. For example, Armstrong and Sappington assert the role of government's interference and anti-market policies in transitional countries. They reveal that features of the low group policy, such as state-controlled monopolies and specifying market share targets are inhibiting the development of long-term industry competition (Armstrong and Sappington 2006).
51. The productivity divergence asserts the model of Gates, Milgrom and Roberts, who show that promoting complementary competitiveness measures leads to positive interaction among the various policy instruments, which results in private companies engagement in positive added-value activities. Thus privatization, price liberalization and competitiveness improve efficiency when implemented together at a high rate (Gates, Milgrom and Roberts 1996).
52. This observation is supported by de Melo and colleagues who found that the level of transition process has a two-way relation to initial economic conditions. Low initial economic condition depresses the transition process, which is the leading factor for a country's level of income (de Melo et al. 2001).
53. Cieślik and Hagemejer show that the European Agreement (EA) was more effective than other free trade agreements (FTAs) in stimulating trade for CEE countries. The success of the EA hints that the effect of trade increase is not solely due to bilateral tax reduction, but also due to related policies, such as abolishing protectionism and capital related restrictions (Cieślik and Hagemejer 2011).
54. For example, the paper industry in Hungary pressured the government for an import tariff to be reinstated in 1993, but political pressure was blocked due to the trade agreement of the EA.
55. For a review on the process of Europeanization of CEE countries, the evolution of EU membership condition from CEE countries, and how it shaped policy decisions see Grabbe (1999); Grabbe (2001); Dimitrova (2002); Schimmelfennig and Sedelmeier (2005).
56. Although Gray claims that voucher method is the best privatization method for achieving market-oriented objectives, he points to the benefits of direct sales, claiming that the preference for the voucher results from the lack of direct sales feasibility as a large-scale privatization program (Gray 1996).

# References

Acemoglu, Daron, Simon Johnson and James A. Robinson. 2001. 'The Colonial Origins of Comparative Development: An Empirical Investigation'. *American Economic Review* 91(5): 1369–1401.

———. 2005. 'Institutions as a Fundamental Cause of Long-Run Growth'. In *Handbook of Economic Growth*, Vol. 1, edited by Philippe Aghion and Steven N. Durlauf, 385–472. Amsterdam: North Holland.

Ali, Abdiweli, and W. Mark Crain. 2001. 'Institutional Distortions, Economics Freedom, and Growth'. *Cato Journal* 21(3): 415.

Armstrong, Mark, and David E. M. Sappington. 2006. 'Regulation, Competition and Liberalization'. *Journal of Economic Literature* 44(2): 325–66.

Auernheimer, Leonardo, and Susan Mary George. 1997. 'Shock Versus Gradualism in Models of Rational Expectations: The Case of Trade Liberalization'. *Journal of Development Economics* 54(2): 307–22.

Barro, Robert J. 1991. 'Economic Growth in a Cross Section of Countries'. *The Quarterly Journal of Economics* 106(2): 407–43.

———. 2003. 'Determinants of Economic Growth in a Panel of Countries'. *Annals of Economics and Finance* 4(2): 231–74.

Bilsen, Valentijn, and Jozef Konings. 1998. 'Job Creation, Job Destruction, and Growth of Newly Established, Privatized, and State-Owned Enterprises in Transition Economies: Survey Evidence from Bulgaria, Hungary, and Romania'. *Journal of Comparative Economics* 26(3): 429–45.

Birdsall, Nancy, and Augusto de la Torre. 2001. 'Washington Contentious'. *Politica Internazionale* 29(1/2): 95–103.

Botero, Juan C., Simeon Djankov, Rafael LaPorta, Florencio López-de-Silanes and Andrei Shleifer. 2004. 'The Regulation of Labor'. *The Quarterly Journal of Economics* 119(4): 1339–82.

Buterin, Vesna, Marinko Škare and Denis Buterin. 2017. '"Macroeconomic Model of Institutional Reforms" Influence on Economic Growth of the New EU Members and the Republic of Croatia'. *Economic Research/Ekonomska Istraživanja* 30(1): 1572–93.

Carstensen, Kai, and Farid Toubal. 2004. 'Foreign Direct Investment in Central and Eastern European Countries: A Dynamic Panel Analysis'. *Journal of Comparative Economics* 32(1): 3–22.

Cazes, Sandrine. 2002. 'Do Labour Market Institutions Matter in Transition Economies? An Analysis of Labour Market Flexibility in the Late Nineties'. *International Institute for Labour Studies*. Retrieved 18 February 2021 from https://papers.ssrn.com/sol3/papers.cfm?abstract_id=366080.

Cieślik, Andrzej, and Jan Hagemejer. 2011. 'The Effectiveness of Preferential Trade Liberalization in Central and Eastern Europe'. *The International Trade Journal* 25(5): 516–38.

Dewatripont, Mathias, and Gérard Roland. 1992. 'The Virtues of Gradualism and Legitimacy in the Transition to a Market Economy'. *The Economic Journal* 102(411): 291–300.

Dewenter, Kathryn L., and Paul H. Malatesta. 2001. 'State-Owned and Privately Owned Firms: An Empirical Analysis of Profitability, Leverage, and Labor Intensity'. *American Economic Review* 91(1): 320–34.

Dimitrova, Antoaneta. 2002. 'Enlargement, Institution-Building and the EU's Administrative Capacity Requirement'. *West European Politics* 25(4): 171–90.

Djankov, Simeon, and Peter Murrell. 2000. *The Determinants of Enterprise Restructuring in Transition: An Assessment of The Evidence*. Washington: The World Bank Publications.

Djankov, Simeon, Edward Glaeser, Rafael La Porta, Florencio Lopez-de-Silanes and Andrei Shleifer. 2003. 'The New Comparative Economics'. *Journal of Comparative Economics* 31(4): 595–619.

Djankov, Simeon, Caralee McLiesh and Rita Maria Ramalho. 2006. 'Regulation and Growth'. *Economics Letters* 92(3): 395–401.

D'souza, Juliet, and William L. Megginson. 1999. 'The Financial and Operating Performance of Privatized Firms during the 1990s'. *The Journal of Finance* 54(4): 1397–1438.

Easterly, William. 2001. 'The Lost Decades: Developing Countries' Stagnation in Spite of Policy Reform 1980–1998'. *Journal of Economic Growth* 6(2): 135–57.

Edwards, Geoff, and Leonard Waverman. 2006. 'The Effects of Public Ownership and Regulatory Independence on Regulatory Outcomes: A Study of Interconnect Rates in EU Telecommunications'. *Journal of Regulatory Economics* 29: 23–67.

European Bank for Reconstruction and Development (EBRD). 1994. 'Economic Transition in Eastern Europe and the Former Soviet Union'. Retrieved 22 February 2021 from https://www.ebrd.com/publications/transition-report-archive.

———. 1995. 'Transition Report 1995: Investment and Enterprise Development'. Retrieved 22 February 2021 from https://www.ebrd.com/publications/transition-report-archive.

———. 1996. 'Transition Report 1996: Infrastructure and Savings'. Retrieved 22 February 2021 from https://www.ebrd.com/publications/transition-report-archive.

———. 1998. 'Transition Report 1998: Financial Sector in Transition'. Retrieved 22 February 2021 from https://www.ebrd.com/publications/transition-report-archive.

———. 2001. 'Transition Report 2001: Energy in Transition'. Retrieved 22 February 2021 from https://www.ebrd.com/publications/transition-report-archive.

Fries, Steven M., and Anita Taci. 2002. 'Banking Reform and Development in Transition Economies'. European Bank for Reconstruction and Development, Working Paper No. 71. Retrieved 18 February 2021 from https://www.ebrd.com/downloads/research/economics/workingpapers/wp0071.pdf.

Frydman, Roman, Cheryl Gray, Marek Hessel and Andrzej Rapaczynski. 1999. 'When Does Privatization Work? The Impact of Private Ownership on Corporate Performance in the Transition Economies'. *The Quarterly Journal of Economics* 114(4): 1153–91.

Gates, Susan, Paul Milgrom and John Roberts. 1996. 'Complementarities in the Transition from Socialism: A Firm-Level Analysis'. In *Reforming Asian Socialism: The Growth of Market Institutions*, edited by John McMillan and Bary Naughton, 17–38. Ann Arbor: University of Michigan Press.

Gavin, Michael. 1996. 'Unemployment and the Economics of Gradualist Policy Reform'. *The Journal of Policy Reform* 1(3): 239–58.

Grabbe, Heather. 1999. 'A Partnership for Accession? The Implications of EU Conditionality for the Central and East European Applicants'. Working Paper, Florence, European University Institute. Retrieved 18 February 2021 from https://cadmus.eui.eu//handle/1814/1617.

———. 2001. 'How Does Europeanization Affect CEE Governance? Conditionality, Diffusion and Diversity'. *Journal of European Public Policy* 8(6): 1013–31.

Gray, Cheryl W. 1996. 'In Search of Owners: Privatization and Corporate Governance in Transition Economies'. *The World Bank Research Observer* 11(2): 179–97.

Haggard, Stephan. 1991. *Economic Adjustment and the Prospects for Democracy*, Vol. 3. Center for International Affairs, Harvard University.

Hall, Robert E., and Charles I. Jones. 1999. 'Why Do Some Countries Produce So Much More Output per Worker than Others?' *The Quarterly Journal of Economics* 114(1): 83–116.

Hellman, Joel S. 1998. 'Winners Take All: The Politics of Partial Reform in Postcommunist Transitions'. *World Politics* 50(2): 203–34.

Holland, Dawn, and Nigel Pain. 1998. 'The Diffusion of Innovations in Central and Eastern Europe: A Study of the Determinants and Impact of Foreign Direct Investment'. National Institute of Economic and Social Research (NIESR) Discussion Papers. London: National Institute of Economic and Social Research.

Kaufmann, Daniel, Aart Kraay and Pablo Zoido-Lobaton. 1999. 'Governance Matters'. World Bank Policy Research Working Paper, no. 2196.

Knack, Stephen, and Philip Keefer. 1995. 'Institutions and Economic Performance: Cross-Country Tests Using Alternative Institutional Measures'. *Economics & Politics* 7(3): 207–27.

Konings, Joep, and Jan De Loecker. 2006. 'Job Reallocation and Productivity Growth in an Emerging Economy. Evidence from Slovenian Manufacturing'. *European Journal of Political Economy* 22(2): 388–408.

Laban, Raul, and Federico Sturzenegger. 1994. 'Distributional Conflict, Financial Adaptation and Delayed Stabilizations'. *Economics & Politics* 6(3): 257–76.

Lazear, Edward P. 2000. 'Performance Pay and Productivity'. *American Economic Review* 90(5): 1346–61.

Martinelli, Cesar, and Mariano Tommasi. 1993. 'Sequencing of Economic Reforms in the Presence of Political Constraints'. *Economics & Politics* 9(2): 115–31.

Mauro, Paolo. 1995. 'Corruption and Growth'. *The Quarterly Journal of Economics* 110(3): 681–712.

de Melo, Martha, Cevdet Denizer, Alan Gelb and Stoyan Tenev. 2001. 'Circumstance and Choice: The Role of Initial Conditions and Policies in Transition Economies'. *World Bank Economic Review* 15(1): 1–31.

Meon, Pierre-Guillaume, and Laurent Weill. 2005. 'Does Better Governance Foster Efficiency? An Aggregate Frontier Analysis'. *Economics of Governance* 6(1): 75–90.

Mondino, Guillermo, Federico Sturzenegger and Mariano Tommasi. 1996. 'Recurrent High Inflation and Stabilization: A Dynamic Game'. *International Economic Review* 37: 981–96.

Murphy, Kevin M., Andrei Shleifer and Robert W. Vishny. 1992. 'The Transition to a Market Economy: Pitfalls of Partial Reform'. *The Quarterly Journal of Economics* 107(3): 889–906.

North, Douglass C. 1990. *Institutions, Institutional Change and Economic Performance*. New York: Cambridge University Press.

Qimiao, Fan, and Mark E. Schaffer. 1994. 'Government Financial Transfers and Enterprise Adjustments in Russia, with Comparisons to Central and Eastern Europe'. *Economics of Transition* 2(2): 151–88.

Paarsch, Harry J., and Bruce Shearer. 2000. 'Piece Rates, Fixed Wages, and Incentive Effects: Statistical Evidence from Payroll Records'. *International Economic Review* 41(1): 59–92.

Renelt, David. 1991. 'Economic Growth: A Review of the Theoretical and Empirical Literature'. Policy Research Working Paper Series 678, The World Bank.

Rio, Fernando Del, and Francisco-Xavier Lores. 2017. 'Regulation and Rent-Seeking: The Role of the Distribution of Political and Economic Power'. *Journal of Public Economic Theory* 19(5): 986–1008.

Rodrik, Dani. 2000. 'Institutions for High-Quality Growth: What They Are and How to Acquire Them'. *Studies in Comparative International Development* 35(3): 3–31.

Roland, Gerard. 1994. 'The Role of Political Constraints in Transition Strategies'. *Economics of Transition* 2(1): 27–41.

Roy, Kartik C., and Clement A. Tisdell. 1998. 'Good Governance in Sustainable Development: The Impact of Institutions'. *International Journal of Social Economics* 25(6/7/8): 1310–25.

Schimmelfennig, Frank, and Ulrich Sedelmeier. 2005. *The Europeanization of Central and Eastern Europe*. Ithaca: Cornell University Press.

Shearer, Bruce. 2004. 'Piece Rates, Fixed Wages and Incentives: Evidence from a Field Experiment'. *The Review of Economic Studies* 71(2): 513–34.

Shleifer, Andrei, and Robert W. Vishny. 1993. 'Corruption'. *The Quarterly Journal of Economics* 108(3): 599–617.

———. 1994. 'Politicians and Firms'. *The Quarterly Journal of Economics* 109(4): 995–1025.

Stiglitz, Joseph, and Robert M. Pike. 2004. 'Globalization and Its Discontents'. *Canadian Journal of Sociology* 29(2): 321.

Tommasi, Mariano, and Andres Velasco. 1996. 'Where Are We in The Political Economy of Reform?' *The Journal of Policy Reform* 1(2): 187–238.

Ulubasoglu, Mehmet A., and Chris Doucouliagos. 2004. 'Institutions and Economic Growth: A Systems Approach'. Australasian Meetings 63, Econometric Society.

Vijayaraghavan, Maya, and William A. Ward. 2001. 'Institutions and Economic Growth: Empirical Evidence for a Cross-National Analysis'. Working Papers 112952, Clemson University, Center for International Trade.

Yergin, Daniel, Joseph Stanislaw and Robert Bothwell. 1998. 'The Commanding Heights: The Battle Between Government & the Marketplace'. *International Journal* 53(2): 362.

# PART II

# Development Strategies on the Economic, Entrepreneurial and Individual Level

CHAPTER 3

# The Middle-Income Trap and Its Narrow Escape Hatches
*Dependent Development and FDI-Led Growth in Romania*

Cornel Ban and Zoltán Mihály

## Dependence and Export-Led Growth

During the past three decades East-Central Europe converged on a growth regime that for all its internal variation between Slovenia and Romania is based on the common denominator of its reliance on export-led growth. Indeed, after 1990 the economic transformations of the former communist countries have been predominantly shaped by foreign capital. They were coupled with local promoters' ideas associated with variations in neoliberalism (Ban 2016) and embedded into a mosaic of domestic and transnational interests and institutional configurations (Bruszt and Karas 2019). There is now a consensus that these configurations yielded three main modes of balancing markets and society: social democracy (Slovenia), embedded neoliberalism (Visegrád) and disembedded neoliberalism (the Baltics, Romania and Bulgaria) (Bohle and Greskovits 2012; Ban 2016, 2019). This embeddedness also led to different growth regime subtypes: financialized growth in the Baltics, export-led industrial growth in the small open economies of Visegrád as well as Bulgaria and a somewhat more balanced export and domestic consumption regime sub-type prevailing in the region's largest countries: Poland and Romania (Bohle 2018; Ban and Adăscăliței 2020). However, overall, even in Poland and Romania, with their relatively large consumer base, the contribution of exports to growth remains considerably above that of the consumption-led regimes identified by Baccaro and Pontusson (2016) (Ban and Adăscăliței 2020).

Most strikingly, if one uses the World Bank measurements, the countries of ECE that joined the EU avoided the middle-income trap. This term was originally coined in the context of the economic slowdown in Asia throughout the late 1990s to refer to the marked slowdown in growth observed when an economy approaches the upper/middle-income level but does not 'make it' into the high-income level. The updated high-income level was set by the World Bank at 12,535 per capita dollars (in 2011 terms). By that level, between 2000 and 2019 all ECE countries except for Bulgaria moved from the upper-middle to the high-income bracket.[1] To see a visualization of World Bank high income economies in 2019, please visit this site: https://blogs.worldbank.org/opendata/new-world-bank-country-classifications-income-level-2022-2023.

However, the twelve thousand dollar threshold has been questioned by international financial institutions, with the EBRD using less trenchant cut-off points. For the EBRD economists, the key element is not income per capita but more Schumpeterian aspects such as productivity. Coinciding with this is the hypothesis that once the initial growth spurt powered by FDI inflows is exhausted, productivity gains decline and, with them, per capita income (EBRD Transition Report 2017–18).[2] The EBRD report finds that middle-income economies, on average, tend to experience a slowdown in productivity growth at income levels of between one and two thirds of the United States, a more demanding benchmark than that of the World Bank. The erosion of these productivity gains is best understood as endogenous to the structure of the economy in the region: lower complexity and labour-intensive activities based on low capitalization costs. Therefore, countries at risk of getting stuck in this trap need to distance themselves from the low-cost model and move towards competitive cost and high value, with economies based on innovation (particularly of the green kind) and ideas, rather than cheap labour. The cost of this can be getting stuck in the middle income, the lower end of the high income or even a reversion to middle income, as the examples of Argentina, Colombia or Russia show. For the EBRD, most ECE countries face this situation. We believe this is a more realistic approach as well.

In many ways this export-led developmental trajectory based around manufactured goods superficially resembles that of East Asia. However, missing, is the developmental state and large domestically owned business groups that played a critical role in South Korea, Taiwan and Singapore's breaking from the middle-income trap regardless of measuring indicators (Wade 2018). Other countries in that region (e.g., Thailand, Malaysia) failed to do so despite pursuing a similar strategy. In the end, they (and all of Latin America for that matter) experienced a significant rise in wages, while their products remained in the low-and-middle skill segment and per capita GDP plateaued in the upper-middle income zone (Doner and Schneider 2016; Raj-Reichert 2020).

This comparative glance allows one to reflect on the ways in which East-Central Europe – where similar trends as those in Thailand have been observed (albeit from higher levels of income) – increased its risk of falling into the middle-income trap, as well as what this potential entrapment looks like in regard to the way in which labour is managed in key export sectors of the FDI-led growth model. The first question is descriptive, but the second question is more analytically important because MNC (multination corporation) practices tend to differ in subsidiaries when compared to countries of origin, or, as Ferner, Quintanilla and Sanchez-Runde (2006: 1–23) argue, local corporate practices are the outcome of interactions between parent and host countries' national managerial styles (Boyer and Freyssenet 2002). These are critical and neglected aspects in the ongoing debate surrounding the middle-income trap because the organizational failure to graft these strategies and policies onto local realities can generate known dynamics of income stagnation and adaptation via increased work intensity, the opposite of the dynamics observed in countries that avoided the middle-income trap.

Through a comparative case study of Romania, one of East-Central Europe's most dynamic economies, this chapter begins by questioning the conventional wisdom of an imminent middle-income trap looming in the region's dependent market economies and export-led growth models. The main argument here is that governments attempted to alter the low-wage structure of the economy through sectoral policies, with the overall result including some niches of excellence but not the structural transformation required to avert the dynamics of the middle-income trap in the long run. Next, the chapter descends to the shop floor level of the country's strategic export sector (automotive) to reveal the concrete mechanisms of dependence that plague work organization, reinforcing the region's mass exodus, a downplayed causal generator of wage increases.

The case study of Romania is particularly interesting for a book on the middle-income trap because it is the ECE country with the largest increases in wages, exports and consumption since the recovery began in 2012. It is the last ECE country to make it above the 12,000 dollars threshold (in 2019) but it is also singled out by the EBRD as the most likely candidate for the middle-income trap.

## MNCs, Growth and Complexity

The consensus on development (narrowly defined as GDP growth) in the Global South is that thirty years after the 1989 revolution, Asia was on top. Yet, the former communist countries now inside the EU have been just as successful, unless you compare them with the crushing case of China. In contrast, Latin America and the rest of Asia severely lagged in comparison. However, the 'communist' Asian cases (with GDP increases, Vietnam sevenfold and China eighteenfold) outperform the best East European cases of growth (Slovakia, Romania, the Baltics and Poland). Overall, with a fourfold increase in its GDP over the past thirty years, Romania stands out as one of the fastest growing economies. In 2020 all former communist states that joined the EU, with the exception of Bulgaria, were defined as high-income economies by the World Bank,[3] a fact that undermines the downbeat evaluation of the region by the EBRD's Middle-Income Trap Transition Report of 2017–18.

Growth in low- and middle-income countries is driven either by finance (think of tax and regulatory havens like Singapore or Latvia) or productivity growth driven by manufacturing and knowledge-intensive complex services. By inserting most of East-Central Europe into complex pan-European supply chains for industrial and service sector MNCs, FDI has contributed to sustained GDP and purchase power growth, improved financial credibility and helped increase productivity and export complexity while slowing down the pace of deindustrialization. Countries that did not benefit from these inflows by virtue of being outside the EU (Montenegro, Ukraine, Georgia) have seen their economies hampered in relative terms. Furthermore, the ECE region reclaimed its comparative advantages in medium-skilled segments of manufacturing industries and some high-end services such as ITC and medical (Guga and Spatari 2021; Skorupinska and Torent-Sellens 2017).

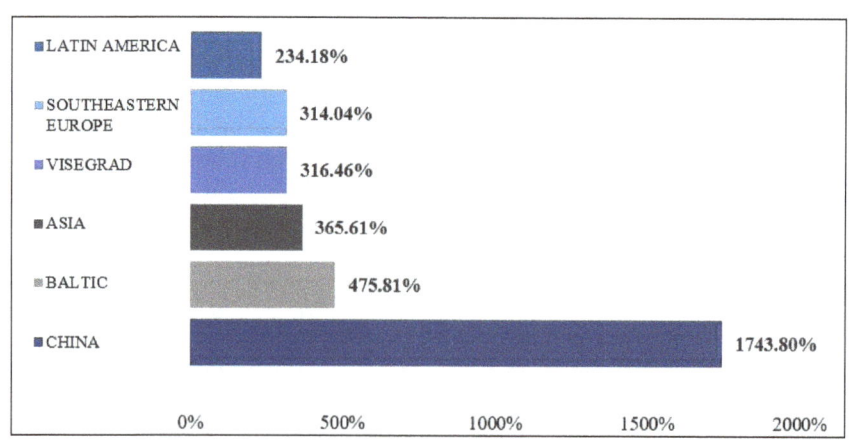

| Region | Growth |
|---|---|
| LATIN AMERICA | 234.18% |
| SOUTHEASTERN EUROPE | 314.04% |
| VISEGRAD | 316.46% |
| ASIA | 365.61% |
| BALTIC | 475.81% |
| CHINA | 1743.80% |

**Figure 3.1.** Percentage growth in GDP (PPP-adjusted) 1990–2018 in selected regions. Source: authors' calculations based on IMF World Economic Outlook data series. Created by authors.

## Figure 3.2.

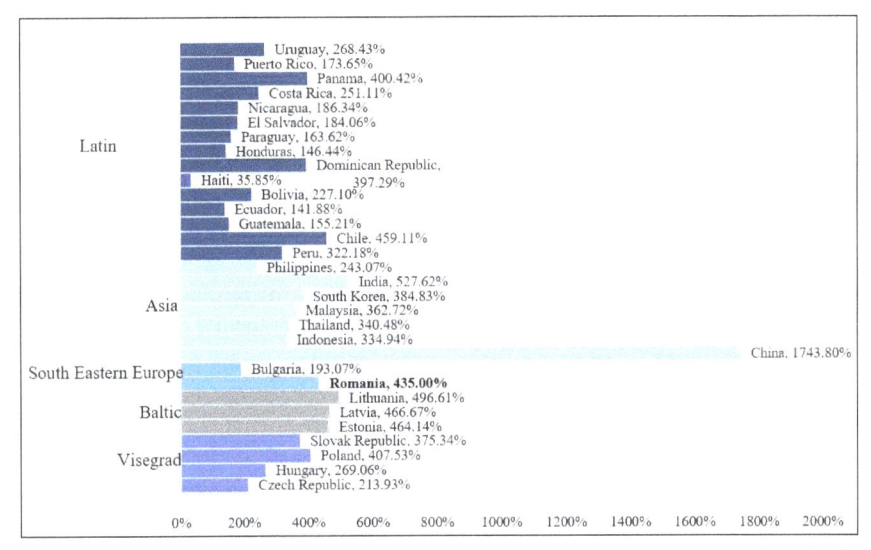

Latin:
- Uruguay, 268.43%
- Puerto Rico, 173.65%
- Panama, 400.42%
- Costa Rica, 251.11%
- Nicaragua, 186.34%
- El Salvador, 184.06%
- Paraguay, 163.62%
- Honduras, 146.44%
- Dominican Republic, 397.29%
- Haiti, 35.85%
- Bolivia, 227.10%
- Ecuador, 141.88%
- Guatemala, 155.21%
- Chile, 459.11%
- Peru, 322.18%

Asia:
- Philippines, 243.07%
- India, 527.62%
- South Korea, 384.83%
- Malaysia, 362.72%
- Thailand, 340.48%
- Indonesia, 334.94%
- China, 1743.80%

South Eastern Europe:
- Bulgaria, 193.07%
- Romania, **435.00%**

Baltic:
- Lithuania, 496.61%
- Latvia, 466.67%
- Estonia, 464.14%

Visegrad:
- Slovak Republic, 375.34%
- Poland, 407.53%
- Hungary, 269.06%
- Czech Republic, 213.93%

**Figure 3.2.** Percentage growth in GDP (PPP) 1990–2018. Source: authors' calculations based on World Bank data. Created by authors.

These are important developments. Dani Rodrik discovered that manufacturing decline in low- and middle-income countries is a structural change that has resulted in growth-reduction in these countries. Moreover, avoiding what he called 'premature deindustrialization' is important because as manufacturing shrinks, informality grows. This is a result of the labour force moving into services; the economy-wide productivity figures and, with them, the chances of claims to higher wages being met are set to suffer. While premature deindustrialization, the ultimate scourge of the post-communist transition, definitively ravaged Latin America and some of the more industrialized parts of the former USSR (Rodrik 2016), since the 2000s it has not affected most of the NMS to the same extent (Figure 3.2). Indeed, it has stabilized close to or above German levels largely because of German investment (with the notable exception of the Baltics, where manufacturing petered out in GDP in the same fashion it did in the Ukraine or Brazil). Virtually, every European Semester and IMF Article IV report indicates that exports of manufactures have been the principal drivers of growth for the East-Central European region. The contrast of the traditional US 'hinterland' (Latin America) and the fate of manufacturing in former communist countries outside the EU could not be more glaring and underscores the importance of the region's proximity to core European capitalism. The critical role of ECE countries in the German export sector also qualifies Dani Rodrik's finding that, 'the sizable shift in global manufacturing activity in recent decades went towards East Asia, and China in particular, with both Latin America and sub-Saharan Africa among the developing regions as the losers' (Rodrik 2016: 16). Where concern with the region's economic future is well placed is in the quality of this arrested deindustrialization. The Czech Republic aside, the manufacturing value added as a percentage of GDP is below East Asia and consistently below China, the region's most important global competitor. The picture becomes darker still if one looks at research and development spending, which is a fraction of South Korean and considerably less than Chinese levels as a share of GDP in the ECE region, including in the more sophisticated Czech and Slovene economies. To see figures of (1) the share of manufacturing as a percentage of GDP and (2) the manufacturing value added as a percentage of GDP, both from World Bank national accounts data, and OECD National Accounts data file, please visit this site: https://data.worldbank.org/indicator/NV.IND.MANF.ZS?end=2022&locations=RO-CN-DE-HU-PL-CZ-LV-LT-EE&start=2002. To see a visualization of the research and development spending as a share of GDP from data on the OECD gross domestic spending on R&D, please see visit the following site: https://data.oecd.org/rd/gross-domestic-spending-on-r-d.htm.

Furthermore, the ECE fits a successful East-Asian profile in terms of its insertion into manufacturing and ITC-based global value chains that extended to the region increasingly complex production capabilities and information technology spin-off activities. This is important because growth is being driven by a process of diversification to enter more, and increasingly complex, production. Growth economists Hausmann and Hidalgo found that:

> the return to the accumulation of new capabilities increases exponentially with the number of capabilities already available in a country and the convexity of the increase in diversification associated with the accumulation of a new capability increases when either the total number of capabilities that exist in the world increases or the average complexity of products, defined as the number of capabilities products require, increases. (Hausmann and Hidalgo 2010)

This convexity in turn defines what they termed as an *acquiescence trap*, or a *trap of economic stasis*: countries with few capabilities tend to have negligible or no return to the accumulation of more capabilities, while simultaneously countries with many capabilities will experience large returns – in terms of increased diversification – to the accumulation of additional capabilities (Hausmann and Hidalgo 2010). Thus, even though a country might avoid the middle-income trap, it might hover perilously above the cut-off line because of these factors, as is evident in the case study of Greece.

Therefore, one may be tempted to view the ECE region in its entirety as eluding the acquiescence trap. In 2017, the Czech Republic, Hungary and Slovenia were in the top twenty most complex exporters, ahead of the US, Italy, UK and France.[4] Even in Romania, a country devastated by deindustrialization in the 1990s, the export profile showed remarkable dynamism in both volume (a nearly 800 percent increase) and complexity between 1999 and 2019, a transformation that exceeds the performance of Asian states that experienced the middle-income trap, such as Thailand and the Philippines, plus all of Latin America except for Mexico. Indeed, the only non-(traditional) core economy that has more complex exports than the new member states is China. This is a drastic change from 1995, when only former Czechoslovakia and Hungary performed in a similar manner.[5] To see a visualization of the complexity of Romanian exports in 1999 and in 2019 from the MIT Atlas of Economic Complexity, please the following figures at this site: https://atlas.cid.harvard.edu/explore?country=185&queryLevel=location&product=undefined&year=2019&productClass=HS&target=Product&partner=undefined&startYear=undefined.

However, despite this remarkable ascendance, it does not compare favourably to Asia. Among the most complex countries, the greatest improvements in the decade ending in 2017 have been made by China, Singapore and South Korea. Moreover, the data aggregator developed at MIT used for these rankings is plagued by problems of uniform measurement in which a gearing box for Mercedes assembled in Romania but designed in Germany counts as a highly complex export, on par with one produced in Korea for a Korean company that designed it and thus profited from all the technology rents.

## Romania: Hovering above the Middle-Income Trap

In conventional terms (GDP, industrial recovery, wages) Romania has had a good run compared to other semiperipheral CEE economies. This is an example of the well-worn argument that dependence can cohabit with development, at least as conventionally understood. Since the crisis, Romania has had the strongest economic recovery in the region and the highest rate of export growth. All this resulted from increasing FDI and an increasingly export-oriented growth model that has only recently received a wage-led modulation in both Romania and its neighbours. Romania is also a case of a dependent market economy that experienced massive transformations from a cocktail of institutional characteristics to a form of capitalism that looks increasingly like Visegrád's, and this dynamism is analytically interesting from the perspective of the scholarly conversation on sources of stability and change in the political economy of East-Central Europe (Ban 2019).

However, for a number of reasons, the EBRD highlights Romania as a candidate most likely for the middle-income trap. The Transition Reports identify negative annual growth in capital stock after 2008, little or no convergence between the most productive industries in Romania and their German counterparts, an abundance of micro-sized firms that fail to grow to employ at least ten people, poor road and rail infrastructure and an effectiveness ranking of political and institutional frameworks and business environments below Russia and Serbia. The EBRD's formula has been institutional reforms based around improved governance and wage moderation. In the spotlight, was the fact that in 2017 and 2018 Romania had Europe's highest wage growth. After inflation, the average wage earner saw their income rise by 9.8 percent in 2017 and 11.1 percent in 2018.

While the EBRD is correct to identify the threat of a middle-income trap in Romania, we believe that this is not imminent. Therefore, the threat should not be used to caution against wage increases, as the EBRD does. Unremarked by the EBRD was the fact that wage increases in Romania have been lower than productivity increases between 2011 and 2018. Since 2015 the trend has reversed, yet the fear of a productivity squeeze remains unwarranted because Romania had both the highest productivity *and* the highest wage increases in Europe. Moreover, double digit minimum wage and public sector wage increases abetted by the upward pressure put on the cost of labour by continuing outmigration (Cosma, Ban and Gabor 2020). This eventually raised the wage share in GDP by 7 percent since 2015, making the labour share reach 57.9 percent of GDP in 2019 (compared to 63 percent in the EU) (Guga 2020). Some of the largest wage increases were in the export-oriented sectors (ITC and auto), with lower value-added sectors (textiles and footwear) experiencing the smallest increases. Finally, in contrast to subsequent work (Guga 2020: 41–43; Ban and Rusu 2020), the EBRD's warning about the middle-income trap via the wage channel does not factor in the weight of transfer pricing, a massive phenomenon in dependent market economies like Romania. To see the GDP per capita in 2010 dollars sourced from the World Bank national accounts data, and OECD National Accounts data file, please visit the following site: https://data.worldbank.org/indicator/NY.GDP.PCAP.KD?end=2022&locations=RO-HU-PL-CZ-LV-LT-EE-ES-BG&start=1990.

An in-depth study of wage increases, and productivity (Guga 2020), challenges the conventional thesis that Romania is in imminent danger of a middle-income trap while alerting about this risk in the long term. On cost competitiveness, Romania continues to have ample space for manoeuvring since the growth in the cost of labour is so slow that even the significant wage increases of the 2012–19 period failed to noticeably reduce the cost gap to core Europe. Sure, low productivity levels are a constraint on wage growth, yet this is not yet a problem in Romania, where wage growth remains far below productivity growth.

Moreover, Guga shows that if the growth rate of wages and productivity from the past decade would have the same gap, it would take years before Romania's current wage competitiveness would be threatened. However, in the long term, given the low and medium skill structure of the economy, both productivity and wage increases will become unsustainable and the middle-income trap dynamics would develop. To alter this structure, the country would have to invest substantially more in innovation, managerial training, health, and in upgrading the skills demanded by the export sector, while attracting higher value-added investments with management practices that would be superior to those prevailing in the economy.

Yet such EBRD boilerplate reforms have found little fertile land in Romania, where the exhaustion of the low-wage model is met with political pushback against wage increases. Indeed, as the next sections show, the Romanian state attempted to alter this structure through sectoral policies, while doing little about skill upgrading. The overall result has included some areas achieving excellence but not the structural transformation required by the task of averting the middle-income trap in the long run. Furthermore, since 2019, the reaction of both the state and employers has been to increase the labour supply to limit wage rises through hiring overseas labour and moving people off the country's meagre welfare schemes. The post-2019 liberal governments also acted to limiting minimum wage increases, in line with Romania's older disembedded neoliberal approach to economic policy (Ban 2016).

## The High Road to Development: The Case of the Romanian ICT Sector

Like other countries in the region, Romania alleviated the overall low-to-middle skill and income profile of its economy with the high road represented by ITC services. Guga and Spatari (2021) demonstrated that the nearly 200,000 people strong labour force employed in this sector are definite winners in both absolute and relative terms. The sector's share in GDP grew from 0.5 percent in 2003 to 6 percent in 2019 while the share of exports of ICT services in the total export *of services* grew from 9.5 to 16 percent during the same period (Guga 2020). Critically, the gross value-added share of the sector in nominal GDP was 4.2 percent in 2014. This figure is the third largest in the EU (average value 3.3 percent), placing Romania in the same league with Estonia, Ireland, the UK and the Nordics. Despite Romania's low level of ITC exports, its ITC sector has some of Europe's highest shares of total exports at 3.7 percent (only Finland, Sweden and Ireland do better). ICT exports grew from €279 million in 2013 to €1,182 million in 2019. Employment in the sector grew from 65,000 employees in 2000 to 190,000 in 2019. Even if one controls for the price transfers that formally reduce taxable profits in this sector, ITC has also been one of the most profitable sectors in Romania and Europe (the sixth most profitable in the EU), with 15 percent returns not being unusual, as well as the highest profits per employee.

The ICT sector provides the most reputable jobs in the country and surpasses even the financial sector in this regard. Net wages (€1,600) are more than ten times higher than the minimum wage, significantly above average and for two decades showed the highest wage growth of any sector. Adjusted by purchase power in terms of the much lower local prices, they deliver a competitive option to emigration for what is a famously mobile workforce. Of the twenty countries surveyed by Eurostat, Romania has had the third fastest growth of ITC sector jobs and although the productivity of ITC workers is comparable to that of other sectors such as automotive or retail, the share of wages in total value added is much higher in ITC (84 percent) relative to automotive (30–55 percent). If the ratio between the average wage in the economy and the average wage in ITC was 1.41 in 2001, by 2013 it stabilized at 2.2, with an 11 percent yearly net wage increase becoming the new normal during the past decade (the yearly growth had been 24 percent a year between 2006 and 2011) (Guga and Spatari 2021).

However, the IT sector's future development remains plagued by the problems of dependent development. First, in 2016, 73 percent of the income generated in the sector came from foreign-owned firms, with a similar percentage of firms' income coming from exports. This reinforces the dependent dynamics discussed above and, because of lower wage Asian countries, exposes the local ITC labour market to a looming income plateau. Second, the fact that the contribution of ITC to total gross value (6 percent) is Europe's sixth largest, far ahead of France, Germany, Poland, the Czech Republic, or Hungary, should be interpreted with care because Romania's overall productivity levels are lower. Third, much of Romanian IT operates in assembly platform mode (outsourcing) and has, therefore, not enabled the emergence of the 'fourth industrial revolution' industries such as artificial intelligence, robotics, nanotech or biotech. As Guga (2020) explained, the share of R&D jobs in the sector is four to five times lower than in Poland, Hungary and the Czech Republic and is only slightly higher than in Latvia and Croatia.

Most importantly, the composition of ITC jobs shows a modest share for R&D employment. In 2018, Romania had 2,170 workers in R&D, while countries with half of Romania's labour force had 3,100 (Bulgaria), 4,700 (Hungary) and 9,500 (Czech Republic). Moreover, R&D spending in the sector is five times lower than in Poland and Bulgaria and ten times lower than in Germany. Fourth, as a result of poor state-capital coordination, the university system graduates only 7,000 specialists a year, while ITC firms need 15,000. Finally, ITC is not as large an exporter as in other countries. According to World Bank data (moving averages for five years), the share of IT in *total* exports is quite low (2.88 percent), particularly in comparison to Slovakia's (16 percent), the Czech Republic's (13 percent) or Hungary's (11.6 percent). For a sector so heavily subsidized by tax measures, Romania's figures are mediocre (Manelici and Pantea 2021).

Are there any 'high roads' beyond FDI? The Social Democrats' attempts to challenge dependence in ways that bypass MNCs altogether between 2016 and 2019 have not been successful. After years of using state aid for a 'trickle-down' innovation policy, the state employed a more direct role after 2011 when it mobilized EU and local resources to establish large public research institutes in frontier technologies. The biggest project to date has been the €300 million Extreme Light Infrastructure Nuclear Physics based in Măgurele. The project was very promising and mobilized significant domestic firepower in a cutting-edge technology. However, by 2020 it became clear that the project was heavily mismanaged, leading to the side-lining of the Romanian operation in the research consortium it was part of.[6] Similarly, the government's moves to establish a sovereign wealth fund and a public development bank, both tasked to act as public venture capitalists for innovation among others, fell apart amidst partisan trench digging, with the sovereign wealth fund project shelved by the liberal coalition that came to power in 2019.[7]

For all its fragilities, ITC has been a dependable high road for income gains in Romania and delivers a superior alternative to employment in any other sector of the privately-owned sectors of the economy. The story of both its spectacular rise *and* of its fragilities is quite straightforward and has already been documented (Ban 2019; Guga and Spatari 2021). A 2001 government decision (OG 7/2001) provided an income tax waiver for workers in this sector at a time when the industry was predominantly domestically owned. Attracted by tax exemptions, competitive wages and cultural proximity to Western markets, multinational investment grew exponentially after the mid-2000s.

But giving a tax break on a permanent basis to the highest-paid employees is illogical in terms of taxation fairness especially when one considers that Romanian ITC is mostly outsourcing-based. Guga (2020) calculated the size of this tax break and found that as the number of ITC workers ballooned, the tax waiver accounted for 0.26 percent of total government revenues (and no less than 7.33 percent of income tax–based revenues), up from merely 0.05 percent in 2010. The tax subsidy covered newer areas of the sector via three waves of tax reforms and as the 2019 debates over scrapping the tax break showed, this tax policy is clear evidence for the existence of an enterprise policy regime and against sweeping claims about market radicalism. At the same time, governments of all types kept Romania at the bottom of the EU pile in terms of public R&D spending while failing to create synergies between ITC, universities and leading sectors such as manufacturing and road transport. The result is a sector that delivered twenty years of strong income growth. However, it remains little more than a 'cost centre' (Guga and Spatari 2021) for the multinational firms that control it. At the current pace of wage increases, it is but a matter of time before the hard wage plateau appears.

In short, Romania managed to develop a remarkably dynamic ITC sector that extracted the sector's workers from the low-wage paradigm of the Romanian labour market. For all its problems (low R&D content, assembly-line software, average productivity growth, etc.), it is one of the few bright spots in what is otherwise an economy of low-to-medium complexity. Even in the best-case scenario for workers and the economy as a whole, progress hinges on a tax rent that camouflages structural weaknesses, which does not bode well for avoiding the problems associated with the middle-income trap dynamics. As the next section highlights, state intervention also played a key role in carving areas of excellence in the manufacturing sector, without denting the general landscape of a low-to-medium skill manufacturing sector.

## The Middle Road: Escape Hatches in Manufacturing

While state elites in East-Central Europe trumpeted the virtues of 'free' markets, they also tried to break the locks of dependence in favour of more domestically generated, high value-added production, with investor loyalty and the higher costs of MNC relocation as additional benefits. Moreover, as Vukov (2019) showed, the EU helped tilt the domestic political balance in favour of development strategies based upon foreign direct investment (FDI) and it increased the capacities of East European states to use generous and EU compliant state aid as a key industrial policy instrument. Romania is no exception, with critical decision-makers sharing (at least in theory) the idea that policy should extract industry from its low complexity trap of the late 1990s, when textiles, footwear and timber were critical exports, and – however unevenly – using the fiscal space generated by EU funds to do this.

Indeed, a study of the list of state aid beneficiaries demonstrates that between 2005 and 2015, €778 million in state aid was targeted at sectors concentrated in middle- and high-complexity manufacturing. As well, some of the state aid was targeted for investments with significant R&D schemes.[8] Specifically, of the fifty largest recipients, forty-four firms were foreign owned, with all recipients in the critical auto sector being foreign. Large investments in the automotive sector (Renault, Ford, Delphi, Bosch, Draxlmaier, Honeywell, Pirelli), aircraft (Premium Aerotec), white goods (deLonghi), oil equipment (Lifkin), electronics (Nokia) and IT (IBM, Oracle) were only completed following the granting of significant state subsidies (30 percent of total investment on average). In car parts, state aid covered 28 percent of multinational investments (Guga, Spatari and Chelaru 2018, 87). The 2016 to 2018 state aid program prioritized relatively low skill employment in white goods automotive. Of these projects the Bosch transmission gear factory in Sebes and the Sonaca aircraft parts factory in Cluj generated middle-skill industrial jobs.[9] By the late 2010s state aid schemes grew markedly to 250–300 million euro a year, but so did the share of state aid schemes targeted at sectors of questionable value-add, such as resorts, sports centres and fossil fuel subsidies (with coal power plants receiving aid to buy green certificates).

However, most importantly, state-led enterprise policies were explicitly targeted not only at high-employment sectors such as car parts (19 percent of the new jobs in car parts during the 2009–16 period were the result of state aid schemes) but also at developing a locally-anchored innovation infrastructure (albeit in outsourcing mode) (Guga et al. 2018). This is particularly the case, with innovation clusters in the auto and ITC sectors, both of which have benefited from extensive state aid, income tax cuts, tax exemptions and large – often rigged – government purchases.

Perhaps the biggest showcase of attempts to break out of the low-skill trap is Renault. As far back as the 2000s Renault set up one of its largest R&D centres and testing and engineering platforms in Titu, close to Bucharest. The government offered Renault €70 million in subsidies and extended guarantees for a €100 million loan during the 2008 to 2011 period in which Renault decided to establish the R&D centre. Built with local firms, managed largely by Romanian managers, and hiring thousands of local engineers, often straight out of university, Renault Technologie Roumanie (RTR) has design, testing and engineering platforms in three cities. RTR hires engineering students at the completion of training and tests them through internships, with no fewer than seven hundred young engineering students having taken up this opportunity so far.[10] By 2020, the centre designs cars from scratch and is no longer a second-rate Renault operation in designing car components. Indeed, RTR engineers had a direct contribution in designing the latest car platform for all the Groupe Renault,[11] and the multinational's best seller Duster SUV was entirely designed at RTR.[12]

RTR is not an isolated case. As a result of similar state-led enterprise policy, Continental (tires and auto parts), Siemens (railway equipment), Bosch (transmission), Alcatel-Lucent (telecom and software), Intel (software), GlaxoSmithKline (pharma), Oracle (software) and Ina Schaeffer (ball bearings) have also spent tens of millions of euros on new R&D centres based in cities with universities with specializations in engineering; they have hired thousands of young engineers there.

However, such important episodes of industrial policy should not be mistaken for a paradigm shift, where such activities would form part of an integrated innovation system, enabling the economy to move rapidly up the value-added ladder and close the wide wage gap that separates it from the EU core. Rather than approximate Korean-style technology 'jumps' benefiting local firms, they operate in transnational R&D schemes whose eventual innovation outcomes generate technology rents for non-residents, with known consequences for investment and taxation. Still unsystematic and with poor horizonal effects, they are best seen as recalibrations of the status quo that do not even amount to a paradigmatic half-turn, lagging far behind the scale and complexity of the state-led enterprise policy that Brazys and Regan (2017) identified in the case of Ireland, let alone those of the Asian (neo)developmental states.

Furthermore, if the vigour of the R&D sector is an indicator of a country's capacity to avert the middle-income trap, Romania is the region's most likely candidate to fail this eluding manoeuvre. The evidence in this regard is overwhelming. Public spending on R&D is one of the lowest in Europe and domestic capital is even less likely to invest in innovation compared to the government.[13] Overall, since 2008 the private sector's share of R&D spending is up to a tenth of West European countries, where manufacturing has a similar share of GDP (e.g., Austria or Sweden). As Guga (2020) showed, the overall share of R&D employment in Romanian manufacturing was barely 0.3 percent, comparatively low to not just Germany's (4.3 percent) but also Hungary's (1.2 percent), Bulgaria's or Poland's (0.9 percent). Indeed, for all these areas of excellence, Romania has the lowest share of R&D jobs in manufacturing in Europe and its R&D spending in manufacturing adjusted per capita is the lowest in the region (and seven times lower than in Hungary and ten times lower than in the Czech Republic). In 2018, the share of R&D employment in total employment was a miniscule 0.1 percent, eight times lower than the EU average and far below neighbouring countries. Moreover, only 2.1 percent of employment was in knowledge-intensive sectors compared to the EU average of 3 percent (Guga 2020). This relative positioning suggests that absent structural change, Romania's chances of hitting a middle-income trap in the future are, along with Latvia's and Croatia's, some of the highest in the region.

While more than half of R&D in the EU is comprised of private firms, in Romania this percentage is barely 23 percent, with most R&D still originating in the public sector, with only 12 percent of CEOs in Romania believing that developing an ecosystem of innovation fostering growth should be a government priority (Tarlea 2018, 10). Alternative market-based sources of funding R&D are late in arriving and the Bucharest Stock Exchange has failed to promote equity finance or project finance on an adequate level.[14] Venture capital for start-ups went from virtually non-existent in 2012[15] to barely noticeable in 2018.[16]

The prospects of averting the symptoms of a middle-income trap are further compounded if we look at the administrative infrastructure necessary to move the economy up the value-added scale. Thus, rather than a coordinated neo-developmental apparatus, Romania has a mosaic of poorly coordinated institutions dealing with innovation while spread across several ministries, not the highly centralized and autonomous enterprise policy agency of Ireland that has kept Irish tech ahead of the curve by enlisting Silicon Valley firms into Ireland's industrial ecologies.

As Brazys and Regan showed, it takes a broader variety of tools (not just tax incentives and state aid) and closer state-corporate coordination for such a strategy to develop a country into a global leader in high-tech exports. Such tasks entail not just departures from the crude neoliberal ideas that prevail in Romanian politics but also a level of state capacity that is unlikely to be developed in the short term in what the literature rightly sees as one of the region's weakest states (Ban and Bohle 2020; Bohle and Greskovits 2012; Vukov 2019). The specifics of this weakness, particularly in the area of R&D, are striking. At first glance, industrial policy is managed by the Ministry of the Economy, the agency in charge of the official industrial policy blueprint for the 2014 to 2020 period (the National Strategy for Competitiveness and Exports). However, upon closer inspection, its specific functions (research, state aid, energy costs, export market targeting) are handled by five different ministries and government bodies, with no central coordination (or 'nodal') agency connecting them. Specifically, the agency for the integration of foreign investment into industrial policy footprints (Agenția Română pentru Investiții Străine) was dismantled in 2009 after barely seven years of (relatively obscure) existence. Industrial innovation is managed by Education, free assembly zones by Regional Development and Public Administration, state aid by the Ministry of Finance, energy infrastructure by the Chief of Staff of the Prime Minister, and foreign trade by the Ministry for the Business Environment, Trade and Entrepreneurship, as well as partly by the Ministry of Foreign Affairs.

Furthermore, the state does not have the capacity to act as a public venture capitalist via promotional banking. This contrasts with Poland and Croatia, where there is no public development bank to at least informally coordinate the existing industrial policy funds and tap into the vast (at Romania's scale) resources of the European Investment Bank and the European Fund for Strategic Investment. There is no integrated document tracing the industrial policy performance of these institutions relative to the objectives set by the National Strategy for Competitiveness and Exports. The establishment of an indicative planning body (Consiliul de Programare Economică) in 2018 reflects growing anxieties about institutional fragmentation in designing and conducting industrial policies. However, the lack of a clear mandate for enforcing institutional coordination for this body suggests that more work needs to be completed. Moreover, after the Social Democrats lost power in 2019 and again in 2020, the planning body was rendered inactive by the new ruling liberal coalition. Finally, coordination between the government and the most important faction of capital (MNCs represented in the Coalition for the Development of Romania) is being pursued in an ad hoc manner via memoranda of understanding, where foreign employers' associations have thus far brought little more than an orthodox supply-side growth agenda and complete obliviousness to the industrial policy blueprint for the 2014 to 2020 period.

With a disorganized state and low mobilization for transition to the knowledge economy, most of the Romanian economy remains stuck in low and at best medium skill activities. Unfortunately, as the next section shows, the organizational micro-foundations of this economic structure seem to reinforce more than to undermine the looming threat of the middle-income trap.

## Entrapment Risks and Organizational Models in the Automotive Industry

Both profit strategies and product policies are determined by host-country labour market characteristics. Certain features (corporate culture and work organization) tend to be identical in host countries, while industrial relations are adapted to specific regulatory frameworks (Meardi et al. 2009). As is often the case, while home country regulations tend to be strict, subsidiaries are placed in deregulated contexts, such as those currently in CEE. Thus, MNCs adapt managerial and productive practices to flexibility requirements, often by transferring labour intensive processes to host-country facilities while also delegating managerial autonomy to these sites.

While automotive MNC's R&D capabilities in Romania are notable and tend to overcome the middle-income trap, DME's still encapsulate contrasting cases. Dependent economic profiles based on low-cost labour and low-complexity production profit strategies aiming to export to Western markets can create the conditions which underlie work crises and reduced employee motivation – particularly when situated in contexts of declining union representation and lack of viable job alternatives. Despite Japanese organizational models being widespread in Western automotive companies, which can indicate elevated production complexity, the shortcomings of these management strategies in settings with reduced technological capabilities can continue to exemplify the middle-income trap. To accurately describe these predicaments, a case study focused on lean production's implementation in a French MNC's Romanian subsidiary is posited (Mihály 2021).

In the studied case, management attempts to mirror the lean framework embedded in France without alterations. The practices transferred are a mix of the German and US 'ideal types' described by Meardi et al. (2009): subsidiaries are directly controlled (managers are often delegates), direct employee participation is encouraged, teamwork is posited as autonomy-inducing, and contracts are primarily permanent with minimal agency workers. The plant is centrally supervised and governed via a home country delegate. Production is project-based, entailing orders from clients passed down from France. The quantity of desired product is negotiated by the parent company, often resulting in the specification of a weekly supply output. Usually, headquarters expect a benchmarked productive output of one component every two minutes, resulting in a total of 50,000 products per month.

Following the launch of a new model by various automobile brands, primary materials are sourced and imported by the parent company, while dashboard moulds are manufactured and delivered by a Chinese company. After the plastic injection process, products pass through at least one more local or global intermediary firm that assembles the plastic pieces before sending them directly to various well-known automobile manufacturers. While the company in question supplies the outer components of automobile interior sub-assemblies, these collaborators manage the mechanical and electrical parts. The importance of finished sub-assembly producers varies: a certain intermediary client based in Timișoara (300 km west of Cluj) is responsible for 60 percent of regional demand, while other collaborations (located in Sibiu and Brașov, both in the range of 200–250 km) are only seasonal. Furthermore, the company directly exports to Slovakia and Mexico, and in certain cases can import specialized moulds from Spain, Portugal and Germany. Thus, the plastic components hold a midlevel position in supply chains that compose the inner workings of a number of automobile models.

Acting as a dependent agent embedded in the automobile industry, the factory's products are part of material flows of commodities, circulating irrespective of state borders, a central trait of the contemporary global economy. Product design is relayed from clients, the company lacking any input in component conception. In the event of minor productive issues, clients communicate the desired modifications and in-house technicians apply them by adjusting mould parameters. Major problems occur when production is reset due to inadequate materials, cases in which clients change primary material types. The client–supplier relation is largely one-sided, the former setting requirements while also solving the majority of production difficulties.

As the production process generally lacks complexity, operators have a limited range of activities. For instance, the singular and repetitive task of managing the products emerging from machine conveyor belts. The skills required are vocational and attained mostly from general education, a proven feature of the 'low-road employment model' (Šćepanović 2013). Technicians, on the contrary, have technical qualifications or are former operators promoted for their proven abilities, and are tasked with maintaining the machines.

A referral system streamlines the recruitment process and optimizes the instruction periods: experienced employees help the inexperienced to adapt and learn job traits. The prestige conferred by well-known automobile brands is invoked simultaneously with quality maximizing kaizen principles. For example, during the hiring interview, the blend of product uniqueness and quality standards is clearly stated for motivation purposes. The HR specialist informs them: 'you might think that it's only a simple plastic piece, but it's not, it's something that has to be made responsibly because no one else in the world does this'. HR visibly seeks to accentuate this fact and give the impression that this represents an important 'selling point' of the factory. Emphasis is placed on client satisfaction, considered the solution to everyone's well-being: 'if the client is appeased then he will place more orders and we will expand, hiring even more personnel'. Disappointing the company is tantamount to a lack of dedication and attention towards the client and thus considered a weak link in an efficient chain of production. This is exemplified by the failure to spot a potential production flaw or to maintain the work pace, embarrassing the firm. As a result, employee dedication is measured by maintaining quality standards, while the resulting pressure contributes to work intensification.

On the shop floor, work teams per shift are defined based on the products' technological profiles, resembling cellular work-focused strategies (Nohara et al. 2014). Work dynamics are fragmented, operating independently from each other, the main indicator of operator autonomy in an otherwise repetitive workflow. Given the daily production of numerous product types in parallel and the number of employees per shift (eighty to ninety), a certain shift can have close to a dozen teams operating side by side. However, even this operator autonomy is determined solely by machine output. Thus, circumstances in which operators have control over their work intensity are few and far between, depending mostly on management decisions.

While the designated 'team member' plays a prominent role in management rhetoric, in practice, interaction between team members is rare during production. Issues are often corrected by technicians, while operators in proximity continue to attend to their duties. As a result, it is mostly technicians and operators who interact during production, a fact in tune with Durand, Stewart and Castillo's (1999) assertion of supervisor-induced kaizen principles. Operators are required to signal any defects and negotiate whether a piece will satisfy or fail the quality inspection with the technicians. These collaborative efforts ensure intermediate product quality, before the final check, performed by quality officers. In contrast, during breaks, technicians and operators form separate groups which rarely interact, while senior personnel also spend their breaks in a separate area.

The presence of agency workers (employed by a temporary work agency) is used as a safety net in the event of major errors in production: when certain types of items need to be repackaged or re-made entirely. Agency worker involvement can range from a few days to a few weeks or even months. Their work tasks are similar to those of directly employed operators: managing plastic pieces from the conveyor belt, packaging products, or the lengthy re-packaging process of already finalized deficient batches. Major production errors have occurred more frequently in recent years because of increased client demands, thus having a flexible reserve workforce on standby is welcomed: 'It is better like this, they don't have contracts with us, you can tell them any day not to come anymore . . . there are no headaches, you don't need to fire them' (M, Maintenance Technician, fifty-three years old). Agency employees originate from the neighbouring Republic of Moldova, and, on the shop floor, they are equipped with distinctive red T-shirts inscribed with the agency's name, instead of the white protective equipment worn by direct employees. Personnel turnover is low among operators and technicians but more frequent among warehouse employees and agency workers.

Work intensification is perceived as a constant rush to meet urgent deadlines for different products: 'This (product) is urgent now, the last was urgent as well, everything is urgent nowadays' (M, Technician, twenty-seven years old). The same respondent also mentioned that experienced employees reminisce over their past experiences when employment relations permitted more informal interactions and less focus on performance and quality standards. Higher expectations tend to raise stress levels and generate conflicts. The lack of other viable options maintains this situation, 'we are cheap labour and have to tolerate everything, other options are worse', this underlines the significance of the local context outlined above. Management also exploits the local context: 'This workplace is better, so we [employees] should stop complaining . . . if it is not satisfactory, then we can go back to where we were' (F, Operator, 42 years old).

In addition, while providing employees with the opportunity to offer suggestions for improvement was intended as a means of empowerment, it is rarely used except for complaints. As a result, employee job satisfaction is generally adequate but at the same time it is strongly determined by the local context. Moreover, management contradicts their own rhetoric of inter-rank communication by invoking the unfavourable context for employees when they voice their dissatisfaction. During production, operators have no direct control over machines, as they require assistance from technicians when stopping or restarting production. Individual employee decision-making (for adjusting errors or voluntary stoppages) is altogether absent. There are no standard visual signals (*kanban*), instead, machines shut down automatically when overloaded or for safety reasons via their built-in motion detectors.

Health complaints range from heat stress to back and leg pain resulting from the continuous production. While there are chairs in the vicinity of each machine, employees rarely have time to rest due to the work pace. Furthermore, resting can attract resentment from nearby colleagues: 'If sitting, the others watch questioningly . . . look, he is sitting again' (M, Technician, twenty-seven years old). The management and mediation of disputes are attempted by invoking the rhetoric of client satisfaction, product quality and worker empowerment. Typically, managers articulate lean principles in the event of conflicts: (1) by emphasising just-in-time production alongside various narratives about quality with the intent of increasing responsibility towards a renowned client; (2) by invoking teamwork as a mild scolding incentive focusing on 'the good of the company'; and (3) by using partial job rotation (assigning guilty parties to distant workstations until the next break period) if all other measures fail. Nevertheless, this approach yields only temporary solutions. The legitimacy of the management rhetoric is only maintained through appeals to authority figures, generally the company administrator or HR specialist, two of the most senior managers.

As described by other studies of different countries (Durand et al. 1999; Durand and Hatzfeld 2003; Stewart et al. 2009), production complexity and lean principles, such as waste reduction and the use of visual indicators, can all favour employee autonomy. However, these components lose their importance in the repetitive workflows predominant in dependent market economies. Incremental improvements are unlikely in a highly refined process with virtually no space for further efficiency gains: the goal is surviving rather than innovating. *Kanban* procedures are also futile in a context lacking employee empowerment on the shop floor. Operators are deprived of the ability to deliberately halt machines. Instead, machines stop when the workflow is interrupted or products overflow, resulting in operators being seen either as negligent or unable to cope with the work pace. Implementing non-financial methods of employee motivation is also difficult under these circumstances. Furthermore, the lack of employee consultation when attempting to increase work intensity via lean production and the subsequent shortcomings in daily practices highlight the dissociation between rhetoric and practice on the shop floor. As a result, lean production's rhetorical and ideological character is perhaps even more evident in DME's than in other contexts. A factor that potentially exhibits the pitfalls of the middle-income trap.

## Conclusions

This chapter's primary objective was to analyse the methods in which East-Central Europe amassed the risk of falling into the middle-income trap. It also focused on what this potential entrapment looks like in the way in which labour is managed in key export sectors of the FDI-led growth model. The findings make four contributions to the literature on the middle-income trap in this region. First, while the analysis is in line with cautionary remarks about why most of the region faces this predicament, it nevertheless highlights ECE's exceptionally good performance relative to other regions, with FDI-led growth appearing to have been critical in this regard.

Second, the chapter questions the conventional wisdom of an imminent middle-income trap emerging via the channel of wage increases. By looking at the case of Romania's economy and focusing on its most dynamic export sectors (the automotive industry and ICT), we highlight that while the causal generators of the middle-income trap (disorganized state, lack of sustained policies aimed at altering the structure of the economy away from the cost centre paradigm, etc.) are in place, that the trap is far from being imminent via the wage channel. Indeed, on current trends, it will be years before Romanian wages will be uncompetitive. Third, the Romanian case illustrated that the Romanian state is aware of the middle-income trap risk and used industrial policy to build attempts to break out of the middle-income trap. These policies landed some successes in high-valued added sectors, disrupting the uniformity of the institutional and structural forces captured in the DME framework. Yet, on balance, because of the weak institutional capacity of the state and the shortcomings of an R&D averse corporate management, they have not had systemic effects in the sense of shifting the economic structure itself upwards beyond a few areas of innovation economy excellence.

Finally, the chapter descended to the shop floor level of the country's strategic export sector (automotive) to reveal the concrete mechanisms of dependence that plague work organization, reinforcing the country's mass exodus, a downplayed causal generator of wage increases. Specifically, the analysis uncovered a strong incompatibility between low-wage, low-complexity strategies typical of Romanian automotive and lean production (Japanese, middle-income trap breaking) organizational models. The mistranslations of these models by local management, has led to coping rather than innovation emerging as the typical outcome on the shopfloor, a micro-level predictor of middle-income trap dynamics.

**Cornel Ban** is Associate Professor of International Political Economy at Copenhagen Business School. Prior to this he was Reader at City University of London, Assistant Professor at Boston University and Research Fellow at Brown University in the United States. He has written two books and over twenty articles on the politics of economic expertise in international settings, organizational shifts in international financial institutions, and capitalist diversity in Brazil, Spain, Hungary and Romania. His most recent book, *Ruling Ideas: How Neoliberalism Goes Local* (2016), received the 2017 Political Economy Award from the British International Studies Association.

**Zoltán Mihály** is an associate teacher and researcher in the Department of Sociology, Babeș-Bolyai University in Cluj-Napoca, Romania. His research focuses on work, employment and human resources management embedded in regional political economies. Recent publications include studies on lean production in a dependent market economy, corporate management transfers and global dependencies in the chemical industry.

## Notes

1. World Bank, Country classification by income level, World Bank, retrieved 5 April 2021 from https://blogs.worldbank.org/opendata/new-world-bank-country-classifications-income-level-2020-2021; for measurement issues see: https://datahelpdesk.worldbank.org/knowledgebase/articles/378831-why-use-gni-per-capita-to-classify-economies-into.
2. The middle-income trap from a Schumpeterian perspective, EBRD, retrieved 5 April 2021 from https://www.ebrd.com/publications/working-papers/middle-income-trap.
3. High income economies in 2019, World Bank, retrieved 5 April 2021 from https://en.wikipedia.org/wiki/World_Bank_high-income_economy#/media/File:High-income_economies_2019.png.
4. Economic complexity legacy rankings, OEC, retrieved 5 April 2021 from https://oec.world/en/rankings/country/eci/.
5. Country and product complexity rankings, retrieved 5 April 2021 from http://atlas.cid.harvard.edu/rankings/1995?country=http://atlas.cid.harvard.edu/rankings/2017?country=.
6. 'Nature, about Laser from Măgurele: Accusations of corruption envelop the project in Romania', retrieved 5 April 2021 from https://www.hotnews.ro/stiri-esential-24236485-nature-despre-laserul-magurele-acuzatiile-coruptie-invaluie-proiectul-imensului-laser-european-din-romania.htm.
7. 'Zeci de proiecte respinse în Camera Deputaților: Înființarea Fondului Suveran de Investiții, la introducerea pensiilor speciale pentru primari', retrieved 5 April 2021 from https://cursdeguvernare.ro/zeci-de-proiecte-respinse-in-camera-deputatilor-infiintarea-fondului-suveran-de-investitii-la-introducerea-pensiilor-speciale-pentru-primari.html.
8. Ministry of Finance, 'Lista agenților economici care au primit acorduri de finanțare emise de MFP în anul 2012', retrieved 5 April 2021 from http://www.mfinante.ro/listafinantare.html?pagina=domenii See also a ten-year report put together by the financial media: http://cursdeguvernare.ro/lista-ajutatilor-cat-si-cui-din-mediul-privat-acorda-statul-roman-ajutoare-de-stat.htm.
9. 'Cine urmează? Zece companii multinaționale care au luat ajutoare de stat pentru investiții au creat 2800 de locuri de muncă în doi ani', retrieved 5 April 2021 from https://www.zf.ro/eveniment/cine-urmeaza-zece-companii-multinationale-care-au-luat-ajutoare-de-stat-pentru-investitii-au-creat-2-800-de-locuri-de-munca-in-doi-ani-17518793.
10. Renault Technologie Roumanie, retrieved 5 April 2021 from www.renault-technologie-roumanie.com.
11. 'Alexander Simionescu, Renault Technologie Roumanie: România are competențe de a produce mașini 'de la zero', retrieved 5 April 2021 from https://www.zf.ro/companii/alexander-simionescu-renault-technologie-roumanie-romania-are-19803819.
12. 'Proiectarea viitoarelor modele Dacia a dus centrul de inginerie Renault Technologie Roumanie la peste 1 miliard de lei în 2018', retrieved 5 April 2021 from https://www.zf.ro/auto/proiectarea-viitoarelor-modele-dacia-a-dus-centrul-de-inginerie-renault-technologie-roumanie-la-peste-1-miliard-de-lei-in-2018-18148994.
13. Author interview with Romanian government officials, 2017.

14. Author interview with Vincenzo Calla, BNP Paribas, 2012; Cristian Socol, government economic advisor, 2017.
15. Author interview with Irina Anghel-Ionescu, European Venture Capital Association, 2012.
16. Conversation with Banca Transilvania chief economist, 2017.

## References

Baccaro, Lucio, and Jonas Pontusson. 2016. 'Rethinking Comparative Political Economy: The Growth Model Perspective'. *Politics & Society* 44(2): 175–207.
Ban, Cornel. 2016. *Ruling Ideas: How Global Neoliberalism Goes Local*. Oxford: Oxford University Press.
———. 2019. 'Dependent Development at a Crossroads? Romanian Capitalism and Its Contradictions'. *West European Politics* 42(5): 1041–68.
Ban, Cornel, and Dragoș Adăscăliței. 2020. *The FDI-Led Growth Regimes of the East-Central and the South-East European Periphery*. Copenhagen Business School. CBDS Working Paper No. 2020/2.
Ban, Cornel, and Dorothee Bohle. 2020. 'Definancialization, Financial Repression and Policy Continuity in East-Central Europe'. *Review of International Political Economy*. https://doi.org/10.1080/09692290.2020.1799841.
Ban, Cornel, and Alexandra Rusu. 2020. *Romania's Weak Fiscal State: What Explains It and What Can (Still) Be Done about It*. Friedrich Ebert Stiftung. Retrieved 5 April 2021 from http://library.fes.de/pdf-files/bueros/Bukarest/15914.Pdf.
Bohle, Dorothee. 2018. 'European Integration, Capitalist Diversity and Crises Trajectories on Europe's Eastern Periphery'. *New Political Economy* 23(2): 239–53.
Bohle, Dorothee, and Béla Greskovits. 2012. *Capitalist Diversity on Europe's Periphery*. New York: Cornell University Press.
Boyer, Robert, and Michel Freyssenet. 2002. *The Productive Models: The Conditions of Profitability*. London: Palgrave Macmillan.
Brazys, Samuel, and Aidan Regan. 2017. 'The Politics of Capitalist Diversity in Europe: Explaining Ireland's Divergent Recovery from the Euro Crisis'. *Perspectives on Politics* 15(2): 411–27.
Bruszt, László, and David Karas. 2019. 'Diverging Developmental Strategies beyond "Lead Sectors" in the EU's Periphery: The Politics of Developmental Alliances in the Hungarian and Polish Dairy Sectors'. *Review of International Political Economy* 27(5): 1020–40.
Cosma, Valer Simion, Cornel Ban and Daniela Gabor. 2020. 'The Human Cost of Fresh Food: Romanian Workers and Germany's Food Supply Chains'. *Review of Agrarian Studies* 10(2). http://ras.org.in/ed61b9bf7c750c6dad2956551e558163.
Doner, Richard F., and Ben Ross Schneider. 2016. 'The Middle-Income Trap More Politics Than Economics'. *World Politics* 68: 608.
Durand, Jean-Pierre, and Nicholas Hatzfeld. 2003. *Living Labour: Life on the Line at Peugeot France*. New York: Palgrave Macmillan.
Durand, Jean-Pierre, Paul Stewart and Juan Jose Castillo. 1999. *Teamwork in the Automobile Industry: Radical Change or Passing Fashion?* New York: Palgrave Macmillan.
Ferner, Anthony, Javier Quintanilla and Carlos Sanchez-Runde. 2006. 'Introduction: Multinationals and the Multilevel Politics of Cross-National Diffusion'. In *Multi-

*nationals, Institutions and the Construction of Transnational Practices*, edited by Anthony Ferner, Javier Quintanilla and Carlos Sanchez-Runde, 1–23. New York: Palgrave Macmillan.

Guga, Ștefan. 2020. *The Question of Productivity: Controversies and Clarification*. Friedrich Ebert Stiftung. Retrieved 5 April 2021 from http://library.fes.de/pdf-files/bueros/bukarest/16384-20200819.pdf.

Guga, Ștefan, and Marcel Spatari. 2021. *The Exception That Proves the Rule: Evolutions in Romanian IT*. Friedrich Ebert Stiftung. Retrieved 5 April 2021 from http://library.fes.de/pdf-files/bueros/bukarest/17691-20210401.pdf.

Guga, Ștefan, Marcel Spatari and Diana Chelaru. 2018. 'Situația salariaților din România. Syndex'. Retrieved 5 April 2021 from https://www.syndex.ro/sites/default/files/files/pdf/2019–06/Situa%C8%9Bia%20salaria%C8%9Bilor%20din%20Rom%C3%A2nia%20%282018%29.pdf.

Hausmann, Ricardo, and Cesar Hidalgo. 2010. 'Country Diversification, Product Ubiquity, and Economic Divergence'. *HKS Working Paper* No. RWP10–045.

Meardi, Guglielmo, Paul Marginson, Micheal Fichter, Marcin Frybes, Miroslav Stanojevic and András Tóth. 2009. 'Varieties of Multinationals: Adapting Employment Practices in Central Eastern Europe'. *Industrial Relations* 48(3): 489–511.

Manelici, Isabela, and Smaranda Pantea. 2021. 'Industrial Policy at Work: Evidence from Romania's Income Tax Break for Workers in IT'. *European Economic Review* 133. https://www.sciencedirect.com/science/article/abs/pii/S0014292121000271.

Mihály, Zoltán. 2021. 'Transnational Transfer of Lean Production to a Dependent Market Economy: The Case of a French-Owned Subsidiary in Romania'. *European Journal of Industrial Relations* 27(1): 1–19.

Nohara, Hiraki, Uichi Asao, Eishi Fujita, Yutaka Tamura, Saruta Masaki, Tomas Engstrom, Lars Medbo and Lennart Nilsson. 2014. *The Same Problem, the Same Approach to Solve and the Different Target for the Solution*. Paris: Gerpisa Colloquium.

Raj-Reichert, Gale. 2020. 'Global Value Chains, Contract Manufacturers, and the Middle-Income Trap: The Electronics Industry in Malaysia'. *The Journal of Development Studies* 56(4): 698–716.

Rodrik, Dani. 2016. 'Premature Deindustrialization'. *Journal of Economic Growth* 21: 1–33.

Šćepanović, Vera. 2013. 'FDI as a Solution to the Challenges of Late Development: Catch-up without Convergence'. PhD diss., Central European University.

Skorupinska, Aleksandra, and Joan Torrent-Sellens. 2017. 'ICT, Innovation and Productivity: Evidence Based on Eastern European Manufacturing Companies'. *Journal of the Knowledge Economy* 8(2): 768–88.

Stewart, Paul, Ken Murphy, Andy Danford, Tony Richardson, Mike Richardson and Vicki Wass. 2009. *We Sell Our Time No More: Worker Struggles in the UK Automobile Industry from 1945–2006*. London: Pluto Press.

Tarlea, Silvana. 2018. 'Low-and High-Skills Equilibria in Central and Eastern Europe: What Role for the Government?' *East European Politics and Societies*. https//:doi.org/10.1177/0888325418777059.

Vukov, Visnja. 2019. 'European Integration and Weak States: Romania's Road to Exclusionary Development'. *Review of International Political Economy* 27(5): 1041–62.

Wade, Robert H. 2018. 'The Developmental State: Dead or Alive?' *Development and Change* 49(2): 518–46.

CHAPTER 4

# Between Domestic Entrepreneurship and Global Technology Chains
*Upgrading Paths of Two Large IT Firms from Poland*

Grzegorz Lechowski

## Introduction

The industrial development model followed by countries in East Central Europe (ECE) since the early 1990s has recently come under increased scrutiny within the literature (Drahokoupil and Galgóczi 2017; Myant 2018; Szent-Iványi 2017). The neoliberal reform policies adopted in the region after 1989 triggered new kinds of industrialization processes driven by inflows of foreign capital into manufacturing sectors and by insertion of the domestic production capacities into globalized value-chain structures (Nölke and Vliegenthart 2009; Bohle and Greskovits 2012; King 2007; Bohle 2018; Jürgens and Krzywdzinski 2010; Pavlínek 2017). In a much-quoted article from 2009, Nölke and Vliegenthart (2009) described the emerging capitalist models of the four Visegrád countries – Czechia, Hungary, Poland and Slovakia – as 'dependent market economies' (DME), characterized by a strong presence of foreign multinational firms (MNCs), weak domestic innovation systems, and institutional frameworks geared towards the needs of the incoming foreign capital. In a more recent contribution, Myant (2018) used the concept of the middle-income trap to argue that the neoliberal reform policies in the region may have created barriers to further growth by stabilizing the national economies on the path of low wage-driven industrialization. At the same time, other authors have indicated that the perceived limitations of the earlier growth strategies have already led the governments of some ECE countries – and especially, the

Polish government – to implement more 'developmentalist' industrial policies that emphasize the importance of local entrepreneurship and state intervention (Bluhm and Varga 2019; Jasiecki 2019).

The purpose of the present chapter is to add to the literature on the perspectives of industrial development in the post-communist Central Europe by highlighting the question about the historical performance of domestically owned technology firms. Establishing internationally competitive businesses controlled by domestic capital is often perceived as an important factor that may allow emerging countries to develop critical knowledge-intensive industrial capabilities and, in this way, avoid the middle-income trap (Kharas and Kohli 2011; Szent-Iványi 2017). At the same time, the existing literature on the post-communist Central Europe from the comparative capitalism (CC) perspective mostly reproduces the picture of a general failure by domestic firms from the region to respond to the challenges of global competition (Myant 2018) or limits the discussion to the case of some relatively successful small and medium-sized enterprises (SMEs) (Nölke and Vliegenthart 2009). Against this background, I will use this chapter to argue that domestic firms from the ECE countries represent a more complex case and still require substantial empirical analysis. While the research on the post-communist Central Europe from the DME perspective assumes the presence of one homogeneous regional mode of economic coordination, the case of the domestic-driven industrial dynamics requires us to start exploring the diversity of sectoral production systems, institutional frameworks and firm strategies that have developed within the region's national economies since the early 1990s (Bluhm 2014).

In empirical terms, this chapter will contribute to the understudied area of domestic firm development in the post-communist Central Europe through an explorative historical analysis of relatively successful Polish companies from the IT sector. The case study focuses on two large firms, Asseco and Comarch (see Table 4.1 for some basic data), which, despite a strong local presence of foreign competitors, have gained significant shares in the domestic market for enterprise IT solutions (hereafter EIT).[1] In addition, both companies have extended their operations into a number of developed foreign markets – which remains a rather exceptional achievement in the context of the Polish IT industry. However, the apparent commercial success of these two firms needs to be placed in relative terms. So far, neither has managed to develop products that would become successful innovations in the global market. Furthermore, as indicated by historical revenue structures (PwC 2016), the business models of the two companies have focused on the relatively less technology-intensive segments of the EIT value chain such as integration services or the provision of tailor-made solutions to big domestic buyers.

**Table 4.1.** Basic data on the two case-study firms (from company reports).

|  | Asseco Group | Comarch Group |
| --- | --- | --- |
| Sectoral specialization | Enterprise software and services | Enterprise software and services |
| Year established | 1991 | 1993 |
| Worldwide employment 2019 | ca. 26,800 | ca. 6,300 |
| Consolidated revenue 2019 | 10.67 billion PLN (ca. €2.3 billion) | 1.43 billion PLN (ca. €330 million) |

Sources: Asseco (2020); Comarch (2020).

The main goal of the present case study is to improve our knowledge about the domestic-driven industrial dynamics in Poland by exploring the mechanisms that have enabled – or also limited – the successful growth of the two selected companies. My argument is organized in three main parts. Following this introduction, in the chapter's *second section*, I use literature review and archival data to develop hypotheses regarding the key conditions that have shaped the upgrading paths of the two Polish IT firms. In doing so, I focus both on the impact of the national political-economic context and on the characteristics of the globalized value-chain arrangements of the IT sector (Thun and Sturgeon 2019). The chapter's *third section* presents the results of the historical case study. The analysis suggests, *first*, that the successful development of the two companies was related to such characteristics of the national economic system as: the country's relatively well-functioning capital market; the availability of various low-cost segments in the domestic EIT market; or the presence of large public buyers of EIT solutions. Furthermore, the analysis provides also anecdotal evidence that, more recently, restructuring processes have taken place within the country's innovation system resulting from European integration and the adoption of the more 'developmentalist' industrial-policy agenda by the national government since around 2015 (Bluhm and Varga 2019). My *second* set of observations relates to the specific mode of transnational value-chain integration of the two Polish EIT firms. The analysis shows that the product strategies of both Asseco and Comarch have historically relied on various platform technologies provided by leading US-American IT firms – which has led to both positive and negative developmental outcomes for the two firms. In the chapter's *final section*, I discuss the implications of the case study for the future research on industrial upgrading processes in Poland and the ECE region.

## Situating the Enterprise IT Sector in the Polish Context

Existing literature provides a number of important indications that I will use to develop more specific hypotheses regarding the mechanisms explaining the relatively successful development of the two Polish EIT producers. First, many authors analysing the emergence of the IT industry in the ECE region after 1989 have pointed to the role of transnational technology transfer and partnerships with foreign technology firms (Sadowski 2001; Linden 1998). Second, regarding the influence of the national political-economic context, the literature often emphasizes the positive impact of labour market characteristics and the availability of highly skilled workforces (Capik and Drahokoupil 2011; Hardy and Hollinshead 2016; Micek 2015). This factor was highlighted, for instance, in the few empirical analyses of successful domestic IT companies from the region – such as the two globally active antivirus-software producers from Czechia and Slovakia examined in-depth by Beblavý and Kureková (2014). In addition to the labour supply, an earlier analysis of the Polish IT sector by Kubielas (2000) pointed to the positive impact of the relatively large domestic capital market and the significant internal demand for IT products and services.

In the remaining part of this section, I will expand on these observations by providing a more systematic review of the historical research literature and relevant statistical data. In doing so, I will focus on the following four aspects of the sectoral production system from the Polish perspective: (1) the fragmentation of the transnational value-chain structures and the product strategies of the dominant global EIT firms; (2) the market entry opportunities for emerging domestic producers in Poland; (3) the availability of external funding for technology firms in the country; and (4) the external supply of relevant innovation capabilities within the national innovation system.

### *Globalized Production Regime*

Existing analyses from business studies and political economy literature indicate that, in the 1980s, the globally dominant US-American IT industry underwent a dramatic process of value-chain fragmentation that created significant entry opportunities into relatively independent technology production for companies from emerging countries (Borrus and Zysman 1997). While historically, the industry was dominated by large and vertically integrated firms (such as IBM), around the 1980s, a more complex organizational ecosystem emerged in the sector, which involved a large number of more specialized suppliers producing different and 'modularized' (Langlois 2003) system components within a common technological framework. Among the most important globally active US-American firms specialized in enterprise IT that represented this new organizational model were Oracle and Informix – two companies providing software products (e.g., database software), or Cisco – the well-known producer of network equipment (Campbell-Kelly 2004).[2]

Regarding specific implications of this vertical disintegration process for emerging-country firms, we can highlight in particular the following two. First, the technological fragmentation of the EIT solutions has increased the demand for integration services – that is, for the labour inputs that are required to manage different technological components and combine them into well-functioning EIT systems that are delivered to specific organizational clients (Dosi et al. 2005). Given that integration services require relatively low levels of innovative capability, it is generally assumed that they represent a major entry opportunity for emerging-country firms in the IT sector (Schware 1987). Second, existing literature from business studies suggests that the technological 'modularization' processes have been related to the adoption of platform-based business models by many of the globally leading software producers (Gawer 2014). These kinds of business models facilitate technological innovation by the relatively less advanced firms, who are encouraged to develop their products by building on the more infrastructural components provided by the global players. A well-known example of this kind of 'platform-based' technological partnership between a developed- and a developing-country firm from the EIT sector was the Indian company i-flex Solutions, whose successful business applications for the financial industry relied on the database management systems provided by Oracle (Baba and Tschang 2004).

## *Domestic EIT Market*

As to the role of the domestic demand, existing historical data suggest that, in a regional comparison, Poland has had a relatively large internal EIT market. For instance, in 2012 (EITO 2013), the domestic turnover in 'project-based IT services' in Poland reached the level of €1.2 billion.[3] This was significantly more than the turnovers reported in other Visegrád countries – on average, almost twice as many as in the case of Czechia and roughly four times more than in the case of Hungary (EITO 2013).

At the same time, existing literature points to the impact of some country-specific regulatory and institutional characteristics that have variously affected the competitive positions of domestic firms vis-à-vis their potential foreign competitors. For one thing, the liberal reform policies of the early 1990s (Lipton et al. 1990) have rapidly opened the country's EIT market to multinational companies. One important aspect of this process has been the decision of the Polish government to adopt public procurement rules based on open international standards (Computerworld 1991) – which has facilitated the entry of foreign firms into the country's large public administration segment.[4] On the other hand, however, existing literature also suggests that establishing a strong position in the Polish market has not always been an easy task for multinational IT players. This was related, for instance, to entry barriers created by country-specific organizational practices of various kinds of large EIT buyers (Kubielas 2000); or to idiosyncratic product requirements in different market niches such as business applications for SMEs or IT solutions for smaller financial institutions (Kubielas and Yegorov 2000).

## Funding Opportunities for Firms

Concerning the accessibility of external funding for firms, the comparative capitalist literature from the DME perspective emphasizes the central role of foreign-owned banks within the financial systems of the ECE economies (Nölke and Vliegenthart 2009). According to Martin (2013), this historical dominance of foreign capital created some disadvantages for domestic firms related to the fact that the foreign-owned banks may have preferred to lend their money to the more secure businesses of multinational companies (Martin 2013). In the Polish case, the foreign capital has dominated the financial system at least until 2015, when the new conservative government initiated a renationalization process in the banking sector.

However, in addition to the bank-based funding, we must also recognize the presence of a relatively well-developed capital market as a possible alternative source of external funding for domestic firms in Poland. Since its launch in 1991, the Warsaw Stock Exchange (WSE) has become the largest stock market in the post-communist Central Europe – both in relative and absolute terms (World Bank 2021). In the 1990s, the growth of the WSE was boosted by the country's intensive privatization processes (Tamowicz 2006) and by the emergence of private pension funds, which were required by law to make significant investments in WSE-listed companies (Wilinski 2012). In addition to its mere size, also some regulatory characteristics of the Polish capital market may have created supportive conditions for domestic companies seeking external funding. One example of this was the relatively lax regulation of shareholder rights (Martin 2013) that may have enabled WSE-listed firms to combine extensive equity financing with relatively concentrated forms of corporate control.

## National Innovation System

Fourth and finally, with regard to the external supply of innovation-relevant technological capabilities for firms, there are two rather contrasting developments to note. On the one hand, the literature suggests that the Polish national innovation system has encountered significant challenges throughout the entire post-communist era (Hardy 2007; Martin 2013; Jasiecki 2013; Breznitz and Ornston 2017). This observation is reflected, for instance, in historical data on the national R&D expenditures. In 2001, the total spending on R&D in Poland amounted to only 0.6 percent of GDP – which was low even in regional comparison (e.g., compared to Hungary, with 0.9 percent, or the Czech Republic, with 1.1 percent GDP; see: OECD 2017b). The data on public R&D expenditures between 2007 and 2011 quoted by Jasiecki (2013) suggest that Poland, with 0.5 percent of GDP, lagged behind the Czech Republic (0.7 percent) in this category as well, while scoring only slightly better than Hungary or Slovakia (both 0.4 percent). A similar picture emerges when we consider academic research. According to OECD data (UIS 2017), between 1996 and 2014, the total value of R&D performed at the Polish universities was around 0.2 to 0.3 percent of GDP – comparable to other Visegrád economies, but, again, significantly lower than the levels characteristic of typical advanced capitalist countries (e.g., Germany with 0.5 percent GDP in 2014). Considering these statistics, we may generally expect that emerging technology firms from Poland have likely received only limited support from domestic R&D institutions.

But at the same time, we should acknowledge also the possible positive impact of the availability of a highly skilled workforce in the domestic labour market on firms' technological innovation efforts. This characteristic is related to the transformation of the Polish skill-formation system since the 1990s, which brought about a significant expansion of academic education at the expense of vocational training (Kogan, Gebel and Noelke 2013). Statistical data indicate, for instance, that the share of the Polish population aged between twenty-five and thirty-four with tertiary qualifications almost tripled between 1995 and 2016 (rising from 14.6 to 43.5 percent) – and was much higher than in other Central European economies (e.g., Czechia with 32.6 percent or Germany with 30.5 percent; see OECD 2017c). More specifically, this expansion was also reflected in the number of graduates in computer sciences. Based on OECD (2017a) data for the years 2003–12, the absolute numbers of IT graduates in Poland were comparable to (and periodically even higher than) the ones in Germany – a country whose population is twice the size.

## Upgrading Paths of the Two Large Polish IT Firms

Building on the above insights into the evolving governance structures of the globalized EIT sectoral production system and the selected key characteristics of the national political-economic context, in the present section, I will explore the historical upgrading paths of the two case-study companies, Asseco and Comarch. Concerning the influence of the transnational value-chain relations, I will focus on observing how the development of the two firms may have been impacted by the organizational fragmentation of the sectoral production system. More specifically, the analysis will reconstruct the firms' evolving strategies regarding the scope of internalized production activities and their relations with external technology partners. Second, concerning the role of the political-economic context, the case study will describe how Asseco and Comarch have historically navigated the domestic EIT market, the Polish financial landscape and the country's national innovation system.

In methodological terms, the following empirical analysis relies on a rich dataset of online archival materials covering the period from the early 1990s, when both companies were founded, until the end of 2017, when the data collection ended (see Table 4.2 at the end of the chapter for more details). In addition to the archival material, statistical data and some rare scholarly articles on the development of the two firms (mostly from management studies) will be quoted in the study.

### *Market Positions*

Starting with the case of Asseco, the company's market positioning strategy has evolved through four main historical periods. In the early 1990s, the company – operating under its previous name, COMP Rzeszów[5] – started supplying information systems for cooperative banks located in the relatively less developed southeastern part of the country. At that time, typical cooperative banks in Poland were characterized by their small size, which prevented them from adopting state-of-the-art IT solutions due to financial constraints. However, the company was able to use the experience accumulated in this particular niche of the domestic market to gradually diversify towards more lucrative market segments – such as universal or retail banks.

The second historical period began in the mid-2000s, when the firm took over two significantly larger domestic companies with established market positions. In 2007, Asseco acquired Softbank,[6] which, since 1989, had been providing IT solutions to some of the biggest financial institutions in Poland. For instance, in the mid-1990s, Softbank's key client was PKO BP, Poland's largest universal bank (Szafrański 2011). Later, in 2008, Asseco acquired another domestic big player, Prokom – at that time, the country's largest IT firm. In the 1990s, Prokom's ERP applications were used by a number of key Polish state-controlled companies such as KGHM, the multinational copper-mining company, or PZU, the country's biggest insurer. Over time, however, Prokom redefined its business model and started focusing on tailor-made IT systems for the public sector. In this segment, the company was able to benefit from the not always transparent procurement practices of the large technology buyers. The best example of this was the huge contract from the national Social Insurance Institution (ZUS), which lasted a few years longer than planned and allowed Prokom to earn a total of 2.1 billion PLN – much more than the initially agreed budget of 700 million PLN (Forbes 2010).

The beginning of the third historical period can be dated back to around 2010, when Asseco started diversifying into foreign markets. In 2012, the revenues from abroad already amounted to 70 percent of the firm's total sales; and in 2016, the share further increased to 80 percent. Importantly, however, the company has adopted a particular approach to penetrate foreign markets by refraining from exporting its own products or establishing new subsidiaries abroad. Instead, Asseco has focused on acquiring foreign IT firms with already established market positions (Radło 2016). Its most important takeover to date took place in 2010, when the company obtained a controlling interest (50.2 percent) in Formula Systems – a NASDAQ-listed and globally active IT holding from Israel.

Finally, the fourth and still open-ended phase in Asseco's market development began in 2015, when the company's domestic operations were negatively affected by the new and leaner public procurement policies introduced by the country's new conservative government. While Asseco has remained a strong player in the Polish banking and public administration sectors, its revenues from these markets dropped significantly around 2015.

The historical market positioning strategy of the second case-study company, Comarch, shows many similarities to the one of Asseco. In the early 1990s, the firm became a key provider of IT solutions for Telekomunikacja Polska SA (TPSA), which was the state-owned telecom monopolist in Poland at that time. An important role in the development of this partnership played interpersonal ties with TPSA, which the future CEO and founder of Comarch established already as a researcher at the AGH University in Krakow. The close collaboration between the companies lasted for several years, during which Comarch kept receiving ever larger and more technologically complex orders from the telecom partner. While the IT producer was active also in other segments of the Polish market (e.g., domestic banks, insurance companies, or SMEs), TPSA remained its main organizational client. However, the cooperation ended abruptly in the early 2000s, when the telecom company shifted its technological strategy and initiated the construction of one countrywide billing platform, integrating all of its regional operations. To the surprise of many observers, the order to develop the new platform was awarded not to Comarch, but to one of its relatively smaller domestic competitors.[7]

The sudden shift in the procurement strategy of TPSA led to dramatic revenue losses for Comarch and forced the company to fundamentally revise its business model. For one thing, already in the early 2000s, Comarch started expanding its operations into foreign markets. One of its main achievements at that time were the successful entries into several low-cost telecom markets in Western Europe – including France and Germany (Przybylska and Pilarska 2005). As of 2017, foreign sales already amounted to more than half of the firm's total revenues. Second, apart from expanding internationally, Comarch has also diversified its domestic operations. One of the niches in which the company has been particularly successful is ERP software for SMEs. As indicated by the data from 2014, Comarch controlled more than half of this market segment in Poland.

At the same time, however – and similar to what we have observed in the case of Asseco – the company started experiencing significant difficulties in the domestic market around 2015, when the leaner public procurement policies have been introduced by the national government.

*Corporate Finance*

Turning now to corporate finance, a key moment in the historical development of Asseco was the company's initial public offering (IPO) on the Warsaw Stock Exchange in 2004. During the entire listing process, Asseco was actively supported by the US-American private-equity fund Enterprise Investors (EI; see Kaszuba 2010), which held a 50-percent interest in the Polish firm since 2003.

The successful IPO allowed Asseco to rely on the stock market to secure funding for its further expansion. Perhaps most importantly, the company has used the capital collected on the WSE to implement its aggressive merger and acquisition strategy focused on both domestic and foreign IT enterprises. For instance, in 2008, when Asseco acquired Prokom (itself a WSE-listed company since 1997), it first entered into a credit agreement for up to 580 million PLN with the foreign-owned BPH bank and then, when the merger had already been settled, it issued a large amount of shares targeted at institutional investors (worth over 325 million PLN) in order to quickly repay the loan. In a similar manner, the takeover of the Israeli IT holding Formula Systems in 2010 was financed through an issue of new shares on the WSE (worth about 270 million PLN).

However, the reliance on the capital market has come at a significant cost for the company. In order to deliver the 'shareholder value', Asseco had to follow a very generous redistributive agenda – including regular, and increasingly high, dividend payments (Kaszuba 2010). In the first year after its IPO, the company paid out 35 percent of its profit as dividends. Later, between 2007 and 2016, the dividend payouts at Asseco Poland[8] amounted, on average, to around 54 percent of the firm's annual income – reaching as much as 83 percent in 2016.

The second company, Comarch, has also listed its shares on the WSE. In the late 1990s, the management came to the conclusion that this move would not only create new opportunities to raise capital, but also enhance the firm's prestige in the eyes of organizational clients. Following several months of preparation, the IPO took place in May 1999 and was very successful. The firm's initial offering was oversubscribed by almost twenty times – which was a WSE record at that time. Interestingly, though, the company decided to enter the stock exchange through the 'free market' – the least prestigious floor of the WSE – and only gradually progressed towards the main floor. We may speculate that this strategy was related to the fact that, during its IPO, Comarch could not rely on organizational support comparable to the one provided by the EI fund to Asseco.

Following the IPO, Comarch started using the stock market to finance its further growth. For instance, in late 1999, the management decided to issue a large number of shares to collect capital for various strategic goals, including the construction of new production and office facilities in Krakow, new software product development, or a diversification into the then-emerging market of online services for individual users. Similarly, in the early 2000s, the capital market played a key role in the company's response to the sudden withdrawal of the main organizational client, TPSA. In late 2001, when Comarch's share price fell to historically low levels, the management decided to issue a large amount of convertible bonds (instead of shares) targeted at institutional investors.

But at the same time, we must recognize that, overall, Comarch's financial strategy has relied on the stock market to a much smaller degree than the one of Asseco. In fact, the company has followed a rather 'hybrid' approach that combined equity funding with bank loans in a rather balanced way. Resulting from this, Comarch did not have to implement any extensive redistributive measures to deliver the 'shareholder value' – or at least not to the extent that we have observed in the case of Asseco.

## Technological Innovation

Finally, let us discuss the strategies of the two firms regarding technological innovation and the scope of internalized value-chain activities. Overall, the collected empirical material suggests that both companies have relied heavily on partnerships with established global EIT producers – and that building strong in-house innovation capabilities is still a major challenge ahead of them.

In the case of Asseco, all of the company's three predecessor firms (Softbank, Prokom and COMP Rzeszów) were using third-party technology to develop their early product strategies in the domestic market. The first of the three companies, Softbank, was for some time even directly controlled by the British-Japanese IT multinational ICL and operated as the exclusive distributor and integrator of ICL's hardware in the Polish market (Kubielas 2004; Linden 1998). The software products developed by the second company, Prokom (e.g., its ERP or financial applications) relied on various high-tech components supplied by US-American vendors (Kubielas 2004). The last of the three firms, COMP Rzeszów, established a long-term collaboration with Oracle – the leading global provider of database software.

Regarding Asseco's more recent technological innovation strategy, the company has largely maintained the focus on higher-level business applications and integration services, and still relies on various third-party platform technologies (e.g., database or middleware software) for many of its key products. But at the same time, there are also indications that, throughout the years, Asseco has managed to upgrade its in-house technological capabilities in the domain of EIT application development. The company has achieved this, to a large extent, through domestic and foreign acquisitions. For instance, between 2006 and 2007, the Polish producer established an entirely new subsidiary, Asseco Business Solutions (specializing in the production of software for SMEs) by merging a few smaller Polish and German ERP vendors. Moreover, our empirical material indicates that the firm's in-house R&D activities have intensified and are being increasingly supported through both national and EU-level policies. For instance, over 30 percent of the recent 80 million PLN investment in the company's new R&D centre in Rzeszów (which was launched in 2020 and will create around four hundred new jobs at the firm's headquarters) was provided by the Polish government via EU funds. In addition, as was observed by Melnarowicz (2017), Asseco has recently strengthened its links to domestic universities – although, not too long ago, the company's management perceived this kind of collaboration as ill-suited to the demands of the commercial IT sector (Melnarowicz 2017).

The second company, Comarch, has developed a very similar value-chain position within the EIT industry to the one of Asseco. In the 1990s, the firm's key software products (e.g., its ERP applications or information systems for telecom operators) relied on third-party platform technologies. Especially important were the components provided by one foreign producer – Oracle, which has become Comarch's long-term strategic partner.

However, in addition to this platform-based innovation strategy, the company has also made significant efforts to develop in-house technological capabilities. In contrast to what we have seen in the case of Asseco, this upgrading process has relied on mergers and acquisitions only to a very limited degree. Based on our empirical data, the largest foreign takeover by Comarch took place in 2008, when the company paid around €11 million to acquire a German producer of ERP software for SMEs (SoftM AG).

Relatively more important for the development of technological capabilities at Comarch have been investments in organic growth. One example of this is the construction of the company's central hub in Krakow, which, throughout the years, has grown to include production and office facilities for a workforce of a few thousand people. The development of this site began in 1999, when Comarch received the permission to relocate to a Special Economic Zone in the Krakow region – the Kraków Technology Park. In addition to the production and office infrastructure, another important element of the firm's upgrading strategy have been its collaborations with external R&D partners. From early on, Comarch has maintained close links to various universities in the Cracow region – such as the AGH or the Cracow University of Technology. More recently, as was observed by Kozioł-Nadolna (2013), the company has also established collaborations with foreign European universities – benefiting from various EU-funded frameworks supporting the transfer of academic knowledge to the industry.

## Summary and Conclusions

The purpose of this chapter was to contribute to the ongoing debate on the perspectives of industrial development in the ECE region by highlighting the question of the historical performance of domestic firms and by empirically exploring the case of two relatively successful IT companies from Poland, Asseco and Comarch. The empirical case study reconstructed the upgrading paths of these two firms in order to reveal both country-specific and transnational-sectoral mechanisms that have enabled – or also limited – the firms' successful growth. Let us summarize the main insights from the case study and discuss their broader implications for the research on the domestic industrial dynamics in Poland and the ECE region.

First, the analysis has demonstrated that integration into the *globalized production networks* of the EIT industry has created important developmental opportunities for the two case-study firms. Strategic collaborations with various foreign suppliers of platform technologies have enabled the Polish companies to enter autonomous software development despite the relatively weak technological capabilities of their own. Both firms have become innovative IT producers within their value-chain specializations by developing business applications or information systems well-suited to the particular needs of various domestic clients – such as the telecom industry, the cooperative banking sector, or SMEs. On the other hand, however, we need to observe that neither of the two firms has been able to introduce to the market its own products that would become successful innovations on a global scale. Moreover, none of them has extended their operations into the production of the more technologically demanding, and potentially more profitable, EIT components – such as database management systems or key ERP applications. Considering this, we may even argue that the integration into transnational value chains driven by the globally leading EIT companies has locked the two Polish companies into the relatively low value-added segments of the sectoral production system.

At the same time, however, we need to also acknowledge that the organizational structure of the global EIT sector described in the present study – shaped by the 'modularization' processes of the 1980s and 1990s – is already a largely historical phenomenon and that, in recent years, this industry has started developing in entirely new directions. It remains to be seen, for instance, how such technological and market developments as the growing importance of capital-intensive cloud-computing infrastructures and the shift towards internet-based provision of software services for commercial and industrial clients (Lechowski and Krzywdzinski 2022) will influence the upgrading opportunities of emerging-country EIT firms.

In addition to the transnational value-chain integration, the case study has placed the upgrading paths of the two Polish IT companies within the context of the national political-economic conditions. Regarding the firms' *corporate finance* strategies, we have shown that both Asseco and Comarch have been able to use the capital raised through the stock exchange to finance their growth. This finding confirms the expectation developed in the second section of the chapter, according to which the country's relatively well-functioning capital market should be able to provide some relevant support to emerging domestic technology firms.

However, our analysis also indicated that, despite their common reliance on the stock market, the two case-study firms have, in fact, followed quite different corporate finance strategies – which have entailed different kinds of risks and developmental opportunities. The first company, Asseco, has used the capital collected on the WSE to pursue an aggressive merger and acquisition strategy. Throughout the three decades of its existence, the company has managed to acquire several big domestic and foreign IT firms with significant technological capabilities and established market positions. But at the same time, this strategy has generated significant costs and may have also negatively affected the firm's technological upgrading in the long run. Perhaps most importantly, large parts of the company's income had to be redistributed to its shareholders by means of increasingly high dividend payments. The second firm, Comarch, has followed a rather 'hybrid' finance strategy – combining equity funding with bank loans in a more balanced way. There were no spectacular mergers and acquisitions in the history of this company and, resulting from this, its overall growth has been relatively slower. On the other hand, however, Comarch's upgrading path has been less dependent on short-term economic interests of external shareholders.

Concerning the firms' *market positioning strategies*, the analysis revealed significant developmental opportunities related to various characteristics of the domestic demand. First, both case-study firms have been able to supply diverse cost-effective EIT solutions, which were not a viable business model for MNCs selling software products designed primarily for high-income markets. These low-cost product strategies (e.g., the competencies in the production of ERP applications for SMEs) have become key resources on which the two Polish firms relied when extending their operations into Western markets.[9] The second important characteristic of the Polish EIT market was the presence of large public technology buyers. Our analysis has shown that, in the past, both firms were able to secure many lucrative contracts from domestic public institutions or state-controlled enterprises. At the same time, however, the long-term influence of this market strategy on the development of the two firms was not always positive. In some of the cases described in the analysis (such as the infamous contract awarded by ZUS to Prokom), the relations between the two firms and the public technology buyers displayed typical characteristics of 'crony capitalism' (Enderwick 2005) and have inhibited rather than stimulated technological innovation. In this respect, it would be important to investigate what kind of long-term implications for domestic technology companies may result from the leaner public procurement approach that was adopted by the Polish government around 2015.

Finally, the third aspect of the national political-economic context considered in the case study was the *external supply of innovation capabilities*. Our starting point was the observations in the research literature regarding the ongoing difficulties in establishing a well-functioning national innovation system in Poland. The picture emerging from the analysis of the two case-study firms is largely consistent with existing literature. During the early years of their existence, none of the studied companies significantly benefited from interactions with research organizations and, in both cases, the early commercial success resulted from entrepreneurial rather than technological innovation. At the same time, the picture was perhaps slightly different in the case of Comarch, which, indeed, has originated in the domestic academic environment and whose development was closely tied to its founder's earlier career as a researcher in telecommunication technology.

However, from the perspective of the future research on the national innovation system in Poland, the most important observations were likely those related to the more recent (and still ongoing) transformative processes. Drawing on the anecdotal evidence discussed in the case study, we may point out in particular two developments that would be worth investigating in more detail. First, there is the question of the possible implications of the European integration. Both case-study firms have recently been involved in various technological innovation projects financially supported by the EU. Considering this, it would be interesting to find out to what extent the well-documented weaknesses of the Polish R&D and technology-transfer infrastructures may have been overcome through the involvement of the EU funds – and what kind of effect this may have had on different kinds of firms and different technology sectors. Second, there emerges the question about the implications of the country's new 'developmentalist' industrial-policy agenda. The example of the corporate R&D centre co-financed by one of the studied companies together with the government (via EU funds) suggests that a shift from the earlier 'hands-off' neoliberal policy paradigm towards a more direct involvement of state actors in guiding the sectoral innovation processes may already be taking place in the Polish IT industry. If that is indeed the case, another important issue to address concerns the relationship between such proactive involvement of the Polish government and the evolving discourses on competition and industrial policy at the EU level (see e.g., Bulfone 2022; Meunier and Mickus 2020; Lechowski, Krzywdzinski and Pardi 2022).

**Grzegorz Lechowski** is a researcher at the WZB Berlin Social Sciences Center and the Helmut Schmidt University in Hamburg. His work focuses on the processes of technological, organizational and regulatory change in the globalized industrial economy. His current research topics include in particular the policy discourse of the EU's 'digital sovereignty' and the implications of the transition to electromobility for the transnational organization of work and production in the automotive industry.

**Table 4.2.** Sources of historical online data (1990–2017).

| Type of collected data | Main sources |
|---|---|
| 1. Company data | Resources published online by the two case-study companies (for Asseco see: inwestor.asseco.com; for Comarch see: www.comarch.pl/relacje-inwestorskie/), including such materials as:<br>• current and annual reports<br>• financial statements<br>• press releases<br>• promotional presentations |
| 2. Media coverage | Articles from Polish trade and mainstream media including the following online services:<br>• Bankier.pl (www.bankier.pl)<br>• Computerworld (www.computerworld.pl)<br>• Polska Agencja Prasowa (infostrefa.com)<br>• Parkiet (www.parkiet.com)<br>• Puls Biznesu (www.pb.pl) |

In sum, the empirical analysis used around 9,200 sources from the period between 1990 and 2017 to reconstruct the upgrading paths of the two case-study firms.

## Notes

1. For the purpose of the present analysis, the enterprise IT (EIT) industry is defined as the subset of IT firms involved in the supply of information systems to organizational clients – including the production of both enterprise software and hardware, and the provision of related integration or maintenance services.
2. From a technological standpoint, we can distinguish the following key components of EIT solutions: (1) a complex layer of enterprise hardware, containing such different technologies as data-centre servers, storage systems or network equipment; and, building on this: (2) a number of different software layers such as database software, the middleware, or end-user business applications (Kumar, Esteves and Bendoly 2011)
3. The year 2012 was the last data point reported by EITO (2013). The category of 'project-based IT services' was proposed by EITO (2013) and includes three kinds of activities: IT consulting, systems integration, and applications development. Excluded are, for instance, revenues from standard enterprise software.
4. In other countries, the adoption of public IT procurement policies based on open international standards was a more disputed topic – see, for example, Anchordoguy (2000) on the Japanese case.
5. Rzeszów is a city of around 200,000 inhabitants in southeastern Poland.
6. Not to be confused with the Japanese multinational SoftBank, which was not related to the Polish integrator.
7. Interestingly, this company was a subsidiary of Prokom (acquired by Asseco in 2008).

8. However, one should also note that the other WSE-listed companies within the Asseco Group (e.g., Asseco Business Solutions) followed less generous dividend policies than Asseco Poland.
9. Regarding the risks related to the adoption of low-cost product strategies by emerging-country firms see Krzywdzinski, Lechowski and Jürgens (2018).

## References

Anchordoguy, Marie. 2000. 'Japan's Software Industry: A Failure of Institutions?' *Research Policy* 29(3): 391–408.
Asseco. 2020. *Asseco Group Annual Report for the Year ended December 31, 2019*. Retrieved 17 May 2021 from https://inwestor.asseco.com/en/reports/financial-reports/2019/.
Baba, Yasunori, and F. Ted Tschang. 2004. 'Corporate Strategies in Information Technology Firms'. In *The New Economy in East Asia and the Pacific*, edited by Peter Drysdale, 172–202. New York: Routledge.
Beblavý, M., and L. M. Kureková. 2014. 'Into the First League: The Competitive Advantage of the Antivirus Industry in the Czech Republic and Slovakia'. *Competition and Change* 18(5): 421–37.
Bluhm, Katharina. 2014. 'Capitalism Theory in Central Eastern Europe. A Critical Review'. *emecon.eu* 1: 1–11.
Bluhm, Katharina, and Mihai Varga. 2019. 'Conservative Developmental Statism in East Central Europe and Russia'. *New Political Economy* 25(4): 642–59.
Bohle, Dorothee. 2018. 'European Integration, Capitalist Diversity and Crises Trajectories on Europe's Eastern Periphery'. *New Political Economy* 23(2): 239–53.
Bohle, Dorothee, and Béla Greskovits. 2012. *Capitalist Diversity on Europe's Periphery*. Ithaca: Cornell University Press.
Borrus, Michael, and John Zysman. 1997. 'Globalization with Borders: The Rise of Wintelism as the Future of Global Competition'. *Industry and Innovation* 4(2): 141–66.
Breznitz, Dan, and Darius Ornston. 2017. 'EU Financing and Innovation in Poland'. Working Paper No. 198. London: European Bank for Reconstruction and Development.
Bulfone, F. 2022. 'Industrial Policy and Comparative Political Economy: A Literature Review and Research Agenda'. *Competition and Change* 27(1): 22–43.
Campbell-Kelly, Martin. 2004. *From Airline Reservations to Sonic the Hedgehog: A History of the Software Industry*. Cambridge, MA: MIT Press.
Capik, P., and J. Drahokoupil. 2011. 'Foreign Direct Investments in Business Services: Transforming the Visegrád Four Region into a Knowledge-Based Economy?' *European Planning Studies* 19(9): 1611–31.
Comarch. 2020. *Annual Report 2019*. Retrieved 17 May 2021 from https://www.comarch.com/files-com/file_570/Annual_report_2019_EN_17_6.pdf.
Computerworld. 1991. *Informatyka w służbie państwa i obywateli*. Retrieved 17 May 2021 from https://www.computerworld.pl/news/Informatyka-w-sluzbie-panstwa-i-obywateli,313490.html.
Dosi, Giovanni, Mike Hobday, Luigi Marengo and Andrea Prencipe. 2005. 'The Economics of Systems Integration: Towards an Evolutionary Interpretation'. In *The

*Business of Systems Integration*, edited by Andrea Prencipe, Michael Hobday and Andrew Davies, 95–113. Oxford: Oxford University Press.

Drahokoupil, Jan, and Béla Galgóczi. 2017. *Condemned to Be Left Behind? Can Central and Eastern Europe Emerge from Its Low-Wage Model?* Brussels: ETUI.

EITO. 2013. *ICT Market Report 2013/14*. Berlin: European Information Technology Observatory, Bitkom Research GmbH.

Enderwick, Peter. 2005. 'What's Bad about Crony Capitalism?' *Asian Business & Management* 4(2): 117–32.

Forbes. 2010. *Maszyneria Trurla za Trzy miliardy*. Retrieved 17 May 2021 from https://www.forbes.pl/wiadomosci/maszyneria-trurla-za-trzy-miliardy/jl3kfs5.

Gawer, Annabelle. 2014. 'Bridging Differing Perspectives on Technological Platforms: Toward an Integrative Framework'. *Research Policy* 43(7): 1239–49.

Hardy, Jane. 2007. 'The New Competition and the New Economy: Poland in the International Division of Labour'. *Europe-Asia Studies* 59(5): 761–77.

Hardy, Jane, and Graham Hollinshead. 2016. '"Clouds" in the Desert? Central and Eastern Europe and Ukraine in the New Division of Labour for Business Services and Software Development'. In *Space, Place and Global Digital Work*, edited by Jörg Flecker, 83–103. London: Palgrave Macmillan.

Jasiecki, Krzysztof. 2013. *Kapitalizm po polsku: Między modernizacją a peryferiami Unii Europejskiej*. Warszawa: IFiS PAN.

———. 2019. 'Conservative Modernization and the Rise of Law and Justice in Poland'. In *New Conservatives in Russia and East Central Europe*, edited by Katharina Bluhm and Mihai Varga, 130–54. London: Routledge.

Jürgens, Ulrich, and Martin Krzywdzinski. 2010. *Die neue Ost-West-Arbeitsteilung. Arbeitsmodelle und industrielle Beziehungen in der europäischen Automobilindustrie*. Edited by Martin Krzywdzinski. Frankfurt: Campus.

Kaszuba, Krzysztof. 2010. 'Rozwój Asseco Poland SA jako przykład tworzenia międzynarodowej grupy kapitałowej'. *Studia i Prace Kolegium Zarządzania i Finansów* 101: 108–16.

Kharas, Homi, and Harinder Kohli. 2011. 'What is the Middle-Income Trap, Why Do Countries Fall into It, and How Can It Be Avoided?' *Global Journal of Emerging Market Economies* 3(3): 281–89.

King, Lawrence. 2007. 'Central European Capitalism in Comparative Perspective'. In *Beyond Varieties of Capitalism: Conflict, Contradictions, and Complementarities in the European Economy*, edited by Bob Hancké, Martin Rhodes and Mark Thatcher, 125–45. Oxford: Oxford University Press.

Kogan, Irena, Michael Gebel and Clemens Noelke. 2013. 'Educational Systems and Inequalities in Educational Attainment in Central and Eastern European Countries'. *Studies of Transition States and Societies* 4(1): 69–83.

Kozioł-Nadolna, Katarzyna. 2013. 'The Analysis of R&D Internationalization – Case Study of Comarch Enterprise'. *Folia Oeconomica Stetinensia* 13(1): 136–49.

Krzywdzinski, Martin, Grzegorz Lechowski and Ulrich Jürgens. 2018. 'The Inevitability of Change in Chinese and Indian Automakers' Low-Cost Productive Models'. *La nouvelle revue du travail* 12: 1–20.

Kubielas, Stanislaw. 2000. 'Restructuring the Computer and Software Industries in Poland'. In *The Globalization of Industry and Innovation in Eastern Europe: From*

*Post-socialist Restructuring to International Competitiveness*, edited by Christian von Hirschhausen and Jürgen Bitzer, 283–312. Cheltenham: Edward Elgar.

———. 2004. 'Product Fragmentation and Alliances in the Central European Computer and Software Industries'. In *International Industrial Networks and Industrial Restructuring in Central and Eastern Europe*, edited by Slavo Radosevic and Bert M. Sadowski, 59–77. Dordrecht: Kluwer.

Kubielas, Stanislaw, and Igor Yegorov. 2000. 'Strategic Alliances and Technology Transfer in Central and Eastern Europe'. *Science and Public Policy* 27(4): 265–73.

Kumar, Sanjay, José Esteves and Elliot Bendoly. 2011. *Handbook of Research in Enterprise Systems*. New Delhi: SAGE Publications India.

Langlois, R. N. 2003. 'The Vanishing Hand: The Changing Dynamics of Industrial Capitalism'. *Industrial and Corporate Change* 12(2): 351–85.

Lechowski, Grzegorz, and Martin Krzywdzinski. 2022. 'Emerging Positions of German Firms in the Industrial Internet of Things: A Global Technological Ecosystem Perspective'. *Global Networks* 22(4): 666–83.

Lechowski, G., M. Krzywdzinski and T. Pardi. 2022. 'A Government-Driven Sectoral Transformation? French and German Policy Responses to the COVID-Crisis in the Automotive Industry'. *International Journal of Automotive Technology and Management* 23(1): 5–21.

Linden, Greg. 1998. 'Building Production Networks in Central Europe: The Case of the Electronics Industry'. Berkeley Roundtable on the International Economy Working Paper 126, July 1998, University of California, Berkeley.

Lipton, David, Jeffrey Sachs, Stanley Fischer and Janos Kornai. 1990. 'Creating a Market Economy in Eastern Europe: The Case of Poland'. *Brookings Papers on Economic Activity* 1990(1): 75–147.

Martin, R. 2013. *Constructing Capitalisms: Transforming Business Systems in Central and Eastern Europe*. Oxford: Oxford University Press.

Melnarowicz, Krzysztof. 2017. 'Rozwój zewnętrzny jako czynnik wspomagający innowacyjność w przedsiębiorstwach'. *Studia i prace Kolegium Zarządzania i Finansów* 156: 9–23.

Meunier, S., and J. Mickus. 2020. 'Sizing up the Competition: Explaining Reform of European Union Competition Policy in the Covid-19 Era'. *Journal of European Integration* 42(8): 1077–94.

Micek, Grzegorz. 2015. 'FDI Trends in the Business Services Sector: The Case of Poland'. In *Foreign Investment in Eastern and Southern Europe after 2008: Still a Lever of Growth?* edited by Béla Galgóczi, Jan Drahokoupil and Magdalena Bernaciak, 297–318. Brussels: ETUI.

Myant, Martin. 2018. 'Dependent Capitalism and the Middle-Income Trap in Europe and East Central Europe'. *International Journal of Management and Economics* 54(4): 291–303.

Nölke, Andreas, and Arjan Vliegenthart. 2009. 'Enlarging the Varieties of Capitalism: The Emergence of Dependent Market Economies in East Central Europe'. *World Politics* 61(4): 670–702.

OECD. 2017a. 'Graduates by Field of Education: Computing (ISC 48)'. Retrieved 17 May 2021 from http://stats.oecd.org/Index.aspx?DatasetCode=RGRADSTY.

———. 2017b. 'Gross Domestic Spending on R&D'. Retrieved 17 May 2021 from https://data.oecd.org/rd/gross-domestic-spending-on-r-d.htm.

———. 2017c. 'Population with Tertiary Education, 25–34 Year-Olds, % in Same Age Group'. Retrieved 17 May 2021 from https://data.oecd.org/eduatt/population-with-tertiary-education.htm.

Pavlínek, Petr. 2017. *Dependent Growth: Foreign Investment and the Development of the Automotive Industry in East-Central Europe*. Springer: Cham.

Przybylska, Krystyna, and Czesława Pilarska. 2005. 'Proces internacjonalizacji przedsiębiorstwa na przykładzie firmy ComArch SA'. *Zeszyty Naukowe Akademii Ekonomicznej w Krakowie* 686: 5–30.

PwC. 2016. 'Emerging Markets Top 30 Software Companies'. Retrieved 17 May 2021 from https://www.pwc.com/globalsoftware100.

Radło, Mariusz-Jan. 2016. *Offshoring, Outsourcing and Production Fragmentation: Linking Macroeconomic and Micro-Business Perspectives*. Basingstoke: Palgrave Macmillan.

Sadowski, Bert M. 2001. 'Towards Market Repositioning in Central and Eastern Europe: International Cooperative Ventures in Hungary, Poland and the Czech Republic'. *Research Policy* 30(5): 711–24.

Schware, Robert. 1987. 'Software Industry Development in the Third World: Policy Guidelines, Institutional Options, and Constraints'. *World Development* 15(10–11): 1249–67.

Szafrański, Bohdan. 2011. 'Dwie dekady informatyki w bankowości polskiej'. *Miesięcznik finansowy Bank* 5: 130–35.

Szent-Iványi, Balázs. 2017. 'Conclusions: Prospects for FDI-Led Development in a Post-Crisis World'. In *Foreign Direct Investment in Central and Eastern Europe*, edited by Balázs Szent-Iványi, 241–57. Cham: Springer.

Tamowicz, Piotr. 2006. 'Corporate Governance in Poland'. In *Handbook on International Corporate Governance: Country Analyses*, edited by Christine A. Mallin, 91–105. Cheltenham: Edward Elgar.

Thun, Eric, and Tim Sturgeon. 2019. 'When Global Technology Meets Local Standards: Reassessing the China's Mobile Telecom Policy in the Age of Platform Innovation'. In *Policy, Regulation and Innovation in China's Electricity and Telecom Industries*, edited by Loren Brandt and Thomas G. Rawski, 177–221. Cambridge: Cambridge University Press.

UIS. 2017. 'R&D Activities Performed by Higher Education as a Percentage of GDP'. Retrieved 17 May 2021 from http://data.uis.unesco.org/Index.aspx?DataSetCode=SCN_DS.

Wilinski, Witold. 2012. 'Internationalisation through the Warsaw Stock Exchange: An Empirical Analysis'. *Post-Communist Economies* 24(1): 145–54.

World Bank. 2021. 'Market Capitalization of Listed Domestic Companies (% of GDP)'. Retrieved 17 May 2021 from https://data.worldbank.org/indicator/CM.MKT.LCAP.GD.ZS?locations=PL-DE-SK-CZ-HU.

CHAPTER 5

# The Value of Return Migration
## *The Case of Bulgaria*

Birgit Glorius

## Introduction

After the fall of the communist regimes in Eastern Europe and the political and economic transformations during the 1990s and 2000s, all CEE countries have faced significant emigration processes, notably in the context of EU integration. It is estimated that between only 2003 and 2007, about 2.2 million citizens from CEE countries moved to the West (Nadler and Lang 2014, 5). The departure of young and well-educated citizens especially has raised concerns about an ongoing brain drain to the detriment of the economic and social development of the countries of origin. However, empirical evidence suggests that most emigration decisions are not definite; emigrants usually maintain strong ties to their homelands and a large proportion returns home, bringing back money as well as knowledge and innovative ideas (de Haas 2007; Klein-Hitpaß 2016; Predojevic-Despic et al. 2016). The share of emigrants who leave their host region within the first five years after arrival – many of them returning home – is estimated to be between 20 and 50 percent (OECD 2008, 163).

That is, return migration is not a marginal phenomenon and must be seen as an important source for human resources and economic development in the countries of origin. A crucial point regarding the efficiency and sustainability of return is the question of whether returnees are able to find suitable labour market positions that match the pay gap between the Western and Eastern European economies. The study of return migration to CEE countries is a field of research that entails a close monitoring of socioeconomic framing features as well as of migration dynamics. A crucial issue is the human factor, meaning the unpredictability of individual subjectivities and fluidity of life course decisions, which are an inherent part of migratory decision making (Kley 2011; Wingens et al. 2011).

Focusing on the phenomenon of return migration to CEE countries, this chapter discusses the effects of return migration on the economic and social development of Bulgaria, focusing on the expectations, decisions and experiences of returning migrants. It presents a case study on educational migrants returning to Bulgaria after university graduation abroad and discusses how and to what extent the Bulgarian economy and society can benefit from emigration and return. In doing so, rather than drawing on statistical data and seeking to answer the research question from a quantitative point of view, the chapter adopts a phenomenological approach and takes the perspective of migrants, shedding light on the complexity of return decisions as one episode in the migratory trajectory.

The chapter draws on academic literature and empirical studies on return migration, return and development, and mobility of knowledge. It also benefits from the results of an empirical research project on return decisions of Bulgarian educational migrants, which was carried out between 2016 and 2018. This study, which is titled 'Return migration and life course decisions – the example of returning graduates to Bulgaria', was designed as a comparative qualitative study comprising sixty biographical interviews with Bulgarian educational migrants in Germany and returnees in Bulgaria as well as eleven semi-structured interviews with experts in the fields of migration, education and German-Bulgarian relations.[1]

This chapter first gives a short overview of the academic literature on the topic and presents the main conceptual approaches, key findings and open questions in the field. Then, it presents the case study on Bulgarian returnees, highlighting the transnational aspects of their mobility trajectories, the complexity of return decisions, experiences of return and their considerations regarding the sustainability of the decision to return. The final section summarizes the findings against the backdrop of the focus of this volume.

## Key Concepts and Findings from Research on CEE Countries

Similar to emigrants, returnees, too, can be distinguished by their main motivations for moving back, which often also relate to reintegration trajectories as well as the individual and collective value of the return. A typology with regards to return motivation was developed by Cerase (1974) based on his research on Italians returning from the US and has to this day remained valid. In this typology, Cerase distinguishes four groups of returnees: return of conservatism, which refers to migrants who have had satisfactory careers abroad and returned home because their strategic goal of migration was reached (also labelled as 'target earners' in migration literature); return of failure which characterizes emigrants who have returned as a consequence of difficulties in the host country; return of retirement, comprising migrants who have reached pension age and returned in order to make the most of their pension; and return of innovation which characterizes returnees with the clear expectation to reinvest their new ideas, values and economic capital for the benefit of their country of origin. While the first three groups are anticipated to have no or few intentions of business investment or knowledge transfer after return, the latter is perceived as the most dynamic category of return migrants (Smoliner et al. 2013, 14).

While migration research has generally supported Cerase's typology, it is obvious that migration intentions are complex, so that a clear distinction of motives, as suggested by Cerase, is rather an ideal type than a reflection of migratory reality. Furthermore, while Cerase focuses on only the economic output of returnees for his typology, recent research reveals also social aspects as a major driver for return decisions (Dustmann 2001; Gibson and McKenzie 2009; Geddie 2013). Thus, we can add 'social return' to the abovementioned typology, defined as a return decision which is mainly influenced by personal or emotional aspects such as health problems, marriage, birth of children, emotional attachment to the home region or the desire to live closer to family and friends (Lang et al. 2014, 10).

A second important conceptual strand of return research is Cassarino's (2004) concept of preparedness. With regard to the pre-return and post-return conditions, Cassarino differentiates between return migrants with a high level of preparedness, those with a low level of preparedness and those without any preparation and he uses this differentiation to draw conclusions regarding the efficiency of return policies (Cassarino 2004, 19ff). For the first group, that is, the well-prepared migrants, he sees a high propensity for entrepreneurial activities in and knowledge transfer to the country of origin. Well-prepared returnees may consider policies that support return to be a positive signal, but these policies are not incremental for their return decisions. For the second group, state programmes fostering return can be of crucial importance for successful reintegration into both the labour market and social life. The third group might do less well after remigration even if assisted by state programmes. Based on his desk research, Cassarino (2004) criticizes programmes with a single focus on the economic motives or social aspects for supporting return migrants. Rather, he recommends a combination of both aspects mirroring the multifaceted motives of migration as well as the relevance of framing features for successful return migration.

Return migration to CEE countries has increasingly been a focus of research since the EU accessions of 2004–2007. Findings suggest a high level of fluidity and circularity in the migration processes between countries of origin and destination (Engbersen and Snel 2013; McCollum and Findlay 2015; McCollum, Shubin et al. 2013; McCollum, Apsite-Berina et al. 2017). A comparative study on emigrants and returnees from six CEE-countries carried out in the years 2011 and 2012 shows that, before emigration, 21 percent of actual returnees and 39 percent of actual emigrants with no return intention had no precise idea about the length of their stay abroad, and the majority of respondents planned to stay abroad less than five years (Lang et al. 2014, 28f). This phenomenon of rather open or unprecise migration strategies – also labelled as 'intentional unpredictability' by British researchers (Eade, Drinkwater and Garapich 2006) – can be explained by the changed institutional frameworks for migration, the unpredictability of economic and political developments at home and abroad and changed sociodemographic profiles of migrants engaging in post-accession migration (Coniglio and Brzozowski 2018; Karolak 2020; Zaicev and Zimmermann 2012).

A notable change in the institutional frameworks has been the shift from mainly temporary work contracts to more open labour markets following the EU accession, which certainly means that migrants have to build up their competences in order to find jobs fitting to their skill level and in order to avoid deskilling, discrimination or exploitation (Glorius, Grabowska-Lusinska and Kuvik 2013, 10). Likewise, there are few institutionalized structures to support reintegration of returnees and to secure adequate deployment of the entire range of their skills (Kovács et al. 2013, 63).

Also, the individual profiles of migrants have changed after the EU enlargement. While pre-accession migrants were rather family-oriented 'target-earners' sending most of their income as remittances back home, a significant proportion of the 'new' migrants have less targeted ideas concerning the duration and monetary outcome of their migration. Their life plans and career prospects are rather open-ended and they are less concerned about a thorough preparation for both emigration and return migration (Eade et al. 2006; Glorius et al. 2013, 10). A growing proportion of these 'new' migrants consists of university graduates at the beginning of their professional careers. For the case of Poland, it has been shown that a disparity between structures of higher education and the needs of the transition economy led to accelerated emigration after 2004. This was due to a boom of higher education, producing strongly increasing numbers of university graduates which could not be absorbed by the labour market (Pietka et al. 2013, 142; Trevena 2013, 172). Furthermore, the expansion of higher education infrastructure was mostly led by private companies, which focused on less expensive programmes in terms of provision such as social sciences or business management and were generally less critical regarding the quality of applicants (World Bank 2004). Thus, many graduates of those times were rather poorly qualified or lacked extra skills that would have helped them outshine the mass of similarly qualified graduates. Temporary emigration was rationalized as a strategy to gain additional cultural capital. Arriving unprepared, many entered the labour market in the destination countries below their skill level in order to secure an income. While deskilled labour might not be detrimental for a shorter period of time, this strategy may lead to deskilling, depreciation of skills and degradation in the long run (Pietka et al. 2013; Trevena 2013). After returning, many of these migrants realized that their occupational or educational biographies were not appreciated in their home country's labour market, which eventually led to decisions for further emigration.

Thus, studies reveal a high level of unpreparedness and missing knowledge about the structures of the home economy on the side of returnees, just like they do in the case of emigration. Furthermore, as home countries' economies are still in the process of transition, structures and thus labour market demands can change rapidly, which pressures return migrants also to adapt their skills. In this case, returnees cannot rely on experiences of earlier cohorts of returnees, either (Wolfeil 2013). Using the example of Poland, Wolfeil (2013) and Klein-Hitpaß (2016) show that a successful re-integration into the home country's labour market depends not only on the match of formal skills and labour market demand but also on soft forms of social capital such as trust, social networks or shared migration experiences.

As a comparative study on emigrants from six CEE-countries shows, most emigrants anticipate return migration to be a challenging endeavour. However, although more than 60 percent of potential returnees expected a return to be difficult, among those who actually returned, around 70 percent reported no significant difficulties regrading re-adaptation (Lang et al. 2014, 35). This leads to the conclusion that it is not merely the reality at home but also the perception of this reality which influences migratory decisions. Nonetheless, there are surely compromises that returnees have to make back at home in comparison to their life abroad. For example, in the comparative survey by Lang et al. (2014, 32f), about 27 percent of the returnees accepted a less profitable professional situation or salary compared to their pre-return experience. However, as the main motive for return was in the field of private life, the reunification with family members and family resulted in a high satisfaction with the return decision. These findings once again highlight the fact that migration decisions cannot be interpreted solely within the neoclassical paradigm, but that the full complexity of human life has to be taken into consideration.

## Return to Bulgaria – Motives and Experiences of Returnees

Like many other Central and Eastern European States, Bulgaria has been experiencing a massive wave of emigration since the fall of the Iron Curtain. The country's accession to the European Union in 2007 and the full freedom of movement in the Union since 2014 has further accelerated emigration, particularly among younger populations. About one third of the emigrants of 2017 were in the age group of fifteen to twenty-four, while the share of the same age group among immigrants to Bulgaria was only 9 percent (Republic of Bulgaria National Statistical Institute 2018). Regarding the age and skill selectivity of migration, emigration for educational purposes is of specific importance for Bulgaria, because studying abroad constitutes a significant pathway into the host country's labour market and, thus, into long-term or permanent emigration (Dreher and Poutvaara 2011; Pratsinakis et al. 2017). Students returning from abroad, on the other hand, are seen as an important element for the economic and social development of a country, as they can reinvest the skills and knowledge that they have acquired while studying abroad (Ghimire and Maharjan 2015; Le Bail and Shen 2008).

The following section presents a case study on return intentions and experiences of Bulgarians who completed a university degree abroad. Most of the interviewees graduated from a German university. In total, sixty biographical interviews with migrants were carried out between September 2015 and November 2017. Thirty of these migrants had returned to Bulgaria at the time of the interview. The selection of migrant interviewees followed the snowball method, aiming at reaching a high diversity of gender, field of study and migratory period (Table 5.1).

At the time of the interview, most interviewees were in their twenties and thirties. Most of them had emigrated either before Bulgaria's EU accession in 2007, or between 2007 and 2013. Among the returnees, five had returned before 2010, twelve between 2010 and 2013 and thirteen after 2014. Many interviewees had returned to Bulgaria several times and re-emigrated either before studying or during the university education – for example, some went to Bulgaria as Erasmus students, many returned after obtaining their first degree, started working and later decided to re-emigrate for a Master's degree. These details already point to the fluidity of migration and migratory decisions, illustrating that emigration, immigration and settling should always be understood as conditional and bound to people's current living situation and subjective assessments, resulting in further migratory episodes throughout the life-course (Kley 2011; Wingens et al. 2011). The remainder of this section presents results on main return motivations, as

**Table 5.1.** Key characteristics of the interviewed migrants.

|  | Interviewees in Germany | Interviewees in Bulgaria |
|---|---|---|
| **Number of interviewees** | 30 | 30 |
| **Gender** | | |
| male | 11 | 13 |
| female | 19 | 17 |
| **Age** | | |
| 21–29 years | 14 | 14 |
| 30–39 years | 15 | 12 |
| 40–49 years | 1 | 4 |
| **Field of study** | | |
| Economics/Management/Communication | 13 | 12 |
| Natural sciences/Technical Sciences/Architecture | 6 | 4 |
| Social sciences/Humanities | 5 | 3 |
| Area Studies/Geography/Tourism | 4 | 6 |
| Law | 1 | 3 |
| Other | 1 | 2 |
| **First emigration** | | |
| before 2007 | 14 | 17 |
| 2007–13 | 14 | 13 |
| since 2014 | 2 | 0 |
| **Latest return** | | |
| before 2010 | — | 5 |
| 2010–13 | — | 12 |
| since 2014 | — | 13 |
| **Family status** | | |
| single | 15 | 20 |
| with partner | 15 | 10 |
| **Have child(ren)** | 4 | 5 |
| **Occupation** | | |
| Self-employed/entrepreneur | 5 | 4 |
| Employee | 15 | 24 |
| Enrolled in higher education | 9 | 0 |
| Unemployed | 1 | 2 |

Source: author compilation.

well as the experience and the sustainability of return. It highlights the necessity to understand migration, return and the transfer of knowledge and innovation within a transnational explanatory framework.

## Motives for Returning

The comparison of return decisions with the decision to stay abroad after graduation shows significant similarities in the motives for the respective decision, with social and professional considerations being the strongest ones for both decisions. Thus, it is of particular relevance how those decisions are substantiated with individual contextual conditions.

The first strong reason is linked to the social life of interviewees. Many returnees argue that they missed their parents, friends and relatives and wanted to be closer to them during important biographical events such as weddings, childbirth or birthdays. This motive is not limited only to the social events taking place in Bulgaria but also to the migrants' own biographical stages such as family formation and having children. For instance, one interviewee reports that he and his wife returned from the US when they felt they wanted to have children. He emphasizes the irrationality of their decision, as they both had good careers in the US and evaluated their living conditions very positively. However, especially the interviewee's wife realized that she needed to have the 'safe haven' of her home country and her close relatives around in order to face the challenge of motherhood:

> Half of the reason was also 'cause we were at the age when we had to have kids, and she was too scared to have it abroad without her mom, without people to talk to. In Bulgaria it's more common in the first months to have somebody with you. She said, maybe she will not understand the doctors, when they speak to her. Even though she understood the language. So, we went back. And, of course, in this time we were trying for, for a baby, it didn't work. It worked on the third day when we came back home! (Boril, thirty-five, accountant in an international company in Bulgaria, lines 344–50)[2]

In the case of a binational couple, which frequently was a German and a Bulgarian in our German sample, the same reasoning led to the decision to stay put. This points to the necessity to understand the conditionality and contingency of migration, which is densely interwoven with life-course decisions, and bound to a transnational social space as major reference frame.

Another important motive for (im)mobility decisions is linked to the interviewees' professional development. In addition to their own career goals, other factors such as existing professional contacts, experiences, and the level of information regarding career opportunities in Germany and Bulgaria play a significant role. The interviewees' narratives show that decisions are often made based on incomplete knowledge. Since most of the interviewees left Bulgaria immediately after leaving school, they lack authentic experience or insight into the professional opportunities in their home country and many have rather pessimistic assumptions about the work atmosphere, career paths and salary level in Bulgaria. Therefore, those who have achieved a good position within the German labour market during or immediately after their studies tend to stay abroad.

A possibility for overcoming the problem of alienation from the situation at home and gaining an authentic impression of the realities of working life in Bulgaria is to work as an intern in Bulgaria as part of higher education in Germany. Interviewee Krasi, for example, followed such a path, which in the end paved the way into her actual career:

> During my bachelor program, I had to do a six-month internship. I looked for positions in Germany and Bulgaria. . . . I was invited to two interviews in Germany, but it didn't work out. Then I received an invitation from the German-Bulgarian business chamber in Sofia, and I obtained the position. This was a good opportunity for me, because I could return to Bulgaria. (Krasi, twenty-seven, employee city administration, Bulgaria, lines 91–97)

While the 'stayers' have a common and rather negative imagination about the working conditions and career prospects in Bulgaria, the returnees are much more positive. They argue that they have more and better opportunities in Bulgaria to show the value of their skills, especially their intercultural competences:

> One should not underestimate that for me, who studied in Germany and gained work experience, there were better chances on the Bulgarian labour market compared to the German labour market. Those were the motivating factors. I was *still* in Germany when I got a job in Bulgaria. (Georgi, forty, employed in German-Bulgarian business chamber, lines 63–67)

Furthermore, a third group of interviewees emphasize the role of their interest in post-materialistic life concepts as element of their return decision. They argue that in Bulgaria, they had better opportunities to find a work-life balance and the possibility to pursue private goals besides the paid work.

Even though the interviewees who have just graduated and are standing at the doorstep to their professional career often focus on career aspects when reflecting their return decision, many also relativize these aspects and employ post-materialistic life concepts, which, they feel, can be better pursued in Bulgaria. Given that the job is remunerated appropriately, the low costs of living in Bulgaria help to ease the pressure of everyday life. Besides the pursuit of more leisure time and flexibility, the pleasant Bulgarian climate and the opportunity to enjoy local and healthy food all contribute to the subjective feeling of well-being. Even though the 'good life' is not the crucial factor for returning, several returnees underscore these aspects as significant advantages of living in Bulgaria compared to living in Germany.

> A further important reason is the quality of living. Here, I have more freedom to travel, while in Germany this is also possible but more expensive. I don't need a lot to be happy. I just want to enjoy life. (Nadja, thirty-two, employee in a law firm, lines 224–28)

A further motive of return is the intention to try out innovative business ideas, often combined with the philanthropic goal of doing 'something good' for Bulgaria. Some interviewees even justify their emigration with the aim of transferring the knowledge and experience gained while studying abroad to Bulgaria and thus contributing to the economic, cultural and social development of their home country:

> But I went to Germany with the goal to get the best from my stay and then return to Bulgaria. I wanted to transfer *everything* that I learned abroad to Bulgaria. I knew that this can be a significant contribution for Bulgaria. (Krasi, twenty-seven, employee city administration, Bulgaria, lines 148–52)

The cheap living conditions in Bulgaria and the good digital infrastructure can be a major incentive for establishing a business in Bulgaria rather than abroad. Especially Sofia and Plovdiv offer the appropriate infrastructure and atmosphere for start-ups. Some of the interviewed experts also argue that the status of Bulgaria as a transition country offers plenty of opportunities for business innovations, while Western European markets are perceived more often as closed, particularly for emerging businesses:

> Because a lot of people came back to make something theirs. . . . the entrepreneur scene is growing really fast here. Because a lot of people who have seen that something works where they lived, and they come and make it here. Yeah. But they create it on their own. (Expert 4, NGO for supporting emigration and return, lines 308–11)

This opinion is also shared by some of the interviewees who are active in this field:

> I earn less money here than I would earn in Germany, but for me it is *more important* that I feel good and that I see a sense in my life. . . . I also know that I can contribute to making Bulgaria a better place to live. The feeling that I can develop something to improve life here is very good for me. I have a meaningful life here. In Germany, everything is so well organized that I

wouldn't even want to change anything. (Krasi, twenty-seven, employee city administration, Bulgaria, lines 158–65)

However, careful preparation is necessary for establishing a business start-up, which is not always possible while staying abroad. I touch upon this issue in the next section on experiences of return.

## The Experience of Return

Return decisions, although carefully considered, are sometimes implemented spontaneously, which suggests that they also depend on a significant level of irrationality and emotionality. Many returnees are initially euphoric and have strong emotions during the first months after return, so that a few weeks or months pass before they develop a conscious impression about the ordinary everyday life in Bulgaria. That is, some of the purely positive impressions and emotions at the beginning are later assessed once again and become less positive. Experiences had while living abroad represent an important reference point for assessing everyday life in Bulgaria:

> Also, in Bulgaria, not everything is wonderful. Also, here you need to be tough sometimes. Many things which are well regulated in Germany are not regulated here. And you just have to accept that. (Martin, thirty-eight, lawyer in Bulgaria, lines 187–89)

> To my mind, there is a raft of corruption everywhere, you know, the energy sector, education if you like, medical, the health sector. Everywhere where the government is, to my mind, it doesn't work. (Ivan, thirty-seven, employed in an international company, Bulgaria, lines 753–55)

There is a significant difference between the returnees of the 2000s and the more recent ones regarding their access to labour market and career opportunities. Earlier returnees had to justify their return, which was interpreted as a signal of failure. For example, Reni, who had completed a doctoral degree in Cambridge, reports the disappointment of her parents and the lack of understanding of the social environment when she returned:

> People always asked why I returned. For those people, it was not relevant what I learned abroad and how I would make use of my knowledge back home. It was only interesting *why* I returned, as *returning* is an atypical step, especially back then. Nowadays it is rather usual. More and more people return. (Reni, forty-seven, associate professor, Bulgaria, lines 233–38)

In comparison to her international peers at the University of Cambridge, who reported positive connotations of return and anticipated the opportunity to transfer their new skills, Reni felt that her career took a step backwards:

> In my peer group at the time, the idea of returning had no negative connotation. Here in Bulgaria, the *return* meant a step backwards. And only when I was back in Bulgaria I understood that I didn't come back like the people from India or South Africa to show and develop something new, but for everyone here in Bulgaria I had *unfortunately* taken a step back. (Reni, forty-seven, associate professor, Bulgaria, lines 202–7)

Toni, who returned in 2015, also experienced negative connotations of return:

> I applied for various positions. And always came the question 'Why did you return to Bulgaria, you studied abroad, you speak several languages?' To be frank, this was always the first question, and I always felt very uncomfortable. (Toni, tweny-nine, employed by temp agency, Bulgaria, lines 182–85)

Of those returnees who returned more recently, many profited from the internationalization of the Bulgarian economy, which created a range of attractive positions for people who studied abroad, notably in the larger cities such as Sofia or Plovdiv. Of the thirty returnees in the qualitative sample, six were employed in German companies and thirteen in other international firms. In many cases, the first position after return was situated in call centres or back offices of international companies. This suggests that the language skills rather than the professional knowledge of the returnees were particularly valued. Nonetheless, many interviewees could choose from several job offers and advanced relatively fast in their career:

> There was a lot of outsourcing, call centres of [names of international companies]. The positions were attractive to me. I applied for all of them and was invited by all companies. In the end, I could choose. Actually, I realize that currently in Bulgaria, skilled workers with German language knowledge are *absolutely* wanted. If you know German, you *don't* stay without a job in Bulgaria. (Jana, twenty-nine, employee in a call center, Bulgaria, lines 298–304)

> I started working for a call centre, but only for a very short while, perhaps one or two months. My work was done in English and German. Shortly thereafter, I received a job offer from the Bulgarian labour administration and started working there. (Kiril, thirty, employee in state administration, Bulgaria, lines 152–55)

However, several of our interviewed experts point to mismatches of self-assessment and expectations with the reality of labour market positioning. Thus, many returnees would come back with a 'superiority feeling', signalling excellent professional knowledge to their employers, while completely lacking practical experiences in the Bulgarian economy. Consequently, there is a phase of disillusionment on both sides:

> And then the employee comes and he doesn't know anything about Bulgarian reality, he doesn't know who is who here, he gives some suggestions that are *totally* out of place. . . . So, there is this big need of adapting the people who studied abroad, to adapt our reality and be realistic about it. Not boast about their education abroad, it finally is just an education. . . . And if the one in Bulgaria has done internships, has been working while studying, he is much better prepared and a better use to *any* company, even without the knowledge. He just *does* things. He *knows* how to do things. And you don't. So that's the biggest disappointment from employers and graduates. (Experts 1/2, Education management company, lines 326–37)

Also, for self-employed returnees, 'ground truth' in terms of up-to-date knowledge on local regulations, conditions, social rules and business contacts are crucial. Thus, a spontaneous return in this field is reflected upon critically by an interviewee who returned with the plan to establish a social project in the city of Sofia:

> Then I decided to return to Bulgaria. At this time, I wanted to organize reading centres for children in marginalised neighbourhoods. In those centres, the children should develop their talents. . . . I quit my job. . . . I collected my luggage – well, only half of my luggage, because I did not quit my apartment in Berlin – and came back to Bulgaria. Here I started to talk about my idea. But a friend of mine told me: Come on, let's first implement a smaller project and postpone your big plans. You haven't lived in Bulgaria for eight years. You should first find out how to collaborate with the city administration. (Katja, twenty-nine, employee in international company, Bulgaria, lines 35–45)

After the initial failure of her project, Katja returned to Berlin. She took up her job again but also concentrated on a thorough preparation of her social project in Bulgaria. When she returned for the second time, she had already built up a relevant social network and had a work contract to be able to make her own living.

> Actually, before I *finally* [makes quotation marks gesture] returned, I already ran several social projects and had a social network. I already knew what to expect. (Katja, twenty-nine, employee in international company, Bulgaria, lines 122–24)

The case of Katja also points to the fluidity of return, which is alternatively labelled 'liquid return' (Anacka, Matejko and Nestorowicz 2013) or 'incomplete migration' (Okólski 2001) by Polish migration scholars who report the same phenomenon in the case of Polish migration. Katja's spontaneous return decision is implemented on the condition that she can always return to Berlin, where she maintains her home and her social network, which provides job opportunities. She develops her future in Bulgaria, while moving back and forth in the transnational social space, drawing from her social resources on both sides. Thus, transnational social spaces represent a sort of social capital which can alleviate the hardship of migration.

From a macro-analytical point of view, the experiences of the interviewed returnees point to a considerable 'implementation gap' of knowledge and skills acquired during emigration, leading to 'brain loss'. As highlighted above, this gap has changed over time and has been considerably reduced by international companies moving into the Bulgarian market, which value the intercultural competences of the returnees. However, those companies mostly offered positions where skills matched only partly. Another observation is that the Bulgarian state as facilitator of return, labour market integration or entrepreneurial activities is completely absent in the narrations of interviewees. Instead, as the following section will show, this void was filled by NGOs and migrant networks themselves.

## Transnational Social Networks

As mentioned above, social networks are specifically important in their capacity to build bridges to local stakeholders and multiply relevant contacts. Social networks are – following Putnam's social capital theory – contact networks that consist of strong or weak connections between their members. Both forms of connections have a specific purpose: while strong connections ensure the emotional stability of the in-group, weak connections are the bridge to the outside world established with other groups or local society. In our empirical example, there is a large number of social networks active in the transnational social space. These include informal networks such as chat groups of Bulgarian high school graduates who moved abroad and represent network hubs, as well as institutionalized networks that help to maintain the continuity of social connections, contact points and the flow of information across different (student) generations.

Some of our interviewees, for example, have founded student organizations for Bulgarian students abroad or engaged in transnational organizations which have not only focused on connecting with fellow Bulgarians but also offered a possibility to engage back home. One of those transnational NGOs organizes innovation challenges among its members; the winning ideas of the challenge are implemented in Bulgaria. This event takes place every summer and gives a good opportunity for expatriates to reconnect or sustain their connection with Bulgarian society. Additionally, some of the self-employed expatriates among our interviewees connect their professional activities with Bulgaria. Thus, not only locally bound knowledge but also circulating knowledge can turn out beneficial for a country's development.

Institutional transnational social networks are also important for the facilitation of mobility trajectories including return and reintegration. These networks address exactly the mismatch between education abroad and economic reality on the ground, as mentioned above. One such networks is an NGO founded by seven returnees who observed a lack of official support for labour market placement upon return. Their NGO now facilitates the whole mobility circuit of international students and connects them with each other. They organize career fairs for (potential) returning migrants where participants not only get an up-to-date impression on job and career opportunities in Bulgaria but are already matched with potential employers.

> We will do this for the ninth time, the 'Career in Bulgaria'. . . . And last year we had seven companies. And thousand point two, 1,200 candidates. And they are all pre-selected. So, for us it's important, and for the companies as well, to pre-select those candidates who have some experience abroad, at least six months. And, yeah, this is the most popular thing and our biggest project. (Experts 4/5, NGO for supporting emigration and return, lines 103–8)

There are various job fairs, economic speed-dating and other contact events in European metropolises such as Frankfurt, Milan and London sponsored by international companies that are looking for qualified workers for their Bulgarian locations. The above-cited NGO, which is one of the largest actors in the alleviation of return migration to Bulgaria, reports a databank consisting of about ten thousand clients with international profiles.

This example gives an indication of the potentials for return migration and the transnationalization of knowledge in the case of Bulgaria.

## Sustainability of (Im)mobility Decisions

The question of further mobility decisions is, without a doubt, of paramount importance in assessing the long-term effects of emigration and return migration. It constitutes a crucial question also for our interviewees. In their narrations, we can find several strategies of coping with biographical uncertainties and changing context conditions.

The comparative analysis of the interviews reveals that age, duration of emigration and position in the family cycle are relevant causal factors for further mobility decisions. For example, interviewee Kristina, who has lived in Germany for ten years, argues that she prefers not returning except for holidays, substantiating her argument with the long duration of her emigration:

> Actually, I probably wouldn't like to return to Bulgaria. For holidays, yes, but to live there, that's what I cannot imagine after ten years. Especially as my work is here, my husband, I found friends, actually I feel quite comfortable here. (Kristina, thirty-five, employee in a language school, Germany, lines 88–91)

Galja, who has lived in Germany since 2009, too, assumes that the flexibility to adapt to new life situations will decrease over the years:

> Well, I think, in the process of ageing you have more difficulties to adapt. I realize that everywhere I go, in the beginning it was easier, but each time it becomes more difficult. (Galja, thirty-one, employee in a research institute, Germany, lines 378–80)

Among the younger interviewees who are not yet married or bound to family life, there is greater flexibility. Twenty-five-year-old Veselin, for instance, places his full focus on the further development of his professional skills. He says that he would engage in further mobility for his professional development. He connects this spatial flexibility with his independence as a bachelor, which enables him to focus on his individual life goals. At the same time, his narration reveals uncertainty regarding further development opportunities and life goals. In his view, this uncertainty prevents a closer bond to a specific place and its social environment.

> I want to develop my professional skills and right now I do have that chance, because I don't have to think about family, or other people. I can just think about myself. And the opportunity to develop my professional skills is leading currently in my life and that's ... I guess I would be open if I get a good opportunity where I could learn a lot, because that's what's important to me right now, to be able to learn a lot. Both to learn like I used to study in university, but learn from experience and actually doing things.... But for now I am definitely happy here in Sofia, in Bulgaria'. (Veselin, twenty-five, employee in international company, Bulgaria, lines 312–18)

The opportunities for further individual development are of strong relevance for further biographical decisions, and interviewees refer to a transnational reference frame for considering further options. For instance,

Sonja, studying in Germany, deliberates about going back to Bulgaria. For her, opportunities for her professional development are crucial, that is why she compares the options she anticipates in Germany to those in Bulgaria, as well as in other countries that she could move to.

> Nowadays when I talk to people who are planning to return to Bulgaria, I *more and more* realize the career opportunities in Bulgaria. There is also a life for you back there (laughs). But still I am sceptical. I am still not convinced that everything can work out there. I don't want to have too much hope. That's why I want to live in a place where I can develop myself, and that's Germany, first of all, and then maybe other countries, if I have this opportunity. (Sonja, twenty-one, student, Germany, lines 159–66)

Zarina, who migrated several times and has happily been living once again in Bulgaria for six years now, too, is largely open to the idea of re-emigrating for specific purposes:

> I am still interested in all that happens abroad, I don't fully rule out to re-emigrate for work purposes. I am open to relevant job offers. But at the same time, I am feeling *very well* here. I am interested in opportunities abroad, because there is a broader labour market in my field of work. I would like to work abroad and learn something new which I could bring back to Bulgaria. (Zarina, twenty-nine, employee in international company, Bulgaria, lines 140–46)

The interviewees closely monitor the developments in Bulgaria. Being embedded in transnational social networks of many peers with comparable biographies, our interviewees are well aware of return conditions and the long-term development of reintegration processes. Based on her observations, Anelia considers 2009 as a tipping point in the return process, as according to her, the decision to return to Bulgaria no longer occurred on the basis of economic rationality after 2009:

> I think, those who returned before, like myself, came exactly at the tipping point, but my peers from college, who returned even one year earlier, 2008, many went back because the economy improved. I mean, of those who returned, which were not many, but they actually returned because it worked out financially. But now, after 2009, it doesn't work out any more. Now the income gap between Germany and Bulgaria is larger, in relative terms of course. (Anelia, thirty-one, employee in international company, Bulgaria, lines 309–16)

Valentin, too, observes a worsening of living conditions in Bulgaria. He is unemployed at the time of the interview. Empowered by his many migration experiences, he is considering emigrating again:

> Actually, since two years my concerns are growing that I might never find an appropriate job in Bulgaria. Notably after the demonstrations in 2013, the situation apparently deteriorated. After living in Sweden for two years, I am able to compare how it was before and how it is now in Bulgaria. . . . Well, actually I will start applying for jobs abroad. (Valentin, forty-one, unemployed, Bulgaria, lines 321–26)

Especially the younger interviewees highlight their independence regarding their place of residence and further mobility decisions. Even though they feel comfortable in their actual living environment, they do not rule out the option of further mobility decisions. They substantiate their attitude with the general experience of their generation as a 'mobile generation', and with an awareness that decisions always have to be seen as provisional.

> I did not take a decision to stay for good. This is a decision for a certain period of time. I cannot say if this decision is good or bad. I just chose one option, and this option is neither bad nor good. It is just that path that I went on back then. (Desi, twenty-two, employee in state administration, Bulgaria, lines 207–210)

> If external conditions or individual preferences change, further migration decisions are possible. We, the young generation, are constantly moving. We are here and there, and we want to take the best from the world. (Krasi, twenty-seven, employee city administration, Bulgaria, lines 214–18)

As the research results show, the manifold emigration, return and re-emigration experiences of our interviewees have led to the development of a transnational reference frame which stays relevant for further life-course decisions. The results also indicate that all emigration decisions are subject to revision. It is difficult to assess the sustainability of those fluid approaches. Yet, even when further life-stages might entail phases of immobility, we can assume that transnational social spaces and reference frames will stay stable and may even be transferred to the next generations.

## Conclusion

This chapter has shed light on the causes, trajectories and consequences of skilled migration for the development of a country, taking the perspective of mobile individuals. Regionally, it focusses on the transition economies in Central and Eastern Europe, notably Bulgaria as a country that entered the EU relatively late and is thus in a later stage of mobility transition compared to other emigration countries such as Poland. As the literature review on

CEE countries and the qualitative case study data on Bulgarian migrants indicate, post-accession migration from and to Bulgaria has developed the same characteristics as in other post-accession countries in terms of the dynamics of the migration processes as well as the composition of migrant groups, their behaviour and experiences. Since migrants usually are positively selected regarding age and education, their loss could be perceived as brain drain. However, as the interviews illustrate, most emigrants are generally willing to return, notably for social reasons. While return is sometimes performed as a spontaneous practice, potential returnees are sometimes held back by the anticipation of adverse conditions for remigration and reintegration.

Both phenomena need to be addressed in terms of policy implications: spontaneous returns, as research shows, are rather poorly prepared and can thus lead to initial hardship and disappointment. The stage of preparedness is crucial for effective reintegration into the labour market. Accompanying measures should be developed to support returnees' re-employment and efficient utilization of foreign work experience in the home country's labour market. Such measures can especially benefit those returnees with a low level of preparedness. Moreover, measures need to address not only economic but also social issues and start while potential returnees are still abroad, using the same information channels as migrants, such as social media, television and direct communication in (professional) networks.

Regarding the case of potential returnees, policy makers should be aware of the large mismatch between opportunities in the home countries' labour markets and expectations of migrants. As this research has shown, information and support are mainly provided by NGOs in the Bulgarian case, while state initiatives have remained invisible. It appears that there is a certain need for raising awareness of return policies and return support initiatives in order to make existing return initiatives more efficient in reaching the target population.

Particularly in the context of the transnationalization of migration, it is important for institutions in the sending countries to maintain and support connections to those who have emigrated in order to disseminate credible information about return options and to offer support mechanisms. In the post-industrial age and in an economy which entered the European economic space relatively late, the increasing relevance of knowledge economies can be an opportunity for Bulgaria. The case study shows that most migrants consider emigration decisions not as definite. They feel a strong connection to their country of origin and to family members and friends who live there. Many can imagine returning for social reasons and are willing to accept less favourable economic conditions in this case, at least in the beginning. The qualitative data demonstrates that a high life satisfaction can be achieved also on the basis of a comparatively low income, given the lower cost of living in Bulgaria in comparison to Western Europe.

For the young, well-educated migrants who want to pursue a professional career in Bulgaria, the presence of international companies means an opportunity to implement their intercultural skills and achieve good positions. However, many are also interested in other values for their personality development and find the right environment in Bulgaria to realize post-materialistic values or to implement their own business ideas at comparatively low risk. This is especially the case in the knowledge sector, which is fuelled by the relatively good digital infrastructure in the country.

As Cerase (1974) with his empirically grounded returnee typology shows, entrepreneurial and innovative activities of returnees (return of innovation) can only be expected for a certain proportion of returnees. The empirical research has revealed that some of the young and highly qualified emigrants are ready to invest their knowledge, which they have acquired throughout the migratory trajectory, in Bulgaria. Moreover, they bring entrepreneurial spirit to the country.

The assessment of Bulgaria's framework for returning graduates leads to ambivalent results. On the one hand, public institutions are weak and to a certain degree also corrupt and non-transparent, which hampers a smooth return in economic terms. On the other hand, the country apparently offers more niches for creative development and the implementation of novelties than more saturated economies. Regarding the ex-post-evaluation of return decisions, it is important to note that most returnees were at the beginning of their professional career and thus appreciated the opportunities for professional advancement in the economic landscape that was offered by Bulgarian economy, notably by the presence of international companies which largely absorbed the returnees. At this early point in working life, income development was a minor issue for most of the returnees. However, and this was clearly articulated by the more advanced returnees, the middle-income-trap is a relevant concern and may at a certain point in life shift the balance towards re-emigration decisions into a higher income country.

**Birgit Glorius** is Professor of Human Geography with a focus on European migration research at Chemnitz University of Technology, Germany. Her research interests and the majority of her publications are in the fields of international migration, demographic change and geographies of education; her regional research focus is on Germany and Central and Eastern Europe. Her recent projects focused on divergences of the Common European Asylum System, on local reception processes of asylum seekers in rural regions and on circulatory migration processes between Eastern and Western Europe, especially student migration and the question of knowledge transfer.

## Notes

1. The research which led to this chapter was financed by the German Research Foundation under grant number GL 683/3–1.
2. Interviews were conducted in Bulgarian or German and transcribed and translated into English by the author. Underlined words represent agitated speech. Pseudonyms have been used in order to protect the identity of the interviewees.

## References

Anacka, Marta, Ewa Matejko and Joanna Nestorowicz. 2013. 'Ready to Move: Liquid Return to Poland'. In *Mobility in Transition: Migration Patterns after EU Enlargement*, edited by Birgit Glorius, Izabella Grabowska-Lusinska and Aimee Kuvik, 277–307. Amsterdam: Amsterdam University Press.

Cassarino, Jean-Pierre. 2004. 'Theorising Return Migration: A Revisited Conceptual Approach to Return Migrants'. EUI Working Paper RSCAS No. 2004/02. Florence: EUI.

Cerase, Francesco P. 1974. 'Expectations and Reality: A Case Study of Return Migration from the United States to Southern Italy'. *International Migration Review* 8(26) (Summer): 245–62.

Coniglio, Nicola Daniele, and Jan Brzozowski. 2018. 'Migration and Development at Home: Bitter or Sweet Return? Evidence from Poland'. *European Urban and Regional Studies* 25(1): 85–105.

De Haas, Hein. 2007. 'Remittances, Migration and Social Development: A Conceptual Review of the Literature.' Social Policy and Development Programme Paper Number 34. Geneva: United Nations Research Department for Social Development (UNRISD).

Dreher, Axel, and Panu Poutvaara. 2011. 'Foreign Students and Migration to the United States'. *World Development* 39(8): 1294–1307.

Dustmann, Christian. 2001. 'Why Go Back? Return Motives of Migrant Workers'. In *International Migration: Trends, Policies and Economic Impact*, Vol. 3, edited by Slobodan Djajic, 229–49. London: Routledge.

Eade, John, Stephen Drinkwater and Michal Garapich. 2006. *Class and Ethnicity: Polish Migrants in London 1996–2006*. Research report for ERSC, Centre for Research on Nationalism, Ethnicity and Multiculturalism (CRONEM). Guildford: University of Surrey.

Engbersen, Godfried, and Erik Snel. 2013. 'Liquid Migration. Dynamic and Fluid Patterns of Post-Accession Migration Flows'. In *Mobility in Transition: Migration Patterns after EU Enlargement*, edited by Birgit Glorius, Izabella Grabowska-Lusinska and Aimee Kuvik, 21–40. Amsterdam: Amsterdam University Press.

Geddie, Kate. 2013. 'The Transnational Ties that Bind: Relationship Considerations for Graduating International Science and Engineering Research Students'. *Population, Space and Place* 19(2): 196–208.

Ghimire, Anita, and Kabin Maharjan. 2015. 'Student Returnees and Their Reflection on Contribution to Nepal: Use of Knowledge and Skills'. *Migration and Development* 4(1): 90–107.

Gibson, John, and David McKenzie. 2009. 'The Microeconomic Determinants of Emigration and Return Migration of the Best and Brightest: Evidence from the Pacific'. IZA Discussion Paper Series No. 3926. Bonn: The Institute for the Study of Labor.

Glorius, Birgit, Izabella Grabowska-Lusinska and Aimee Kuvik. 2013. 'Introduction'. In *Mobility in Transition: Migration Patterns after EU Enlargement*, edited by Birgit Glorius, Izabella Grabowska-Lusinska and Aimee Kuvik, 7–17. Amsterdam: Amsterdam University Press.

Karolak, Mateusz. 2020. 'Returning for (Dis)Integration in the Labour Market? The Careers of Labour Migrants Returning to Poland from the United States'. In: *Politics of (Dis)Integration*, edited by Sophie Hinger and Reinhard Schweitzer, 101–20. IMISCOE Research Series. Cham: Springer.

Klein-Hitpaß, Katrin. 2016. 'Return Migrants as Knowledge Brokers and Institutional Innovators: New Theoretical Conceptualisations and the Example of Poland'. In *Return Migration and Regional Development in Europe Mobility against the Stream*, edited by Robert Nadler, Zoltán Kovács, Birgit Glorius and Thilo Lang, 55–81. London: Palgrave McMillan.

Kley, Stefanie. 2011. 'Explaining the Stages of Migration within a Life-Course Framework'. *European Sociological Review* 27(4): 469–86.

Kovács, Zoltan, Lajos Boros, Lados Hegedűs and Gábor Lados. 2013. 'Returning People to the Homeland: Tools and Methods Supporting Remigrants in a European Context'. In *Return Migration in Central Europe: Current Trends and an Analysis of Policies Supporting Returning Migrants*, edited by Thilo Lang, 58–94. Forum IfL 21. Leipzig: Leibniz-Institut für Länderkunde e.V. (IfL).

Lang, Thilo, Aline Hämmerling, Stefan Haunstein, Jan Keil, Robert Nadler, Anika Schmidt and Stefanie Smoliner. 2014. '"Migrants" Capacities and Expectations: Empirical Results Concerning Return Migration'. In *Return Migration to Central and Eastern Europe: Transnational Migrants' Perspectives and Local Businesses' Needs*, edited by Thilo Lang and Robert Nadler, 7–46. Forum IfL 23. Leipzig: Leibniz-Institut für Länderkunde e.V. (IfL).

Le Bail, Hélène, and Wei Shen. 2008. 'The Return of the "Brains" to China: What are the Social, Economic and Political Impacts?' *Asie Visions* 11. Paris and Brussel: Centre Asie Ifri. Retrieved 8 January 2021 from https://www.ifri.org/sites/default/files/atoms/files/AV11_ENG.pdf.

McCollum, David, Elina Apsite-Berina, Maris Berzins and Zaiga Krisjane. 2017. 'Overcoming the Crisis: The Changing Profile and Trajectories of Latvian Migrants. *Journal of Ethnic and Migration Studies* 43(9): 1508–25.

McCollum, David, and Alan Findlay. 2015. '"Flexible" Workers for "Flexible" Jobs? The Labour Market Function of A8 Migrant Labour in the UK'. *Work, Employment & Society* 29(3): 427–43.

McCollum, David, Segei Shubin, Elina Apsite and Zaiga Krisjane. 2013. 'Rethinking Labour Migration Channels: The Experience of Latvia from EU Accession to Economic Recession'. *Population, Space and Place* 19(6): 688–702.

Nadler, Robert, and Thilo Lang. 2014. 'Introduction'. In *Return Migration to Central and Eastern Europe: Transnational Migrants' Perspectives and Local Businesses' Needs* edited by Thilo Lang and Robert Nadler, 5–6. Forum IfL 23. Leipzig: Leibniz-Institut für Länderkunde e.V. (IfL).

OECD (Organisation for Economic Co-operation and Development). 2008. 'International Migration Outlook 2008'. Paris: SOPEMI-Continuous Reporting System on Migration.

Okólski, Marek. 2001. 'Incomplete Migration: A New Form of Mobility in Central and Eastern Europe. The Case of Polish and Ukrainian Migrants'. In *Patterns of Migration in Central Europe*, edited by Claire Wallace and Dariusz Stola, 105–28. Basingstoke: Palgrave Macmillan.

Pietka, Emilia, Colin Clark and Noah Canton. 2013. '"I Know that I Have a University Diploma and I'm Working as a Driver" Explaining the EU Post-Enlargement Movement of Highly Skilled Polish Migrant Workers to Glasgow'. In *Mobility in Transition: Migration Patterns after EU Enlargement*, edited by Birgit Glorius, Izabella Grabowska-Lusinska and Aimee Kuvik, 133–54. Amsterdam: Amsterdam University Press.

Pratsinakis, Manolis, Panos Hatziprokopiou, Dimitris Grammatikas and Lois Labrianidis. 2017. 'Crisis and the Resurgence of Emigration from Greece: Trends, Representations, and the Multiplicity of Migrant Trajectories'. In *European Mobility in Times of Crisis – The New Context of European South-North Migration*, edited by Birgit Glorius and Josefina Dominguez-Mujica, 75–102. Bielefeld: Transcript.

Predojevic-Despic, Jelena, Tanja Pavlow, Svetlana Milutinovic and Brikena Balli. 2016. 'Transnational Entrepreneurship in the Western Balkans: A Comparative Study of Serbian and Albanian Migrants and Returnees'. In *Return Migration and Regional Development in Europe: Mobility Against the Stream*, edited by Birgit Glorius, Thilo Lang, Robert Nadler and Zoltán Kovács, 111–27. London: Palgrave McMillan.

Republic of Bulgaria National Statistical Institute. 2018. 'International Migration by Age and Citizenship of Migrants'. Retrieved 13 January 2021 from http://www.nsi.bg/en/content/13040/international-migration-age-and-citizenship-migrants.

Smoliner, Stefanie, Michael Förschner, Josef Hochgerner and Jana Nová. 2013. 'Comparative Report on Remigration Trends in Central and Eastern Europe'. In *Return Migration in Central Europe: Current Trends and an Analysis of Policies Supporting Returning Migrants*, edited by Thilo Lang, 11–57. Forum IfL 21. Leipzig: Leibniz-Institut für Länderkunde e.V. (IfL).

Trevena, Paulina. 2013. 'Why do Highly Educated Migrants Go for Low-Skilled Jobs? A Case Study of Polish Graduates Working in London'. In *Mobility in Transition: Migration Patterns after EU Enlargement*, edited by Birgit Glorius, Izabella Grabowska-Lusinska and Aimee Kuvik, 169–90. Amsterdam: Amsterdam University Press.

Wingens, Matthias, Michael Windzio, Helga de Valk and Can Aybek. 2011. *A Life-Course Perspective on Migration and Integration*. Dordrecht: Springer.

Wolfeil, Nina. 2013. 'Translators of Knowledge? Labour Market Positioning of Young Poles Returning from Studies Abroad in Germany'. In *Mobility in Transition: Migration Patterns after EU Enlargement*, edited by Birgit Glorius, Izabella Grabowska-Lusinska and Aimee Kuvik, 259–76. Amsterdam: Amsterdam University Press.

World Bank. 2004. 'Tertiary Education in Poland'. Report No. 29718. Retrieved 13 January 2021 from http://documents1.worldbank.org/curated/en/452921468299045483/pdf/297180ESW0PL0w1ryEducation01PUBLIC1.pdf.

Zaicev, Anzelika, and Klaus F. Zimmerman. 2012. 'Returning Home at Times of Trouble? Return Migration of EU Enlargement Migrants during the Crisis'. IZA Discussion Paper Series No. 7111. Bonn: The Institute for the Study of Labor. Retrieved 8 December 2021 from http://ftp.iza.org/dp7111.pdf.

# PART III

# The Impact of European Integration

CHAPTER 6
# The Winners and Losers of Economic Openness
*Eastern Europe's Growth Path Post-1989*

Kiril Kossev

## Introduction: Economic Openness as a Path to Convergence

Economic openness has been the critical dimension of the growth path undertaken by the former command economies in Eastern Europe since 1989. Openness and global interactions have had profound direct effects on their economic development. Internationalisation has taken the form of both entry into global markets – sequenced opening up to trade and financial flows – and gradual integration and eventual membership into Western economic governance institutions. The latter has shaped significantly domestic policies and set the key elements of the open markets economic reform agenda, as well as increased economic prosperity. Importantly, this move towards market-oriented economies and openness has been translated into economic success, in particular by those countries that were best able to integrate their economic potential and political institutions with the value chains and institutions of the West.

This success, however, has been neither unqualified nor complete. Linking to global economic and financial patterns has contributed to domestic volatility within the Eastern European Economies. Destruction of pre-1989 industrial centres and trade links, limited demand for existing skills and considerable arbitrage opportunities for insiders have resulted in regional economic disparities, as well as sharp income inequalities. These have produced groups that do not identify as economic winners from the transition. Large-scale migration has opened new channels of skills and money flows, but it has also contributed to a growing demographic problem and increasing skill shortage in Eastern Europe underpinned by outward migration. Increasingly, economic openness and the associated financial and technological transfers from abroad appear to have met their limit as drivers of growth. Macroeconomic convergence appears to be slowing down and the Central and Eastern European economies may need to change their growth model to avoid entering a middle-income trap – a situation of economic stagnation once a certain level of income is attained.

Some thirty years ago the former centrally planned economies of the Soviet bloc embarked on a road to openness, often from a very high degree of economic autarky. The economic transition urgently needed access to foreign technology and expertise as technological underdevelopment was widely recognized as one of the weakest points of the previous system. They also desperately needed access to capital. In most Eastern European countries, the domestic market size was relatively small. Without linking to global value chains – the new mode of international trade focused on complex high technology products and was underpinned by narrower specialization and larger-scale production – they could not benefit from the gains the global market economy could generate. Foreign trade has fostered new production links and flows that generated new skill sets and promoted economic efficiency, while foreign direct investment has created channels for fresh capital but also technologies and modern corporate and managerial expertise. Entry into international institutions, like the World Trade Organization, the European Union and the Organization for Economic Cooperation and Development (OECD), served to quicken the process of reform and entrench its various strands.

Such openness, however, came at a price. Many of the new market economies experienced balance-of-payments crises, exposure to Western financial volatility and widening economic inequalities. The sharp global crisis of 2008/09, for example, transmitted directly into Eastern European financial systems. This was in contrast, to the early banking crises of the 1990s that impacted Eastern European economies and had more to do with domestic institutional and corporate governance difficulties. The closing down of old and uncompetitive centres of heavy industry, soon after 1989, and their eventual substitution with modern manufacturing clusters that are a component of the Western European value chains created one-directional migration patterns coupled with generational and regional income disparities. This was particularly noticeable with wealth and opportunities conspicuously concentrated in metropolitan areas and a select few other large urban centres. Piecemeal removal of trade barriers (among other pro-market reforms of the early transition period), often as a result of internal political bargaining rather than concerns for economic efficiency, allowed for arbitrage and helped small groups of insiders to amass fortunes, further concentrating wealth and economic opportunities (Hellman 1998; Frye and Mansfield 2003).

The growth model, ultimately aimed at convergence with Western living standards, was based on open trade and reliant on foreign investment and technological transfer. It has been successful in overcoming the sharp downturns of the 1990s and starting a period of convergence to the Western European economies. This process of catch-up growth has been slowing down since the years of the Global Financial Crisis. There is a real danger of the Eastern European economies entering a middle-income trap. This economic condition is characterized by a competitive advantage in low-technology and low-value exports, concentrated product specialization at the high technological end, large disparities in income and wealth, labour force that lacks dynamism and human capital that is not (re)generated on a broad basis across the working population. The latter would preclude the creation of numerous innovative economic centres and 'graduating' to a knowledge-based high-income economy (Im and Rosenblatt 2013).

The region must tackle the underlying inefficiencies of unbalanced growth and newly created inequalities and must seek to reinvigorate its economic institutions. This means devising a new growth model that is mindful of regional disparities, can find an economic place for those that have been left behind by the early transition, and provides an incentive to keep institutional modernization reform going. This will assist the Central and Eastern European countries to avoid falling into the middle-income trap and experiencing a long-term economic stagnation.

## The Legacy of Command Economies: A Heavy Burden to Carry

The model of command and planned economies in the Soviet Union and Eastern Europe ran to a grinding halt by the end of the 1980s and in part precipitated the destruction of the totalitarian political order in these countries (Gros and Steinherr 2004). This economic model was defined by a high degree of autarky – that is, of self-sufficiency in the production of goods and services. Foreign trade turnover tended to be low relative to GDP, foreign investment was in most times and places either non-existent or strictly controlled, and – until a relatively late stage – foreign debt was very low. This was an essential feature of the planned economies; at least in those countries where the system remained relatively close to the Soviet model (Kornai 1996).

In the first instance, communist economic planners could not hope to plan the domestic economy unless they also controlled cross-border flows. Therefore, a foreign trade monopoly was required at a minimum. Since the planners likewise lacked control over prices and flows abroad, there was also an incentive to minimize this exposure by limiting foreign trade and thus reducing the economy's exposure to external developments. This autarkic tendency was reinforced by geopolitics: Western restrictions on trade with the Communist bloc and their own reluctance to rely on Western goods and services (Gros and Steinherr 2004). Even within the communist bloc, foreign economic relations tended to be planned, with political considerations rather than economic gain often dominating decision-makers' priorities.

At a microlevel, planning arrangements meant that foreign trade was unattractive to most firms. For industrial managers, this involved considerable bureaucratic hassles and would not necessarily have been more 'profitable' (Holzman 1976; Gros and Steinherr 2004). Their primary motivation and obligation were plan fulfilment, not profitability. Distorted price signals served to conceal the costs and distributional impacts of autarky, as did the use of multiple exchange rates for different types of transactions and the panoply of foreign currency controls that the system of multiple exchange rates entailed.

There were partial exceptions to the general rule of autarky, as some countries – most notably Poland, Hungary and Yugoslavia – began to experiment with greater international openness well before 1989. This process facilitated some post-communist reforms but also entailed certain costs. Poland, for example, experienced prolonged difficulties in managing its foreign debt from the second half of the 1970s. Its indebtedness had made it increasingly dependent upon Western banks and financial institutions and in 1986, it joined the IMF and was required to introduce a series of structural reforms in order find resources to pay its debt –this marked an early start on transition (Rae 2016). Hungary, too, borrowed heavily in the 1970s and 1980s in an effort to sustain consumption, a path that caused it considerable difficulty in the 1990s when the burden of debt service added substantially to its current account deficit (Kornai 1996).

This lack of integration into the wider world economy did help to largely shield communist economies from fluctuations in international markets and from the ups and downs of the capitalist business cycle. It is probably no coincidence that Poland, one of the pioneers of international integration within the then-communist bloc, was the only Eastern bloc country to experience a recession before 1989.

However, there were also drawbacks, particularly in respect to the lack of learning, innovation and technology acquisition. Romer (1993) argues that the failure to exchange ideas rather than the failure to trade objects may have cost the centrally planned economies, since this cut them off from access to foreign expertise in respect to production, marketing, packaging, distribution, inventory, quality control and others – all critical to economic efficiency and dynamism. Even in areas where they were able to import advanced Western technologies, Eastern countries generally found it hard to use them as productively as their Western rivals did, let alone to diffuse them. In the view of many observers, they needed Western management systems more than Western goods or technologies (Brainard 1981).

Internationalisation (opening the domestic economy to global flows and interactions, following reforms consistent with the economic norms and rules recommended by international economic institutions) was thus an essential component of the post-communist transition and was seen as such from the start, even if countries varied somewhat in the speed with which they progressed on different dimensions of openness (Frye 2010). The transition economies greatly needed access to foreign technology and knowledge – technological backwardness was widely recognized as one of the weak points of the old system – as well as access to capital. Moreover, in most countries, the domestic market size was fairly small. Without international trade, they could not benefit from the gains that narrower specialization and larger-scale production could generate. Additionally, while pre-transition trade was limited, the breakdown of the old system in many places served to disrupt important production chains that had to be reconnected or replaced. This was particularly evident in the former Soviet Union and ex-Yugoslavia, where a great deal of domestic trade became foreign trade more or less overnight.

Finally, it is important to recognize that international integration reinforced other reforms – or at least raised the political costs of backsliding on them. For example, foreign direct investment created new constituencies concerned with clear, secure property rights and efficient institutions, while foreign trade quickly created new production links and flows that would be costly to disrupt. Entry into international institutions, likewise, served to entrench various strands of domestic institutional and policy reforms. Openness, however, would also come at a price: many of the new market economies experienced balance-of-payments or financial crises as well as persistent challenges with growing disparities in productivity within country regions, accompanied by increasing income and wealth inequality.

## Economic Convergence during the Transition: A Story Awaiting Completion

Economic convergence was underpinned by the opening up of economies to Western market economies, through a process of internationalisation or integration into a globalized open economy. The aim was to reap economic efficiency gains from the transformation to competitive open markets and eventually converge with the Western economies, which were already driven by complex industrial and knowledge products.

However, this was not a linear process. The 1990s were a volatile and crisis-prone decade for every country in Eastern Europe, where rapid growth in unemployment because of the destruction of old industrial centres was coupled with banking and financial crises. By 2000, almost all of the Eastern European countries had achieved macroeconomic stabilization and began on the path of economic catch-up with the West. The Central European and the Baltic economies saw the most success because of their export-led growth model which itself was fuelled by proximity to the industrial heartland of Western Europe. Other less successful economies, like those in Southeast Europe, adopted the same model, but suffered from poorer economic geography or natural resource endowment (as discussed in greater detail below). This catch-up growth was disrupted by the Global Financial Crisis of 2008/09, which caused considerable damage to the small open economies in the Baltics, and those economies connected to global finance and value-chain trade in Central and Southeast Europe (Kossev and Tompson 2020).

With economic growth slowing down, it appears that the early efficiency gains made as a result of transitioning to market economies (removing price and wage controls, loosening border restrictions, liberalising currency and financial markets, among others) and macroeconomic stabilization (following successful currency and exchange rate reforms, and setting up appropriate institutions for fiscal and financial market supervision) may have dissipated. Yet, convergence to the income levels of the Western economies has also not been achieved yet.

Figure 6.1 and Table 6.1, below, illustrate the growth rate of GDP of Eastern European economies, as compared to the growth rate of the Eurozone and the European Union. The decline in rapid catch-up growth is visible when comparing the two periods 2000–2007 and 2011–19. The early 2000s represented a period of rapid and stable growth. For example, the fastest growing Baltic countries grew over 9 percent per year on average or over six times faster than the Eurozone countries over the same period. Following sharp declines in the growth rate during the period of the Global Financial Crisis (2008–10 in Table 6.1), the recovery and the return to positive growth has been increasingly volatile and weak. The Baltic economies, again the fastest growing Eastern European economies, have been able to achieve growth rates that were four times faster than those of the Eurozone. However, the other regions have slowed down significantly in absolute terms and in relative terms in comparison to the growth rate of the Eurozone.

These growth rates have not been sufficient in closing the gap with the rich economies of the industrialized West, as illustrated by the levels of

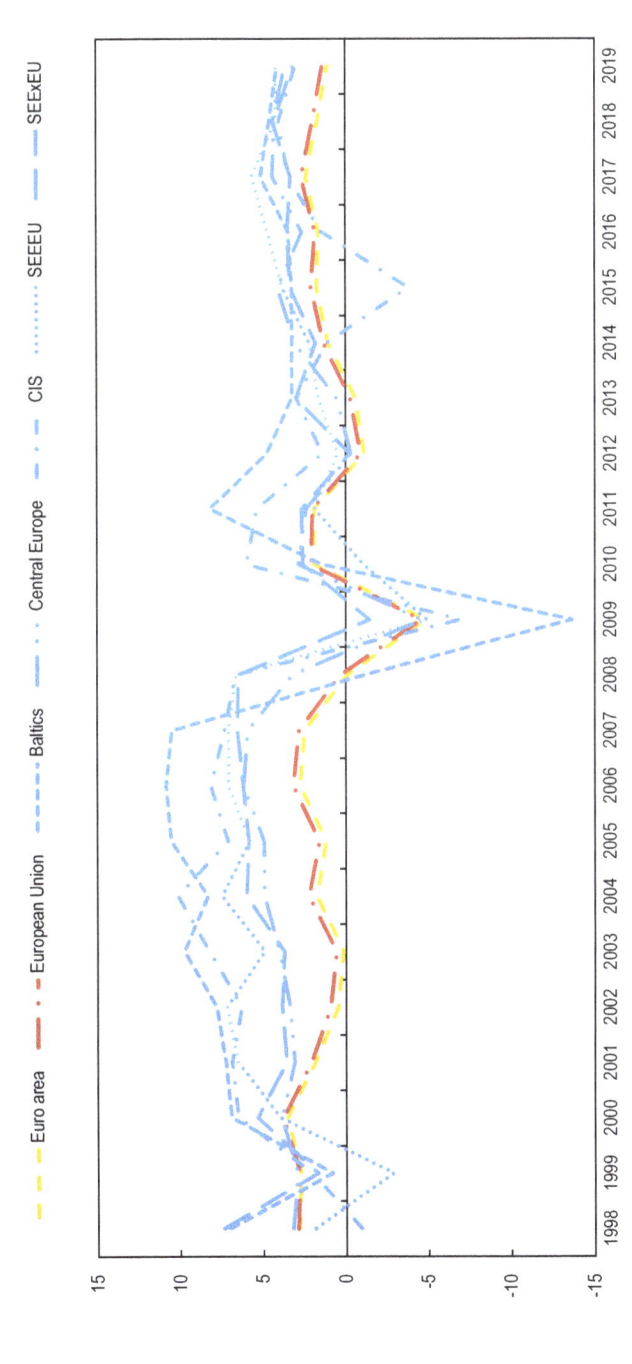

**Figure 6.1.** GDP growth rates across Eastern Europe and the former Soviet Union as compared to the industrialized Western market economies (GDP per capita growth, annual percentage, 1998–2019).[1] Source: World Bank Data. Created by the author.

**Table 6.1.** GDP growth rates across Eastern Europe and the former Soviet Union as compared to the industrialized Western market economies (GDP per capita growth, average annual percentage, 1998–2019).

|  | 1998–2000 | 2001–2007 | 2008–2010 | 2011–2019 |
|---|---|---|---|---|
| **Euro area** | 3.0 | 1.5 | −1.0 | 1.1 |
| **European Union** | 3.1 | 1.9 | −0.7 | 1.3 |
| **Baltics (average)** | 4.9 | 9.3 | −4.5 | 4.4 |
| Estonia | 4.7 | 8.3 | −5.4 | 3.9 |
| Lithuania | 4.1 | 9.3 | −2.1 | 5.0 |
| Latvia | 5.9 | 10.2 | −5.8 | 4.4 |
| **Central Europe (average)** | 3.3 | 4.6 | 0.5 | 2.7 |
| Czech Republic | 1.8 | 4.5 | −0.4 | 2.2 |
| Hungary | 4.1 | 4.0 | −1.3 | 3.3 |
| Poland | 5.0 | 4.1 | 3.7 | 3.7 |
| Slovak Republic | 1.7 | 6.4 | 1.9 | 2.5 |
| Slovenia | 4.0 | 4.1 | −1.4 | 1.8 |
| **CIS (average)** | 2.5 | 7.7 | 1.9 | 2.1 |
| Belarus | 6.4 | 8.7 | 6.3 | 1.2 |
| Moldova | -2.5 | 6.4 | 3.1 | 4.8 |
| Russian Federation | 4.0 | 7.2 | 0.6 | 1.3 |
| Ukraine | 2.2 | 8.6 | −2.4 | 1.0 |
| **SEE, EU (average)** | 1.0 | 6.6 | 0.2 | 3.2 |
| Bulgaria | 0.8 | 7.2 | 1.8 | 3.2 |
| Croatia | 1.9 | 5.2 | −2.1 | 1.9 |
| Romania | 0.2 | 7.3 | 1.0 | 4.4 |
| **SEE, non-EU (average)** | 4.8 | 5.1 | 2.5 | 2.8 |
| Albania | 10.3 | 6.5 | 5.5 | 2.7 |
| Bosnia and Herzegovina | 10.1 | 5.6 | 1.6 | 3.5 |
| North Macedonia | 3.5 | 2.9 | 2.7 | 2.4 |
| Montenegro | −0.2 | 3.9 | 1.2 | 2.8 |
| Serbia | 0.4 | 6.5 | 1.6 | 2.6 |

Source: World Bank Data.

*Note:* Euro Area and the European Union represent the averages for the member countries of these respective institutions.

GDP in Figures 6.2 and 6.3. These illustrate the growth path of GDP levels and labour productivity across Eastern Europe and the former Soviet Union, as compared to the industrialized Western market economies (since 1990 in Figure 6.2 and 2001 in Figure 6.3). They show the overall path of gradual convergence up until the Global Financial Crisis and a stalling of the catch-up process thereafter (Zuk and Savelin 2018, who also provide further evidence of the slowdown). The story is more nuanced and differs between individual countries.

A growth slowdown upon reaching a middle-income status has been linked to entering into the middle-income trap, where further growth trajectory remains low and precludes economies from achieving high-income status (Eichengreen, Park and Shin 2011, 2013). Eichengreen, Park and Shin (2013) have provided estimates of two possible modes of economic growth slowdown – one in the $10,000–$11,000 range and another at $15,000–$16,0000 (where the estimates are in 2005 purchasing power parity, US dollars per capita). Figure 6.2, below, suggests that the wealthier Baltic and Central European economies may currently be around the second income band, while the Southeast European (EU members) remain around the first one. The rest of the Eastern European economies are yet to grow towards such income levels. While the precision of such income per capita bands across the large global sample used may be questioned as further empirical work is conducted, the identification of multiple slowdown points is relevant to the Eastern European economies that are promoting pro-growth reforms. Of increasing relevance are the reasons for falling into a middle-income trap identified by Eichengreen et al. (2013); Felipe, Abdon and Kumar (2012); and Aiyar et al. (2013), among others: not being able to progress up the technology ladder and/or exporting a large share of low-technology products; relatively low levels of secondary and tertiary education among the population; concentration in product specialization leading to an undiversified economy. Furthermore, a report by the European Commission (2020) has emphasized the regional nature of the middle-income trap, where economic stagnation happens at a sub-national level and has a negative effect on country-level growth. Regions that experience lengthy periods of low growth and are in danger of never realizing high-income status, tend to broadly suffer from the characteristics described above.

The process of internationalisation described below and the evidence provided, highlights the slowdown experienced by the Eastern European economies. Integration into Western trade value chains have brought fruitful returns for the more successful Eastern European economies, while others have had a more difficult convergence path. However, the early gains have been spread thinly and the resulting disparities in income, employment, education, and growth opportunities are especially evident in

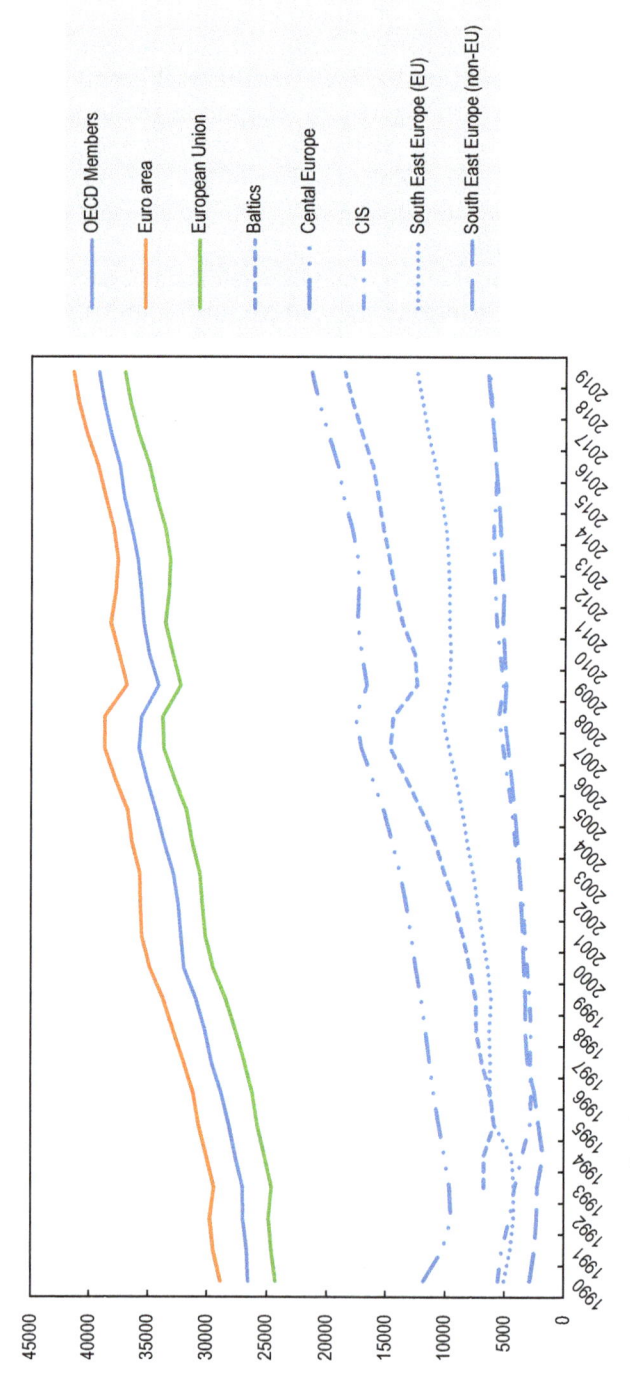

**Figure 6.2.** GDP levels across Eastern Europe and the former Soviet Union as compared to the industrialized Western market economies (GDP per capita, constant 2010 US dollars, 1990–2019).[2] Source: World Bank Data. Created by the author.

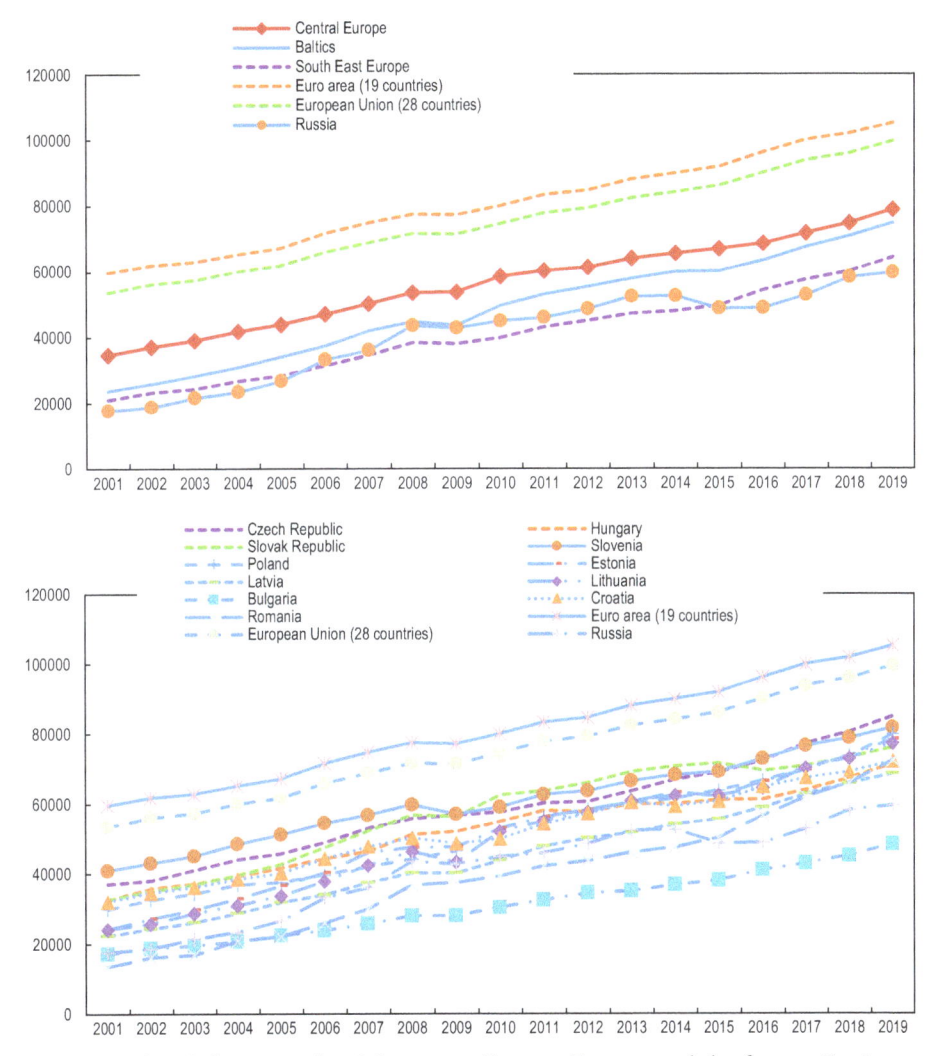

THE WINNERS AND LOSERS OF ECONOMIC OPENNESS        *179*

**Figure 6.3.** Labour productivity across Eastern Europe and the former Soviet Union in comparison to the industrialized Western market economies (GDP per person employed, US dollars, constant prices, constant PPP, base year 2015).[3] Source: OECD data. Created by the author.

intra-country or regional disparities. Large parts of the Eastern European economies are left behind and are a drag on growth (and also generate dangerous political forces like populism, which can itself cause further growth impediments), as the middle-income trap hypothesis illustrates. Early rapid growth has not yet brought Eastern European economies on par with the income levels or institutional development of the West. However, it has concentrated economic success only into some sectors and brought about Western levels of economic inequality. To complete the convergence process and reach the high incomes of the West, a new economic growth model will need to be inclusive of the groups and regions left behind by spreading novel technologies and the broadening of knowledge sectors. This storyline is demonstrated in the analytical narrative below.

*Note:* Euro Area and the European Union represent the averages for the member countries of these respective institutions.

\* \* \*

There are a number of different processes ongoing behind the concepts of 'internationalisation' and 'integration' and various Eastern European countries have pursued these at different speeds and in different combinations, at times with important links among them.

The economic literature assessing Eastern European internationalisation patterns and their success has focused on the effects of investment inflows and trade linkages, resulting in technological transfer and productivity gains. Persuasive evidence has been brought forward by studies tracing the positive productivity impact of foreign direct investment. Djankov and Hoekman (2000) provide evidence of the positive productivity gains from foreign direct investment during the 1990s in the Czech Republic, through the channel of technological transfer and improvements in the local firms. Bijsterbosch and Kolasa (2009) have similarly provided evidence for productivity gains and a catch-up growth in Central and Eastern Europe fuelled by technological diffusion and economic efficiency improvements brought about by capital inflows from the West. Developing successful trade relationships also often depended on foreign capital inflows and collaboration with multinationals. Myant and Drahokoupil (2012) observe that success in exporting complex products from Eastern Europe was almost entirely dependent on the involvement of foreign-owned multinationals, which in turn often depended on geographical proximity and/or close cultural and historical ties. Trade and investment policies were thus closely linked, as were institutional, geographic and historical preconditions.

Kossev and Tompson (2020) follow up this storyline by suggesting that the opening up of Eastern European economies proceeded through four main channels – the liberalization of trade, opening up of financial markets, allowing a movement of people, and integration and adherence to international institutional structures. Along these channels, there were different modes of success and some Eastern European countries fared better than others. Migration of people, mostly outward from Eastern Europe and into the West was a feature of all transition countries. The successes (as will be argued further and illustrated by the patterns in Tables 6.2 and 6.4) were underpinned by longer-term historical path dependence. This entailed the attraction of foreign investment and integration into complex Western trade value chains dependent on geographical and historical ties, which in turn supported institutional integration.

There were (and in some cases still are) significant differences in the speed and extent of change with respect to the dimensions of post-1989 economic growth and internationalisation. This variation was far from random: on the contrary, it is possible to identify a number of distinct patterns of integration. Although there is considerable heterogeneity within groups and some countries that are hard to classify, several broad themes stand out. Table 6.2 provides a rather general classification to allow for

**Table 6.2.** Patterns of economic openness and integration into the globalized market economy post-1989.

|  |  | Gradually open borders, entry into trade, services, migration flows ||
|---|---|---|---|
|  |  | Trade and / or integration into export value chains | Outward migration and / or reliance on remittances |
| Starting endowments of countries | Reliant on or rich on natural resource endowments | Commodity-rich countries of the former Soviet Union, focused on exporting hydrocarbons (Azerbaijan, Kazakhstan, Turkmenistan), metals (Ukraine), or both (Russia). | Southeast European countries, and especially those in the Western Balkan, traded less complex products and reliant on migration and remittances. |
|  | Limited natural resource endowment | Central European economies attracting considerable foreign direct investment and integrating into larger value chains as suppliers of relatively complex goods (Czech Republic, Hungary, Poland, Slovakia). Partially true for Southeast European Countries that eventually gained membership into the EU (Bulgaria, Croatia, Romania). | Countries from the former Soviet space in the Caucasus, Central Asia. |

Source: author's interpretation of patterns of economic openness and integration.

some patterns of the economic models of growth and openness to be identified. There is an important caveat that the boundaries between the four boxes are in fact blurry. Some of the characteristics describing the starting endowments of the various countries or the economic model that describes them, may be shared to various degrees across the groups. For example, gradual openness (to trade, financial services and flows, and people flows) was true for all the countries that emerged from the autarchy of the Soviet-inspired command economy model, although the degrees of variation and the competitive outcomes were also factors. Thus, outward migration was a feature of all the Eastern European economies post-1989. However, in some cases it was the *most* important economic feature of some of the economies such as in the Caucasus. Similarly, some form of natural resource endowment and export of raw materials and/or primary products can be observed across all the economies in the ex-Soviet space. Although, it should be noted that remittances and the export of simple manufactures were more important economic features of the Southeast European economies.

The commodity-rich countries of the former Soviet Union had perhaps the least difficulty in identifying their immediate export opportunities – in particular, the Soviet Union had already been well established as an exporter of hydrocarbons and to a lesser extent metal. Even as oil and metal production in these countries fell sharply for a time in the early 1990s, exports held up relatively well because domestic consumption fell even faster. Broadly speaking, exports of primary products were critical for the Russian Federation (hydrocarbons and metals), for Ukraine (metals), and in the CIS post-Soviet space of Kazakhstan, Azerbaijan and Turkmenistan (exported hydrocarbons). In addition, Estonia, Lithuania and especially Belarus exported petroleum products refined from Russian crude.

The Central European economies, benefiting from proximity to Germany and Austria, moved quickly to reorient their economies towards Western Europe, attracting considerable foreign direct investment and gradually integrating into larger value chains as suppliers of relatively complex goods. In fact, foreign direct investment targeted domestic production aimed at exports and helped link Eastern European products to Western markets. This was especially the case for the Czech Republic, the Slovak Republic, Hungary and, albeit to a lesser degree, Poland. Physical proximity to the heart of the European Union's single market brought other benefits, as it ensured that these countries were a relatively high priority for Western governments seeking to support the transition. This was also coupled with the added ease of accessibility to Western markets and to attract foreign investment, particularly from Germany. The fact that their manufacturing bases were in better shape even at the start of the transition helped them to integrate into German-led supply chains (Roaf et al. 2014; Winiecki 2000).

In other countries within easy reach of Western Europe, trade focused initially on less complex products. Overall, the Balkan countries started in a less promising position than the Central Europeans or even the Baltic states, in terms of economic and political conditions, as well as location. The series of wars that followed the break-up of Yugoslavia, as well as political instability in Albania, Bulgaria and Romania, impeded both domestic reforms and internationalisation throughout the 1990s (Frye 2010). As a result, the exports from this group of countries were dominated by less sophisticated goods and some primary commodities. In many cases, exports were insufficient to cover the cost of imports and they also depended heavily on remittances and access to foreign (often debt) financing. Myant and Drahokoupil (2012) note that countries in this grouping typically had the highest levels of reliance on foreign financing other than FDI: annual financial account inflows less FDI exceeded 10 percent of GDP in the run-up to the global crisis of 2008/09, which Myant and Drahokoupil see as a source of vulnerability.

A large number of economies, particularly in the former Soviet space, were heavily reliant on remittances, exporting labour rather than raw commodities or processed goods. In the case of labour-exporters in Transcaucasia and Central Asia, this implied a high degree of sensitivity to the performance of the receiving economies, particularly the Russian Federation and Kazakhstan. This was true, albeit to a lesser degree, of Central European countries sending workers to Western Europe.

An illustration of the patterns of internationalisation is the Economic Complexity Index, a measure of the relative knowledge intensity of production in specific geographical areas as determined by the export of complex products. Figure 6.4 (and Table 6.3, the index by country) reflect the successful trade links of the Central European economies, which were able to gain competitiveness in complex products or services and find markets in the Western value chains. The Baltics and the Southeast European Economies (EU Members) have also been able to benefit from growing specialization into more complex products with export potential over time. The largest share of this trade has been with Western Europe as a result of the integration of the Eastern European economies into the European Union and its economic sphere (Mann 2015; Eichengreen and Boltho 2008). The least successful when measured in terms of the complexity or knowledge-intensity of their tradeables have been the CIS and the countries from the Western Balkans.

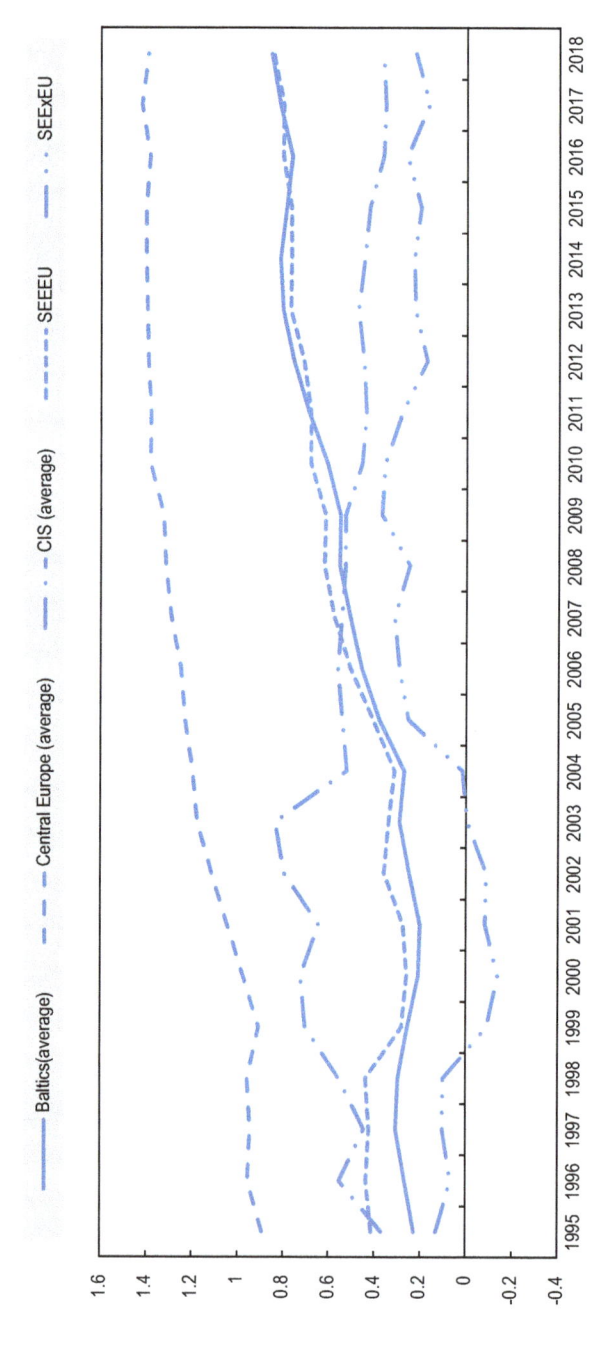

**Figure 6.4.** Economic Complexity Index (index of trade of complex products, 1995–2018).[4] Source: Observatory of Economic Complexity. Created by the author.

**Table 6.3.** Economic complexity index (index of trade of complex products, selected years).

|  | 1995 | 2000 | 2004 | 2008 | 2012 | 2018 |
|---|---|---|---|---|---|---|
| **Baltics** | 0.23 | 0.21 | 0.27 | 0.56 | 0.76 | 0.85 |
| Estonia | 0.33 | 0.30 | 0.38 | 0.66 | 0.91 | 0.99 |
| Lithuania | 0.21 | 0.13 | 0.13 | 0.52 | 0.65 | 0.86 |
| Latvia | 0.14 | 0.21 | 0.30 | 0.49 | 0.71 | 0.71 |
| **Central Europe (average)** | 0.89 | 0.98 | 1.20 | 1.32 | 1.39 | 1.39 |
| Czech Republic | 1.12 | 1.28 | 1.42 | 1.55 | 1.69 | 1.64 |
| Hungary | 0.71 | 0.75 | 1.11 | 1.32 | 1.39 | 1.38 |
| Poland | 0.50 | 0.61 | 0.81 | 0.96 | 1.07 | 1.10 |
| Slovak Republic | 1.03 | 1.08 | 1.09 | 1.25 | 1.26 | 1.27 |
| Slovenia | 1.10 | 1.16 | 1.55 | 1.51 | 1.56 | 1.58 |
| **CIS (average)** | 0.37 | 0.72 | 0.52 | 0.53 | 0.45 | 0.37 |
| Belarus | 0.49 | 0.64 | 0.86 | 0.92 | 0.91 | 0.80 |
| Moldova | 0.00 | 0.00 | −0.21 | 0.05 | 0.00 | −0.12 |
| Russian Federation | 0.30 | 0.89 | 0.75 | 0.56 | 0.38 | 0.34 |
| Ukraine | 0.32 | 0.64 | 0.70 | 0.59 | 0.52 | 0.44 |
| **SEE, EU (average)** | 0.41 | 0.26 | 0.32 | 0.62 | 0.71 | 0.85 |
| Bulgaria | 0.22 | 0.19 | 0.24 | 0.47 | 0.52 | 0.60 |
| Croatia | 0.53 | 0.42 | 0.50 | 0.66 | 0.88 | 0.86 |
| Romania | 0.49 | 0.18 | 0.20 | 0.73 | 0.75 | 1.08 |
| **SEE, non-EU (average)** | 0.13 | −0.14 | 0.02 | 0.25 | 0.18 | 0.23 |
| Albania | 0.00 | 0.00 | 0.00 | 0.10 | −0.30 | −0.40 |
| Bosnia and Herzegovina | 0.00 | 0.00 | 0.26 | 0.42 | 0.51 | 0.49 |
| North Macedonia | 0.13 | −0.14 | −0.22 | −0.09 | −0.05 | 0.18 |
| Serbia | 0.00 | 0.00 | 0.00 | 0.57 | 0.55 | 0.64 |

Source: Observatory of Economic Complexity.

\* \* \*

The disparities *between* the macroeconomic experiences of the post-Soviet bloc countries are also reflected in the important economic disparities *within* these countries. In reality, the two are closely interlinked. The planned economies and the inter-country economic support institution of the Eastern Block, the COMECON, created economic clusters based on artificial incentives and investment flows that were centrally coordinated (Gevorkyan 2018). Once borders were open for competition, many of these clusters lost their markets, and their employees found themselves left out of a job market that no longer needed their obsolete skills. A minority of industrial areas in Eastern Europe benefitted from their geographical proximity to the manufacturing core of the EU and managed to start integrating themselves into its value chains. However, the foreign investment that brought new technologies and updated the plants was concentrated and benefitted only a limited set of workers within certain regions. On the other hand, previously underdeveloped areas found new income streams as a result of tourism, yet again limiting any new investment and new gains to specific regions. Even smaller groups that benefitted substantially from the onset of economic openness and the transition to market economies were the insiders in the process of economic policy making, that drove the direction of the economic transition of their country. They were able to lock in the early arbitrage opportunities of gradual relaxation of domestic price controls, export/import quotas and the panoply of licenses needed for trade and investment, and as a result were able to enrich themselves. Hellman (1998) suggests it was the insiders of the policy-making process and early gainers of transition reform that proceeded to derail reform completion and have thus become a drag on further economic progress: opposition to economic and legal stability came

> from enterprise insiders who have become new owners only to strip their firms' assets; from commercial bankers who have opposed macroeconomic stabilization to preserve their enormously profitable arbitrage opportunities on distorted financial markets; from local officials who have prevented market entry in their regions to protect their share of local monopoly rents; and from super-rich 'mafiosi' who have undermined the creation of a stable legal foundation for the market economy. (Hellman 1998)

Some of the results of these processes were incomplete economic and institutional reforms, concentration – both geographic and sectoral – of successful economic functions, and the concentration of incomes and wealth.

The disparities in the experience of openness and convergence that can be observed within the economies and societies of the East European counties are illustrated in Table 6.4. Gorzelak (2020) proposes a model of mapping the winners and losers of the internationalisation (in terms of geographical regions and the social/economic groups that reside in them) and the convergence process based on the economic experience of regions within Eastern Europe.

The metropolitan regions of Eastern Europe have become the centres of productivity growth in the transition period. Post-1989 these areas went

**Table 6.4.** Patterns of development within regions and societies as a result of openness in and integration into the globalized market economy post-1989.

|  |  | Experience and outcomes of the economic transition ||
|---|---|---|---|
|  |  | Successful integration and benefits of economic openness | Unsuccessful integration into the open markets |
| Legacy of the planned economy | Capitals, economic centres and heavy industrial regions and their populations | Capitals of the majority of the Eastern European economies, large cities with legacy of skilled technical labour in the services sector. | Former centres of Soviet-inspired heavy industry and labour force with obsolete skills. |
|  | Rural and / or peripheral areas and their populations | Areas benefitting from newly developed tourist sectors or foreign investment outside of the metropolis. | Rural areas that have seen outward migration. |

Source: author's elaboration of Gorzelak (2020).

through severe restructuring, often deindustrialising, needing new infrastructure. However, because of their diverse economies, good connectivity, and size, they were able to lead the process of economic transformation by developing the most dynamic sectors of commerce, knowledge-intensive services (finance, insurance, managerial, research). The capital cities of Eastern Europe became productivity leaders by attracting workers from smaller cities and rural areas. They offered greater diversity of jobs, higher wages, better networking connections, better study opportunities. Workers flocked in search of these and in turn created booming demand for new and better housing, which attracted investment. Thus, perpetuating a virtuous economic cycle.

Figure 6.5 illustrates the productivity differences between the capital regions and the rest of the economy (or in some interesting cases other individual regions). The capital metropolitan areas are considerably more productive and thus generate considerably higher incomes for their residents. Hungary (Figure 6.5, Panel C) is an important exception; the Győr region has been competing with the Budapest region for the highest labour productivity due to its excellent connectivity (it is geographically situated in one of the most important transport links in Central Europe, between Budapest and Vienna) and heavy investment in a modern industrial plan (the presence of large factories for the Audi AG).

**Figure 6.5.** Labour productivity across cities in selected Eastern European countries (GDP per person employed, millions of USD, constant prices, constant PPP, base year 2015). Source: OECD data. Created by the author.

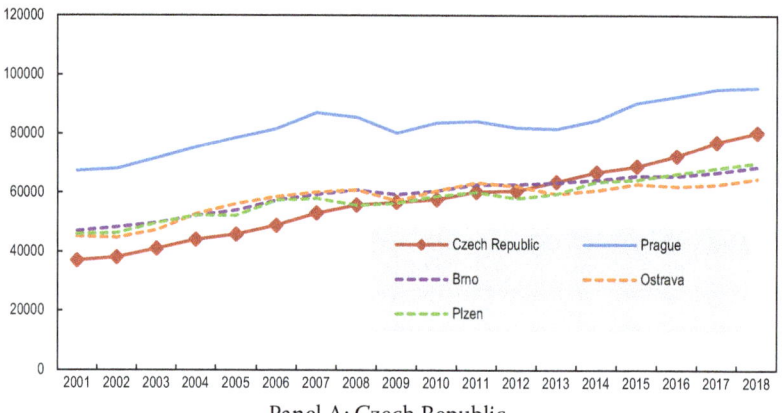

Panel A: Czech Republic

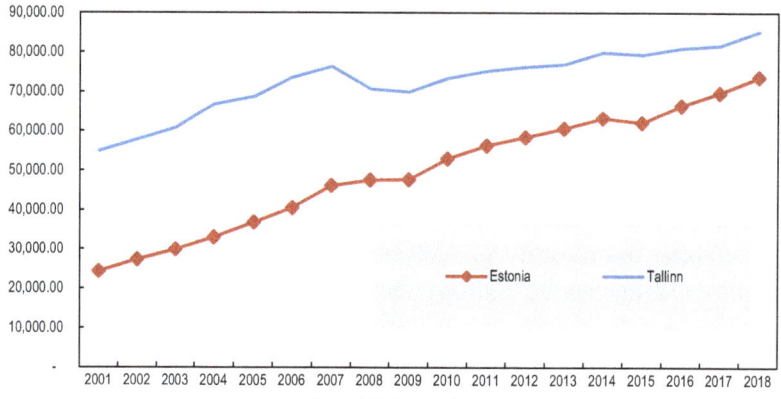

Panel B: Estonia

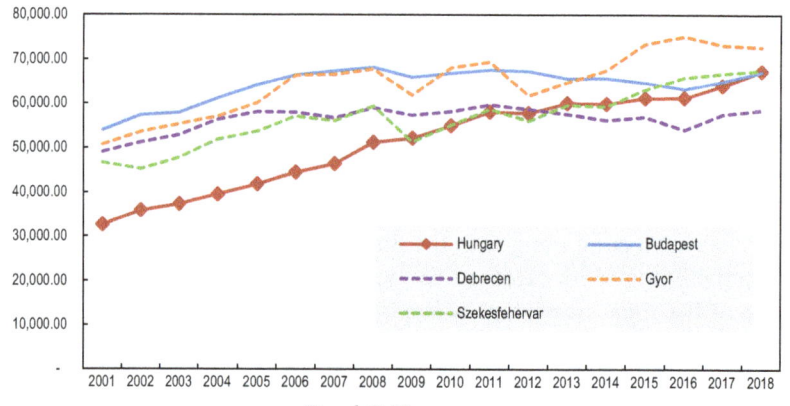

Panel C: Hungary

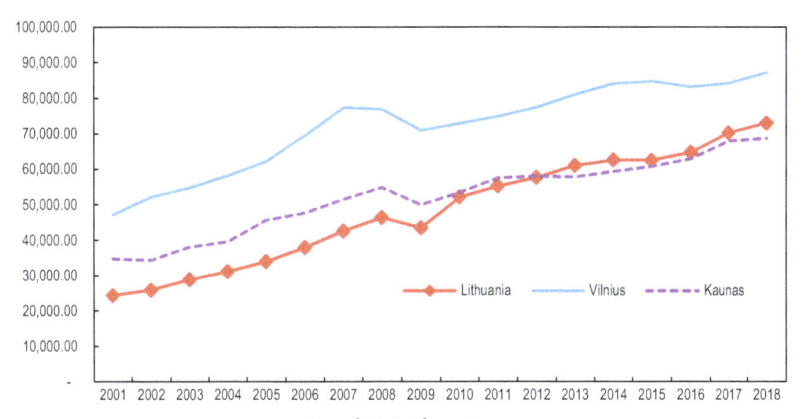

Panel D: Lithuania

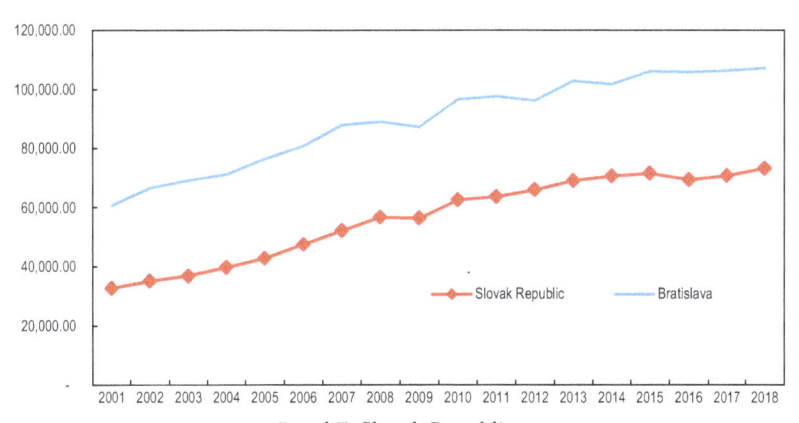

Panel E: Slovak Republic

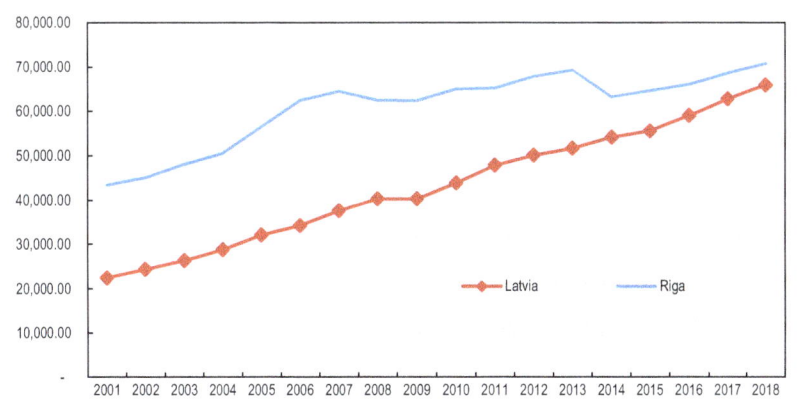

Panel F: Latvia

*(continued)*

**Figure 6.5.** Continued

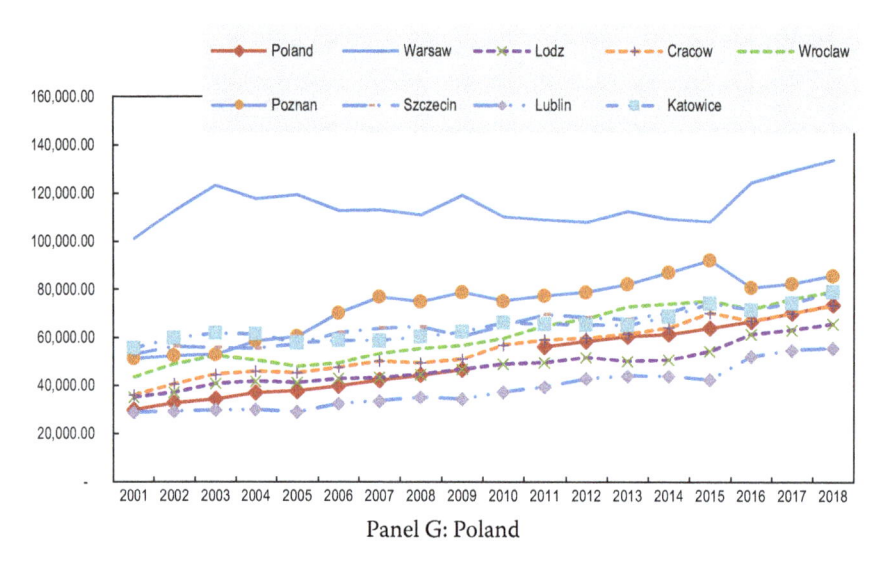

Panel G: Poland

Panel H: Slovenia

Figure 6.6 and Table 6.5 further illustrate the important economic disparity between the capital cities and the urban-rural divide.

THE WINNERS AND LOSERS OF ECONOMIC OPENNESS *191*

**Figure 6.6.** Economic activity by type of region, urban or rural (regional GDP, USD per head, constant prices, constant PPP, base year 2015). Source: OECD data. Created by the author.

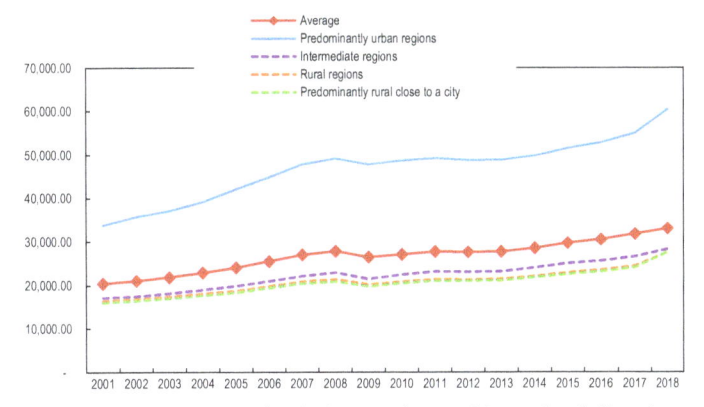

Panel A: Central Europe (includes Czech Republic, Poland, Slovakia, Hungary, Slovenia)

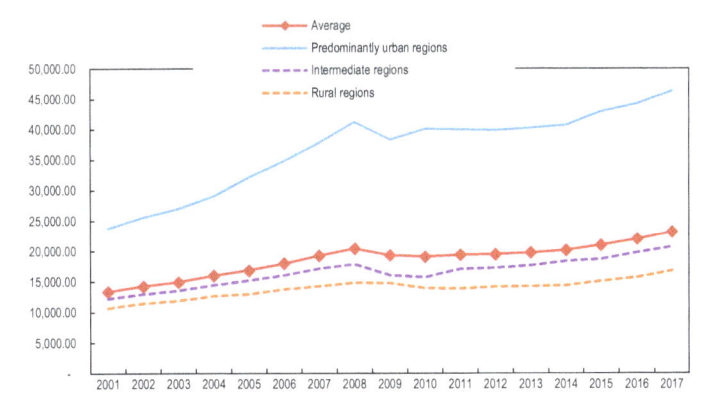

Panel B: Southeast Europe (includes Bulgaria, Croatia, Romania)

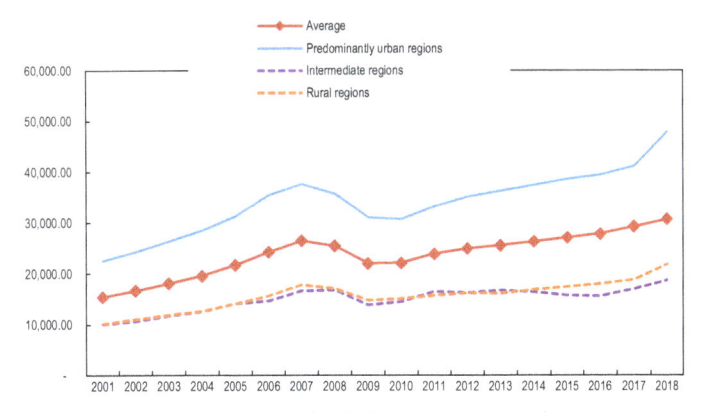

Panel C: Baltics (includes Estonia, Latvia)

Table 6.5. Labour utilization, capital regions versus the average for the country (percent of total employment of population).

| | | 2004 | 2005 | 2006 | 2007 | 2008 | 2009 | 2010 | 2011 | 2012 | 2013 | 2014 | 2015 | 2016 | 2017 | 2018 |
|---|---|---|---|---|---|---|---|---|---|---|---|---|---|---|---|---|
| Czech Republic | Average | 47 | 48 | 49 | 50 | 50 | 49 | 48 | 48 | 48 | 48 | 49 | 49 | 50 | 51 | 51 |
| | Prague region | 67 | 70 | 73 | 72 | 76 | 76 | 74 | 73 | 74 | 73 | 72 | 71 | 71 | 72 | 73 |
| Hungary | Average | 41 | 41 | 41 | 41 | 40 | 40 | 40 | 40 | 40 | 41 | 43 | 44 | 46 | 47 | 48 |
| | Budapest region | 76 | 78 | 80 | 79 | 80 | 79 | 77 | 77 | 76 | 78 | 80 | 82 | 86 | 88 | 90 |
| Lithuania | Average | 42 | 43 | 43 | 45 | 45 | 42 | 40 | 41 | 43 | 44 | 45 | 46 | 48 | 48 | 49 |
| | Vilnius region | 45 | 47 | 47 | 48 | 49 | 45 | 45 | 46 | 47 | 48 | 48 | 50 | 52 | 54 | 55 |
| Poland | Average | 37 | 38 | 40 | 41 | 42 | 40 | 41 | 41 | 41 | 41 | 42 | 42 | 43 | 43 | |
| | Warsaw region | | | | | | | | | | | | 52 | 53 | 54 | |
| Bulgaria | Average | 44 | 46 | 48 | 49 | 51 | 50 | 49 | 48 | 47 | 47 | 48 | 48 | 49 | 50 | 50 |
| | Sofia (South West) region | 47 | 51 | 54 | 58 | 61 | 60 | 59 | 59 | 57 | 57 | 57 | 58 | 59 | 61 | 62 |
| Romania | Average | 43 | 43 | 44 | 45 | 46 | 44 | 43 | 42 | 43 | 43 | 43 | 43 | 43 | 44 | 44 |
| | Bucharest - Ilfov region | 46 | 46 | 49 | 50 | 50 | 50 | 50 | 50 | 50 | 49 | 50 | 51 | 52 | 52 | 52 |

Source: OECD data.

Some peripheral or rural regions that possessed natural advantages for tourism or connectivity (due to proximity to production or service centres in the West, like the Budapest-Gyor corridor, extending to Vienna; for example, discussed above but also see Gorzelak 2020) also benefitted of the post-1989 economic openness. Such regions were able to compete in the new market economy thanks to favourable economic geography; paradoxically it was their prior underdevelopment and potential high marginal return to capital that attracted foreign investment. Such regions have not been as successful as the metropolitan regions or the largest population centres of Eastern Europe (described above). However, they have offered rising living standards to their populations.

On the other hand, poorly performing areas have seen rising outward migration, low employment prospects and relative decline. These have been the old industrial regions, as well as the remote rural areas of the Eastern European countries. These are the areas responsible for stagnating country-level growth rates, populated by people disillusioned with the dislocations of economic transition, and those with political nostalgia for the totalitarian past (Hann 2020).

The old industrial regions had played a leading role in creating and sustaining the socialist command economies. These areas were created through forceful investment in heavy plant and infrastructure and had attracted migrants from the countryside into relatively high-paid jobs. While they offered hard living and working conditions, they also presented promises of a brighter future and a dignified role for their residents in the socialist societies. However, the qualifications of the labour force were relatively low and narrowly specialized, the natural environment deteriorated over time together with the working and living infrastructure (often of poor quality to begin with). As a result, the breakdown of these economic centres throughout the 1990s and the following attempts at restructuring have been long and painful. Some of these industrial cities and regions have only recently been able to re-enter growth paths. The coal and steel region of Upper Silesia, the cities with shipyards along the Baltic Sea, the textile industry regions like Lodz (all in Poland) and the region of Maribor in Slovenia (Gorzelak 2020), the old coal and metallurgy base near Pernik (in Bulgaria), are some examples of industrial regions that are still going through difficult economic restructuring with the resulting high social costs of work/skills dislocation, outward migration and relative poverty.

Remote rural areas, which relied on agriculture during socialist times and still tend to do so, have not only been unable to experience the economic benefits of an open market economy, but have further suffered outward migration contributing to their economic downturn (see Figure 6.5). Interestingly, Gorzelak (2020) has noted that these areas tend to be the eastern or peripheral regions of most Eastern European countries, supporting an economic geography argument of connectivity and economic prosperity. Examples are border regions located on the eastern edge of the European economic core (the Eurozone), like the Sudeten region of the Czech Republic, the northeastern and southeastern regions of Bulgaria, the Baltic regions bordering Russia and Belarus (with the exception of the Lithuanian capital Vilnius). The low and diminishing concentration of people and poor transport links and infrastructure have limited attraction for foreign investment, while domestic capital has been scarce.

These regional disparities present a more complex picture than the relative macroeconomic success of Eastern Europe over the past three decades (discussed at the beginning of this chapter and illustrated in Figures 6.1 and 6.2). The newly created market economies have created wealth and lifted people out of abject poverty. In Table 6.5, below, the last two columns illustrate the fall in absolute poverty headcount between the two periods of early transition (1995–2005) and late transition (2006–14), which was universal across all the countries (with the exception of Croatia, which still exhibited a poverty headcount less than 1percent of its population). The middle two columns, which exhibit poverty headcount at national poverty lines looking at country-specific factors, suggest a less pronounced improvement of living standards across different social/economic groups relative to the total income of the specific country. This suggests that the Eastern European countries unleashed a potential that was pent up pre-1989 and were able to overcome some basic growth challenges such as higher investment levels, greater innovation, and production efficiency as well as higher trade specialization. This has resulted in higher incomes across all income groups of their populations when compared to global poverty levels. However, this achievement was less spectacular in relative terms to the country-specific poverty line and some groups were indeed *left behind* in economic terms. This is to say that as incomes of even the poorest Eastern Europeans did grow, the national incomes grew faster, and some groups obtained a greater part of it while others profited significantly less.

This point is further illustrated by the stagnating or worsening measures of income inequalities at country level (see Table 6.6). The Gini coefficients (a measure of statistical dispersion representing income inequality within the population of a country) of the Central European countries have marginally improved, while those of the Baltic countries (excluding Estonia) and Southeast European countries have worsened. In fact, increasing income inequality has been a persistent feature of the transition economies. Milanovic (1998) early on underlined the likely social costs of transition by pointing to the hollowing out of the middle class (constituting an overwhelming majority of the socialist economies) and the resulting rise in income inequality. Empirical work suggests that the transition to market economies have concentrated the incomes of Eastern European economies at the top end of the income distribution. Gevorkyan (2018) suggests that across a broad sample of Eastern European economies up to 41 percent of total income or consumption is attributed to the richest 20 percent of households, while only 8 percent of total income or consumption is held by the poorest 20 percent of households.

The disparities in income and wealth distribution between top earners and the lowest ones are not dissimilar to those experienced by Western European economies (as is reflected at the end of this section). OECD (2020a) compares income and wealth inequalities across a broad sample of European economies (among others) in its publication *How's Life: Measuring Well-Being* and reports on the ratio of the incomes of the top 20 percent of the distribution to the bottom 20 percent. In Europe the highest income inequality according to this measure in 2017 was in Lithuania (7.8, this is to say that the top 20 percent of the income distribution had income 7.8 times higher than the bottom 20 percent) and Latvia (6.4), but also Spain, Great

Table 6.6. Income inequality and poverty across Eastern Europe, various indicators.

| Region | Country | GINI index 1995–2005 | GINI index 2006–2014 | Poverty headcount ratio at national poverty lines (% of the population) 1995–2005 | Poverty headcount ratio at national poverty lines (% of the population) 2006–2014 | Poverty headcount ratio at 3.2 US Dollars per day (2011 PPP) (% of population) 1995–2005 | Poverty headcount ratio at 3.2 US Dollars per day (2011 PPP) (% of population) 2006–2014 |
|---|---|---|---|---|---|---|---|
| Central Europe | Czech Republic | 26.8 | 26.3 | 10.2 | 9.2 | 0.12 | 0.15 |
| | Slovakia | 28 | 26.4 | 12.5 | 12 | 0.96 | 0.41 |
| | Hungary | 28.9 | 28.5 | 14.7 | 13.6 | 0.44 | 0.28 |
| | Poland | 33.6 | 33.2 | 17.3 | 17.3 | 3.02 | 0.55 |
| | Slovenia | 27.6 | 24.7 | 11.9 | 13.13 | 0.12 | 0.04 |
| Baltic Countries | Estonia | 34.7 | 32.4 | | 21.8 | 4.29 | 1.39 |
| | Lithuania | 33.1 | 34.8 | 20.3 | 20.1 | 3.53 | 2.56 |
| | Latvia | 34.6 | 35.8 | 21.5 | 21.7 | 5.02 | 2.32 |
| Southeast Europe | Bulgaria | 30.9 | 33.9 | 18.4 | 21.6 | 4.54 | 4.38 |
| | Croatia | 29.7 | 31.8 | | 20.2 | 0.24 | 0.9 |
| | Romania | 29.9 | 33.2 | | 23 | 19.68 | 10.19 |
| CIS | Russia | 39.7 | 41.22 | 20.1 | 12.5 | 6.94 | 0.97 |
| | Ukraine | 31.3 | 25.72 | 70.1 | 13.1 | 14.15 | 0.47 |
| | Belarus | 29.8 | 27.7 | 26.5 | 6.6 | 14.91 | 0.35 |
| | Armenia | 36.8 | 30.9 | 48.3 | 32.4 | 6.96 | 2.51 |
| | Georgia | 39.9 | 40.9 | | 18.1 | 37.7 | 34 |

Source: World Bank Data and Gevorkyan (2018).

Britain, Italy and Greece, all had around six times. Inequalities are smallest in some Central and Eastern European countries (i.e., the Czech Republic, the Slovak Republic, Slovenia), as well as in Iceland, Denmark, Finland and Belgium, where the ratio never exceeds four. The distribution of household wealth is much more concentrated than that of household income and it is again broadly comparable across Eastern and Western Europe. In 2016, for example, the wealthiest 10 percent in Latvia owned about 65 percent of total household wealth; the same measure was 58 percent in Germany, 55 percent in Estonia, Austria and Ireland, and around 42 percent in Italy, Belgium, Greece and Poland.

The aggregate inequality story for Eastern Europe is further mapped out by various well-being measures that are available at the regional level. The important differences between metropolitan regions and other regions that appear left behind during the transition are evident. Not only are the best-educated individuals chasing the best employment and livelihood opportunities (see Table 6.7, below) at the capital cities and regions, but they also report higher scores in life-satisfaction and show the highest turnout for elections. The latter exhibits a high degree of civic and political engagement, which in turn results in high social capital, a factor that is an important determinant of successful economies (Putnam 1993).

The geographic dimension of inequality is very important, as the model illustrated by Table 6.4 suggests. In fact, this model suggests that geographic (and historical) factors helped determine the economic development post-1989 and thus the income and wealth levels across various groups in Eastern European societies. The regional disparities are one way of unpacking the inequality story of post-1989 transition. They suggest how groups that do not benefit from the concentration of complex productive economic activity and economic connectivity in metropolitan areas, or of areas that are part of a trade/production value chain, end up at the bottom of the income and wealth ladder.

Concentration of economic activity in certain sectors and/or regions coupled with stagnating regions where the educated and productive individuals emigrate exacerbates the likelihood of an economy falling into the middle-income trap. It may be argued that economic growth, especially under a rapid structural change as in the case of Eastern Europe, inevitably leads to uneven development. However, economic dynamism in Eastern Europe is highly concentrated in the metropolitan areas while the left behind regions in Eastern Europe have seen very little impact by the new knowledge-intensive and fast-growing sectors (see Figures 6.4 and 6.5). The latter have considerably lower levels of income and higher rates of unemployment (Table 6.6, above, and Table 6.7, below). Cingano (2014) has found evidence that high-income inequality leads to lower economic

**Table 6.7.** Regional well-being, various indicators, for Czech Republic, Poland and Slovak Republic in 2014.

| Country / Region | Employ- ment rate % | Labour force with at least secondary education % | Life expec- tancy at birth years | Turnout in general elections % | House- holds with internet broadband access % | Self- evaluation of life satisfaction index[i] |
|---|---|---|---|---|---|---|
| *Czech Republic* | 70.4 | 95 | 78.3 | 59.8 | 76 | 6.5 |
| Prague | 77.6 | 97.7 | 79.8 | 64.1 | 88 | 6.8 |
| Central Bohemian Region | 72.4 | 96 | 78.1 | 61.5 | 77 | 6.2 |
| Southwest | 71.5 | 94.4 | 78.2 | 59.3 | 75 | 6.4 |
| Northwest | 66.8 | 90.1 | 76.3 | 51.7 | 68 | 6.3 |
| Northeast | 70 | 95 | 78.4 | 60.8 | 70 | 6.6 |
| Southeast | 70.5 | 96.1 | 78.7 | 61.4 | 78 | 6.5 |
| Central Moravia | 67.7 | 95.4 | 78 | 60.2 | 76 | 6.6 |
| Moravia-Silesia | 66.2 | 94.1 | 77 | 55.5 | 74 | 6.2 |
| *Poland* | 59.9 | 93.4 | 77.1 | 50.9 | 71 | 5.8 |
| Central region | – | – | – | – | – | – |
| Lodzkie | 74.2 | 91.9 | 75.4 | 51.6 | 66 | 5.8 |
| Mazovia – Warsaw | 71.9 | 94.1 | 77.7 | 58.7 | 75.3 | 5.9 |
| South region | – | – | – | – | – | – |
| Lesser Poland | 57.4 | 95 | 78.5 | 54.9 | 71.7 | 5.8 |
| Silesia | 58.3 | 96 | 76.3 | 52.2 | 68.2 | 5.8 |
| East region | – | – | – | – | – | – |
| Lublin Province | 66.9 | 91.9 | 77.1 | 49 | 70.8 | 5.7 |
| Podkarpacia | 53.5 | 93 | 78.6 | 50.4 | 74.3 | 5.4 |
| Swietokrzyskie | 66.7 | 91.2 | 77.1 | 46.8 | 66.5 | 5.4 |
| Podlasie | 57.9 | 90.5 | 77.7 | 47.1 | 70.8 | 5.8 |
| Northeast West region | – | – | – | – | – | – |
| Greater Poland | 55.2 | 94.4 | 77.2 | 50.2 | 74.6 | 6 |
| West Pomerania | 47.9 | 91.1 | 76.7 | 45.9 | 66.5 | 6.6 |
| Lubusz | 56.5 | 93.1 | 76.3 | 44.6 | 63.3 | 5.9 |
| South-West region | – | – | – | – | – | – |
| Lower Silesia | 54.1 | 94.4 | 76.9 | 49.4 | 71.9 | 6 |
| Opole region | 54.9 | 93.4 | 77.2 | 43.1 | 71.5 | 5.8 |

*(continued)*

**Table 6.7.** Continued

| Country / Region | Employ-ment rate % | Labour force with at least secondary education % | Life expec-tancy at birth years | Turnout in general elections % | House-holds with internet broadband access % | Self-evaluation of life satisfaction index[i] |
|---|---|---|---|---|---|---|
| *Poland continued* | | | | | | |
| North region | – | – | – | – | – | – |
| Kuyavian-Pomerania | 53.8 | 92.3 | 76.9 | 46.4 | 69.9 | 5.9 |
| Warmian-Masuria | 52.3 | 88.9 | 76.3 | 42.3 | 64.1 | 6 |
| Pomerania | 57.1 | 92.7 | 77.9 | 51.9 | 78.8 | 6.1 |
| *Slovak Republic* | 63.3 | 93.4 | 76.5 | 43.4 | 76 | 5.9 |
| Bratislava Region | 73.1 | 96.7 | 78.1 | 52.1 | 78 | 6.5 |
| West Slovakia | 63.8 | 94.4 | 76.8 | 42.8 | 76 | 6.1 |
| Central Slovakia | 59.2 | 92 | 76.2 | 43.3 | 74 | 6 |
| East Slovakia | 56.5 | 92.3 | 76.2 | 40.4 | 78 | 6 |

Source: OECD data.

*Note*: i. The index of self-reported life satisfaction is constructed by the OECD and the higher the number the better the life-satisfaction of the individual.

growth, by hindering human capital accumulation by way of undermining education opportunities for disadvantaged individuals, lowering social mobility and hampering skills development. This provides a stark recall that countries that fall and remain in the middle-income trap tend to be the ones that fail to ensure broad access to education (especially tertiary, least accessible to low-income groups) and fail to export a large share of high-end technological products (Eichengreen et al. 2013). Thus, the incomplete structural transformation of the Eastern European economies, which has resulted in large internal income disparities, can be the break that is stopping them from completing the convergence process to the West and entering the groups of high-income countries.

It is important to acknowledge that rising inequality, as well as concentration of high income and highly educated individuals in the metropolitan areas, are broader phenomena that are also true for a large number of developed Western economies. Milanovic (2016) presents convincing data on the global growth of inequality and middle-class erosion. The most productive regions in France and Great Britain, for example are centred on their capitals Paris and London (this is however not true for Austria, where the city of Salzburg has had higher GDP per capita than the capital of the country, Vienna, since 2016). Regional disparity has been shown to be a blight on the Eurozone and the European Union economies in general (Hudecz, Moshammer and Wieser 2020).

An important difference for Eastern European countries is that their citizens have not yet caught up with the living standards and the consumption levels of their Western counterparts. Neither have they built the resilient and accountable institutions that underpin the Western economies and their high-growth patterns. However, Eastern European citizens are already experiencing the high inequality and volatility of the open market economies; and they are aware of this.

The 2015 *Life in Transition Survey* conducted by the European Bank for Reconstruction and Development (EBRD 2016) finds that in self-assessments of income inequality, perceptions matter. Across Eastern Europe, individuals report a strong belief that income (and wealth) inequality levels have gone up during the three decades since 1989 and that inequality is higher now than in the period pre-1989. The OECD's perception of corruption data for 2014 (the percentage of people that replied 'Yes' with respect to all respondents to the following question: 'Is corruption widespread throughout the government in this country, or not?') suggest that individuals in transition countries – like the Czech Republic (83 percent), Hungary (79 percent) and the Slovak Republic (78 percent) – consider government corruption to be widespread in contrast to individuals in neighbouring Austria (52 percent) or Germany (56 percent) for instance. Estonia is an exception for a former command economy with 54 percent, as well as Italy for a Western market economy with 83 percent (OECD Regional Well-Being dataset 2020). There appears to be a link between the level of income and development of a region within a country and the perception of corruption its citizens feel. For example, 82 percent residents of Prague and its region (who have the highest income in the Czech Republic) consider corruption widespread, while 90 percent of the residents of the Northeast Sudeten region (a below-average income region) do so (OECD Regional Well-Being Dataset 2020). This further accentuates the disparities between regions and individuals in Eastern Europe.

## Conclusions: In Search of a New Growth Model

The three decades since 1989 have seen the former command economies of Eastern Europe on a transition path towards open markets. This has resulted in a successful growth in living standards and consumption opportunities boosted by the inflows of Western technologies, integration into global value chains, and finally, the prospects of catch-up growth given the low starting point for the majority of these economies.

The early gains, however, appear to have dissipated and the economic success they have produced appears narrowly shared. Economically successful regions, largely concentrated around the capital cities, have found their place in the high-income Western economy increasingly driven by high-end technology and knowledge products and services. Many, if not most, other regions appear left behind – they are economically inefficient, they have old infrastructure and people migrate out of them. This disparity is not conducive to further catch-up and convergence growth and will need to be addressed if the Eastern European economies are to avoid economic stagnation and a possible slip into the middle-income trap. The *fruits of economic prosperity* need to be spread out of the bustling metropolitan areas towards the disillusioned residents of stagnating ones, if a political backlash to the open markets and pro-Western economic orientation is to be avoided.

One path to a more broad-based and inclusive growth is to channel investments into education and connectivity, and to seek to develop existing or novel knowledge sectors. The old industrial sectors will not be returning to economic life, as global manufacturing comparative advantage has already moved decisively elsewhere – largely to Southeast Asia. However, new sectors are emerging in the Western developed economies, which seek to utilize green technologies and the digital domain to solve its own problems of economic inequality and uneven growth. The countries of Eastern Europe can benefit only if they cooperate institutionally and seek to compete economically in these domains.

**Kiril Kossev** is a senior economist at the OECD. He has held policy and research positions at the European Bank for Reconstruction and Development (EBRD) and the Bulgarian National Bank, lectureships at the University of Oxford and the American University of Bulgaria, as well as private sector roles in London. He has published on the role of finance in development, banking systems and crises, productivity and growth in historical perspective, and the Eastern European economic transition. He holds a DPhil from Nuffield College and BA/MSc from Hertford College, University of Oxford.

### Notes

1. Euro Area and the European Union represent the averages for the member countries of these respective institutions. The groupings include Baltics (Estonia, Latvia, Lithuania), Central Europe (Czech Republic, Hungary, Slovak Republic, Slovenia, Poland), CIS (Belarus, Moldova, Russia, Ukraine), Southeast Europe (EU) (Bulgaria, Croatia, Romania), Southeast Europe (non-EU) (Albania, Bosna and Herzegovina, North Macedonia, Montenegro, Serbia).

2. OECD, Euro Area, European Union represent the averages for the member countries of these respective institutions. The groupings include Baltics (Estonia, Latvia, Lithuania), Central Europe (Czech Republic, Hungary, Slovak Republic, Slovenia, Poland), CIS (Belarus, Moldova, Russia, Ukraine), Southeast Europe (EU) (Bulgaria, Croatia, Romania), Southeast Europe (non-EU) (Albania, Bosna and Herzegovina, North Macedonia, Montenegro, Serbia).
3. OECD, Euro Area, European Union represent the averages for the member countries of these respective institutions. The groupings include Baltics (Estonia, Latvia, Lithuania), Central Europe (Czech Republic, Hungary, Slovak Republic, Slovenia, Poland), Southeast Europe (Bulgaria, Croatia, Romania).
4. The groupings include Baltics (Estonia, Latvia, Lithuania), Central Europe (Czech Republic, Hungary, Slovak Republic, Slovenia, Poland), Southeast Europe (Bulgaria, Croatia, Romania).

# References

Aiyar, Shekhar, Romain Duval, Damien Puy, Yiqun Wu and Longmei Zhang. 2013. 'Growth Slowdowns and the Middle-Income Trap'. *IMF Working Paper*, Asia and Pacific Department, Authorized for Distribution by Romain Duval.

Bijsterbosch, Martin, and Marcin Kolasa. 2009. 'FDI and Productivity Convergence in Central and Eastern Europe: An Industry-Level Investigation'. ECB Working Paper Series, No. 992. http://ssrn.com/abstract_id=1311396.

Brainard, Lawrence J. 1981. 'Foreign Economic Constraints on Soviet Economic Policy in the 1980s'. *The Soviet Economy: Continuity and Change*, edited by Morris Bornstein. Routledge, 217–33. https://doi.org/10.4324/9780429314735.

Cingano, Federico. 2014. 'Trends in Income Inequality and Its Impact on Economic Growth'. OECD Social, Employment and Migration Working Paper*s*, No. 163. https://doi.org/10.1787/5jxrjncwxv6j-en.

Djankov, Simeon, and Bernard Hoekman. 2000. 'Foreign Investment and Productivity Growth in Czech Enterprises'. *The World Bank Economic Review* 14(1): 49–64.

EBRD. 2016. 'EBRD Life in Transition'. EBRD. https://www.ebrd.com/publications/life-in-transition-iii.

Eichengreen, Barry, and Andrea Boltho. 2008. 'The Economic Impact of European Integration'. Centre for Economic Policy Research Discussion Paper Series, No. 6820. https://papers.ssrn.com/sol3/papers.cfm?abstract_id=1143183.

Eichengreen, Barry, Donghyun Park and Kwanho Shin. 2011. 'When Fast Growing Economies Slow Down: International Evidence and Implications for China'. NBER Working Paper, No. 16919. https://doi.org/10.3386/w16919.

———. 2013. 'Growth Slowdowns Redux: New Evidence on the Middle-Income Trap'. NBER Working Paper, No. 18673. https://doi.org/10.3386/w18673.

European Commission. 2020. 'Falling into the Middle-Income Trap? A Study on the Risks for EU Regions to Be Caught in a Middle-Income Trap'. https://doi.org/10.2776/02363.

Felipe, Jesus, Arnelyn Abdon and Utsav Kumar. 2012. 'Tracking the Middle-Income Trap: What Is It, Who Is in It, and Why?' Levy Economics Institute, Working Paper No. 715.

Frye, Timothy. 2010. *Building States and Markets after Communism: The Perils of Polarized Democracy*. Cambridge Studies in Comparative Politics. New York: Cambridge University Press. https://doi.org/10.1017/CBO9780511779718.

Frye, Timothy, and Edward D. Mansfield. 2003. 'Fragmenting Protection: The Political Economy of Trade Policy in the Post-Communist World'. *British Journal of Political Science* 33(4): 635–57. https://doi.org/10.1017/S0007123403000292.

Gevorkyan, Alexander. 2018. *Transition Economies: Transformation, Development, and Society in Eastern Europe and the Former Soviet Union*. Oxon: Routledge.

Gorzelak, Grzegorz, ed. 2020. *Social and Economic Development in Central and Eastern Europe: Stability and Change after 1990*. London: Routledge.

Gros, Daniel, and Alfred Steinherr. 2004. *Economic Transition in Central and Eastern Europe: Planting the Seeds*. Cambridge: Cambridge University Press. https://doi.org/10.1017/CBO9780511805646.

Hann, Chris. 2020. 'Resilience and Transformation in Provincial Political Economy: From Market Socialism to Market Populism in Hungary, 1970s–2010s'. *Cargo Journal* 16(1–2).

Hellman, Joel S. 1998. 'Winners Take All: The Politics of Partial Reform in Postcommunist Transitions'. *World Politics* 50(2): 203–34. https://doi.org/10.1017/S0043887100008091.

Holzman, Franklin D. 1976. *International Trade under Communism: Politics and Economics*. New York: Basic Books.

Hudecz, Gergely, Edmund Moshammer and Thomas Wieser. 2020. 'Regional Disparities in Europe: Should we Be Concerned?' European Stability Mechanism Discussion Paper Series, No. 13.

Im, Fernando Gabriel, and David Rosenblatt. 2013. 'Middle-Income Traps: A Conceptual and Empirical Survey'. World Bank Policy and Research Paper, No. 6594.

Kornai, János. 1996. 'Paying the Bill for Goulash Communism: Hungarian Development and Macro-Stabilization in a Political Economy Perspective'. *Social Research* 63(4).

Kossev, Kiril, and William Tompson. 2020. 'Political and Economic Integration with the Western Economies since 1989'. *The Economic History of Central, East and South-East Europe: 1800 to the Present*, edited by Matthias Morys, 434–68. London: Routledge. https://doi.org/10.4324/9781315686097.

Mann, Katja. 2015. 'The EU, a Growth Engine? The Impact of European Integration on Economic Growth in Central Eastern Europe'. FIW Working Paper series, No. 136. https://www.fiw.ac.at/fileadmin/Documents/Publikationen/Working_Paper/N_136-Mann.pdf.

Milanovic, Branko. 1998. 'Income, Inequality, and Poverty during the Transition from Planned to Market Economy'. World Bank Regional and Sectoral Studies, Washington, DC, 1998.

———. 2016. *Global Inequality: A New Approach for the Age of Globalisation*. Cambridge, MA: Belknap Press.

Myant, Martin, and Jan Drahokoupil. 2012. 'International Integration, Varieties of Capitalism and Resilience to Crisis in Transition Economies'. *Europe–Asia Studies* 64(1): 1–33. https://doi.org/10.1080/09668136.2012.635478.

OECD. 2020a. 'Broad-Based Innovation Policy for All Regions and Cities'. https://doi.org/10.1787/299731d2-en.

———. 2020b. 'How's Life? 2020 Measuring Well-Being'. https://doi.org/10.1787/9870c393-en.

Putnam, Robert. 1993. *Making Democracy Work*. Princeton: Princeton University Press.

Rae, Gavin. 2016. 'Public Debt and Its Impact on the Polish Economy and Society'. *Journal of Management and Business Administration Central Europe* 24(1): 89–112. https://doi.org/10.7206/jmba.ce.2450-7814.165.

Roaf, James, Ruben Atoyan, Joshi Bikas and Krzysztof Krogulski. 2014. '25 Years of Transition: Post-Communist Europe and the IMF: Regional Economic Issues Special Report'. International Monetary Fund. https://www.imf.org/ /media/Websites/IMF/imported-flagship-issues/external/pubs/ft/reo/2014/eur/eng/pdf/erei_sr_102414.ashx.

Romer, Paul. 1993. 'Idea Gaps and Object Gaps in Economic Development'. *Journal of Monetary Economics* 32(3): 543–73. https://doi.org/10.1016/0304-3932(93)90029-F.

Winiecki, Jan. 2000. 'Successes of Trade Reorientation and Expansion in Post-Communist Transition: An Enterprise-Level Approach'. *BNL Quarterly Review* 53(213): 187–223.

Zuk, Piotr, and Li Savelin. 2018. 'Real Convergence in Central, Eastern, and South-Eastern Europe'. European Central Bank Occasional Paper Series, No. 212. https://www.ecb.europa.eu/pub/pdf/scpops/ecb.op212.en.pdf.

CHAPTER 7

# Developmentalist Illusion?
## *EU Cohesion Policy, Dependent Development and the State in East Central Europe*

Daniel Šitera

### Introduction

The developmentalist illusion describes the historical fate of semiperipheral states in global capitalism: these states consensually integrate into the open global economy to chase a promise that they will catch up with the developmental levels of the core states only to find themselves entrapped in the very same middle-income position in the long run. According to Wallerstein (1988) and Arrighi (1990), such an illusion seems a more tangible developmental ideology there than anywhere else because the semiperipheral states are positioned between the global cores and peripheries. This intermediate position encompasses historically the more advanced states in East Central Europe (ECE), East Asia, Southern Europe or South America. The middle-income position and developmentalist illusion in ECE as in Europe's historical (semi)periphery (Kouli and Müller, Introduction) seems to be generally repeated in the region's otherwise diverse European Union (EU) integrations. Since the eastern enlargement in 2004, most of the ECE states have experienced a partial catch-up with the North-Western European core states. They also remained rather economically resilient to the global economic crisis (GEC) and rather resumed this catch-up in the post-crisis recovery of the 2010s (Bohle 2017). However, after more than fifteen years of their EU membership, the four ECE states remain a European, if not global semiperiphery. Far worse, according to the European Commission (2017, vii–x, 21ff), they reach only the lower ranks of the EU's 'middle-income trap': Czechia, Hungary, Poland and Slovakia are categorized as ranging from 'less' to 'moderately developed' (semi)peripheral states, while falling behind the EU's 'highly developed' North-Western core.

Why then do the ECE states still pursue the developmentalist illusion of overcoming the middle-income trap and catching up with North-Western Europe? Answering this question, I foreground the EU Cohesion Policy and its European Structural and Investment Funds (ESIF). This concerns three EU funds organized under the Cohesion Policy: European Regional and Development Fund, European Social Fund and Cohesion Fund. I also offer the neo-Gramscian reconceptualization of developmentalist illusion for ECE (Bohle 2006; Shields 2020; Gagyi 2016; Bieling, Jäger and Ryner 2016). Because the Cohesion Policy promises a mutual core-peripheral catch-up in the EU under the visions of *economic, social and territorial cohesion* (EC 1996, 2010), I study it as a unique Marshall Plan–type case of redistribution from core states and regions to their peripheral counterparts. The policy forms an intra-EU developmental policy – through which the EU core states supply the (semi)peripheral states and their regions – with ESIF transfers as a de facto developmental aid. This ESIF investment goes into the ECE's human, infrastructural and institutional development. Against this background, I understand the Cohesion Policy as materializing this EU developmentalist illusion for ECE.

From a neo-Gramscian viewpoint, the Cohesion Policy underpins the EU's tendency to forming a hegemonic order, as no such order can be sustained without signalling such ideologies, visions, or illusions (Cox 1983; Jessop 2006; Arrighi 2010). Under the Commission's 'conditional leadership' (Wozniak Boyle 2006), the core states and their (semi)peripheral counterparts have negotiated this key EU policy. Through it, the core states transfer the ESIF investment to (semi)peripheral states and regions as an economic concession in exchange for their subordinate, yet consensual integration. However, I simultaneously investigate how such asymmetric redistributive relations and the Cohesion Policy's developmental ideology entrap ECE states in the illusory catch-up strategies.

Foregrounding the Cohesion Policy's ESIF transfers, this chapter offers two contributions to the Comparative Capitalism scholarship on the ECE's dependent market integrations (Nölke and Vliegenthart 2009; Drahokoupil and Myant 2015) into the EU and globally (Becker and Jäger 2012; Nölke et al. 2015). The first contribution extends this scholarship's preoccupation with the region's dependency on foreign direct investment (FDI), which has flown predominantly from North-Western Europe into the export-oriented complex industries (Ban and Mihály, Chapter 3). By doing so, the ESIF transfers are foregrounded as a still under-researched source of dependency besides the FDI dependency on the decision-making of multinational corporations' (MNC) headquarters from North-Western Europe. As Figure 7.1 shows, the FDI dependency has increasingly been complemented with the ESIF dependency since the late 2000s. Following those researching the Cohesion Policy in ECE (Jacoby 2014; Medve-Bálint 2018; Medve-Bálint and Šćepanović 2020; Vukov 2020), I go further to analyse the two dependencies as *politically* co-constituted in a mutual *FDI-ESIF complementarity* (May and Nölke 2015). In this dual dependency, the ESIF dependency is not only researched as making the FDI-led reindustrialization socioeconomically or infrastructurally sustainable. I mainly study how the Cohesion Policy's developmentalist illusion makes such (semi) peripheral integrations politically legitimate. As documented, the illusion envisions the mutual complementarity of these two dependencies on the North-Western European states and capital as a successful industrial or more broadly developmental strategy for the ECE states in their catch-up with the North-Western developmental levels.

The second contribution innovates the concept of developmentalist illusion in order to explore the asymmetric transnational power struggle over the *ideological content* of Cohesion Policy and the political legitimization of the FDI dependency. I focus on the struggle between the Commission bureaucrats (Wozniak Boyle 2006) – as key supranational decision-makers in the distribution of ESIF transfers – and the ECE state managers or national political and bureaucratic elites. This exposes their asymmetric negotiations over the Cohesion Policy's developmental ideology, which fixes binding investment purpose and targets of ESIF transfers in ECE. Exploring this ideology and the negotiation process of making it a socially resonant and politically legitimate catch-up illusion, I trace them as *hegemonic visions* (Sum and Jessop 2013). In the EU's multilevel governance (Brenner 2004; Walters and Haahr 2005), any ideology becomes a hegemonic illusion of (semi)peripheral catch-up only when it translates into comprehensive multi-scalar visions of European, national and subnational socioeconomic development. These visions are initially produced by the Commission in its EU-level regulation of 'uneven and dependent' (Becker, Jäger and Weissenbacher 2015) core-peripheral relations. They then co-produce the developmental strategies of (semi)peripheral states. Analyzing thus the ideological content of this regulation and these strategies, I recognize the political asymmetry to be conditioned and further reproduced by the dual economic dependency. To enable or overcome the FDI dependency on North-Western capital, the ECE states enter asymmetric negotiations as the dependent ESIF net-recipients with both the North-Western net-paying donors and especially the supranational Commission.

Two arguments answer the question about the ECE's consensual pursuit of the EU's developmentalist illusion. As detailed in the next section, I trace the hegemonic visions in the key strategic documents produced by the Commission and the ECE governments in the Cohesion Policy. First, the Commission bureaucrats have normalized and reproduced the dual

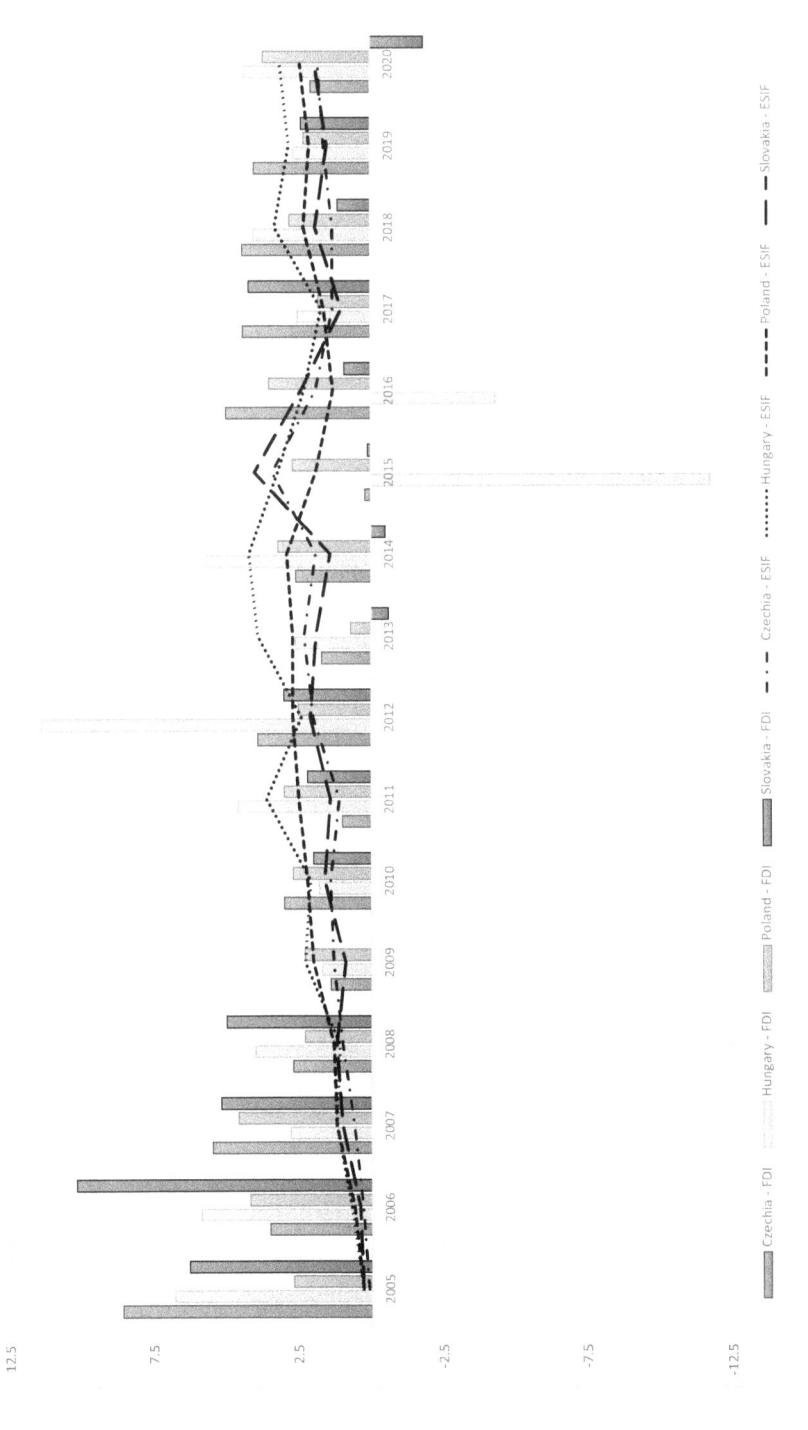

**Figure 7.1.** Comparison of FDI net inflows and ESIF inflows into ECE, 2005–20 (as percentage of GDP). Source: author's own preparation; European Commission (Revenues and Expenditures data) on ESIF under the EU budget headings for the Cohesion Policy, OECD database on FDI. Created by the author.

dependency in the comprehensive visions of FDI-ESIF complementarity. Such *globalist* visions bind the ECE state managers to strategically invest the ESIF transfers into enabling complementary infrastructural and institutional conditions so that their FDI-based and export-led economies are sustained or upgraded in a global economic competition.

Second, the ECE state managers have reappropriated these visions in two nationally varied but still similar types of state strategies: *globalist* catch-up strategies before the GEC in the late 2000s (Drahokoupil 2009; Shields 2012) and the *nationalist* catch-up strategies in the 2010s (Scheiring 2020; Toplišek 2020; Naczyk 2022). Comparing both types and their national variations, I deepen this argument. In the 2000s, the Cohesion Policy's globalist visions behind the ESIF transfers prioritized *globalist* elites and strategies, which enforced the ECE's strategic convergence on the FDI-led dependent economies (Drahokoupil 2009). Since the 2010s, the Cohesion Policy and the ESIF dependency have constrained the rise of *nationalist* elites and strategies in ECE, as epitomized by the post-2010 Hungary and post-2015 Poland. Compared with the EU-level visions and the Czech and Slovak strategies, even the Hungarian and Polish catch-up strategies remain far from abandoning the FDI-ESIF complementarity. Blending the globalist and nationalist visions (Scheiring 2022), they reshape the globalist setting halfway in the manner of 'selective economic nationalism' (Becker 2020). Selectively rebalancing the ESIF investment purpose and aims from prioritizing the locational conditions for foreign capital to the upgrading conditions for national capital, such strategies remain articulated within the EU's developmental visions.

The chapter is structured as follows. I reconceptualize the developmentalist illusion in the Comparative Capitalism scholarship on ECE integrations in the EU. Then, I can trace the ideological origins of FDI-ESIF complementarity in the Cohesion Policy and explore how the Commission has produced and deepened this hegemonic vision in the EU's regulation of core-peripheral relations and ECE semiperipheral integrations. Last, I compare two types of globalist and nationalist catch-up strategies of ECE states to understand their historical and national varieties in re-envisioning the FDI-ESIF complementarity for overcoming the middle-income trap.

## Theorizing Developmentalist Illusion in ECE

This section innovates the concept of developmentalist illusion by bringing it into the Comparative Capitalism debate on the ECE's integrations and the role of the Cohesion Policy therein. Arrighi (1990) used the concept to explain how neither the dependency theory, nor the modernization theory could fully address the semiperipheral catch-up strategies and their failure to cross the persistent divide between the North-Western cores and the Southern and Eastern (semi)peripheries in Europe and globally. With respect to the FDI-ESIF dependency, I follow Arrighi in the somewhat repeated debate on the EU-ECE integrations between the neo-Gramscian/regulationist/dependency scholars (Shields 2012; Becker et al. 2015; Bieling et al. 2016) and the rather neoinstitutionalist dependency approaches (Bohle 2017; Bruszt and Vukov 2017). I thus go beyond explaining the catch-up failure of FDI-led *transnational* reindustralization due to the *internal failings* of ECE states, as implied by the modernization and neoinstitutionalist scholars. I also go beyond explaining how the EU integration and this foreign-led reindustrialization *externally denied* ECE's autonomous catch-up strategies, as implied by the neo-Gramscian/regulationist/dependency scholars. Rather, I refine both these explanations in order to decipher the Cohesion Policy's globalist visions, and why even the ECE's nationalist catch-up strategies selectively pursue them in the 2010s (Arrighi and Drangel 1986; Arrighi, Silver and Brewer 2003; Wallerstein 1988): in the logic of uneven development, *nominal* industrial or any infrastructural and institutional convergence might spill over into a partial but never full *real* socioeconomic catch-up.

From a neo-Gramscian perspective, I use the distinction between nominal convergence/real catch-up to decipher the visions of FDI-ESIF complementarity as a developmentalist illusion. First, I can document how this illusion underpins the EU's hegemonic regulation of its uneven and dependent core-peripheral relations. This is by envisioning the *public* ESIF transfers as an additional state-sponsored investment in translating the *private* FDI-led nominal convergence into the real core-peripheral catch-up. Second, backed-up with credible ESIF transfers, these illusory visions can be interpreted to promote the globalist strategies in the post-accession 2000s and to constrain the nationalist strategies in the post-GEC 2010s. Arrighi (1990, 17f, 29) differentiated two types of semiperipheral catch-up strategies: the "anti-systemic" strategies and the "pro-systemic" strategies. The anti-systemic or anti-integrationist type of strategies against 'exploitation' is associated with the communist semiperiphery in the 1980s (Kouli, Chapter 1) and those of contemporary non-European, large emerging economies (Nölke et al. 2015). Such catch-up strategies challenge the North-Western hegemony of (neo)liberal globalization. However, studying the globalist and nationalist strategies in the ECE states, I interpret the ECE strategies as a mere variation of the pro-systemic or pro-EU/-FDI type of integrationist strategies against market 'exclusion' in open global competition. Epitomized by Southern Europe in the 1980s, such strategies generally accept the EU's neoliberal market order. The anti-systemic or anti-EU/-FDI potential of ECE nationalist strategies might thus selectively challenge the 'hyper-integrationist' (Šćepanović 2013) globalist strategies of the 2000s but remains within the negotiated pro-systemic visions of EU's core-peripheral relations.

The neo-Gramscian perspective (Shields 2012, 2020; Bieling et al. 2016; Sum and Jessop 2013; Cantat 2017) helps to trace how the hegemonic visions of nominal convergence/real catch-up through the FDI-ESIF complementarity are asymmetrically 'created, reproduced, and deepened' (Arrighi 1990, 13) through the Cohesion Policy. The Commission (van Apeldoorn 2002) produces such comprehensive visions to regulate the EU's uneven core-peripheral relations as an essential problem in making the EU a hegemonic market-enabling order. Such visions are reproduced and deepened in the Commission-led multilevel and intergovernmental governance networks (Bachtler and Mendez 2013; Baun and Marek 2014). This happens through their translation into a surveillance system of developmental indicators, indices and coefficients in the Cohesion Policy (Walters and Haahr 2005). In such a transnational context, the Commission not only sets the agenda of the intergovernmental negotiations over the volume of ESIF transfers and the visions about their investment (Wozniak Boyle 2006), it also acts as mediator and institutional guarantor of the final compromise between the core net-payers and the (semi)peripheral net-recipients.

However, the neo-Gramscian/regulationist/dependency analysis must first take the Cohesion Policy seriously as a Marshall-plan type arrangement. By doing so, I go beyond viewing the EU as running on the domination and *exploitation* of (semi)peripheral states by denying an autonomous ECE catch-up (Ivanova 2007; Bohle 2006; Shields 2012; Gagyi 2016; Ryner and Carfuny 2016). Hence, the ESIF dependency incorporates the (semi)peripheral state managers – in the EU's East and South – into consensually accepting the political asymmetries and economic inequalities of their subordinate integrations vis-à-vis the supranational Commission and the North-Western core states. The Cohesion Policy tendentially turns these states into a EU-based (semi)peripheral variety of market integration- 'enabling state' (Streeck 1997 in Van Apeldoorn 2002, 74–75). In other words, the ESIF transfers give the ECE elites more domestic capacity for cultivating their own catch-up strategies, but only if they comply with the Commission-led visions of market-enabling convergence. In this logic, I study how the ESIF dependency has favoured the FDI-based *state-foreign capital nexus* (Shields 2012; Pavlínek 2016) and its globalist strategies. These enabled the MNC interests in exploiting the ECE conditions of cheap (but skilled) labour, investment incentives (but also ready infrastructures) and domestic small and medium-sized enterprises (SME) as (technologically reliable) subcontractors. As well, I also explore how the ESIF dependency enables the anti-FDI challenge of nationalist catch-up strategies in favour of *domestic* capital and consumption as only a selective nationalist upgrade of the FDI-based development (Becker 2020; Scheiring 2022).

Synthetizing the neo-Gramscian/regulationist and neoinstitutionalist dependency scholarships, I take the Cohesion Policy seriously. Although the neoinstitutionalist scholars are aware of the EU hierarchies and the ECE dependency (Bruszt and Vukov 2017), they tendentially neglect the role of or even reify the hegemonic ideology. On the one hand, they reify the Commission's increasing overemphasis on the ECE's institutional incapacities, misuse, or misallocation of ESIF transfers (Surubaru 2017; Fazekas and King 2018; Medve-Bálint 2018). Taking these issues seriously, I still document how the Commission mainstreams such visions of *internal* corruption and institutional incapacity to legitimize the continued failure of ECE states in translating the FDI-ESIF complementarity into a faster or full-scale catch-up. On the other hand, the Cohesion Policy is studied as making even the ECE's nationalist catch-up strategies only a variation of pro-systemic strategies of upgrading global competitiveness against the market-based *exclusion* in the EU and globally (Vukov 2020). The ESIF partially substituted the declining FDI inflows as a growth engine since the GEC (Jacoby 2014; Figure 7.1), while continually sourcing the public investment for sustaining the ECE convergence in the labour skills, infrastructural development and SME structures (Medve-Bálint and Šćepanović 2020).

For tracing the EU's visions and ECE's catch-up strategies, I interpret two sets of documents. The first set includes the so-called Cohesion Reports (EC 1996, 2001, 2004, 2007, 2010, 2014, 2017). Published by the Commission since 1996, the three-year editions of this report periodically evaluate the 'progress made towards achieving economic and social cohesion' (Maastricht Treaty 1993). I also include the shorter Progress Reports, which appear in-between the three-year editions (EC 2008, 2009, 2013). The second set was negotiated by the Commission and the national governments to form the so-called programming documents in ECE states. The Community Support Framework was negotiated for the period 2004–2006 (GoCR 2003; GoRH 2003; GoRP 2003; GoSR 2003) during the accession. In the post-accession period, the National Strategic Reference Frameworks covered the period between 2007 and 2013 (GoCR 2007; GoRH 2007, 2010; GoRP 2007; GoSR 2007). The Partnership Agreements were then negotiated for the post-GEC period between 2014 and 2020 (GoCR 2014; GoRH 2014; GoRP 2014, 2017; GoSR 2014). I decode the Commission's visions of FDI-ESIF complementarity through interpreting the Cohesion Reports, while the programming strategies reveal their concrete national reappropriations in the ECE states.

## European Union: Regulating the 'Less' and 'Moderately Developed' Europe

The analysis starts with reviewing the EU's hegemonic visions. After fifteen years of their convergent integration, the Commissions' mapping of 'development clubs' (EC 2017, 21ff) found the *less developed* Hungary and Poland, and the *moderately developed* Czechia and Slovakia stuck in the lower ranks of the EU's middle-income trap. Table 7.1 documents this contradictory catch-up with the EU's North-Western core and Southern (semi)periphery. I trace how the Commission has produced, reproduced and deepened the convergence/catch-up visions of FDI-ESIF complementarity from the accession period of the 1990s to the post-GEC period of the 2010s. Such visions prioritize the ECE's integration into the German-led export-oriented bloc, which encompasses the Benelux in the West, Scandinavia in the North, Northern Italy in the South and ECE in the East (Becker and Jäger 2012; Jessop 2014; Krpec and Hodulák 2019; Šitera 2020). Since the (post)accession period, the ESIF transfers were re-envisioned as a key public investment in the infrastructural and institutional convergence for the ECE's FDI-led catch-up with the core-like development. As the GEC crisis disrupted the FDI-led catch-up, the ESIF-based convergence and the real catch-up with the debt-driven and diverging Southern European semiperiphery substituted this disruption (Becker et al. 2015; Bohle 2017; Bruszt and Vukov 2017). By the late 2010s, the stalling pace of post-crisis catch-up with the North-Western core was linked with the ECE's internal failings in the institutional and innovation convergence. The restored catch-up visions project thus repurposing the ESIF transfers so that these failings are overcome, while ECE attracts the FDI and upgrades the SME in higher value-added positions in the EU-based global value chains.

Since the 1990s, the Commission has put the FDI-ESIF complementarity into the centre of ECE development. By accepting the FDI-based visions, ECE state managers were expected to replicate the 'Irish experience' as a '"good practice" of the first order' (EC 2001, 71). The Irish strategy relied on channelling the ESIF into the physical and human infrastructures to enable the FDI-led reindustrialization. In order to succeed 'in attracting higher quality investments', the Irish neoliberal strategies of 'low wages, low corporate taxation and generous [investment] incentives' had to be followed (EC 1994, 85; 1996, 54). Ireland's successful upgrade from its initial (semi)peripheral position alongside Greece, Spain and Portugal to reaching the attributes of core development established the catch-up model for ECE. Hence, the early introduction of globalist FDI-oriented strategies was always linked with the (post-)accession promise of ESIF transfers. In the preparations for both tasks, the pre-accession PHARE funds became avail-

Table 7.1. North-West, South and East according to the GDP per capita in PPS, 2000–2018 (index: EU = 100, 4- to 5-year averages).

| Territory | Pre-Accession 2000–2003 | Post-Accession 2004–2008 | Crisis 2009–2013 | Postcrisis 2014–2018 | Developmental Level Late 2010s[i] |
|---|---|---|---|---|---|
| **North-West** | **130** | **129** | **130** | **128** | **Highly Developed** |
| Austria | 130 | 129 | 130 | 130 | Highly Developed |
| Denmark | 127 | 127 | 129 | 129 | Highly Developed |
| Germany | 123 | 120 | 122 | 124 | Highly Developed |
| Netherlands | 142 | 141 | 137 | 131 | Highly Developed |
| **South** | **99** | **98** | **90** | **84** | **Moderately-Highly Developed** |
| Greece | 92 | 96 | 80 | 78 | Moderately Developed |
| Italy | 120 | 111 | 104 | 98 | Highly Developed |
| Portugal | 84 | 84 | 80 | 78 | Moderately Developed |
| Spain | 100 | 103 | 94 | 91 | Highly Developed |
| **East** | **60** | **66** | **73** | **76** | **Less-Moderately Developed** |
| Czechia | 76 | 82 | 84 | 89 | Moderately Developed |
| Hungary | 59 | 63 | 66 | 69 | Less Developed |
| Poland | 49 | 53 | 65 | 69 | Less Developed |
| Slovakia | 54 | 65 | 76 | 75 | Moderately Developed |

Source: Own preparation, Eurostat on the data for the periods 2000–2018 and EC (2017, viii–x, 21–25) on the indication of developmental levels.

Note: i. The developmental hierarchies are discursively produced by the Commission in the Cohesion Policy.

able to assist the ECE states in the 'period of massive economic restructuring and political change' (EC 2001, 154) on their path to the EU.

Making the dual external inflows complementary was made urgent because the eastern enlargement formed 'an unprecedented challenge for the competitiveness and internal cohesion of the Union' (EC 2004, xxv). There was thus 'the importance of restructuring' (EC 2001, 8) the ECE economies due to their 'acute and wide-ranging' institutional backwardness and given their 'worn out, obsolete or non-existent' (EC 2004, 16, 174f) physical and human infrastructures. These infrastructures ranged from transport networks to education and training systems or SME structures. The ESIF had to be channelled into all domains of the infrastructural convergence to enable the locational conditions for the FDI. The market-enabling institutional restructuring was thus linked with such an infrastructural convergence so that the ECE states could 'strengthen their competitiveness' and thus realize their 'catch-up' with the EU averages (EC 2004, xxii, 16). In return, ECE materialized its growth potential for the North-Western core. When matched with this convergent neoliberal restructuring, the combination of industrial legacies, 'lower wages', geographical 'proximity' and 'low corporate taxes' promised economic returns for the core MNC and states as a result of their higher global competitiveness (EC 2007, 73f). The FDI-ESIF complementarity as a win-win strategy thus re-envisioned the new member states from an economic threat to a growth opportunity:

> The challenge for cohesion policy is to help them bring their infrastructure up to date, modernize their education and training systems and create a business environment favourable to investment .... This is not impossible, as the experience of Ireland demonstrates forcibly, but it will require effective support from the EU .... Given the increasing interdependencies which exist in trade and investment, the economic development of the new Member States can potentially provide the dynamic to initiate and sustain higher rates of growth throughout the EU .... Structural deficiencies in endowment of infrastructure and human capital mean that these countries, as well as many lagging and problem regions in the EU15, are not able to contribute as much as they might to the competitiveness of the EU as a whole .... The gains to Germany and Italy, in particular, of stimulating growth in the new Member States are, therefore, substantial, though all existing EU countries stand to benefit from this and from the higher growth of the EU market. (EC 2004, 14f)

Observing the post-accession catch-up as 'occurring' and likely to 'continue' (EC 2007, viii, x, 9), the Commission has also fixed its limits due to the global competition and crisis since the late 2000s. These limits were articulated as inscribed externally in the global structure to save the legitimacy of FDI-led reindustrialization and also to find new investment horizons for the ESIF. Before the GEC outbreak, the ECE strategies were thus re-envisioned in the new 'global context [where] catching up takes different forms' (EC 2007, iv). While the core states had to compete with their developed global rivals, the ECE's catch-up became conditioned by the continued infrastructural upgrade and export-oriented 'cost competitiveness' against the 'competition from the emerging Asian economies' (EC 2007, xviii, 153). As the crisis outbreak stalled the catch-up due to the 'rapid reduction' (EC 2013, 10) in the EU intra-trade and intra-investment flows, the legitimacy of the FDI-led development had to be saved. Although being 'volatile and highly sensitive to the economic cycle', the investment and trade links formed 'an opportunity to develop a strong cluster' and thus facilitate 'positive knowledge spillovers' in ECE (EC 2009, 32; 2010, 8).

Although the 'available resources [were directed] back to "mother" companies' in the North-Western core, the precrisis 'rise [in FDI stock] was never reversed' in ECE (EC 2013, 8ff). The crisis of globalist integration through the FDI was thus rearticulated as an external challenge to be overcome over time and through increased global competitiveness rather than as a factor behind the ECE's vulnerabilities and stalled catch-up.

Emerging from the GEC, the ESIF transfers and the South European debt-driven crisis were offered as a substitution for this stalled catch-up with the North-Western Europe since the early 2010s (Table 7.1). The Eurozone debt crisis in the Baltics and especially Southern Europe foregrounded the FDI-led reindustrialization in Czechia, Hungary, Poland and Slovakia as the most resilient catch-up strategies. The four ECE economies could thus be envisioned to 'perform relatively well' or 'recover quite quickly' in contrast to Southern Europe (EC 2010, 3; 2013, 7). The ESIF were found to substitute for the FDI when accounting 'for half or more of the total' (EC 2014, 54) governmental investment. The ESIF transfers not only constituted 'a substantial contribution to growth and jobs' but formed also a 'growth-friendly expenditure' on supply-side conditions for resuming the post-crisis catch-up (EC 2014, 54; 2017, 166f). While Southern Europe became associated with diverging in both real terms such as the GDP and nominal ones like unemployment, ECE was often associated with the convergent trajectory. Poland 'escaped the crisis relatively unscathed' (EC 2013, 17). Slovakia integrated into the high and medium-tech manufacturing cluster around 'the central part of Europe, notably in Germany, Northern Italy and the Czech Republic' (EC 2008, 28; 2013, 8). Most of the city-regions 'in Poland, Germany, Sweden, Slovakia and Czechia' (EC 2013, 32) were observed as generally resilient to the crisis.

Because the transnational integration did not explain the stalling catch-up, the Commission bureaucrats identified the internal failures as its cause. Indeed, the 'competitiveness as measured remained largely unchanged' (EC 2017, 51) in ECE, among other states. Since the early 2000s, these internal barriers shifted from the gap in physical infrastructures to the inadequate institutional performance such as the governance and innovation capacities. During the GEC, these visions of inadequate institutional convergence were foregrounded. While the 'questionable' expertise of state managers and the 'ostensibly high' but outdated skills of the ECE workforce were expected to be repaired by the ESIF- and FDI-based knowledge and policy spillovers (EC 2004, 16, 174f), ECE populations failed as proper students in this regard. In the 2010s, the 'corrupt or inefficient government' is emphasized (EC 2017, 136). Despite the 'improvements' and 'increases', such indicators remain on 'relatively low scores' in ECE (EC 2014, 166; 2017, 142). The low scores on governance capacity not only explain the ECE backwardness anew but also legitimize the reorientation of developmental targets in this way. The lacking governance capacity explains the lower 'innovation and entrepreneurship' (EC 2014, 163f; 2017, 136) because such spillovers remain sensitive to the inefficient institutions in the state apparatus and the domestic SME structures. Therefore, the new conditions of resumed catch-up require going beyond 'offering low cost land and labour' to improve 'the quality of their institutions and business ecosystem' (EC 2017, 25).

By the late 2010s, the Commission observes ECE as an integrated global semiperiphery, which however fails in advancing enough from its peripheral positions in the EU-based 'global value chains' (EC 2017, 11). Only its capital city-regions accumulate the higher value-added FDI to be observed as highly developed islands 'located in catching up countries' (EC 2010, 42). This creates the vision for the other city-regions to catch-up through additional 'spillovers' (EC 2010, 71; 2017, xii) once their infrastructural and institutional convergence improved enough. On the one hand, the new visions of channelling the ESIF into moving up the value chains signalled an update for the globalist catch-up strategies in the (semi)peripheral states. On the other, the increased orientation of such visions at corruption and institutional inefficiencies signalled the Commission's readiness to delegitimize detours from these visions by the post-GEC nationalist rise in these states.

## East Central Europe: Managing the Dual Dependency

This section studies the impact of the Commission's visions and the ESIF dependency on the two types – globalist and nationalist – of state strategies in ECE. There was an FDI-led convergence on the globalist strategies in the 2000s (Drahokoupil 2009). Epitomized by the post-2010 Hungary under the Fidesz governments and the post-2015 Poland under PiS governments (Scheiring 2020; Toplišek 2020), the post-GEC emergence of nationalist strategies is studied in ECE. While the globalist strategies were asymmetrically enforced during the ECE's subordinate economic integration into the EU's neoliberal order (Bohle 2006; Shields 2012), the nationalist strategies challenge the FDI dependency within this crisis-ridden (semi)peripheral integrations. I document how the Cohesion Policy has been inherent to this asymmetrical transnationalization of the ECE state. As Figure 7.1 shows, the FDI dependency has become increasingly complemented with the ESIF dependency over time. Figure 7.2 further documents how the ECE general government investment has become highly reliant on the steady ESIF transfers since the GEC, also in comparison to the EU average. Making the catch-up illusion in ECE more tangible (Arrighi 1990; Gagyi 2016),

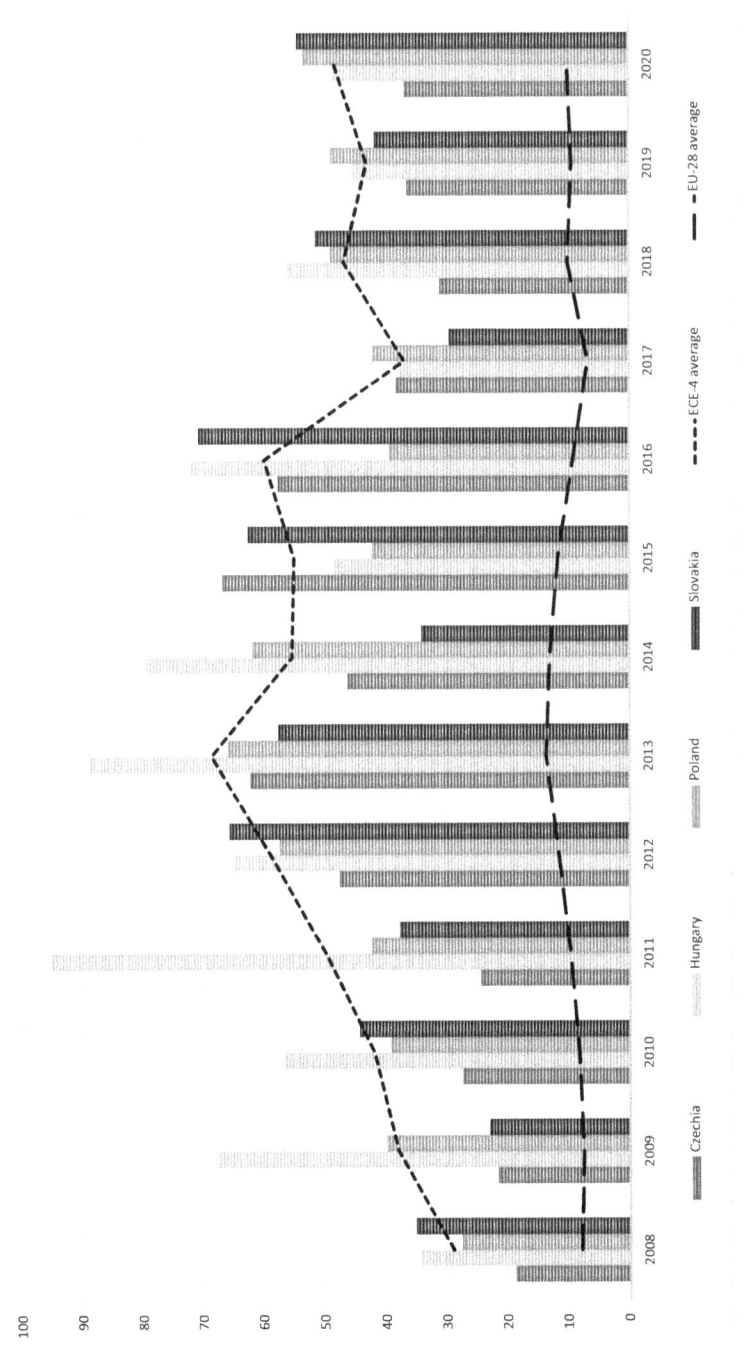

**Figure 7.2.** Share of ESIF in the General Government Investment, 2008–20 (by percent). Source: author's own preparation; European Commission (revenues and expenditures data for the EU budget headings for the Cohesion Policy) and Eurostat (general government gross fixed capital formation). Created by the author.

I thus argue that the ESIF dependency has co-produced both – globalist and nationalist – types of catch-up strategies in ECE as merely varieties of *pro-systemic* state strategies.

To support this argument, I search for commonalities and differences through an inter-temporal and inter-spatial comparison. I follow Arrighi (1990, 17) to observe how the ECE state managers, when deciding between the pro-systemic/-FDI/-EU tendencies and the anti-systemic/-FDI/-EU ones, have relied 'more on one than on the other' and tended to 'alternate or combine the two' as well. Temporarily, I compare the globalist strategies of the 2000s and the nationalist strategies of the 2010s. Spatially, I compare the Polish and Hungarian showcases of nationalist strategies with those of the 2010s strategies in Czechia and Slovakia. Based on such comparing, I claim that the ESIF transfers enabled the hyper-integrationist tendencies (Šćepanović 2013; Medve-Bálint and Šćepanović 2020) in the globalist strategies as they made the FDI-led neoliberal restructuring more socioeconomically and infrastructurally sustainable, and thus politically legitimate in the 2000s. In the 2010s, the very same effect limited the anti-systemic tendencies by co-producing the strategies of selective economic nationalism (Toplišek 2020; Becker 2020; Scheiring 2022). As finally shown, the main difference between these two types of strategies relates to the ESIF-FDI complementarity. While the globalist strategies favoured the ESIF investment into attracting the foreign MNC, the nationalist selectively shift it to support domestic SME. As somewhat expected by Wallerstein (1988) and Arrighi (1990), the main commonality of these catch-up strategies consists in sustaining the ECE populations as a skilled but relatively cheaper labour for both foreign and domestic capital.

## Globalist Strategies

In the 2000s, the globalist strategies were enforced by the EU and privileged by the emerging ECE 'state-foreign capital nexus' (Bohle 2006; Pavlínek 2016) to consolidate the intra-regional convergence on the FDI-led development. While there were nationalist elites and tendencies, as documented below, the globalist strategies overwhelmingly prevailed (Drahokoupil 2009). As the growing FDI dependency was exhaustive for the ECE states, it established conditions for the ESIF dependency. This made the ESIF transfers indispensable for the political legitimacy of globalist elites and their industrial or broader strategies of enabling 'sustainable development based on competitiveness' (GoCR 2003, 54). As economic concessions, the ESIF transfers filled the growing funding gap in the neoliberalizing 'race to the bottom' (Bohle 2009; Pavlínek 2016) over the FDI: low capital taxes, enforced flexibilization of labour codes in combination with the public subsidies for workforce retraining, cheap or free infrastructural sites for the investment localization and tax holidays. As a trade-off, the ESIF transfers simultaneously legitimized the globalist strategies among labouring populations and domestic capital because they formed resources for the 'modernization and catching-up to the EU-15 average' (GoRH 2007, 20). Three key investment areas of physical redevelopment, workforce adaptation and firm development dominated the convergence/catch-up visions.

The physical infrastructures such as the transport links but also general urban redevelopment were prioritized. The 'connection' (GoRH 2003, 138), 'sustainability' (GoCR 2003, 38) and 'attractiveness' (GoRP 2003, 117) of ECE could be improved as a result. First, the connectivity navigated the physical integration of the newly accessed economies. Therefore, the 'backward' (GoCR 2003, 15), 'missing' (GoHR 2003, 112) and 'highly unsatisfactory' (GoRP 2007, 136) transport links had to be upgraded on all scales from the intra-regional and intra-national transport networks to the trans-regional and trans-border links. Thus, integrating the ECE capital metropoles and second-tier city-regions into the Trans-European Transport Networks, the highways, airports, ports, but also energy transmission networks became involved. Given that the ECE economies were prone to excessive pollution, the 'environmental infrastructure' (GoSR 2003, 130) became another priority due to sustainability. Such investment ranged from the greening of their industrial production to the renewal of urban infrastructures like the water supply and waste disposal networks or the air pollution control facilities. In these visions of urban redevelopment, the environmental sustainability could then be matched with the 'economic and social attractive[ness]' (GoRH 2007, 83) of ECE city-regions with respect to the localization of foreign investment.

The ESIF-based infrastructures have a dual use because they are consumed by local populations but must inevitably attract foreign investment into ECE. The same goes for 'human capital through better education and improved qualifications' (GoRH 2003, 57) of ECE populations. Ranging from workers to developers, researchers to qualified managers, this was lagging behind the 'labour demands of international companies' (GoRH 2007, 27). The following conditions needed to be fixed: the 'low effectiveness of' (GoRP 2007, 21) labour markets and welfare states, 'outdated' (GoRH 2007, 38) social and health infrastructures, and 'inadequate' (GoSR 2007, 18) educational and training systems. First, the flexible labour markets had to fix the lack of '[profession and spatial] mobility' so that the low 'adaptability' of workforce and firms to the structural and technological restructuring could be increased (GoCR 2007, 45). Modernizing the labour market through *active* labour market policies, the institutional capacities of employment offices had also to be increased for sustaining the highly employable workforce. Last, the modernization of education and training systems from elementary schools to universities was to make them responsive to 'matching the qualification supply with the demand' (GoCR 2007, 32) by investors who appreciate 'healthy and highly qualified labour resources' (GoRP 2007, 68). Indeed, the health infrastructures from hospital facilities to their effective management required modernization because a 'healthy population is a synonym for a prosperous and productive workforce creating higher profit' (GoSR 2007, 70).

The available 'business infrastructure' for both domestic and foreign investors was then privileged besides other 'nonmarket' incentives such as a 'favourable investment environment, which is characterized by skilled labour power, low labour costs, low tax burden' (GoSR 2007, 27, 32, 53). This infrastructure included the preparation of industrial zones and parks or innovation centres for the arrival of greenfield investment or the regeneration of industrial brownfields. Although the ESIF could not serve as direct incentives like the tax holidays, they complemented them as an 'indirect support' (GoCR 2003, 55, 61, 94). This business infrastructure aimed at integrating the domestic SME into 'supplier' functions to the foreign MNC, and thus integrating the whole domestic economy into the global 'subcontracting chains' (GoRH 2007, 80f). To succeed in this endeavour, the lagging SME structure had to be equally modernized because the 'multinational firms are not willing to subcontract with firms that lack appropriate management skills, products, trained workforces and modern technology' (GoRH 2003, 21). Therefore, the modernization needs of domestic capital were understood but simultaneously subordinated to the major aim of embedding the MNC into the ECE production structures.

Such globalist visions of FDI-ESIF complementarity were broadly similar, yet nationally varied in Czechia, Hungary, Poland and Slovakia. Their state managers generally followed the hyper-integrationist visions where the ESIF investment would reinforce the FDI-led trajectories toward convergence on the 'higher value-added' economic activities (GoRH 2007, 77ff; GoRP 2007, 59ff; GoSR 2007, 26f). In these visions, the threat of remaining stuck in the low value-added positions was thus the outcome of the region's persistent internal failures, that is the low innovation capacities and the incapacity to fully utilize the spillover opportunities offered by the FDI-ESIF complementarity. However, the Hungarian and Slovak strategies were more prone to the promotion of FDI-led development than the Polish and Czech strategies. Czechia articulated the middle-income-trap threats emanating from the globalist strategies, which would underpin the nationalist turn in the post-crisis ECE:

The strong FDI inflow over the last seven years has significantly changed the character of the Czech economy and increased its competitiveness. The future threat lies in the fact that the low-cost strategy of some foreign investors may lead to their departure from Czechia, which would have serious social consequences. For sustainable growth, it is necessary to change the current strategy and focus on strengthening the competitiveness and its resources . . . . Czechia shows signs of a dual economy, the downside of which is the lagging behind of SME controlled by domestic entities, which is reflected in their weak level of innovation, low share of domestic sales, low success in foreign markets and insufficient intensity of ties with foreign companies at home and in international networks. In the case of the existence of a dual economy, the economy is driven mainly by the segment of large companies, often with foreign owners. In the case of small businesses, this is a significant threat to the future that is only very slowly being overcome. (GoCR 2007, 6ff)

The explanation of this restrained position was the political representation in the Czech government. The Czech strategic documents rigorously stressed the interests of 'domestic and foreign' (GoCR 2007, 35, 41, 51) capital during the programming period between 2007 and 2013. During its final negotiation and the whole implementation, the Czech governments were led by a neoliberal but *nationalist* ODS in coalition with the small globalist centre-right parties. Similar political challenges to the globalist strategies appeared also in the other three states before the GEC (Drahokoupil 2009). However, the governmental alternation had a little effect on the change of globalist strategies in this period. Rather, it remained constrained by the transnationalization of ECE states through the asymmetric negotiations with the Commission and the powerful representation of the MNC interests in the state–foreign capital nexus.

## Nationalist Strategies

This explains the post-GEC rise of nationalist strategies as a rather *selective* departure from the globalist ones (Becker 2020). Although there is a national difference among the ECE states, the nationalist strategies generally redirect the ESIF away from their FDI-oriented complementarity (Vukov 2020). By doing so, they assist the domestic capital without necessarily abandoning the neoliberally tinted FDI-led development. They also legitimize the domestic capture by national technocrats or capitalists rather than putting the interests of ECE populations outside their treatment as skilled but cheap and available labour. Hence, the ESIF transfers allowed the post-2010 Hungary under Fidesz-led governments and the post-2015 Poland under PiS-led governments to articulate a more selective state-led developmentalism and make it credible (Toplišek 2020; Naczyk 2022; Scheiring 2022). However, this only deepened the Czech nationalist approach under the ODS-led governments from before the crisis with a more state-led orientation in ECE but did not substantively differ from the Czech and Slovak strategies in the 2010s. Such state strategies also only shifted from the FDI dependency to the ESIF dependency. The nationalist strategies remain thus broadly within the Commission's visions of innovation-oriented upgrading to higher positions in the EU-based global value chains.

Such strategies open the question of 'dual economy' at full scale (GoRH 2014, 20f; GoSR 2014, 16). The dual economy denotes the semiperipheral coincidence of the FDI-led production structures and the underdeveloped sectors of domestic production structures as their outcome. Besides exploiting the skilled but cheaper labour, other problems like the declining FDI inflows and the rising outflow of profits condition this strategic reorientation (Galgóczi, Drahokoupil and Bernaciak 2015; Figure 7.1). The Hungarian nationalist reorientation shows it:

> As close links between the global corporate sector and the domestic SME sector have only partially developed.... The great challenge of Hungarian economic policy for two decades has been how to connect these two sectors more closely, how small and medium-sized [domestic] enterprises can catch up with large [foreign] enterprises in technology, business knowledge and productivity.... In order to improve the growth potential of SME, it is essential to develop resource-deficient SME in a focused and differentiated way, including the creation and expansion of already developed capacities of enterprises belonging to key sectors, regions and target groups of entrepreneurs. These developments will help bring the production and service infrastructures of SME closer to the level represented by large enterprises, thus enabling SME to enter markets, retain their markets and expand further. (GoRH 2014, 21f)

Branded as the Széchenyi 2020 (GoRH 2014), the Hungarian strategy was symbolic in the nationalist rhetoric. It expanded the so-called New Széchenyi Plan (GoHR 2010), which was introduced shortly after the Fidesz's return to the government in 2010 to correct the earlier globalist strategy (GoRH 2007). Titled after the nineteenth century economic reformer István Széchenyi, the strategic plans were framed as a patriotic program of economic renewal. In Poland, the Strategy for Responsible Development 2020 was prepared to promote the very same renewal. Colloquially known as the Morawiecki Plan after the PiS minister of development/finance and then prime minister Mateusz Morawiecki, it also served to rearticulate the earlier Polish strategy of 2014 (GoRP 2014, 2017). Both sets of documents blamed the globalist strategies for deepening the risk of 'middle-income trap' (GoRP 2017, 25) and the 'declining competitiveness' (GoRH 2010, 8) as a result. They offered to repair it through the comprehensive industrial policy for the domestic strategic sectors. For example, this included prospective innovation-led domestic enterprises in IT sectors (Lechowski, Chapter 4). For these efforts, the 'EU and state funds' (GoRH 2010, 16f; 2017, 52) had to be mobilized. This nationalist reorientation in Hungary and Poland was however fully consistent with the strategic shifts in the two other ECE states as the Slovak strategy explains:

> The Slovak economy is dependent on the economic performance of large multinational corporations operating in export-oriented manufacturing industries. Although some SME have successfully integrated into the supply structures of these MNC, a large number of SME, especially in non-manufacturing sectors, where the vast majority of SME operate, face numerous problems resulting from the loss of target markets due to disruption of organic ties to specialized innovation process and systematically educated human capital. The situation became significantly more complicated after 2008, when the global economic crisis led to a significant drop in the economic condition and viability of SME. (GoSR 2014, 17)

The Czech post-GEC approach goes even further than the Slovak one even though its response is not different from the Hungarian and Polish receipts: using the ESIF to support the domestic enterprises. Therefore, Czechia had to support the domestic SME but also 'large firms, which have bigger capacity to systematically invest into the R&D' (GoCR 2014, 39f), in order to restore the domestic determinants of economic growth. Irrespective of the political forces in ECE governments, all of them had to deal with the FDI-based disruptions and declining inflows by finding a new catch-up strategy. Rather than repudiating it, the FDI dependency was pragmatically upgraded through fixing the dual characteristics of ECE production structures. The ESIF transfers were to be rechannelled for the support of national capital so that the domestic enterprises gained more upward positions in the global and innovation 'supply' (GoCR 2014, 40; GoSR 2014, 70) and 'value chains' (GoRP 2014, 98ff; 2017, 65) or capacity to succeed alone in the global competition.

However, the ECE populations remained reincorporated into these strategies only as a source of more skilled and qualified but still relatively cheaper labour for the new rounds of ECE catch-up. These innovation-led visions bring the flexible labour markets more tightly together with the (tertiary) education and training systems. The education system is thus paired with the effective labour market as a producer of high-quality human resources especially in the IT and other innovation sectors, which are both key for the 'non-price competitiveness' but simultaneously 'lacking' in ECE (GoCR 2014, 10). It is essential to offer a 'qualified and adaptable workforce', which is 'the source of competitive advantage for the domestic enterprises and attracts investment from those multinational ones' (GoCR 2014, 18). As producers of a qualified workforce, universities and research institutions are instrumentalized as intermediating platforms for technological transfers. They are integrated into the new business infrastructures such as the 'science-technological' (GoRP 2014, 90), 'R&D' (GoSR 2014, 11), and 'innovation' (GoRH 2014, 80ff) parks and centres of excellence. Through them, the MNC are expected to localize higher-valued activities such as the innovation and development centres, while the domestic SME integrate into the innovative production networks.

By the late 2010s, the nationalist strategies show a realization of the FDI-based middle-income trap. At the same time, they remain a showcase of selective adaptation of the formerly hyper-integrationist pro-systematic strategies rather than any anti-systemic/anti-FDI/anti-EU strategies. In efforts to overcome such a middle-income trap, they shift the ESIF transfers from primarily promoting the MNC locational interests to those of upgrading the domestic SME and large enterprises. On the one hand, the Cohesion Policy enables such a selective shift through the ESIF as economic concessions. On the other, shifting away from the FDI dependency, the ECE state managers must rely much more on the Commission-led ESIF dependency. In effect, Poland and Hungary's state-led developmentalism was overall neither distinctively different from the globalist strategies, nor from Czechia and Slovakia, and nor were all ECE nationalist strategies radically different from the Commission's visions.

## Conclusion

This chapter analyses the Cohesion Policy's role in the (semi)peripheral integrations of ECE states into the EU. By doing so, I try to answer why the ECE state managers still pursue the developmentalist illusion of overcoming the ECE's middle-income trap and catching up with North-Western Europe. First, this is because the Cohesion Policy offers the ESIF transfers as an economic concession to ECE states in core-peripheral relations, while simultaneously conditioning such transfers with these states' consensual integration into the EU's asymmetric regulation of such relations. Second, since the 1990s, such Commission-led visions fixed the ECE integrations by pairing the North-Western FDI inflows and the Commission-led ESIF transfers. Third, such visions of FDI-ESIF complementarity have offered rather credible material conditions for sustaining the visions of future convergence/catch-up but simultaneously established power constraints within this dual dependency in ECE. In the 2000s, the Cohesion Policy politically enforced but simultaneously legitimized the region's globalist convergence on the FDI dependency. In the 2010s, the ESIF dependency has enabled nationalist strategies but simultaneously helped to constrain them into a more or less selective adaptation of rather than abandoning the FDI dependency.

Such findings extend the emerging studies on the role of the Cohesion Policy and its ESIF in shaping the state strategies in the FDI-led dependent market economies (Vukov 2020; Medve-Bálint and Šćepanović 2020). By doing so, I study the developmental ideologies, visions, or illusions that the Cohesion Policy co-produces, reproduces and deepens in the ECE's state economic strategies. Exploring such an ESIF dependency, this also nuances the neo-Gramscian/regulationist/dependency scholarship on the EU's regulation of uneven and dependent core-peripheral development (Becker et al. 2015; Ryner and Carfuny 2016). Taking the Cohesion Policy seriously, I explore how the EU's hegemonic tendencies co-opt the (semi)peripheral state managers, and thus reproduce the core-peripheral relations in the process. Last, among other (trans)national determinants, this all allows a better understanding of the emergence of the nationalist state strategies in the manner of selective rather than a full-blown economic nationalism (Becker 2020; Toplišek 2020; Scheiring 2022).

Are there any alternatives for ECE to change the allegedly successful but still FDI-led and EU-based march to the 'middle-income trap' (EC 2017, 21ff)? One legitimate way is to push and enable the ECE states to make their economies more innovative (Ban and Mihály, Chapter 3) and their domestic enterprises global leaders (Lechowski, Chapter 4). However, such strategies would have to abandon the competitiveness-oriented and firm-centred catch-up imperative that mainly benefits – domestic or foreign – capital, the leading metropolitan city-regions vis-à-vis the peripheral city-regions, while reducing the ECE populations into a skilled but cheaper and easily available labour (Wallerstein 1988; Arrighi 1990; Gagyi 2016). Much of this would require a systemic change of the EU which is nowadays a globalist neoliberally tinted order that prioritizes exportist competitiveness over Europeans' socioeconomic protection. Such an order would have to be socially protective and nonhierarchical across the EU's multilevel governance. In such an order, Cohesion Policy would sponsor the EU's social, economic and territorial cohesion in this socially protective way rather than sponsoring (semi)peripheral catch-ups through the mutual intra-European competition in the name of enhancing Europe's global competitiveness. In the 2020s, the EU flagship strategies such as the European Green Deal have become more aware of this need.

However, they could easily end up as a greenwashing of the very same developmentalist illusion.

## Acknowledgements

This work was supported by the European Regional Development Fund project 'Creativity and Adaptability as Conditions of the Success of Europe in an Interrelated World' (reg. no.: CZ.02.1.01/0.0/0.0/16_019/0000734) implemented at Charles University, Faculty of Arts. The project is carried out under the ERDF Call 'Excellent Research' and its output is aimed at employees of research organizations and PhD students. This work was also supported by the institutional funding of the Institute of International Relations Prague.

**Daniel Šitera** is Head of the Centre for Global Political Economy of the Institute of International Relations and Researcher in the Department of Politics at the Faculty of Arts of the Charles University, both in Prague. His work has been published in the *Journal of International Relations and Development* and *New Perspectives*. He specializes in the international political economy of East Central Europe.

## References

Arrighi, Giovanni. 1990. 'The Developmentalist Illusion: A Reconceptualization of the Semiperiphery'. In *Semiperipheral States in the World-Economy*, edited by William Martin, 11–42, New York: Praeger.
———. 2010. *The Long Twentieth Century: Money, Power, and the Origins of Our Times*. New York: Verso.
Arrighi, Giovanni, and Jessica Drangel. 1986. 'The Stratification of the World-Economy: An Exploration of the Semiperipheral Zone'. *Review* 10(1): 9–74.
Arrighi, Giovanni, Beverly Silver and Benjamin Brewer. 2003. 'Industrial Convergence, Globalization, and the Persistence of the North-South Divide'. *Studies in Comparative International Development* 38(1): 3–31.
Bachtler, John, and Carlos Mendez. 2013. *EU Cohesion Policy and European Integration: The Dynamics of EU Budget and Regional Policy Reform*. London: Routledge.
Baun, Michael, and Dan Marek. 2014. *Cohesion Policy in the European Union*. London: Palgrave Macmillan.
Becker, Joachim. 2020. 'Selektiver Wirtschaftsnationalismus und Klassenprojekte: Fidesz und PiS im Vergleich'. In *Autoritärer Populismus*, edited by Carina Book, Nikolai Huke, Norma Tiedemann and Olaf Tietje, 150–64. Münster: Westfälisches Dampfboot.

Becker, Joachim, and Johannes Jäger. 2012. 'Integration in Crisis: A Regulationist Perspective on the Interaction of European Varieties of Capitalism'. *Competition & Change* 16(3): 169–87.

Becker, Joachim, Johannes Jäger and Rudy Weissenbacher. 2015. 'Uneven and Dependent Development in Europe: The Crisis and Its Implications'. In *Asymmetric Crisis in Europe and Possible Futures: Critical Political Economy and Post-Keynesian Perspectives*, edited by Johannes Jäger and Elisabeth Springer, 81–96. London: Routledge.

Bieling, Hans-Jürgen, Johannes Jäger and Magnus Ryner. 2016. 'Regulation Theory and the Political Economy of the European Union'. *Journal of Common Market Studies* 54(1): 53–69.

Bohle, Dorothee. 2006. 'Neoliberal Hegemony, Transnational Capital and the Terms of the EU's Eastward Expansion'. *Capital & Class* 30(1): 57–86.

———. 2009. 'Race to the Bottom? Transnational Companies and Reinforced Competition in the Enlarged European Union'. In *Contradictions and Limits of Neoliberal European Governance: From Lisbon to Lisbon*, edited by Bastian van Apeldoorn, Jan Drahokoupil and Laura Horn, 163–86. London: Palgrave Macmillan.

———. 2017. 'European Integration, Capitalist Diversity and Crises Trajectories on Europe's Eastern Periphery'. *New Political Economy* 23(2): 239–53.

Brenner, Neil. 2004. *New State Spaces: Urban Governance and the Rescaling of Statehood*. Oxford: Oxford University Press.

Bruszt, Laszlo, and Visnja Vukov. 2017. 'Making States for the Single Market: European Integration and the Reshaping of Economic States in the Southern and Eastern Peripheries of Europe'. *West European Politics* 40(4): 663–87.

Cantat, Celine. 2017. 'Cohesion Policy and Perceptions of the European Union in Hungary: A Cultural Political Economy Approach'. *CPS Working Papers* 2017/2018: 1–30.

Cox, R. W. 1983. 'Gramsci, Hegemony and International Relations: An Essay in Method.' *Millennium: Journal of International Studies* 12(2): 162–75.

Drahokoupil, Jan. 2009. *Globalization and the State in Central and Eastern Europe: Politics of Foreign Direct Investment*. London: Routledge.

Drahokoupil, Jan, and Martin Myant. 2015. 'Putting Comparative Capitalisms Research in Its Place: Varieties of Capitalism in Transition Economies'. In *New Directions in Critical Comparative Capitalisms Research*, edited by Matthias Ebenau, Ian Bruff and Christian May, 155–71. London: Palgrave Macmillan.

European Commission (EC). 1994. *Fifth Periodic Report on the Social and Economic Situation and Development of the Regions of the Community*. Luxembourg: Office for Official Publications of the European Communities.

———. 1996. *First Report on Economic and Social Cohesion*. Luxembourg: Office for Official Publications of the European Communities.

———. 2001. *Unity, Solidarity, Diversity for Europe, Its People and Territory: Second Report on Economic and Social Cohesion*. Luxembourg: Office for Official Publications of the European Communities.

———. 2004. *A New Partnership for Cohesion: Convergence, Competitiveness, Cooperation. Third Report on Economic and Social Cohesion*. Luxembourg: Office for Official Publications of the European Communities.

———. 2007. *Growing Regions, Growing Europe: Fourth Report on Economic and Social Cohesion*. Luxembourg: Office for Official Publications of the European Communities.

———. 2008. *Fifth Progress Report on Economic and Social Cohesion: Growing Regions, Growing Europe*. Luxembourg: Office for Official Publications of the European Communities.

———. 2009. *Sixth Progress Report on Economic and Social Cohesion. Creative and Innovative Regions*. Luxembourg: Office for Official Publications of the European Union.

———. 2010. *Investing in Europe's Future: Fifth Report on Economic, Social and Territorial Cohesion*. Luxembourg: Office for Official Publications of the European Communities.

———. 2013. *Eighth Progress Report on Economic, Social and Territorial Cohesion. The Urban and Regional Dimension of the Crisis*. Luxembourg: Office for Official Publications of the European Communities.

———. 2014. *Investment for Jobs and Growth: Promoting Development and Good Governance in EU Regions and Cities. Sixth Report on Economic, Social and Territorial Cohesion*. Luxembourg: Office for Official Publications of the European Communities.

———. 2017. *My Region, My Europe, Our Future: Seventh Report on Economic, Social and Territorial Cohesion*. Luxembourg: Office for Official Publications of the European Communities.

Fazekas, Mihály, and Lawrence King. 2018. 'Perils of Development Funding? The Tale of EU Funds and Grand Corruption in Central and Eastern Europe'. *Regulation & Governance* 13(3): 405–30.

Gagyi, Agnes. 2016. '"Coloniality of Power" in East Central Europe: External Penetration as Internal Force in Post-socialist Hungarian Politics'. *Journal of World-Systems Research* 22(2): 349–72.

Galgóczi, Béla, Jan Drahokoupil and Magdalena Bernaciak, eds. 2015. *Foreign Investment in Eastern and Southern Europe after 2008. Still a Lever of Growth?* Brussels: ETUI.

Government of the Czech Republic (GoCR). 2003. *Rámec podpory Společenství – Česká republika 2004–2006* [Community Support Framework – Czech Republic 2004–2006]. Prague: Ministry of Regional Development of the Czech Republic.

———. 2007. *Národní strategický referenční rámec ČR 2007–2013* [National Strategic Reference Framework of Czech Republic 2007–2013]. Prague: Ministry of Regional Development of the Czech Republic.

———. 2014. *Dohoda o partnerství pro programové období 2014–2020* [Partnership Agreement for the Programming Period 2014–2020]. Prague: Ministry of Regional Development of the Czech Republic.

Government of Republic of Hungary (GoRH). 2003. *Community Support Framework – Republic of Hungary 2004–2006 – Objective 1 of the Structural Funds*. Budapest: National Development Agency of the Republic of Hungary.

———. 2007. *The New Hungary Development Plan – National Strategic Reference Framework of Hungary 2007–2013*. Budapest: National Development Agency of the Republic of Hungary.

———. 2010. *New Széchenyi Plan: The Development Strategy of Recovery and Progress* (Preliminary, Abridged Version for Public Review). Budapest: Ministry for National Economy of the Republic of Hungary.

———. 2014. *Magyarország Partnerségi Megállapodása a 2014–2020-as fejlesztési időszakra*, [Hungarian Partnership Agreement for the 2014–2020 Programme Period]. Budapest: Office of the Prime Minister, Ministry of National Economy and the Office of the National Economic Planning of the Republic of Hungary.

Government of Republic of Poland (GoRP). 2003. *Narodowy Plan Rozwoju 2004–2006 (Dokument przyjęty przez Radę Ministrów w dniu 14 stycznia 2003 r.)* [National Development Plan 2004–2006 (Document Approved by the Council of Ministers on 14 January 2003]. Warsaw: Ministry of Regional Development of the Republic of Poland.

———. 2007. *National Strategic Reference Framework 2007–2013 – National Cohesion Strategy*. Warsaw: Ministry of Regional Development of the Republic of Poland.

———. 2014. *Programowaniie perspektywy finansowej 2014–2020 – Umowa Partnerstwa* [Programming of Financial Perspective 2014–2020 – Partnership Agreement]. Warsaw: Ministry of Regional Development of the Republic of Poland.

———. 2017. *Strategia na Rzecz Odpowiedzialnego Rozwoju do roku 2020 (z perspektywą do 2030 r.)* [Strategy of the Responsible Development 2020 (with a Perspective of 2030)]. Warszawa: Ministry of Regional Development of the Republic of Poland.

Government of Slovak Republic (GoSR). 2003. *Národný rozvojový lan* [National Development Plan]. Bratislava: Ministry of Construction and Regional Development of Slovak Republic.

———. 2007. *Národný strategický referenčný rámec 2007–2013* [National Strategic Referential Framework 2007–2013]. Bratislava: Ministry of Construction and Regional Development of Slovak Republic.

———. 2014. *Partnerská dohoda SR na roky 2014–2020* [Partnership Agreement of Slovak Republic 2014–2020]. Bratislava: Ministry of Transport, Construction and Regional Development of Slovak Republic.

Ivanova, Maria. 2007. 'Why There Was No "Marshall Plan" for Eastern Europe and Why This Still Matters'. *Journal of Contemporary European Studies* 15(3): 345–76.

Jacoby, Wade. 2014. 'The EU Factor in Fat Times and in Lean: Did the EU Amplify the Boom and Soften the Bust?' *Journal of Common Market Studies* 52(1): 52–70.

Jessop, Bob. 2006. 'Spatial Fixes, Temporal Fixes and Spatio-Temporal Fixes'. In *David Harvey: A Critical Reader*, edited by Noel Castree and Derek Gregory, 142–66. Oxford: Blackwell Publishing.

———. 2014. 'Variegated Capitalism, das Modell Deutschland, and the Eurozone Crisis'. *Journal of Contemporary European Studies* 22(3): 248–60.

Krpec, Oldřich, and Vladan Hodulák. 2019. 'The Czech Economy as an Integrated Periphery: The Case of Dependency on Germany'. *Journal of Post Keynesian Economics* 42(1): 59–89.

May, Christian, and Andreas Nölke. 2015. 'Critical Institutionalism in Studies of Comparative Capitalisms: Conceptual Considerations and Research Programme'. In *New Directions in Critical Comparative Capitalisms Research*, edited by Matthias Ebenau, Ian Bruff and Christian May, 83–100. London: Palgrave Macmillan.

Medve-Bálint, Gergő. 2018. 'The Cohesion Policy on the EU's Eastern and Southern Periphery: Misallocated Funds?' *Studies in Comparative International Development* 53(2): 218–38.

Medve-Bálint, Gergő, and Vera Šćepanović. 2020. 'EU Funds, State Capacity and the Development of Transnational Industrial Policies in Europe's Eastern Periphery'. *Review of International Political Economy* 27(5): 1063–82.

Naczyk, Marek. 2022. 'Taking Back Control: Comprador Bankers and Managerial Developmentalism in Poland'. *Review of International Political Economy* 29(5): 1650–1674.
Nölke, Andreas, Tobias ten Brink, Simone Claar and Christian May. 2015. 'Domestic Structures, Foreign Economic Policies and Global Economic Order: Implications from the Rise of Large Emerging Economies'. *European Journal of International Relations* 21(3): 538–67.
Nölke, Andreas, and Arjan Vliegenthart. 2009. 'Enlarging the Varieties of Capitalism: The Emergence of Dependent Market Economies in East Central Europe'. *World Politics* 61(4): 670–702.
Pavlínek, Petr. 2016. 'Whose Success? The State–Foreign Capital Nexus and the Development of the Automotive Industry in Slovakia'. *European Urban and Regional Studies* 23(4): 571–93.
Ryner, Magnus, and Alan Carfruny. 2016. *The European Union and Global Capitalism: Origins, Development, Crisis*. London: Palgrave Macmillan.
Šćepanović, Vera. 2013. 'FDI as a Solution to the Challenges of Late Development: Catch-up without Convergence?'. PhD diss., Central European University.
Scheiring, Gábor. 2020. *The Retreat of Liberal Democracy Authoritarian Capitalism and the Accumulative State in Hungary*. London: Palgrave Macmillan.
———. 2022. 'The National-Populist Mutation of Neoliberalism in Dependent Economies: The Case of Viktor Orbán's Hungary'. *Socio-Economic Review* 20(4): 1597–1623.
Shields, Stuart. 2012. *The International Political Economy of Transition*. London: Routledge.
———. 2020. 'The EBRD, Fail Forward Neoliberalism and the Construction of the European Periphery'. *The Economic and Labour Relations Review* 31(2): 230–48.
Šitera, Daniel. 2020. 'Transition Redux: Global Warehousing in Europe's Westernmost East'. In *Steel Cities: The Architecture of Logistics in Central and Eastern Europe*, edited by Kateřina Frejlachová, Miroslav Pazdera, Tadeáš Říha and Martin Špičák, 176–89. Zürich: Park Books.
Sum, Ngai-Ling, and Jessop, Bob. 2013. *Towards a Cultural Political Economy: Putting Culture in Its Place in Political Economy*. Cheltenham: Edward Elgar.
Surubaru, Neculai-Cristian. 2017. 'Administrative Capacity or Quality of Political Governance? EU Cohesion Policy in the New Europe, 2007–13'. *Regional Studies* 51(6): 844–56.
Toplišek, Alen. 2020. 'The Political Economy of Populist Rule in Post-Crisis Europe: Hungary and Poland'. *New Political Economy* 25(3): 388–403.
Van Apeldoorn, Bastiaan. 2002. *Transnational Capitalism and the Struggle over European Integration*. New York: Routledge.
Vukov, Visnja. 2020. 'More Catholic than the Pope? Europeanisation, Industrial Policy and Transnationalised Capitalism in Eastern Europe'. *Journal of European Public Policy* 27(10): 1546–64.
Wallerstein, Immanuel. 1988. 'Development: Lodestar or Illusion?' *Economic and Political Weekly* 23(39): 2017–23.
Walters, William, and Jens-Henrik Haahr. 2005. *Governing Europe: Discourse, Governmentality and European Integration*. London: Routledge.
Wozniak Boyle, Jennifer. 2006. *Conditional Leadership: The European Commission and European Regional Policy*. Lanham, MD: Lexington Books.

CHAPTER 8

# East-Central Europe
## *The Eternal Periphery of the EU?*

Christian Schweiger

## Introduction

The member states in the East-Central region of the European Union have been characterized as the new member states due to their late accession in 2004 and 2007. They have also remained an integral part of the European periphery both in terms of their position as economic laggards and as predominantly passive policy-takers. This chapter examines the extent to which the ECE countries have managed to extricate themselves from their role as the Eastern European periphery in the wake of the global financial crisis in both economic and political terms.

The ECE region has been united in their joint challenge of having to overcome the remainders of the economic and political legacy of state-planned communism. This resulted in a profound overhaul of the foundations of domestic policies, economies, welfare states and established cultural ties. The main aim of the ongoing transformation was to reduce the development gap between the region and the EU-15 average, a process in which the ECE countries have made overall relatively good progress under persistently adverse external conditions. This chapter critically examines the economic and political transformation process of the ECE countries in the context of their membership of the European Union, which has been dominated by a period of almost consistent crisis conditions, ranging from the effects of the financial crisis to the Eurozone, the migration crises, the disintegration as a result of the Brexit process and the current Covid-19 pandemic. The first part of the chapter outlines the background to the peripheralization of the region. In the second part, the focus lies on the prospects for the ECE member states to emerge from their peripheral position in the post-Brexit EU under the conditions of an increasingly unpredictable external environment and a new tendency towards autocratic renationalization in their domestic policies.

## Accession to the EU: The Good Europeans

The first group of eight ECE accession countries (ECE-8) that joined the EU in January 2004 aspired to integrate smoothly by adopting the position of compliant Europeans (Dimitrov 2012, 308). As a result, they accepted an accession strategy of strictly conditional Europeanization, which was based on the newly established Copenhagen membership criteria (Sedelmeier 2015, 427) and initially excluded Bulgaria and Romania due to their failure to show the ability to implement solid governance and effectively combat corruption. The same approach was adopted in the eurozone, where the ECE countries were not given the same benefit of the doubt that their Southern European counterparts had when the euro was established as a hard currency in 2002. The noticeable gap in gross domestic product (GDP) per capita between the ECE-8 (and after 2007, the ECE-10) accession candidates and the EU-15 average at the time of the pre-accession negotiations was a major concern for Western European governments considering the prospect of a 'Big Bang' enlargement of the EU towards the post-communist countries in the ECE region (Goetz 2005, 256). What was branded as good governance hence became a priority for the EU-15 in the assessment of the ability of the ECE-8's readiness to join the Union under the newly established Copenhagen membership criteria. Romania and Bulgaria were excluded from the initial accession group and could join only in 2007, due to the concerns raised by the European Commission about the two countries' readiness to join. Even in economic terms, strict conditionality was applied. It was only in 2007 that Slovenia became the first ECE member state to join the eurozone.

The EU-15 countries were most of all concerned about the potential economic, budgetary and social impact of accession of the new member states from the ECE. Among these, the budgetary costs to support the new members in their transition efforts and the potential impact of a mass influx of workers from the ECE to EU-15 domestic labour markets raised the greatest concern, as there was a noticeable gap in GDP per capita between the ECE-8 (and after 2007, the ECE-10) accession candidates and the EU-15 average. Apart from the Czech Republic, Slovenia and Hungary, the ECE candidates remained below 60 percent of GDP per capita of the EU-15 average, and in some cases, such as Bulgaria and Romania, only around 30 percent. There was also reason for concern found in the levels of unemployment amongst the ECE accession group, which had reached double figures in Bulgaria, Estonia, Latvia, Lithuania, Poland and Slovakia in 2000. A particular case for concern was Poland, where unemployment was steadily rising and had substantially increased between 2000 and 2004 (Figure 8.1).

These figures resulted in a profound discussion amongst the EU-15 countries about whether the ECE accession candidates should be brought into the EU as a larger group or stage by stage in smaller groups in line with their economic and social levels of development. Consensus on allowing a bigger group to join as part of a 'Big Bang' enlargement could only be reached on the basis of clearly determined budget restrictions for the eastward enlargement and the introduction of transitional periods for the free movement of workers from the ECE members. Particularly the German government led by Social Democratic Chancellor Gerhard Schröder insisted on the latter in order to counter mounting public concerns in Germany about the potential adverse effects of the eastward enlargement on the domestic labour market. The German position reflected the overall concerns in the EU-15 about a potential race to the bottom regarding labour market standards after the accession of a group of new countries whose wage levels remained substantially below the EU-15 average.

The EU-15 ultimately agreed to go ahead with the 'Big Bang' eastward enlargement by allowing eight states from the ECE to join in May 2014 but only based on the strict application of the Copenhagen criteria. The ECE new member-state candidates consequently faced firm conditionality in the assessment of their application. This was partly the result of considerations

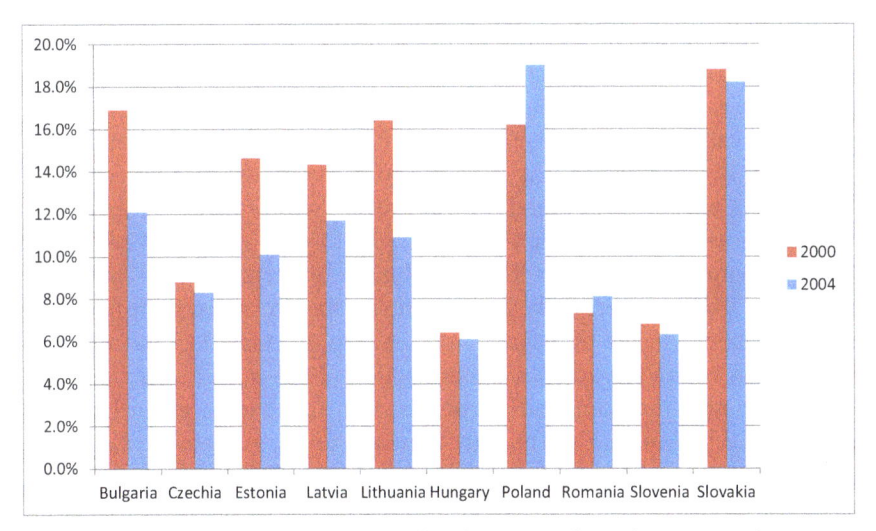

**Figure 8.1.** Unemployment annual data by sex and age (1992–2020). Source: Eurostat 2022. Created by the author.

about the management of past waves of enlargement, particularly towards South-Eastern Europe, which could have been more effective if stricter conditionality had been applied. In the case of Bulgaria and Romania, the strict conditionality resulted in a delay in their entry due to concerns about corruption and inefficient state structures, which were considered to be unfit to manage the integration into the EU acquis. The ECE-8 group also faced restrictions on access to EU structural funds and to the Western labour markets, with the exception of the United Kingdom, Ireland and Sweden. In the years following the accession, the 2004 group had to be content with receiving less financial support than previous accession groups – especially Ireland and the Southern European group, that is Greece, Portugal and Spain. The 2004 newcomers, including Cyprus and Malta, received on average as little as €21 million (for Malta) and as much as just over €4 billion (for Poland). Poland as the largest country in the accession group was substantially lagging behind the EU-15 average in terms of social cohesion. It nevertheless received only about one third of the EU's total cohesion fund (€4.1 billion) between 2004 and 2006. In contrast Spain, which had joined in 1986 and consistently been subject to substantial cohesion fund support, had received €56.3 billion of the total share of the cohesion funds between 2000 and 2006. During the budgetary period of 1993–99, Spain had already received €42.3 billion, which illustrates its status as the main recipient of cohesion fund support since it had joined the European Community in 1986 (European Commission 2008, 17ff).

The compromise, which was reached under the pre-enlargement Agenda 2000 at the March 1999 EU Council summit in Berlin under the German presidency, determined that the EU-15 would allocate a total of €18.7 billion for pre-accession support for the period between 2000 and 2006 for the ten accession candidates that were bound to join in 2004. In addition, the EU-15 allocated €58 billion for structural fund payments to the new member states. By comparison, the EU had spent 168 billion ECUs (which are fully equivalent to euros based on the 2004 1:1 conversion) on structural and cohesion funds between 1994 and 1999. Of this amount, 42.4 billion went to Spain, 21.7 billion to Italy, 18.2 billion to Portugal and 17.7 billion to Greece. The Southern European countries had for more than two decades been beneficiaries of massive financial support from EC/EU cohesion funds. Even in the previous budgetary round (1989–93) of structural and cohesion funds, the Southern European countries had received between 8.2 and 14.2 billion ECUs. The East-Central European member states, on the other hand, had to wait for an increase in financial support until 2007, when the EU allocated €67.3 billion to Poland, €26.7 billion to the Czech Republic and €25.3 billion to Hungary under a substantially enhanced total cohesion budget of €347 billion (European Commission 2008, 25).

The eastward enlargement was strongly supported by a joint British-German effort, spearheaded by British prime minister Tony Blair and German chancellor Gerhard Schröder. Schröder branded the eastward enlargement of the EU as a historic chance to finally bring an end to the more-than-four-decades-long artificial division of Europe under the Cold War. It was the reflection of the widely shared domestic sentiment in Germany that bringing the ECE region back to the heart of Europe represented a moral duty to return the countries in the region to their rightful place at the heart of Europe. At the same time, Germany had concerns about the impact of the freedom of movement of workers from the acceding low-wage ECE member. Schröder consequently demanded the temporary restriction of the free access of ECE workers to the German labour market. He justified these demands with the widespread domestic public concerns in Germany about the impact of large-scale labour migration from low-wage countries in the ECE: 'We need identification with the enlargement process .... Without this identification and without transitional periods it will be really difficult to find the necessary consent' (Schröder 2001). Germany hence negotiated the ability to impose transitional restrictions on the freedom of movement for citizens from the ECE member states for up to seven years after their accession to the EU. This had never occurred during previous rounds of enlargement and illustrated how the ECE countries were treated as second-class citizens in comparison to their Western and Southern European neighbours. In contrast, the British Labour government under Tony Blair granted unrestricted access for workers from the ECE member states to the UK labour market. This was replicated by Ireland and Sweden. In this respect, Blair emphasized that his government considered the influx of ECE workers as an opportunity for the booming British economy and labour market, which struggled to fill vacancies in the services industry and the National Health Service (NHS).

The strict conditionality for the 2004 ECE-8 group and even more so for the late joiners in 2007 – Bulgaria and Romania – became even more obvious in relation to their widespread ambition to join the eurozone. Germany and France had permitted the fragile Southern European economies, including Greece, to join the founding group of the eurozone in 2002. This occurred even though especially Italy and Greece entered the euro with large budget deficits of over 100 percent of GDP. They were consequently in clear breach of the budgetary criteria which were essentially a German design but never strictly implemented (Schweiger 2014, 68). The acceptance of the Southern European economies into the eurozone on predominantly political grounds stood in stark contrast with the strict conditionality that the ECE applicants faced. In the case of the Southern Europeans, economic concerns outweighed the overall ambition to engage these countries in a prolonged process of coercive 'Europeanisation' (Börzel 2005), which would ensure their long-term economic, political and social modernization. Membership of the core project of the monetary union was hence considered to be indispensable to avoid the peripheralization of the Southern region while embedding it into a monetary union that was supposed to be driven by collective responsibility. The failure to strictly apply conditionality by enforcing the Stability and Growth Pact (SGP) criteria and to define overall membership principles, especially in the area of good governance, allowed Southern Europeans to adopt a free-rider position with predominantly superficial levels of Europeanisation (Magone 2016, 92).

The ECE members were not granted this flexibility in the eurozone. The European Central Bank (ECB) applied the complete set of SGP criteria in the assessment of their readiness to join, including inflationary targets. This came as an addition to the determination of the precise political and economic entry preconditions under the 1993 Copenhagen membership criteria. Overall, the combination of these factors justifies the classification of their treatment as that of second-class members (Åslund 2010, 8). The latter's self-perception as second-class members of the EU has been the hallmark of the process of reintegration into the European mainstream in the ECE region.

## The Transformation Process: The Patchy Success of Conditionality

The stricter conditionality applied to the ECE members can be counted at least as a partial success when it comes to the overall economic convergence process. All member states, apart from Slovenia, managed to increase their GDP per capita in the decade since their accession to the EU. In Slovenia's case, the GDP per capita declined only slightly from a relatively higher position. Substantial increases in comparison to the 2005 figures are noticeable for Bulgaria, Estonia, Latvia, Lithuania, Poland, Romania and Slovakia (Figure 8.2). In Poland, GDP per capita increased by almost 20 percent, and in Romania, even more than 20 percent. The EU hence witnessed noticeable economic convergence between the EU-15 and the new ECE members in the decade after accession and before the onset of the global financial crisis.

This occurred because of annual GDP growth rates in the ECE, which surpassed those of the EU-15 average. Before the onset of the global financial crisis, all ECE member countries except for Hungary grew by more than 2 percent annually. Baltic states of Estonia, Latvia and Lithuania recorded substantial growth rates between 7 and 11 percent between 2004

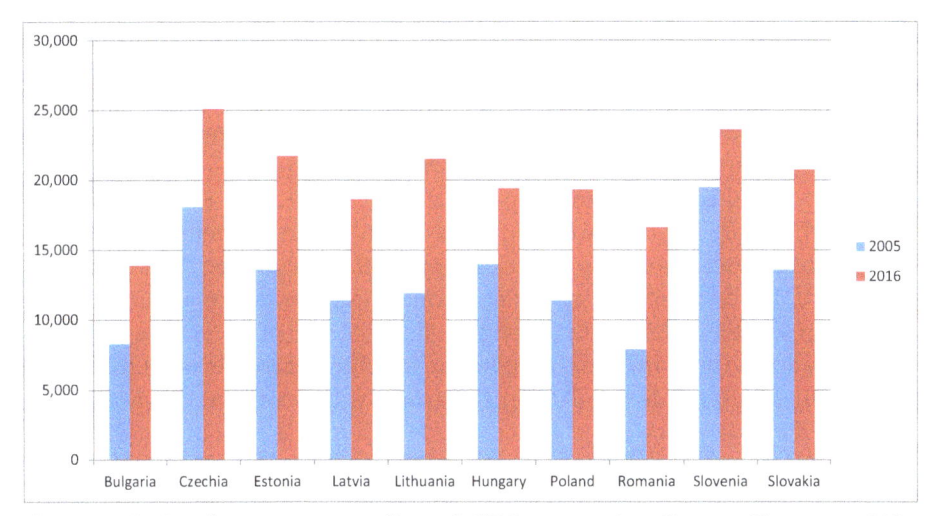

**Figure 8.2.** Purchasing power adjusted GDP per capita. Source: Eurostat 2023a. Created by the author.

and 2007. Among the EU-15, this was matched only by Ireland, which recorded similar foreign direct investment (FDI) as the Baltic states and the wider ECE region. Like the Irish *Celtic Tiger* economy, the overall economic transition of the ECE was one of dependent industrialization. In the case of the Baltics, the transition was characterized by openness to financial-service investments particularly from Sweden (Arrak 2013, 138). In the case of the Visegrád countries, dependence on the German manufacturing chain became the prominent feature of the process of economically catching up based on the externally financed growth model, with the largest share provided by German FDI (Farkas 2018, 62). In the background of the attractiveness of the ECE for external finance lays the low-wage culture in this region, which on the one hand represents a competitive advantage for the region but on the other hand manifests the challenge of overcoming the middle-income trap which has taken hold in ECE societies. This became an integral part of their perceived competitive advantage, despite the noticeable adverse effects on cohesion in their domestic societies (Galgoczi 2014, 367). The low-wage culture has to be considered also in combination with budgetary austerity in many countries, which was implemented to meet budgetary criteria in preparation for eurozone entry. This has resulted in low levels of social expenditures in the region. The latest thematic assessment of the European Commission on social inclusion under the Annual Semester policy cycle of the impact of social transfers on reducing poverty in the EU reveals that all ECE member states belong to the group of countries with low levels of welfare spending (excluding pensions). Romania,

Bulgaria, Estonia and Latvia are positioned at the very bottom of the scale both in terms of spending levels and overall poverty reduction (European Commission 2016).

Economic growth and budgetary austerity became preconditions for the successful entry of five new ECE member states (Slovenia, Slovakia, Estonia, Latvia and Lithuania) into the eurozone between 2007 and 2015. This was remarkable, as it occurred during a period when budgetary crises in existing member states in Southern Europe were threatening the future of the euro. In the aftermath of the eurozone crisis, the desire to adopt the euro has waned considerably among the current ECE outsiders, especially in Poland, Hungary and the Czech Republic, which currently form the Eurosceptic group inside the EU. For the group of five countries that joined during the peak of the crisis, concerns about potential limitations of their economic sovereignty and apprehension about having to contribute to the financial support system of the European Stability Mechanism (ESM) were outweighed by the anticipated positive economic and political effects of joining the EU's core project (Haughton 2016, 257).

Thirteen years after the 'Big Bang' enlargement and despite noticeable progress, the ECE region continues to be positioned on the economic and social periphery of the EU. Economically, the peripheralization of the region predominantly stems from three factors: (1) lack of an indigenous base for long-term economic competitiveness; (2) strong reliance on externally financed growth, even though the origin and scope of the FDI in individual cases has gradually become more diverse (Hancke 2011, 169); and (3) the inability to escape the middle-income trap under which wage ranges stagnate and the stagnation has become an integral part of the region's competitive economic advantage. As Figure 8.3 illustrates, gross wages in the ECE region have remained at the bottom end of the EU levels and grown, with the exception of Slovenia, only modestly. The middle-income trap is consequently a significant feature of the economic and social transformation in East-Central Europe.

In social terms, the middle-income trap in the ECE region manifests itself in the inability to recover from its peripheral status, persistently lower standards of living and higher poverty levels than the EU average. In recent years, the ECE countries have been surpassed only by the crisis countries in Southern Europe in this respect. Figure 8.4 shows that the share of people who are at risk of poverty remains above the EU average (changing compositions) in most ECE member states, apart from the Czech Republic, Hungary, Poland, Slovakia and Slovenia. Particularly Bulgaria and Romania also have a noticeably high ratio of population classified as being severely materially deprived (19.5 and 14.5 percent of the total population, respectively). Eurostat describes this as a situation of abject poverty in which individuals

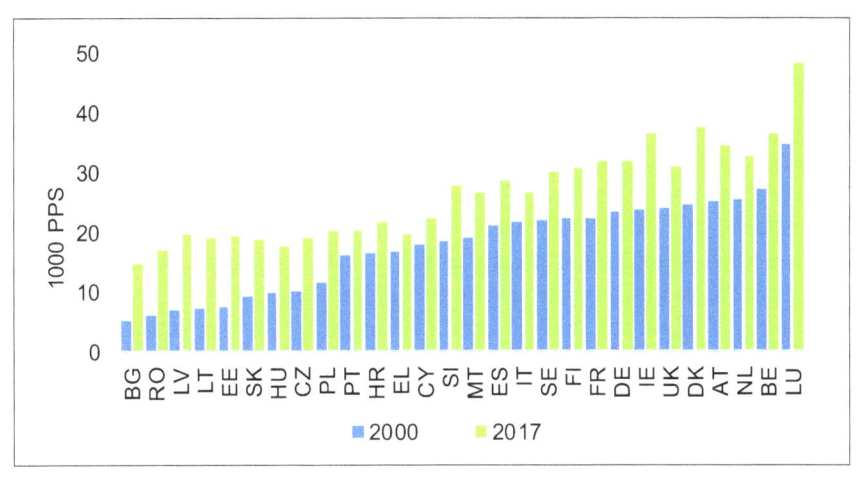

**Figure 8.3.** Gross wages and salaries per employee in 1,000 PPS in 2000 and 2017. Source: European Commission (2018, 117). Created by the author.

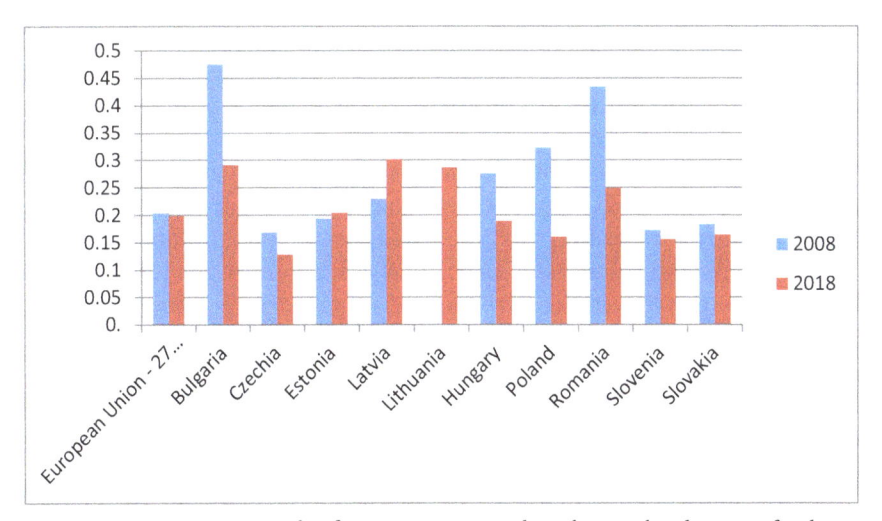

**Figure 8.4.** Persons at risk of poverty or social exclusion by degree of urbanisation – EU 2020 strategy. Source: Eurostat (2023b). Created by the author.

in question lack core elements essential for a decent standard of living such as being able to afford good-standard housing, heating for their dwellings, or meals containing meat or fish every second day. These figures are also above the EU average in Estonia, Latvia, Lithuania and Slovakia (Eurostat 2023b).

The relative success in catching up with the EU-15 average in terms of economic growth has therefore not been matched by uniform progress in the social area in the region toward higher levels of social cohesion in the ECE member states. Overall, the region continues to be part of the EU's social periphery, with a distinctive low-wage culture and high levels of social deprivation.

These conditions have started to spill over into the political arena, where the trend towards 'democratic backsliding' has slowly been encroaching in the region (Agh 2014, 35). This phenomenon has its roots in the growing public desire to deviate from the political mainstream of the EU and its inherent values of economic and political liberalization. In this respect, the ECE region follows the overall trend in Europe, which has witnessed a noticeable rise in support for populist and Eurosceptic parties that promote protectionist economic nationalism. This was most noticeable in the UK, where the majority support for Brexit was grounded in a mixture of concerns about national sovereignty and economic deprivation in the predominantly English regions. In the ECE member states, the relatively shallow democratization processes have been widely documented. The 2019 Economist Intelligence Unit (EIU) Democratisation Index classifies the entire wider ECE region as displaying 'hybrid/authoritarian' tendencies or 'flawed democracies' the latter of which have a democratization index of less than 6 percent. The overall index consists of an assessment of functioning of electoral processes and pluralism, government, and political participation function and the extent to which political culture and civil liberties are guaranteed. The EIU report classifies all EU member states in ECE as flawed democracies, as they all display weaknesses in their domestic democratic checks and balances, in particular with regard to the power of the executive. In the report, the EIU emphasizes that 'Eastern Europe's democratic malaise persists amid a weak political culture, difficulties in safeguarding the rule of law, endemic corruption, a rejection by some countries of "liberal" democratic values and a preference for "strongmen" who bypass political institutions, all of which creates a weak foundation for democracy' (The *Economist* Intelligence Unit 2020, 30).

This is supported by the Progress Report on the first two decades of social and political development in the ECE member states; the report highlights that the recent tendency to backslide from an already-superficial democratization towards a new authoritarianism in countries such as Hungary and Poland has its origins in the negative social effects of globalization, which initially was embraced in the ECE region. The openness to FDI and the resulting modest-to-strong economic growth in the region has been accompanied by an overall 'negative social process' which has failed to create more inclusive societies (Agh 2013, 59). Since the onset of the global financial crisis, the adverse social effects of the ECE region's embrace of the Washington consensus have resulted in an increasingly obvious desire by the new member states to evolve from their role as passive policy-takers. Under the conditions of economic crisis, the established political agenda of the EU has come under increasing scrutiny because of the breakdown of the permissive consensus between the political elites and the public (Schweiger 2016, 26). ECE governments have tried to use this opportunity to take a more active role in reshaping the EU's policies (Koller 2014, 74), which has more recently positioned them in opposition to Germany, their traditional close ally and as such the EU's liberal core.

## Challenging the EU's Liberal Core

The newly found self-confidence in parts of the ECE has resulted in a more sceptical view of the Eurozone's governance architecture (Visvizi and Tokarsi 2014, 461; Stryjek 2013, 59), which has contributed to a backsliding in the overall reform process. The financial crisis has hence enhanced the existing differentiation of the ECE region from the EU's core led by Germany, which keeps promoting liberal economic and social values. Instead, the ECE's peripheral economic and social position in the EU risks turning it into a new political periphery that increasingly questions the liberal political status quo. This is symbolized by the recent firm and united opposition by the Visegrád states to Germany's liberal migration policy. This differentiation has opened a new and potentially dangerous cleavage in the EU, which could tear apart the fabric of the traditionally close partnership between Germany and the ECE at a time when the EU urgently needs co-operation in anticipation of the UK's exit.

The relative success in catching up in economic terms with the EU-15 under adverse external conditions has been overshadowed by the growing perception of the post-communist transformation process as a sacrifice in the ECE region. Ultimately, this perception has resulted in an overall feeling of being wounded and victimized, with the dominant opinion that the ongoing profound political, economic and social transformation has been a trauma characterized by insecurity and a loss of cultural belonging (Farkas and Máté-Toth 2018, 37). The persistent status of the region as the EU's periphery that is 'lagging behind in the new, more sophisticated terms of human investment, good governance and social progress' (Agh 2016, 125) has also pushed the region towards political peripheralization. On the positive side, the increased Euroscepticism in the ECE remains an 'insider' Euroscepticism, which is fundamentally hostile towards individual aspects of the EU's agenda, particularly the demands for permanent migration quotas but does not question the EU's overall legitimacy (Bruter 2012, 26). The EU, or more concretely the term 'Brussels', is frequently used as a political scapegoat in ECE domestic politics. This could be seen in the recent anti-EU campaign initiated by Hungarian prime minister Victor Orbán in the run-up to the 2018 national elections in Hungary. Orbán started the controversial 'Let's Stop Brussels' letterbox campaign in which he asked Hungarians to answer suggestive questions on issues relating to national sovereignty in the EU with a particular focus on migration policy. This was echoed by the anti-EU propaganda of the Polish Law and Justice (PiS) government, which published a national defence plan for Poland under former prime minister Szydło who re-emphasized her opposition to migration quotas, which she branded as a 'folly' when she declared, 'We will not participate in any folly of Brussels elites' (Zbytniewska 2017). In recent years Poland has witnessed a continuous trend of weakening of the foundations of the democratic state under the PiS leadership. As a result, serious concerns have emerged about declining judicial supervision of executive powers and respect for the rights of minorities in Polish society (Przybylski 2018, 55). For the EU, Hungary and Poland have consequently become the main focus of concern about the region's trend towards backsliding on post-communist democratic consolidation.

In spite of the growing anti-EU rhetoric in ECE capitals, particularly in Poland, Hungary and the Czech Republic, public opinion in all ECE member states remains favourable towards EU membership. Identifying as EU citizens is currently strongest in Lithuania and Poland (81 percent), followed by Estonia and Hungary (80 percent), Slovakia (79 percent), Latvia (73 percent), Romania (72 percent), the Czech Republic (65 percent) and Bulgaria (56 percent) (European Commission 2019). The majority of the region does not identify with the hard Euroscepticism which has taken hold in the United Kingdom, the first country to exit the EU.

There is nevertheless a real risk that the current predominantly policy-oriented insider Euroscepticism in the ECE could harden and ultimately lead towards the questioning of the purpose of EU membership. In this respect, the future relations between the ECE and their former leading partner, Germany, is crucial. If the end of the Merkel era after the German federal election in 2021 does not result in a more consensual leadership style, the current cleavage between Berlin and the ECEs is likely to grow further. Under Merkel, Germany has pursued a leadership approach in the EU resembling a permanent informal presidency, which materialized as one where collective consensual decision-making has been abandoned in favour of a selective intergovernmental approach (Giddens 2014, 19). This selective mode of governance has deepened the divisions in the EU and primarily contributed to the feeling of marginalization in the ECE member states. The German insistence on its own domestic value system as the core of the EU's liberal agenda poses the risk that the Union will be permanently divided between a small liberal core of countries willing to deepen their political cooperation and a periphery of sovereigntist member states that remain on the sidelines (Bulmer and Paterson 2017, 228–29; Webber 2017, 347).

The relationship with Germany continues to be crucial for the ECE member states both in economic and political terms. Germany has been a long-standing close economic and political ally of the countries in the region. The origins of the close relationship go way back to the Cold War and the period of the Ostpolitik of Social Democratic Chancellor Willy Brandt in the 1970s, which promoted change through cooperation. After reunification, Germany maintained its role as mediator between Western and Eastern European interests. For the aspiring EU members in the region, Germany became the focal point of economic and political contact. The country became the prime promoter of eastward enlargement not simply because its leaders considered it an inevitable act of historic reparation for the horrors caused by the Second World War. German leaders, especially of the Schröder government (1998–2005), also spoke openly of the economic opportunity that eastward enlargement would present for Germany's export-oriented economy. Schröder's Green foreign minister Joschka Fischer emphasized this in his landmark speech on the future of the EU at the Humboldt University in Berlin in May 2000: 'Enlargement will bring tremendous benefits for German companies and for employment. Germany must therefore continue its advocacy of rapid Eastern enlargement' (Fischer 2000).

Consequently, Germany almost naturally became the main foreign direct investor in the region. This was strengthened after the enlargement towards ECE as part of a strategy (Galgoczi 2014, 367) in which Germany successfully exported its 'institutional and regulatory structures' to the ECE (Bulmer, Jeffery and Paterson 2000, 114). For the ECE, Germany became the 'hegemonic stabilizer' of the region (Bulmer and Paterson 2013). This hegemony was perceived positively by Berlin's partners in the region since it had an essentially 'cooperative' nature (Kundnani 2014, 110). The close relationship between Germany and the ECE was reflected by Germany's engagement in the so-called Weimar Triangle, which established trilateral cooperation with Poland and France in 1991. This showed that Poland had potentially become an important strategic partner in the enlarged EU, where it had become harder for Germany to set the agenda based on the bilateral cooperation with France (Paterson 2014, 182). This was also visible in the generally positive attitude ECE leaders displayed towards German leadership in the EU. Even during the eurozone crisis, when Germany's leading role became increasingly contested in Southern Europe as well as in the United Kingdom, the ECE leaders pleaded with

Germany to accept its role as the 'reluctant hegemon' of the eurozone (Paterson 2011, 73).

Based on the country's long-standing stabilizing role in the EU, the eurozone countries expected Germany to use its economic resources to support the crisis countries on the Southern periphery. This was particularly true for the ECE members, which expected Germany to lead the eurozone out of a potentially systemic crisis (Bulmer and Paterson 2013, 1397). East-Central Europeans hence stood firmly with Berlin and pointed at the risk of Germany not engaging in a profound crisis for the euro. The Polish foreign minister Radoslaw Sikorski publicly warned about the potential negative effects of the absence of German leadership at a time of profound crisis during his widely noticed speech on Poland's role in the EU, in Berlin in 2011 (Sikorski 2011). At the 2013 GLOBSEC summit, his Slovak counterpart Miroslav Lajcak stated that he was relaxed about his country being part of the extended economic area of, in his words, 'the greater Germany' (Mikulova 2013). This was not only a reflection of the importance of the close economic and political ties with Germany but also based most of all on genuine support for Germany's ordoliberal approach to reforming the eurozone.

The ECE members uniformly backed Chancellor Merkel's uncompromising conditionality towards the debtor countries in the eurozone. Given the strict conditionality they had faced when they applied to join the EU and subsequently the eurozone, the ECE states refused to grant their Southern European counterparts a free ride. From the ECE perspective, Southern Europe had lived above its means for decades before the financial crisis and now urgently needed to engage in fundamental structural reforms (Haughton 2016, 258). The opposition to financial support to what was considered to be an unsustainable Southern economic and social model cumulated in the temporary refusal by Slovakian centre-right prime Minister Iveta Radicova to back the financial support program for Greece under the newly created European Financial Stability Mechanism (EFSF) (Auer 2016, 82). Germany's willingness to base the eurozone on the European Stability Mechanism (ESM) as a permanent support instrument for countries in crisis in the eurozone has substantially contributed to growing scepticism about the euro in the ECE countries that are still outside the euro. Figure 8.5 illustrates that amongst the group of ECE euro outsiders with the exception of Hungary and Romania, public scepticism towards adopting the euro is now substantial. This corresponds with the stern refusal to consider euro entry by political elites in Poland and the Czech Republic. Only Viktor Orbán in Hungary faces a predominantly pro-euro sentiment by the Hungarian public, which is at odds with his own hostility towards monetary union.

EAST-CENTRAL EUROPE    245

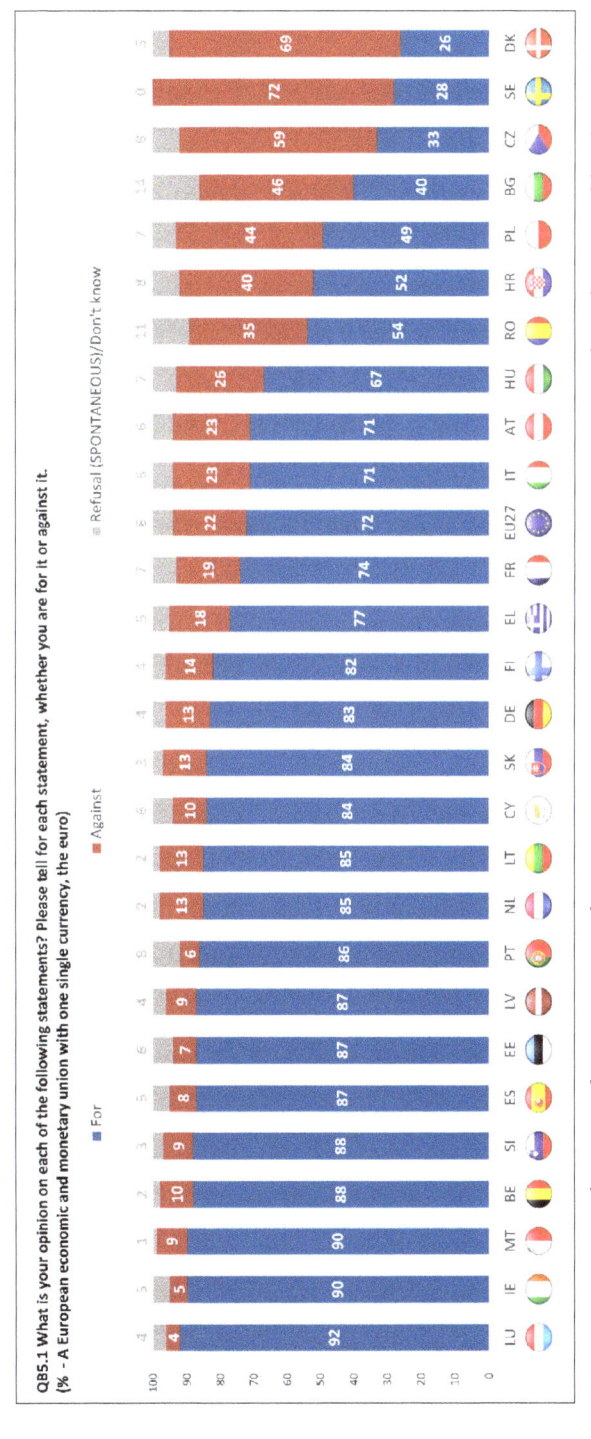

**Figure 8.5.** Attitudes towards economic and monetary union. Source: European Commission (2022). Created by the author.

As much as the ECE countries supported Chancellor Merkel's uncompromising stance in the eurozone crisis, they actively started to oppose German leadership when Merkel adopted the same approach to the resolution of the migration crisis which hit the EU in the summer of 2015. Merkel's self-branded 'moral imperative', with which she attempted to implement binding migration distribution quotas in the EU, significantly changed the ECE perception of German leadership, which was increasingly seen as 'self-righteous' (Streeck 2016) and uncooperative. Merkel's uncompromising and progressively more unilateral leadership style has consequently drawn a new political division between Western Europe and the ECE, which is no longer limited to the economic and social core-periphery division discussed earlier. The positive perception of German hegemony as an essentially stabilizing force in the EU under multiple crisis conditions has been waning. German power is instead seen as an ever more constraining force in the ECE region, which increasingly perceives Berlin's European policy as one predominantly oriented towards transferring Germany's liberal value system towards the EU (Bulmer and Paterson 2017, 229). The firm and unified opposition of the Visegrád-4 (V4) against Germany's migration policy (Schweiger 2016, 116) has instilled a new sense of unity in the ECE region, which overall remains patchy and has frequently characterized by disunity between individual countries (Törő, Butler and Gruber 2014, 393).

## A Question of Leadership: Bridging the Core-Periphery Gap in the EU

The emerging split between Germany and its former close allies in the ECE is predominantly the result of the growing doubts about the German capacity to offer inclusive and stabilizing leadership in the face of the emergence of multiple internal divisions under crisis conditions. The growing electoral support for anti-EU populism in ECE countries, most noticeably in Hungary and Poland, has been enhanced by anti-German overtones. In his recent speeches, Hungarian prime minister Viktor Orbán has pushed his generally Eurosceptic rhetoric to new limits by comparing the 1956 Hungarian uprising against the Soviet dictatorship to the electoral successes for populist parties, which he claimed were based on an 'uprising' of civil society against the liberal European agenda, which excessively promoted 'political correctness' and economic liberalization (Orbán 2017). Orbán has also warned that ECE interests in the EU would be under fundamental threat because 'Brussels is taking our powers away from us one by one, and then they do not know what to do with them' (Orbán 2019). Orbán's warnings are echoed by the PiS leader who has warned the Poles against catching the EU's 'social diseases' (Euractiv 2018). Orbán managed to maintain his strong power base in Hungary at the national elections on 3 April 2021, where his Fidesz-KDNP alliance increased its share of the electoral vote even further by almost 5 percent against a united alliance of opposition parties under the leadership of Péter Márki-Zay. The 2021 national election marks the fourth consecutive election victory for Fidesz in Hungary. In Poland, PiS also increased its share of the electoral vote at the 2019 national parliamentary elections but faces the electorate again in 2023. The prospect of an alternative government without PiS remains slim as opinion polls indicate that the party will once again emerge as the strongest political force in the forthcoming national election (Politico 2022). Hopes for the possible reversal of the trend towards democratic backsliding in the two key Viségrad countries have hence turned out to be preliminary. The EU and here particularly Germany will consequently have to establish ways to deal with the political status quo in the region and to develop a critical but ultimately constructive dialogue with difficult partners in ECE.

The Ukraine crisis has illustrated the neglect of developing an effective common foreign and security policy for the EU. Under Germany's semi-hegemonial leadership the EU neglected this area in favour of focusing on the management of the eurozone crisis. The ECE countries, particularly Poland, have made several attempts to regain Germany's attention to this matter but to very little avail (Handl and Paterson 2013, 334). Germany can no longer afford to neglect this important policy area for the future of Europe's security. A renewed Franco-German leadership impetus to deepen the EU's foreign and security policy cooperation and enhance military capabilities will therefore substantially depend on cooperation with the ECE member states. This is even more important because with the exit of the United Kingdom the EU has lost a key security actor. As the future involvement of the UK as an outsider in the development of European defence capabilities remains profoundly uncertain, the V4 countries and here particularly Poland as the leading player in the area of defence and security, could play a key role in enhancing this crucial policy area. The V4 cooperation has been actively promoting deeper security cooperation through the establishment of joint battlegroups (Suplanta 2013). The problematic case in this area remains Hungary, as its commitment towards strengthening EU defence and security capabilities in response to Russia's military incursion into Ukraine remains lukewarm. Hungary under Orban is therefore likely to remain 'an autocratic thorn in the EU's side' (Matthijs 2022), especially when it comes to foreign and security policy. In spite of the domestic flirt with Orban's illiberalism, Poland stands in stark contrast to the Hungarian position towards Russia. Poland has been a strong advocate of a tough stance towards Russia over Ukraine and a staunch advocate of strengthening the EU's defence and security capabilities in cooperation with NATO (Terlikowski 2022). Poland's cooperation with the remaining big players, that is Germany and France, will be indispensable to ensure that the EU matches its capabilities to the mounting external challenges. Here, the trilateral Weimar cooperation format could potentially play a crucial role but has in recent years become increasingly irrelevant.

The Ukraine crisis has substantially disrupted supply chains and increased inflation in countries across Europe. Combined with the lingering adverse effects of the Covid-19 pandemic, the crisis poses a profound economic and social challenge for the EU, which at the same time offers the opportunity to narrow the gap between the EU core and the ECE periphery. Inflation has particularly affected the low-wage economies in ECE (Barber 2022), which brings a new dimension to the challenge of the middle-income trap in the region. Under these circumstances retreating into self-isolation will not be a viable option for even those countries in ECE which have in recent years pursued an illiberal turn away from the EU's liberal mainstream. At the same time the EU core and, foremost Germany, depends on maintaining its manufacturing supply chains from and export markets in its Eastern neighbourhood. The liberal Western and the partly illiberal Eastern part of EU is consequently bound together by the necessity to cooperate to tackle existential and unprecedented challenges. The new joint recovery facility *NextGenerationEU* offers the basis for a renewed dialogue between the core and the periphery, both in East-Central and in Southern Europe, on shaping a common policy agenda for the future of the EU. The EU core rightly insists that the precondition for cooperation with the ECE countries is their respect for the core elements of the Copenhagen membership criteria, most of all democratic values and respect for the basic rights of minorities. Hungary and Poland will consequently only receive much needed financial support for crisis recovery if they accept these basic parameters and do not continue down the path of democratic backsliding towards autocracy. The triggering of the EU's new 'rule of law mechanism' against Hungary over corruption charges regarding the misallocation of EU funds is a clear warning shot against Poland and other countries in the region who fail to take the EU membership standards seriously (Bayer 2022). This was further underlined by the call of the European Parliament for the Hungarian and Polish national plans under the Recovery and Resilience Facility not to be approved by the European Commission and the Council until 'both countries comply fully with all European Semester recommendations in the field of rule of law, and only after they implement all relevant judgements' (European Parliament 2022). If the governments in Budapest and Warsaw fail to comply, they risk being cut off from urgently needed financial support for economic recovery from the current crises. The EU's new tough line towards ECE illiberalism represents an indispensable basis for cooperation. It nevertheless leaves room for unity in diversity with the need to accept the impact of historically divergent pathways between the EU-15 and the ECE member states who experienced four decades of state-controlled socialism. If Hungary and Poland are willing to abide by the EU's democratic values, they should be offered the chance to pursue policy differentiation from the EU core in other areas, such as migration and energy policy.

## Conclusion: ECE as the Eternal Periphery?

The ECE member states are currently facing a watershed that will not only determine their own position in the EU but also the future of the entire Union. A more central role for the region in the EU will substantially depend on two factors. Firstly, if the ECE governments continue down the path of backsliding on the democratic reforms they adopted during their initial transformation process and move further towards autocratic structures, they will not only alienate the EU's liberal core but also jeopardize their potential to contribute to the shaping of the EU's post-Brexit political agenda. Secondly, the possibility for the ECE countries to move closer to the EU core and abandon their peripheral status as passive policy-takers will strongly depend on relations with Germany, which remains the leading player in the EU. Germany's status as the EU's reluctant hegemon has been strengthened further by France's fragile economic standing and waning power resources. In addition, the UK's exit from the EU has substantially reshaped the EU's internal power structure and strengthened Germany's influence even further.

The ECE governments therefore need to maintain an intensive dialogue with Germany, which remains an indispensable economic and political partner for the region, despite the current fundamental disagreements over issues such as migration, the eurozone and deepening integration. At the same time, the new traffic light coalition under the leadership of chancellor Olaf Scholz, which has governed Germany since the September 2021 federal election, cannot afford to leave the ECE members in their current peripheral political, economic and social position. Given the mounting challenges that the EU is facing, neither Germany nor the ECEs can risk putting their traditionally close partnership in jeopardy at a time when cooperation is most needed. The extent to which the ECE region can be brought back into the EU's core will substantially depend as much on the shape of their domestic policies as on their commitment towards a pro-

European vocation. Even more important will be Berlin's and Paris's willingness to include the ECEs, that is, particularly, on a more inclusive policy agenda given the conditions of an impending Brexit. The success or failure of bringing the ECEs back into the heart of Europe will ultimately not just determine the future of the ECE but also the EU.

**Christian Schweiger** holds the Chair for Research Methods at the University of Cooperative Education Saxony in Germany. His research concentrates on comparative politics and comparative political economy in the European Union, particularly social and labour market policies. His most recent publications include 'Governance under the Covid-19 Pandemic: Comparative perspectives on Germany and Hungary', *Zeitschrift für Vergleichende Politikwissenschaft* (2022), 'The German Economic Model: from Germany's Social Market Economy to Neoliberalism?', in Klaus Larres, Holger Moroff and Ruth Wittlinger (eds.), *Oxford Handbook of German Politics* (Oxford: University Press, 2022), 251–64, and 'Eurozone Membership, Economic Gains and Losses', in Krisztina Arató, Boglarka Koller, Anita Pelle (eds.), *The Political Economy of the Eurozone in Central and Eastern Europe* (London and New York: Routledge, 2021), 102–23.

## References

Agh, Attila. 2013. *Progress Report on the New Member States: 20 Years of Social and Political Developments*. Budapest: College of Communication and Business.
———. 2014. 'Ten Years of Catching-Up Story in the European Union: Differentiated Integration and Multilevel Governance in ECE'. In *10 Years After: Multi-Level Governance and Differentiated Integration in the EU*, edited by Attila Agh, Tamasz Kaiser and Boglarka Koller, 31–61. Budapest: Blue Ribbon Research Center.
———. 2016. 'The Increasing Core-Periphery Divide and New Member States: Diverging from the European Union's Mainstream Developments'. In *Core-Periphery Relations in the European Union*, edited by José M. Magone, Brigid Laffan and Christian Schweiger, 117–29. Oxon: Routledge.
Arrak, Andres. 2013. 'Estonia: From a Bubble to Austerity'. In *From Reform to Growth: Managing Economic Crisis in Europe*, edited by Vít Novotný, 133–52. Brussels: Centre for European Studies.
Åslund, Anders. 2010. *The Last Shall Be the First: The East European Financial Crisis*. Washington, DC: Peter G. Peterson Institute for International Economics.
Auer, Stefan. 2016. 'Will the Centre Hold? Germany, Ireland and Slovakia and the Crisis of the European Project'. In *Core-Periphery Relations in the European Union*, edited by José M. Magone, Brigid Laffan and Christian Schweiger, 72–86. Oxon: Routledge.
Barber, Tony. 2022. 'Inflation Rears Its Head in Central and Eastern Europe', 21 April. Retrieved 30 May 2022 from https://www.ft.com/content/0e8b905f-1c4a-469e-99a7-cebea61a63fe.

Bayer, Lili. 2022. 'In Major First, EU Triggers Power to Cut Hungary's Funds over Rule-of-Law Breaches'. *Politico*, 27 April. Retrieved 30 May 2022 from https://www.politico.eu/article/eu-european-commission-rule-law-mechanism-hungary-funds/.

Börzel, Tanja A. 2005. 'Europeanization: How the European Union Interacts with Its Member States'. In *The Member States of the European Union*, edited by Simon Bulmer and Christian Lequesne, 25–44. Oxford: Oxford University Press.

Bruter, Michael. 2012. 'The Difficult Emergence of a European People'. In *European Disunion: Between Sovereignty and Solidarity*, edited by Jack Hayward and Rüdiger Wurzel, 17–31. Basingstoke: Palgrave Macmillan.

Bulmer, Simon, Charlie Jeffery and William E. Paterson. 2000. *Germany's European Diplomacy: Shaping the Regional Milieu*. Manchester: Manchester University Press.

Bulmer, Simon, and William E. Paterson. 2013. 'Germany as the EU's Reluctant Hegemon? Of Economic Strength and Political Constraints'. *Journal of European Public Policy* 20(10): 1387–1405.

———. 2017. 'Germany and the Crisis: Asset or Liability?' In *The European Union in Crisis* edited by Desmond Dinan, Neil Nugent and William E. Paterson, 212–32. Basingstoke: Palgrave Macmillan.

Dimitrov, Veselin. 2012. 'The Central and East European Countries: From Weak Latecomers to Good Citizens of the Union'. In *European Disunion: Between Sovereignty and Solidarity*, edited by Jack Hayward and Rüdiger Wurzel, 298–313. Basingstoke: Palgrave Macmillan.

The *Economist* Intelligence Unit. 2020. 'Democracy Index 2019: A Year of Democratic Setbacks and Popular Protest'. Retrieved 4 November 2020 from http://www.eiu.com/Handlers/WhitepaperHandler.ashx?fi=Democracy-Index-2019.pdf&mode=wp&campaignid=democracyindex2019.

Euractiv. 2018. 'Defiant Kaczynski Says Poland Must Avoid EU's "Social Diseases"', 2 September. Retrieved 11 October 2020 from https://www.euractiv.com/section/eu-elections-2019/news/defiant-kaczynski-says-poland-must-avoid-eus-social-diseases/.

European Commission. 2008. 'European Union Regional Policy: Inforegio panorama 26 (June)'. Retrieved 24 January 2021 from https://ec.europa.eu/regional_policy/sources/docgener/panorama/pdf/mag26/mag26_en.pdf.

———. 2016. 'European Semester Thematic Factsheet: Social Inclusion'. Retrieved 4 October 2020 from https://ec.europa.eu/info/sites/info/files/file_import/european-semester_thematic-factsheet_social_inclusion_en_0.pdf.

———. 2018. 'Labour Market and Wage Developments in Europe: Annual Review 2018'. Retrieved 25 January 2020 from https://ec.europa.eu/social/main.jsp?catId=738&langId=en&pubId=8139&furtherPubs=yes.

———. 2022. 'Standard Eurobarometer 97 Summer 2022: First Results'. Retrieved 10 February 2023 from https://europa.eu/eurobarometer/api/deliverable/download/file?deliverableId=83378.

European Parliament. 2022. 'MEPs Demand More EU Action to Protect Common Values in Hungary and Poland', 5 May. Retrieved 30 May 2022 from https://www.europarl.europa.eu/news/en/press-room/20220429IPR28226/meps-demand-more-eu-action-to-protect-common-values-in-hungary-and-poland.

Eurostat. 2022. 'Unemployment by Sex and Age (1992–2020) – Annual Data'. Last modified 12 April 2022. Retrieved 10 February 2023 from https://ec.europa.eu/eurostat/databrowser/view/UNE_RT_A_H__custom_4761273/default/table.

———. 2023a. 'Purchasing Power Adjusted GDP per Capita'. Last modified 6 January 2023. Retrieved 10 February 2023 from https://ec.europa.eu/eurostat/databrowser/view/SDG_10_10/default/table.

———. 2023b. 'Persons at Risk of Poverty or Social Exclusion by Degree of Urbanisation – EU 2020 Strategy'. Last modified 1 February 2023. Retrieved 10 February 2023 from https://ec.europa.eu/eurostat/databrowser/view/ILC_PEPS13__custom_4763215/default/table.

Farkas, Beáta. 2018. 'Central European Relations in Turbulent Times'. In *Central and Eastern Europe in the EU*, edited by Christian Schweiger and Anna Visvizi, 57–73. Abingdon: Routledge.

Farkas, Beáta, and András Máté-Toth. 2018. 'A Rift in European Integration? Neglected Shadows of the Central and Eastern European Transformation'. In *Central and Eastern Europe in the EU*, edited by Christian Schweiger and Anna Visvizi, 22–43. Abingdon: Routledge.

Fischer, Joschka. 2000. 'From Confederacy to Federation: Thoughts on the Finality of European Integration'. Last modified 12 May 2020. Retrieved 11 October 2020 from http://ec.europa.eu/dorie/fileDownload.do?docId=192161&cardId=192161.

Galgoczi, Bela. 2014. 'The Tale of Two Peripheries in a Divided Europe'. *Perspectives on European Politics and Society* 15(3): 359–69.

Giddens, Anthony. 2014. *Turbulent and Mighty Continent: What Future for Europe?* Cambridge: Cambridge University Press.

Goetz, Klaus H. 2005. 'The New Member States and the EU: Responding to Europe'. In *The Member States of the European Union*, edited by Simon Bulmer and Christian Lequesne, 254–85. Oxford: Oxford University Press.

Hancke, Bob. 2011. 'Varieties of European Capitalism and Their Transformation'. In *Developments in European Politics 2*, 2nd ed., edited by Erik Jones, Paul M. Heywood, Martin Rhodes and Ulrich Sedelmeier, 155–72. Basingstoke: Palgrave Macmillan.

Handl, Vladimir, and William E. Paterson. 2013. 'The Continuing Relevance of Germany's Engine for CEE and the EU'. *Communist and Post-Communist Studies* 46: 327–33.

Haughton, Tim. 2016. 'Central and Eastern Europe: The Sacrifices of Solidarity, the Discomfort of Diversity, and the Vexations of Vulnerabilities'. In *The European Union in Crisis*, edited by Desmond Dinan, Neil Nugent and William E. Paterson, 253–68. Basingstoke: Palgrave.

Koller, Boglárka. 2014. 'Unity in a "Different Way" or the New Logic of EU Integration: The Special Focus on the Post-Enlargement Period of ECE Countries'. In *10 Years After: Multi-Level Governance and Differentiated Integration in the EU*, edited by Attila Agh, Tamás Kaiser and Boglárka Koller, 62–83. Budapest: Blue Ribbon Research Centre.

Kundnani, Hans. 2014. *The Paradox of German Power*. London: C. Hurst & Co.

Magone, José M. 2016. 'From "Superficial" to "Coercive" Europeanization in Southern Europe: The Lack of Ownership of National Reforms'. In *Core-Periphery Relations in the European Union*, edited by José M. Magone, Brigid Laffan and Christian Schweiger, 87–98. Oxon: Routledge.

Matthijs, Matthias. 2022. 'Does Orban's Victory in Hungary Change the EU's Calculus on Russia?' *Council on Foreign Relations*, 5 May. Accessed 30 May 2022 from https://www.cfr.org/in-brief/does-orbans-victory-hungary-change-eus-calculus-russia.

Mikulova, Kristina. 2013. 'Central Europe's Pivot to Germany: What does the US Stand to Gain'. *Huffington Post*, 1 May. Retrieved 11 October 2020 from http://www.huff ingtonpost.com/kristina-mikulova/central-europes-pivot-to-_b_3194342.html.

Orbán, Viktor. 2017. *State of the Union Address*, 10 February.

———. 2019. *State of the Union Address*, 10 February.

Paterson, William E. 2011. 'The Reluctant Hegemon? Germany Moves Centre Stage in the European Union'. *Journal of Common Market Studies*, Annual Review, 49: 57–75.

———. 2014. 'Germany and the European Union'. *Developments in German Politics 4*, edited by Stephan Padgett, William E. Paterson and Reimut Zohlnhöfer, 166–87. Basingstoke: Palgrave Macmillan.

Politico. 2022. *Poland – National Parliament Voting Intentions*. Retrieved 30 May 2022 from https://www.politico.eu/europe-poll-of-polls/poland/.

Przybylski, Wojciech. 2018. 'Explaining Eastern Europe: Can Poland's Backsliding Be Stopped?' *Journal of Democracy* 29(3): 52–64.

Schröder, Gerhard. 2001. 'Statement on the Nice European Council at the German *Bundestag*', 19 January 2001.

Schweiger, Christian. 2014. *The EU and the Global Financial Crisis: New Varieties of Capitalism*. Cheltenham: Edward Elgar.

———. 2016. *Exploring the EU's Legitimacy Crisis: The Dark Heart of Europe*. Cheltenham: Edward Elgar.

Sedelmeier, Ulrich. 2015. 'Enlargement: Constituent Policy and Tools for External Governance'. In *Policy-Making in the European Union*, edited by Helen Wallace et al., 407–35. Oxford: Oxford University Press.

Sikorski, Radosław. 2011. 'Poland and the Future of the European Union'. Speech delivered in Berlin, 28 November. Retrieved 11 November 2020 from http://www.mfa .gov.pl/resource/33ce6061-ec12–4da1-a145–01e2995c6302:JCR.

Streeck, Wolfgang. 2016. 'Scenario for a Wonderful Tomorrow'. *London Review of Books* 38(7): 31. Retrieved 11 November 2020 from https://www.lrb.co.uk/v38/n07/ wolfgang-streeck/scenario-for-a-wonderful-tomorrow.

Stryjek, Joanna. 2013. 'Economic Security Aspects of the Potential EMU Membership of Poland'. *Yearbook of the Institute of East-Central Europe* 11(5): 47–65.

Suplanta, Milan. 2013. 'The Visegrád Battlegroup: Building New Capabilities for the Region'. *Policy Brief*. Bratislava: Central European Policy Institute Bratislava.

Terlikowski, Marcin. 2022. 'Poland and NATO's Next Strategy: Deterring Russia and Making European Defence Work (for the Alliance)'. *Real Instituto Elcano*, 16 February. Retrieved 30 May 2002 from https://www.realinstitutoelcano.org/en/analyses/ poland-and-natos-next-strategy-deterring-russia-and-making-european-defence-work-for-the-alliance/.

Törő, Csaba, Eamonn Butler and Károly Gruber. 2014. 'Visegrád: The Evolving Pattern of Coordination and Partnership after EU Enlargement'. *Europe-Asia Studies* 66(3): 364–94.

Visvizi, Anna, and Pawel Tokarski. 2014. 'Poland and the Euro: Between Lock-In and Unfinished Transition'. *Society and Economy* 36(4): 445–68.

Webber, Douglas. 2017. 'Can the EU Survive?' In *The European Union in Crisis*, edited by Desmond Dinan, Neil Nugent and William E. Paterson, 336–60. Basingstoke: Palgrave Macmillan.

Zbytniewska, Karolina. 2017. 'Trans-Europe Express: The Foundations of Fortress'. *EURACTIV*, 26 May 2017. Accessed 4 November 2002 from http://www.euractiv .com/section/all/news/trans-europe-express-the-foundations-of-fortress-poland/.

CHAPTER 9

# Cohesion Policy for Escaping the Middle-Income Trap

Andrea Filippetti and Raffaele Spallone

## Introduction: Cohesion Policy in Europe

Cohesion Policy was implemented with the aim of reducing territorial disparities across the European Union. It was based on a fundamental intuition: a larger and integrated common market would exacerbate economic disparities across rich and poor regions (i.e., economic divergence), jeopardizing social cohesion. The rationale was that the most advanced regions could attract financial resources, skilled labour force, foreign direct investments and the most dynamic companies. This would increase the differences in the economic activities, ultimately aggravating income disparities across regions (Leonardi 1995a; Myrdal 1957). As a consequence, a large fraction of the EU budget has since then been devoted to Cohesion Policy by means of structural funds aimed at avoiding the divergence process by narrowing down the disparities in the level of income across regions (Barry 2003; Bazo-Lopez et al. 1999; Filippetti and Peyrache 2013). Hence, Cohesion Policy was adopted as an instrument to make the common market not only more efficient but also more equal. In other words, it was meant to avoid the offsetting of the increase in efficiency by an increase in the inequality due to a larger market for goods and service, which would put the entire European integration project at risk.

Certainly, uneven economic development across regions and territories precedes the establishment of the common market and in some instances – such as the Italian case – predates even the creation of the nation states themselves (Díez-Minguela et al. 2017). Furthermore, territorial disparities cannot be attributed entirely to the establishment of the common market; the effect of national policies in creating such disparities should also be acknowledged.

As for today, the promise of even development in Europe is only partially fulfilled (Crescenzi, de Blasio and Giua 2018; Ederveen, de Groot and Nahuis 2006). While it is true that income disparities among EU-15 regions had declined up until the mid-1990s, in the past two decades they have been broadening (Díez-Minguela et al. 2017; Ertur, Le Gallo and Baumont 2006). Moreover, regional disparities among a number of Member States, in particular in the Central and Eastern European (CEE) countries, have also increased (Michelis and Monfort 2008). In fact, while we were used to observing inequality as a vertical phenomenon based on differences of social class, over the past decades, we have observed inequality as a horizontal phenomenon occurring across regions and places rather than across social classes. Today, the place where one lives and works is more important in determining one's income than it was some twenty, thirty, or fifty years ago.

When Cohesion Policy was created, the middle-income regions were placed in the south of Italy and Spain, the north of the UK, and Portugal. Today, the regions that are trying to escape from the middle-income trap mostly belong to the CEE-economies. Ever since they joined the European Union (EU), the CCE economies have been receiving considerable structural funds in order to close their income gap with the Western European member states. In fact, the CEE-economies have grown at a larger pace compared to the other member countries. Yet, these countries are suffering from growing inequality *within* their borders. We witness that the regions around the capital cities such as Warsaw or Prague have become more and more advanced and attracted investment, brainpower, entrepreneurship and financial capital, giving rise to a vibrant environment for innovation, start-ups and new technologies. These capital regions today resemble their peers in the Western European countries, rich of talented, dynamic and international creative classes (Iammarino and McCann 2013, 2006). The downside effect of this phenomenon is the progressive deterioration of the social and economic conditions of the inner and rural regions: today, it is these regions that need the Cohesion Policy in order to escape from the middle-income gap.

This process has recently been discussed in terms of negative spillovers. The economic dynamism in the most dynamic regions bears some costs such as congestion expenses (i.e., traffic, house prices, pollution), not only on these dynamic regions themselves but also on the less developed regions (Iammarino, Rodriguez-Pose and Storper 2017; Rodriguez-Pose and Crescenzi 2008a). These costs result in a process of diversion of resources from poor to rich regions, whereas the latter also see their most skilled labour force as well as financial capital and the most dynamic companies migrating to the former (Petraglia and Vecchione 2020). Quite often, national policies exacerbate this unbalanced process of development by disproportionally investing in more advanced regions in terms of, for example, infrastructure, universities and public transportation. The underlying idea behind such disproportionate investments is that national competitiveness depends more and more on a few very dynamic places and, therefore, it is relatively more efficient to strengthen these strategic areas further.

Overall, although we can certainly argue that the promise of a more efficient functioning of the economic system has been made possible with the integration to the common market, we cannot suggest that Cohesion Policy has been effective in making the market also less uneven. Today, Europe is running the risk of becoming an area characterized by islands of prosperity in a sea of poverty (Díez-Minguela et al. 2017).

## Middle-Income Gap at the Region Level

A recent report of the European Commission titled 'Falling into the Middle-Income Trap? A Study on the Risks for EU Regions to Be Caught in a Middle-Income Trap' has introduced the concept of a regional development trap into the case of the EU and 'deployed [the concept] to identify EU regions that have lost their competitive edge and hence face significant structural challenges' (European Council 2020, 1). The concept of a development trap at a regional level was derived from the theoretical notion of the middle-income trap. It has been used to understand the reasons why certain countries that have successfully transitioned from low- or middle-income status subsequently experience durable declines in economic growth and, as a result, struggle to move up to a higher income level, often for a long time. Two factors make it necessary to apply this concept at the regional level in the EU. First, as briefly illustrated above, the process of economic development in Europe is increasingly marked by sizeable differences among regions both within and across countries. Second, the application of the concept allows linking the notion of middle-income gap to Cohesion Policy, which is articulated at the regional level.

In this chapter, we explain the function of Cohesion Policy in relation to the characteristics of the capitalistic model in which this policy has been adopted since it was first created. We focus on Cohesion Policy and its role in boosting economic development in disadvantaged regions, that is regions struggling with the middle-income trap. We take a comparative perspective by comparing Cohesion Policy before and after the most recent enlargement of including the EEC countries into the EU. Our main argument is that Cohesion Policy has been taking place in the context of two very different modes of capitalistic accumulation. First, the Keynesian policy approach, which has characterized Cohesion Policy since the 1980s, takes place within the industrial model of capitalism. Second, after the more recent enlargement, we observe a knowledge-driven policy approach in Cohesion Policy, which takes place within the post-industrial environment of the 'knowledge economy' (Avdikos and Chardas 2016). We argue that this major paradigmatic shift in the capitalist mode of accumulation has made it harder for Cohesion Policy to be effective and has made it more challenging for EEC countries and regions to escape the middle-income trap.

## The Shift from the Industrial Mode of Production to the Knowledge Economy: State Rescaling and Regionalization of Public Policy

In this section, we illustrate the major transition that has involved the capitalistic system during the 1980s. We depict two ideal types: the industrial and the knowledge-economy mode of production. The former had characterized the most advanced economies since the Second Industrial Revolution and reached its maturity in the aftermath of the Second World War until the 1980s. The latter has characterized Europe starting from the new globalization wave of the 1980s following the two major recessions that took place during the 1970s and interrupting the relentless period of intense economic growth since the end of the war.[1] We emphasize the major differences of the two models in which the economic production system has been organized. We also describe the mechanisms though which public development policies have been designed in these two models with a particular focus on the territorial configuration of economic development policies, which have represented the ground upon which Cohesion Policy itself was designed.

To briefly describe the major differences among the two ideal types of economic models – the industrial and the knowledge economy – it should be noted that capital is the more important input in the former, while in knowledge is more important in the latter. The particular, that is, the economic nature of capital and knowledge has shaped the entire organization of the economic activity in the space and the design of public policy accordingly.

What we mean by capital is fixed capital, such as machineries, instruments, tools and computers. These were the key elements that characterized the rise of the factories during the gloomy days in the docklands in London as described by Charles Dickens, as they marked the introduction of the assembly lines introduced by Ford at the beginning of the twentieth century in the United States up to the gigantic blast furnaces and moulds in the steel industry. This is the capital as described by Karl Marx around which capitalism has been organized, shaping not only the economic sector but the whole social organization of life. In a single word, it is industrialization: possibly one of the most significant transitions experienced in social life in the entire history of humankind. Capital has been the most important driver also in the economic development of the first part of the twentieth century when the manufacturing sector became the first mover of economic growth, labour productivity and technological innovation.

By contrast, what we mean by knowledge is the immaterial articulation of information, which today is at the core of the knowledge economy. Knowledge is neither visible nor tangible, although part of it can be articulated into codes, that is, the codified knowledge. But for the most part, the crucial knowledge in today's mode of production cannot be articulated and therefore cannot be written down into codes and procedures (Cowan, David and Foray 2000). This is the knowledge that Alfred Marshall grasped with a seminal intuition back at the beginning of the twentieth century, when he observed that companies tend to concentrate in certain areas where one can sense that the knowledge is 'in the air' (Marshall 1920). Hence, if you want to 'breathe' that knowledge, that is, if you want to benefit from it by employing it in the production process of your firm, you have to carry your business to that particular location. This simple fact constitutes the cornerstone of the territorial organization of the economy.

In the manufacturing-based mode of production, the organization of the economy revolved around the characteristics of capital. The aim was to improve the productivity of capital. Hence, the number of large firms in those sectors, in which economies of scale are the most relevant driver of productivity, increased. The scientific organization of production, which was introduced by Taylor in the automotive sector, aimed at reducing the time of production, thus increasing productivity. Later on, the just-in-time organization introduced in Toyota also aimed at increasing the productivity of the assembly line. The shift from the mass production towards the flexible production, however, did not change the fundamental fact that the organization of the production was still driven by the functioning of capital.

By contrast, in the model of knowledge economy, the organization of production is driven by the economic properties of knowledge. In particular, agglomeration economies and increasing returns are the two most relevant features that have been reshaping the organization of the economic processes. The transformation of the economy has been further accelerated by the rise of the service sector and the relative decline of the manufacturing sector. The reorganization of production around knowledge and in the service sector has profoundly changed the territorial – that is, geographical – articulation of the economic processes, requiring a new approach of local development policies.

As mentioned before, the two models depicted here are quite broad and general, as they encompass important differences and could be described much further. However, our objective here is to illustrate the major shift in the economy that has been observed since the 1980s. This shift has profoundly altered the territorial articulation of the economies and the very mechanisms of economic growth and innovation. Our aim is to show its effect also on development policies, with a specific focus on European policies. Innovation plays a fundamental role in the story that we tell. In the manufacturing mode of production, innovation was prominently technological and mostly embodied in new capital (e.g., numerical control machines, new materials, new techniques of production); that is, it was centred on capital and aimed at improving capital's productivity (Clark, Freeman and Soete 1984; Freeman 1998; Rosenberg 1974). Contrarily, in our ideal typical model of the knowledge economy, innovation is mostly immaterial – and not embodied in new machines or equipment – and, most importantly, does not aim at increasing the productivity of capital but rather at developing new products in hi-tech industries and new services in the so-called knowledge-intensive sectors. Hence, innovation is at the root of both the modes, but its nature and aims are rather different (Djellal and Gallouj 2001; Gallouj and Savona 2009).

## Development Policies in the Industrial Mode of Production

The industrial mode of production emerges by the end of the nineteenth century and reaches its maturity after the Second World War. In Western European countries, these are the years of the spectacular economic growth, during which they modernized their economy and caught up with the United States. In this model, the industrial policy has been described as Keynesian welfare policy, which has the following major characteristics: (1) it is based on massive investments in fixed capital in the manufacturing sector; (2) it is a national policy eventually articulated on the territory; (3) it is aimed at narrowing the disparities in the level of income across rich and poor territories and regions (Brenner 2004; Storper 1995).

Development policies in the Industrial Era were based on industrial policy. The main idea was that the whole territory would have benefited from the linkages of the industry, both inward and outward, by implanting a new factory in the more competitive manufacture industry. The multiplier effect was to be driven by the network of suppliers which needed to feed the manufacturing process and by the complementary services developed. Hence, a big push of massive investment driven by the public hand would have spurred a sustainable and reinforcing growth mechanism in the whole territory surrounding the new plant.

Public policy in the Italian Mezzogiorno is a case in point. The regions in the south of Italy had a significantly lower level of income depending on a lower level of economic development. The state designed a big push policy, the so-called extraordinary intervention, aiming at closing the gap with the rest of the country. The policy was based on two instruments: a series of incentives to attract the big industry that was settled in the north to move to the south (in particular in the mechanical and automotive sectors) and establishing public companies in the region (in particular in the chemical and in the iron and steel sectors) (Felice and Lepore 2017; Leonardi 1995b). The policy was thus based on massive investment in some strategic sectors in areas characterized by a low level of economic activity and a large ration of unemployed people or an underemployed workforce, such as people employed in the informal agricultural sector. The interventions were designed at the centre level, in the ministries of Rome, which would choose the areas of destination. The philosophy of the intervention was Keynesian welfare, in the sense that it aimed at levelling out the most dramatic differences between the Mezzogiorno and the rest of Italy by means of massive public investment.

This policy, which has been partially successful especially in the two decades after the Second World War, was reinforced by the nature of capital itself. First, and somehow in a counterintuitive way, capital is highly mobile. This does not mean that one can easily move a factory from one place to the other. Instead, one can choose where to locate a new factory. Especially in those manufacturing sectors in which a low-skilled labour force is needed, there are no major constraints about the location of these policy interventions. In the case of Italy, in fact, large plants were established in poor areas of Campania, Puglia, Sicily and Sardinia. Second, a large fraction of the population could immediately be employed as a direct result of the public policy. When new large industries were established in these areas, people would flock looking for a job. Quite often the management and the more skilled workers came from the Northern plants, however, the big bulk of the manpower was recruited on the spot. As a result, thousands of new jobs were created directly out of the public policy as well as indirectly thanks to the rise of a network of suppliers. Eventually, as income in the area would rise, new services would be on demand, spurring new jobs in the service sector. As a final outcome, a few thousand new jobs would be created with the policy intervention and a new economic ecosystem would emerge out of it.

Public policy was not always successful; several other factors could hamper the effectiveness of the policy, such as a lack of an efficient transport system, low management skills, poor local institutions and corruption. A case in point has been the 'cathedrals in the desert', which were massive investments in industries which did not manage to create a network with the territory and therefore were not successful in activating a multiplying effect on the local economy. The lack of complementary investment in infrastructures such as transportation has also resulted in the only partial success of public policies. However, the Industrial Age offered a fertile economic environment to design a development policy that would raise the economic level of the less advanced regions and create thousands of new jobs by means of public investment in the industrial sector.

## Development Policies in the Knowledge Economy

Life is harder in the knowledge economy for governments trying to design effective development policies. Economic growth, which was previously centred on capital and technological innovation embodied in new capital, has evolved into something different. In the knowledge economy, knowledge is the main input in the economic process; whereas the manufacturing sector has been transformed into a more flexible and innovation-based organization, and the service sector has gained in prominence and the crucial investment is no longer in tangible asset but in intangible asset. In several advanced economies, investment in intangible assets has surpassed those in tangible ones. While the latter such as buildings, machineries, hardware, equipment and vehicles were the fundamental driver in the Industrial Era, the former – software, research and development (R&D), design, marketing, engineering – are the quintessential drivers in the knowledge economy mode of production (Corrado et al. 2012; Den Hertog, Bilderbeek and Maltha1997).

To understand how the very mechanism of growth has changed, we need to look at the economic nature of the knowledge generation and the knowledge diffusion processes. First, knowledge can be codified, that is translated into a codebook, or it can be tacit. The former type of knowledge, however, constitutes only a fraction of the latter. Remarkably, it is the latter that makes a firm unique. As management scholars would put it, tacit knowledge is the source of competitive advantage (Kogut and Zander 1993; Teece and Pisano 1994). Second, knowledge is quite sticky. Contrary to the initial enthusiasm when it was envisaged that the web would have allowed the transmission of information at no cost and almost immediately, it has been later understood that knowledge does not travel as easily (Storper and

Venables 2004; von Hippel 1994). Third, knowledge is a public good. This implies that knowledge is freely available and accessible, at least in principle. In practice, however, getting knowledge outside the company and employing it in a competitive way within an organization are not as easy as plugging in a radio and turning it on. Employing knowledge in a productive and profitable way requires substantial costs for searching, learning and adapting from prospective users (Archibugi and Filippetti 2015a; Bell and Pavitt 1993; Filippetti and Guy 2020).

Once we put together these three characteristics of knowledge, we can explain the most visible phenomenon of the knowledge economy: spatial agglomeration (Bathelt, Malmberg and Maskell 2004; Lorenzen and Mudambi 2012; Martin and Sunley 2003). In the present day, the organization of production process in most relevant industries – that is, in those that produce high returns and job creation – is more and more spatially bounded. As knowledge is the most relevant input, companies and a skilled labour force tend to stay put in the same place. People acquire new knowledge by being where it gets generated and by interacting among themselves. Informal and social networks play a paramount role in the exchange of tacit knowledge: meeting a peer at a school party can increase productivity more than reading a codebook or the content of a patent. More technically speaking, the productivity of a person regarding a company's knowledge depends on the amount of knowledge surrounding them. The greater the amount in a working environment, the greater the value of the knowledge that one possesses.

Hence, the value of the same piece of knowledge is not the same around the world: that is, 'the world is not flat' (McCann 2008; Rodríguez-Pose and Crescenzi 2008b). This explains why both large and small companies, prospective entrepreneurs (or startuppers), financial investors and high-skilled workers all tend to concentrate in certain areas. Notably, this concentration happens quite often around the greater producers of knowledge-as-a-public-good of our age: universities and research centres, as is the case in some much-celebrated clusters such as Cambridge and Oxford, Cambridge, MA, and Silicon Valley. Hence, Aristotle has finally been proved right, as he seems to have said that if one wants a city in a hundred years' time, they need to establish a university today.

The reorganization of economic activity around the nature of its new and most relevant input has had profound impact on the geography of the economy and of the society as a whole. The most macroscopic result has been the rise of global cities and global clusters, which have been steadily growing since the mid-1980s. These centres have grown in population, kept attracting high-skilled workers, international capital and investors and startuppers (Archibugi and Filippetti 2015b; Iammarino and McCann

2006; Sassen 1991). The same trend is observed in European countries, where economies are increasingly more dependent on a few major cities. Countries such as France and the UK have become almost totally dependent on their capital cities. More advanced regions and cities tend to establish close networks among them. Networks are nurtured by the mobility of high-skilled people, financial capital and fresh ideas with the multinational corporations playing an important role (Iammarino and McCann 2013).

This trend is also observed in the EEC countries. The most dynamic regions in the EEC countries are around the capitals: cities like Warsaw, Prague and Bratislava have been radically transformed into new internationalized knowledge and service hubs. At the same time, most peripheral regions have been lagging behind. Hence it is observed that the same dynamics are taking place in all member states; the capital regions becoming more dynamic and richer, broadening the distance with peripheral regions. As a result, income disparities within countries are on the rise both in EU-15 and the EEC economies.

However, the other side of the coin shows a progressive deterioration in the economic and social conditions of inner and rural regions. The 'Europe of Regions' has seen a rise of inequality mostly within national borders. While countries have become more similar, regions within them have become more different. This is the result of the self-reinforcing process that has characterized regional knowledge-driven economic growth (Iammarino et al. 2017).

This is where local development policy steps in. Territorial policy in the knowledge era is caught in a dilemma. On the one hand, efficiency consideration might encourage investing in the reinforcement of dynamic regions, as national competitiveness – the new mantra of public policy – depends on these knowledge-hubs. The knowledge-hubs need to compete internationally to attract the best ideas, people, abundant capital and corporations. This requires public investment in some enabling factors. Some of these elements such as first-class universities and research centres, local and international public transportation, facilities and housing have an economic nature, while others – including amenities such as theatres, opera houses – are of a softer nature (Florida 2005; Florida, Adler and Mellander 2016; Storper 2013). A quick look at the transformation of the capital cities around Europe is sufficient to comprehend the extent of these competitiveness-enhancing investments.

On the other side of the dilemma lies the question of what kind of policy needs to be implemented in the less advanced regions that are left at the margins of the knowledge economy and the international flows of wealth. As illustrated above, in the Industrial Age, industrial policy would bring or produce new, large industry (both private or public) to spur economic activity and create jobs. Far from being a perfect mechanism, it nonetheless helped some places and regions to escape from poverty, isolation and underemployment.

In the knowledge economy boosting economic growth in marginal regions however is far more complex. Various approaches have been taken in this regard. The first was to replicate the mechanism that spurred development in the dynamic regions. In a kind of one-size-fits-all fashion, cluster policies have been designed to help poor regions activate their own agglomeration of dynamic firms and knowledge-generation process. These were also the heydays of the technological hubs, transfer-technology centres and incubators (Tola and Contini 2015). Typical examples of this trend are the proliferation of cluster policies, which came under various names such as innovation poles and meta-district. The idea was to induce a self-reinforcing process of agglomeration economies by encouraging linkages between the university and the industry as well as within firms. Crucially, these policies have proven to be more successful in most developed regions, and less in regions lagging behind (Bertamino et al. 2016; Chatterji, Glaeser and Kerr 2014; Crescenzi, Filippetti and Iammarino 2017; Lerner 2009).

More recent approaches in European policy making have evolved towards the so-called place-based policies (Barca, McCann and Rodríguez-Pose 2012; Mendez 2013). The idea is that policies need to be tailored to the territory and adapted to the local conditions, in terms of local capabilities, human capital and industrial specialization, among others. Each region and territory has to find its own policy consistently with its own technological trajectory through a process of self-discovery. Here, top-down approaches are avoided. This approach has also been the acknowledgement that the notion that every region should have its own Silicon Valley is deemed to fail. With this approach, we observe the final rescaling of state policies. National policies are no longer articulated on the territory through a top-down process of regionalization but at the regional level through a process of recognition of regional diversity that led to the rise of Regionalism. It is not a coincidence that this major rescaling of state policies went hand in hand with an increase in the regional authority. During the same years, we have observed institutional reforms in many countries – devolution or fiscal federalism – aimed at decentralizing power, legislative authority and financial resources from the centre to the subnational levels of governments (Filippetti and Sacchi 2016; Canaleta, Pascual and Rapún 2004; Martinez-Vazquez, Lago-Peñas and Sacchi 2016).

Today, this approach is far from posing a clear theoretical picture of economic development for less advanced regions. One argument is that agglomeration economies are relentless and are here to stay; as such, the most sensible policy is to encourage mobility towards the most dynamic regions, to invest in public service in the knowledge-hubs to make their growth sustainable (Glaeser 2011) and to compensate marginal regions with welfare instruments and fiscal transfer – which has been the case in the UK. The opposite argument is that local development should be boosted in the more marginal regions by means of differentiated approaches (Iammarino et al. 2017).

The crux of the matter is that in the knowledge economy, one cannot simply build a three-thousand-worker factory. Instead, one needs to engineer an endogenous mechanism that favours economic growth and local development led by innovation. This brings us to the paradoxical argument that knowledge, compared to capital, is less mobile. This statement merits some further qualification: creating the condition to start a process of knowledge generation and diffusion that generates agglomeration economies and ultimately a process of self-reinforcing pace of economic growth has its roots in complex alchemies. Studies on the birth and development of clusters have shown that these processes are based on a complex interrelation of historical, social and contingent factors. Sometimes they are rooted in centuries of accumulation of tacit knowledge, as in the case of the industrial districts in Italy; sometimes they are the result of a favourable social environment where the establishment of universities has prompted a self-reinforcing process of growth, as has been the case for the most celebrated US-American clusters of Silicon Valley and Cambridge, MA. The key implication for policy is that knowledge-based growth mechanisms are hard to formulate into a recipe and therefore to replicate (Saxenian 1996).

By contrast, activating growth-enhancing processes based on capital – for example, investment in the industry – is easier. In fact, it was precisely the industrial policy that we have described above. Hence, what we mean by 'mobile' here is not mobility per se. In this respect, information, contrary to capital, is extremely mobile as it travels in virtually no time and negligible cost. Mobility here relates to the ex-ante options of the policy maker to replicate successful development policies across territories. In this sense, unlike capital, which was quite a versatile tool in the hand of policy makers, knowledge is now far harder to manipulate and transfer.

Moreover, the argument of creating the conditions for innovation is far from a vigorous theory. How does one establish trust, create informal networks or attract investors to move from London, Paris or Milan to less developed regions? At present, few robust theories have been developed in this respect. Furthermore, the mantra about more investment in education and human capital too faces two problems. First, in a weak economic environment, the return to education investments is lower: from the perspective of lack of good employment, the perceived risk of education investments would tend to rise. Second, high-skilled human capital in poor regions increasingly tend to move towards richer regions.

Finally, in the knowledge economy time is not on the side of policy makers. Successful processes of growth take time, while unemployment and social distress need short-term answers. Hence in order to make the transition viable, the development process should be accompanied by welfare interventions and fiscal redistribution.

## The Evolution of Cohesion Policy between Convergence and Competitiveness

As explained above, economic convergence among European regions has always been a fundamental pillar in the policy design of the European Union (EU). This is stated clearly in Article 174 of the 'Treaty on the Functioning of the European Union' (TFUE): 'The Union shall aim at reducing disparities between the levels of development of the various regions and the backwardness of the least favored regions' (European Union [Official Journal of] Article 174). In addition, the prevalence of the cohesion over other policy objectives has been restated once again before the foundation of the policy itself back in 1986: *'all other policy interventions in the EU should not hamper the aim of economic convergence among the European regions'* (TFUE, Art. 175). About one-third of the EU budget has been spent to support structural actions in less developed regions with the goal of achieving convergence.

However, while the general idea of fostering growth in less developed regions has remained constant over time, the nature of Cohesion Policy itself as well as its instruments, measures and priorities have changed significantly from one budget period to another (Drometer and Nam 2018). The objectives of the European structural and investments funds have been transformed from time to time in response to the revision of the strategies and policy directions dictated by the European Commission – adjustments which, in turn, reacted to the profound changes that have occurred in the economy in the last three decades.

From 1989 onwards, regional policy was conceived to provide aid to less developed regions, seeking to ensure that the single market did not undermine itself by exacerbating regional inequalities (Brunazzo 2016). Indeed, the previous budget periods of 1988–93 and 1994–2000 were characterized by the redistribution-oriented Cohesion Policy. Since the 2000s, there has been an increasing emphasis away from redistribution toward stimulating new growth opportunities through innovation (Van den Broek, Rutten and Benneworth 2018). In short, cohesion evolved from a passive policy with redistributive aims into a dynamic one aimed at creating resources through investment in regions and people (Barnier 2003).

In addition, the need for a reform was dictated by a series of challenges – the slow economic growth in the EU area in the late 90s, the increasing competitiveness in the emerging economies, and the transformation of the economy – which have been explained above. All of these elements led to a reflection on the need to reconceive the whole economic policy of the EU. The Lisbon Agenda, which was agreed on at the summit in March 2000, had the explicit aim of making the EU *'the most competitive and dynamic knowledge-based economy in the world, capable of sustainable economic growth with more and better jobs and greater social cohesion'* (European Council 2000, 3, original emphasis). To achieve this goal, the agenda set the target of increasing R&D investment in the EU to 3 percent of the GDP by 2010. The focus on R&D and innovation, at least until the outbreak of the crisis (Filippetti and Archibugi 2011), resulted in considerable increases in the R&D expenditure, which was also favoured by the profound revision of the priorities and guidelines of the Cohesion Policy.

In part, the transformation of Cohesion Policy and the reconsideration of its added value have been supported by two main arguments. On one hand, there was a lack of consensus about the effectiveness of Cohesion Policy (Leonardi 2006). The convergence process took place very slowly without the action of the Structured Funds being significant. This criticism was also supported by the fact that the action of funds was not able to prevent polarization at the regional level, which, in some cases, was slowing down the specialization process (see Boldrin et al. 2001; Neven and Goyette 1995; Cappelen, Fagerberg and Verspagen 1999). On the other hand, there was growing interest in regional innovation policies among scholars and policymakers who underlined the distinctive character of the innovation process for regions and sectors due to diverse technological and institutional trajectories and put emphasis on the need to move the axis of place-based policies towards supporting research and innovation on the local level.

Regional innovation policies were linked to regional innovation systems (RIS) theories. The RIS approach emerged in the 1990s in connection to both the literature on national innovation systems (NIS) and contemporary contributions on economic geography and cluster theory (Cantwell and Iammarino 2003; Cooke 2001). It was seen as an instrument to trigger local and self-sustained growth dynamism, especially in those areas that lagged behind. Growing emphasis was put on supporting infrastructures for innovation, technological parks and centres, and on the provision of services by innovation centres or agencies for innovation. Cooperation both among different players involved in innovation – such as enterprises and universities – and among institutions (best practices) was a crucial aspect of the new strategy.

However, the transformation of the Cohesion Policy around the new priorities took place not by rupture but in a rather gradual way. The policy priority of promoting regional innovation systems was presented for the first time during the programming period from 2007 to 2013 and extended to all regions. The R&D and innovation promotion scheme, which was implemented in the cohesion framework, included mainly the following measures: (1) financial support for the innovation activities of companies (in particular SMEs); (2) promotion and expansion of public R&D capacity; and (3) support for projects aimed at the creation and establishment of regional innovation systems (i.e., cluster information).

Later on, the key priorities of knowledge, R&D and Innovation, have further been strengthened as part of 'Europe 2020', the EU's political strategy adopted in response to the economic crisis and aimed at supporting competitiveness, social cohesion and regional development during the period of 2014–20. As a tool to foster innovation on the regional level, the European Commission encouraged the design of national and regional research and innovation strategies for Smart Specialization (the so-called S3 strategies) as a means to deliver a more targeted structural fund support and a strategic and integrated approach to harness the potential for smart growth and the knowledge economy in all regions. The concept of Smart Specialization has been promoted by the Communication 'Regional Policy contributing to smart growth in Europe 2020' and, although initially designed not as a regional policy, Smart Specialization soon became a key pillar for the Cohesion Policy of the European Commission for the period 2014–20 (see Fitjar, Benneworth and Asheim 2019).

The promotion of innovation has been a central feature in the Cohesion Policy programmes for 2014–20, which has devoted about €65 billion to innovation and research. Some 30 percent of the total Cohesion Policy allocations has been invested in innovation in the wider sense. In the next section, we provide a broad overview of the evolution of budget allocation on competitiveness policy, in general and on innovation promotion, in particular.

## The Evolution of Budget Provisions

From 2000 onwards, cohesion and innovation policy has turned into a common economic strategy. The set of place-based policy and the funds available in the EU became the instruments to boost innovation and competitiveness in European regions. In this light, the Lisbon Agenda effectively set the dial towards productivity and economic growth by fostering R&D investments particularly within the scope of the European Regional Development Fund.

Looking at numbers on the evolution of budget provisions, one can observe a dramatic increase of funds dedicated to research and development. Compared to the 2000–2006 period, the level of financial resources dedicated to innovation and R&D more than tripled between 2007 and 2013. EU Cohesion Policy instruments provided some €83 billion almost 24 percent of the total budget) to R&D and innovation. Out of this total, €50.5 billion went to R&D and innovation in the narrow sense,[2] €8.4 billion to entrepreneurship – including €5.2 billion for advanced support services for firms and €3.2 billion to support self-employment and business start-ups – €13.2 billion to innovative information and communication technologies in order to foster the demand side of ICT and €14.5 billion to education and human capital development.

For the 2014–20 period, stricter rules for priority spending targets were introduced (thematic concentration) leading to a greater focus by the European Research and Development Fund (ERDF) on a few key objectives: research and innovation, information and communication technology, SME competitiveness, and the low carbon economy.[3] A total of €64 billion has been dedicated to the thematic objective research and innovation in the narrow sense, which has become the first item financed with the ERDF funds (around 21.5 percent of the total). In this particular case, R&D and innovation activities have also been supported under other thematic objectives, particularly SME competitiveness, low-carbon economy, information and communication technologies (the second priority in terms of budget allocation) and Educational and Vocational Training.

In order to provide a broad idea about the evolution of cohesion spending, we can look at the weight of R&D and innovation promotion in a selection of Member States over the five programming periods by only considering the objective 1 regions – for example, the less developed regions that are the largest beneficiaries of Cohesion Policy (see Table 9.1). Before going in depth with the analysis, however, it is important to clarify that a comparison across the different programming periods is not straightforward, given both the quality of data available and the fact that budget items evolved over time. Additionally, as transparency further decreases with the number of funds increased, only ERDF funds and cohesion funds have been taken into consideration. Hence, our estimates should be seen only as a general indication of the direction of Cohesion Policy.

In the first three programming periods, even if there were some attempts to strengthen enterprise involvement in technology development as well as to encourage technology transfer from the most developed to the least developed regions, the percentages of fund allocation to R&D and innovation remained under 10 percent in all cases thus testifying to the limited importance given to the topic. As previously highlighted, the emphasis during the periods of 1989–93 and 1994–99 was heavily on infrastructure and capacity enhancement with a lesser concern paid to the innovation performance of regions.

As can be seen in the Table 9.1, the increasing trend of R&D allocation has been dramatic, considering that we are only accounting for the thematic objective research and innovation without taking into account the funds allocated to R&D and innovation under other thematic objectives. In the sample considered, the research and innovation allocation as percentage of total ERDF and cohesion funds move from 3.4 percent in the period 1988–93 to 15.7 percent in the last seven years of the programming period. The increase has impacted all countries under analysis, as they move from a percentage weight of RTD of 3.4 percent to almost 35 percent between 2014 and 2020. However, the performance of Ireland is especially noteworthy as the ERDF funds have been used intensely to invest in research and innovation in the country. In contrast, Greece even with an increase of around seven percentage points remains the country with the lowest percentage share of funds dedicated to R&D and innovation.

It is important to underline that the increase in R&D expenditure in the periphery regions has not yielded the expected broader socioeconomic benefits. Indeed, the net effect on economic growth and employment and, consequently, on the reduction of divergence has been modest. Under-

**Table 9.1.** R&D and innovation allocation in former objective 1 regions, percentage of total ERDF and cohesion funds.

| Objective 1 Regions | 1988–1993 %RTD | 1993–1999 %RTD | 2000–2006 %RDT | 2007–2013 %RDT | 2014–2020 %RDT |
|---|---|---|---|---|---|
| Spain | 2.2 | 4.8 | 7.7 | 14.7 | 14.2 |
| Italy | 4.9 | 6.4 | n.a.[i] | 21.4 | 14.5 |
| Ireland | 3.7 | 5.6 | n.a. | 39.8 | 35.1 |
| Greece | 0.9 | 4.2 | n.a. | 7.1 | 7.8 |
| Portugal | 4.5 | 6.9 | n.a. | 30.2 | 17.02 |

Source: European Commission, author's elaboration. Data from https://cohesiondata.ec.europa.eu/ and https://ec.europa.eu/regional_policy/en/policy/evaluations/data-for-research/.

*Notes:* Objective 1 regions in the framework of Cohesion Policy in the programming period of 2000–2006 became less developed and transition regions in the framework of the EU Cohesion Policy 2014–20.

i. n.a. = not available.

standing the reasons behind this low impact is out of the scope of this analysis. However, the limitedness of socioeconomic benefits may be explained with the so-called European Paradox, that is, the difficultly that peripheral regions face in transforming both basic and applied research into innovation due to: (a) deficits in the supply of suitably skilled human capital, (b) industry specialization and sectoral composition which make them less prone to knowledge-intensive innovative activity, (c) lack of human capital mainly because of the loss of valuable highly qualified personnel and (d) deficient institutional settings (Rodríguez-Pose 2015).

The thematic concentration in structural funds spending has enormous implications, not only for periphery regions of EU-15 but also for Central and Eastern European (CEE) countries, the latter of which have in the last years been experiencing a strong pattern of regional polarization (Kühn 2015). Understanding to what extent the thematic concentration has also affected the eastern regions adds some interesting elements into our analysis.

In the Cohesion Policy programming period of 2007–13, the EU-12 earmarked an average 13 percent of the total allocations for R&D and innovation with large differences between countries (Table 9.2). Bulgaria allocated the smallest share of the ERDF funds on R&D (4 percent), while Slovenia and Estonia earmarked the largest share (25 percent). In the 2014–20 program-

**Table 9.2.** R&D and innovation allocation in less developed regions of CEE countries, percentage of total ERDF and cohesion funds.

| Objective 1 Regions | 2007–2013 %RDT | 2014–2020 %RDT |
|---|---|---|
| Bulgaria | 4% | 7% |
| Poland | 14% | 11% |
| Hungary | 6% | 10% |
| Czech Republic | 17% | 17% |
| Slovenia | 19% | 11% |
| Slovakia | 11% | 17% |
| Lithuania | 14% | 10% |
| Latvia | 15% | 11% |
| Estonia | 19% | 25% |
| Romania | 6% | 4% |
| Croatia | n.a. | 8% |

Source: European Commission, author's elaboration. Data from https://cohesiondata.ec.europa.eu/.

ming period, the average percentage decreased by 2 percentage points.[4] Unlike Table 9.1, we are not able to evaluate the evolution of thematic allocation from 1988 onwards in Table 9.2. A comparison between the two tables makes it nonetheless clear that the allocation on innovation-related objective has been similar between the two groups of countries, that is, the CEEs and Southern countries, with the exception of Ireland.

The data confirm that eastern countries entered into an already defined regional policy framework with little room for manoeuvre for national authorities. The framework was already limited by the compulsory thematic concentration and by the introduction of ex-ante conditionality linked to the requirement of approval of Smart Specialization Strategies (S3). In addition, most of the CEE countries have been highly dependent on Cohesion Policy interventions. It has been an important source of funding (between 2.5 percent and 3 percent of GDP in the CEE and between 0.1 percent and 2 percent in the EU-15) in the last programming periods – that is, respectively, 2007–13 and 2014–20 – and shaped the thematic allocation of domestic regional policy funding due to the co-financing mechanism (Ferry and McMaster 2013).

The little progress towards economic convergence of the CEE countries since accession calls the effectiveness of the European regional policy framework into question. Despite the consequences of the economic crisis of 2008, the impacts of Cohesion Policy are evenly distributed neither across nor within the member states (Crescenzi and Giua 2018). The asymmetry can be further exacerbated in the case of regional aid to research and development where the impact depends not only on a range of socioeconomic and institutional factors but primarily on the manner in which technology is absorbed, as well as on the stock of human capital, knowledge diffusion, the presence of knowledge networks and spillovers, and the accessibility of the region – all the features that typically discriminate between core and periphery regions.

In addition, the focus on innovation and R&D after both the Lisbon Agenda and especially the adoption of the 'Europe 2020' strategy leads to the fact that prosperous regions have obtained a higher share of public contributions than before. This fact has further exacerbated the trade-off between convergence and competition policies in Europe (Lawton-Smith 2003).

The different development trajectories between a club of more dynamic regions and the rest of Europe (included in this group are the less developed regions and the so-called middle-income ones) are becoming more and more evident, pointing to a problem that calls for a reconsideration of the kind of place-based policy that the European Union will need in the future (Iammarino et al. 2017).

## Conclusions

The creation of the common market in Europe has produced several opportunities for the member states. However, a greater market can also generate unbalanced paths of development benefiting the more dynamic and innovative regions while damaging the marginal and rural ones. This problem has been clear ever since the very outset of the common market project and Cohesion Policy has been set up precisely to avoid growth of disparities across regions, thus preserving social cohesion in the whole of Europe. Yet, Cohesion Policy has been only partially successful. The challenge has grown further, with the inclusion of the EEC economies after the recent enlargement process. Less developed regions in both the old and new member states are now stuck in the middle-income trap.

We have analysed the evolution of Cohesion Policy as a means to raise income of less developed regions along with its evolution from a redistributive policy based on capital investment towards a competitiveness policy based on innovation and research. The evolution has followed a major transition from the industrial accumulation model to the knowledge-based one. We have illustrated the most relevant differences between the models. Accordingly, we have argued that Cohesion Policy and the mode of general public policy accumulation model have a clearer theoretical framework and greater potential to be effective especially with regard to helping regions to escape the middle-income gap. Crucially, this is not the case in the knowledge economy: the EEC-economies are developing increasingly uneven with growing disparities within their borders and Cohesion Policy seems to be ineffective in narrowing these differences.

How Cohesion Policies might be modified to address the 'post-industrial environment' of the knowledge economy? Some suggestions have been put forward recently (such as, Iammarino et al. 2017) to improve the capacity of the Cohesion Policy to tailor to the specific characteristics of the territories, in terms of stage of development, tangible and intangible endowments, technological capabilities and human resources. However, at this stage, we lack a clear theoretical understanding about how to spur knowledge-driven economic development in less developed regions.

We can provide some suggestions along the following lines. First, create the conditions to benefit from agglomeration economies also in peripheral regions; here an important role can be played by middle-size cities. In fact, a major problem of peripheral regions is the brain drain process which is increasingly affecting these territories. This results in a progressive lack of those (human) resources which are necessary to make Cohesion Policy itself successful. A case in point is represented by technology and innovation policies – that is, the regional Smart Specialization Strategies – where the loss of high-skilled workers is a major obstacle for these policies to be effective.

Second, increase the connections among more developed regions and less developed regions (as for instance by imposing/encouraging) these types of partnership in European-funded programmes. This is important because while it is hard to avoid the concentration of innovation and knowledge production in the more dynamic regions, public policies can help the circulation of innovation extending its benefits also in the peripheral regions.

Further, exploring the opportunities to reform the governance of Cohesion Policy by relying on the current experience of the Next Generation EU (NGEU). In fact, the governance of the latter differs significantly from that of the Structural Funds, mostly because of its structure of *milestones* and *targets* implemented in the Recovery and Resilience Facility, which is very likely to increase the effectiveness, and possibly the impact, of the investment funded from the NGEU. In the context of an ex-post evaluation of the NGEU funds there will be a significant scope for a comparison between the two systems of governance in order to explore the extent to which successful mechanisms implemented in the management of the NGEU and the Recovery and Resilience Facility can be implemented in Cohesion Policy.

In the absence of a significant increase in the performance of Cohesion Policy especially in peripheral regions, we are likely to observe increasing tensions within the EEC economies, even in the presence of a vital rate of growth. Escaping the middle-income gap in the EEC regions is going to be more complicated than it was for their peers in the 1970s and 1980s. Compensation policies and welfare support are needed in order to mitigate the negative effects of unbalanced patterns of growth, but Cohesion Policy will also need to reinvent itself to restore a sustainable balance of the regional development process.

**Andrea Filippetti** is Research Director at the Institute of Studies on Regional and Federal Systems, National Research Council (CNR) in Rome, Italy; Adjunct Professor at the Luiss University of Rome; and Visiting Fellow at the Centre for Political Economy and Institutional Studies of the University of London, Birkbeck. His research interests focus on the geography of innovation, knowledge economy and technological change, science and innovation policy, and regional institutions and decentralization.

**Raffaele Spallone** is a postdoc researcher at the Institute of Studies on Regional and Federal Systems, National Research Council (CNR) in Rome, Italy. He is currently serving as economic advisor at the cabinet office of the Italian Ministry of the economic development. His research interests focus on cohesion policy, state aid and competition, and industrial economics and innovation policies.

## Notes

1. Our two labels – industrial and knowledge economy are quite general. It becomes clear in as our chapter develops that these models are employed as ideal types of the ways in which economy is organized around the capital in the former and around knowledge in the latter. Surely, there were relevant differences between the industrial models adopted in the United States and in Western Europe. Furthermore, one could observe important differences across countries even within Europe, as it was the case with the Italian model of industrial districts and, later on, with the rise of flexible specialization, which would replace mass production (Piore and Sabel 1984). However, these differences do not affect our main line of reasoning, that is, the role of capital and knowledge respectively in the industrial mode of production and in the knowledge economy.
2. Including €10.2 billion to RTD infrastructure and centres of competence, €9 billion for investment in firms directly linked to research, €5.8 for R&TD activities in research centres, €5.7 billion for assistance to R&TD particularly in SMEs, €5.6 billion for technology transfer and the improvement of cooperation of networks, €4.9 billion in developing human potential in the field of research and innovation and €2.6 billion to assistance to SMEs for the promotion of environmentally-friendly products and production processes.
3. The ERDF resources allocated to these priorities depend on the category of region. In more developed regions, at least 80 percent of funds must focus on at least two of these priorities. In transition regions, the focus is for 60 percent of the funds, and 50 percent in less developed regions.
4. As already highlighted before, it is not possible to fully compare the changes and relative shares of thematic objectives between the two programming periods because the programmes do not sufficiently correspond with each other.

## References

Archibugi, Daniele, and Andrea Filippetti. 2015a. 'Knowledge as Global Public Good'. In *Handbook of Global Science, Technology and Innovation*, edited by Daniele Archibugi and Andrea Filippetti, 483–507. Oxford: Wiley-Blackwell.

———, eds. 2015b. *Handbook of Global Science, Technology and Innovation*. Oxford: Wiley-Blackwell.

Avdikos, Vasilis, and Anastassios Chardas. 2016. 'European Union Cohesion Policy Post 2014: More (Place-Based and Conditional) Growth – Less Redistribution and Cohesion'. *Territory, Politics, Governance* 4(1): 97–117. https://doi.org/10.1080/21622671.2014.992460.

Barca, Fabrizio, Philip McCann and Andrés Rodríguez-Pose. 2012. 'The Case for Regional Development Intervention: Place-Based versus Place-Neutral Approaches'. *Journal of Regional Science* 52: 134–52. https://doi.org/10.1111/j.1467-9787.2011.00756.x.

Barnier, Michel. 2003. 'EU Cohesion Policy: Challenges and Responses'. *Intereconomics* 38(6): 305–10.
Barry, Frank. 2003. 'Economic Integration and Convergence Processes in the EU Cohesion Countries'. *Journal of Common Market Studies* 41(5): 897–921.
Bathelt, Harald, Andres Malmberg and Peter Maskell. 2004. 'Clusters and Knowledge: Local Buzz, Global Pipelines and the Process of Knowledge Creation'. *Progress in Human Geography* 28(1): 31–56. https://doi.org/10.1191/0309132504ph469oa.
Bazo-Lopez, Enrique, Esther Vayà, Antonio J. Mora and Jordi Surinach. 1999. 'Regional Economic Dynamics and Convergence in the European Union'. *The Annals of Regional Science* 33: 343–70.
Bell, Martin, and Keith Pavitt. 1993. 'Technological Accumulation and Industrial Growth: Contrasts between Developed and Developing Countries'. *Industrial and Corporate Change* 2(2): 157–210.
Bertamino, F., Raffaello Bronzini, Marco de Maggio and Davide Revelli. 2016. 'Regional Policies for Innovation: The Case of Technology Districts in Italy'. *Regional Studies* 51(2): 1–14. https://doi.org/10.1080/00343404.2016.1255321.
Boldrin Michele, Fabio Casanova, Jörn-Steffen Pischke and Diego Puga. 2001. 'Inequality and Convergence in Europe's Regions: Reconsidering European Regional Policies'. *Economic Policy* 16(32): 207–53.
Brenner, Neil. 2004. *New State Spaces: Urban Governance and the Rescaling of Statehood*. New York: Oxford University Press.
Brunazzo, Marco. 2016. 'The History and Evolution of Cohesion Policy'. In *Handbook on Cohesion Policy in the EU*, edited by Simona Piattoni and Laura Polvari, 17–35. Cheltenham: Edward Elgar.
Canaleta, Carlos Gil, Pedro Pascual and Manuel Rapún. 2004. 'Regional Economic Disparities and Decentralization'. *Urban Studies* 41(1): 71–94. https://doi.org/10.1080/0042098032000155696.
Cantwell, John, and Simoa Iammarino. 2003. *Multinational Enterprises and European Regional Systems of Innovation*. London: Routledge.
Cappelen, Aadne, Jan Fagerberg and Bart Verspagen. 1999. 'Lack of Regional Convergence'. In *The Economic Challenge for Europe: Adapting to Innovation Based Growth*, edited by Jan Fagerberg, Paolo Guerrieri and Bart Verspagen, 130–48. Cheltenham: Edward Elgar.
Chatterji, A., E. Glaeser, W. Kerr. 2014. Clusters of Entrepreneurship and Innovation. *Innovation Policy and the Economy* 14: 129–66. https://doi.org/10.1086/674023.
Clark, John, Christopher Freeman and Luc Soete. 1984. 'Long Waves, Inventions, and Innovations'. In *Long Waves in the World Economy*, edited by Christopher Freeman, 63–77. London: Frances Pinter.
Cooke, Phillip. 2001. 'Regional Innovation System, Clusters, and the Knowledge Economy'. *Industrial and Corporate Change* 10(4): 945–74.
Corrado, Carol, Jonathan Haskel, Massimiliano Iommi and Cecilia Jona-Lasinio. 2012. 'Intangible Capital and Growth in Advanced Economies: Measurement and Comparative Results'. CEPR Discussion Paper No. DP9061. http://ssrn.com/abstract=2153512.
Cowan, Robin, Paul A. David and Dominique Foray. 2000. 'The Explicit Economics of Knowledge: Codification and Tacitness'. *Industrial and Corporate Change* 9(2): 212–53.

Crescenzi, Riccardo, Guido de Blasio and Mara Giua. 2018. 'Cohesion Policy Incentives for Collaborative Industrial Research: Evaluation of a Smart Specialisation Forerunner Programme'. *Regional Studies* 54(19): 1–13. https://doi.org/10.1080/00343404.2018.1502422.

Crescenzi, Riccardo, Andrea Filippetti and Simona Iammarino. 2017. 'Academic Inventors: Collaboration and Proximity with Industry'. *Journal of Technology Transfer* 42: 730–62. https://doi.org/10.1007/s10961-016-9550-z.

Crescenzi, Riccardo, and Mara Giua. 2018. 'One or Many Cohesion Policies of the European Union? On the Diverging Impacts of Cohesion Policy across Member States'. SERC Discussion Papers No. 0230, Spatial Economics Research Centre, LSE.

den Hertog, P., R. Bilderbeek and S. Maltha. 1997. 'Intangibles: The Soft Side of Innovation'. *Futures* 29: 33–45. https://doi.org/10.1016/S0016-3287(96)00064-X.

Díez-Minguela, Alfonso, Rafael González-Val, Julio Martinez-Galarraga, M. Teresa Sanchis and Daniel A. Tirado. 2017. 'The Long-Term Relationship between Economic Development and Regional Inequality: South-West Europe, 1860–2010'. EHES Working Papers in Economic History, no. 119. http://www.ehes.org/EHES_119.pdf.

Djellal, Faridah, and Faïz Gallouj. 2001. 'Innovation in Services'. *Science and Public Policy* 28: 57–67.

Drometer, Marcus, and Chang Woon Nam. 2018. 'R&D and Innovation Support in the Evolving EU Cohesion Policy'. *CESifo Forum* 19(1): 37–42.

Ederveen, Sjef, Henri L. F. de Groot and Richard Nahuis. 2006. 'Fertile Soil for Structural Funds? A Panel Data Analysis of the Conditional Effectiveness of European Cohesion Policy'. *Kyklos* 59(1): 17–42. https://doi.org/10.1111/j.1467-6435.2006.00318.x.

Ertur, Cem, Julie Le Gallo and Catherine Baumont. 2006. 'The European Regional Convergence Process, 1980–1995: Do Spatial Regimes and Spatial Dependence Matter?' *International Regional Science Review* 29: 3–34. https://doi.org/10.1177/0160017605279453.

European Council. 2000. Presidency Conclusions – Lisbon European Council, 23 and 24 March. http://www.consilium.europa.eu/ uedocs/cms_Data/docs/pressData/en/ec/00100-r1.en0.htm, 8.11.2006.

European Union (Official Journal of). 2012. Consolidated version of the Treaty on the Functioning of the European Union Part Three – Union Policies and Internal Actions Title XVIII – Economic, Social and Territorial Cohesion, Article 174.

Felice, Emanuele, and Amedeo Lepore. 2017. 'State Intervention and Economic Growth in Southern Italy: The Rise and Fall of the "Cassa per il Mezzogiorno" (1950–1986)'. *Business History* 59(3): 319–41. https://doi.org/10.1080/00076791.2016.1174214.

Ferry, Martin, and Irene McMaster. 2013. 'Cohesion Policy and the Evolution of Regional Policy in Central and Eastern Europe'. *Europe-Asia Studies* 65(8): 1502–28. https://doi.org/10.1080/09668136.2013.832969.

Filippetti, Andrea, and Daniele Archibugi. 2011. 'Innovation in Times of Crisis: National System of Innovation, Structure and Demand'. *Research Policy* 40: 179–92.

Filippetti, Andrea, and Frederick Guy. 2020. 'Labor Market Regulation, the Diversity of Knowledge and Skill, and National Innovation Performance'. *Research Policy* 49(1): 1–14. https://doi.org/10.1016/j.respol.2019.103867.

Filippetti, Andrea, and A. Peyrache. 2013. 'Is the Convergence Party Over? Labour Productivity and the Technology Gap in Europe'. *JCMS: Journal of Common Market Studies* 51: 1006–22.

Filippetti, Andrea, and Agnese Sacchi. 2016. 'Decentralization and Economic Growth Reconsidered: The role of Regional Authority'. *Environmental Planning C: Government and Policy* 34(8): 1793–1824. https://doi.org/10.1177/0263774X16642230.

Fitjar, Rune Dahl, Paul Benneworth and Bjørn Terje Asheim. 2019. 'Towards Regional Responsible Research and Innovation? Integrating RRI and RIS3 in European Innovation Policy'. *Science and Public Policy* 46(5): 772–83, https://doi.org/10.1093/scipol/scz029.

Florida, Richard. 2005. *The Flight of the Creative Class: The New Global Competition for Talent*. New York: HarperCollins.

Florida, Richard, Patrick Adler and Charlotta Mellander. 2016. 'The City as Innovation Machine'. *Regional Studies* 51(1): 1–11. https://doi.org/10.1080/00343404.2016.1255324.

Freeman, Chris. 1998. 'The Economics of Technical Change: Trade, Growth and Technical Change'. *Cambridge Journal of Economics* 18(5): 16–54.

Gallouj, Faïz, and Marina Savona. 2009. 'Innovation in Services. A Review of the Debate and a Research Agenda'. *Journal of Evolutionary Economics* 19: 149–72.

Glaeser, Edward. 2011. *Triumph of the City: How Urban Spaces Make Us Human*. Stuttgart: Pan Macmillan.

Iammarino, Simona, and Philip McCann. 2006. 'The Structure and Evolution of Industrial Clusters: Transactions, Technology and Knowledge Spillovers'. *Research Policy* 35(7): 1018–36. https://doi.org/10.1016/j.respol.2006.05.004.

———. 2013. *Multinationals and Economic Geography: Location, Technology and Innovation*. Cheltenham: Edward Elgar Publishing.

Iammarino, Simona, Andrés Rodriguez-Pose and Michael Storper. 2017. 'Why Regional Development Matters for Europe's Economic Future'. Working Papers – European Commission. https://ec.europa.eu/commission/index_en.

Kogut, Bruce, and Udo Zander. 1993. 'Knowledge of the Firm and the Evolutionary Theory of the Multinational Corporation'. *Journal of International Business Studies* 24: 625–45.

Kühn, Manfred. 2015. 'Peripheralization: Theoretical Concepts Explaining Socio-Spatial Inequalities'. *European Planning Studies* 23(2): 367–78. https://doi.org/10.1080/09654313.2013.862518.

Lawton-Smith, Helen. 2003. 'Knowledge Organizations and Local Economic Development: The Case of Oxford and Grenoble'. *Regional Studies* 37(9): 899–909, https://doi.org/10.1080/0034340032000143904.

Leonardi, Robert. 1995a. *Convergence, Cohesion and Integration in the European Union*. London: Macmillan.

———. 1995b. 'Regional Development in Italy: Social Capital and the Mezzogiorno'. *Oxford Review of Economic Policy* 11(2): 165–79.

———. 2006. 'Cohesion in the European Union'. *Regional Studies* 40(2): 155–66.

Lerner, Josh. 2009. *Boulevard of Broken Dreams: Why Public Efforts to Boost Entrepreneurship and Venture Capital Have Failed – And What to Do About It*. New York: Princeton University Press.

Lorenzen, Mark, and Ram Mudambi. 2012. 'Clusters, Connectivity and Catch-up: Bollywood and Bangalore in the Global Economy'. *Journal of Economic Geography* 13(3): 501–34. https://doi.org/10.1093/jeg/lbs017.

Marshall, A. 1920. *Principles of Economics*, 8th ed. London, Macmillan.

Martin, Ron, and Peter Sunley. 2003. 'Deconstructing Clusters: Chaotic Concept or Policy Panacea?' *Journal of Economic Geography* 3(1): 5–35. https://doi.org/10.1093/jeg/3.1.5.

Martinez-Vazquez, Jorge, Santiago Lago-Peñas and Agnese Sacchi. 2016. 'The Impact of Fiscal Decentralization: A Survey'. *Journal of Economic Surveys* 31: 1095–1129. https://doi.org/10.1111/joes.12182.

McCann, Philip. 2008. 'Globalization and Economic Geography: The World is Curved, not Flat'. *Cambridge Journal Regions Economy and Society* 1(3): 351–70. https://doi.org/10.1093/cjres/rsn002.

Mendez, Carlos. 2013. 'The Post-2013 Reform of EU Cohesion Policy and The Place-Based Narrative'. *Journal of European Public Policy* 20(5): 639–59. https://doi.org/10.1080/13501763.2012.736733.

Michelis, Nicola de, and Philippe Monfort. 2008. 'Some Reflections Concerning GDP, Regional Convergence and European Cohesion Policy'. *Regional Science Policy & Practice* 1: 15–22. https://doi.org/10.1111/j.1757-7802.2008.00004.x.

Myrdal, Gunnar. 1957. *Economic Theory and Underdeveloped Regions*. London: Duckworth.

Neven, Damien, and Claudine Goyette. 1995. 'Regional Convergence in the European Community'. *Journal of Common Market Studies* 33: 47–65. https://doi.org/10.1111/j.1468-5965.1995.tb00516.x.

Petraglia, Carmelo, and Gaetano Vecchione. 2020. 'Long-Run Pro-Trade Effects of Diasporas: Evidence on Italian Regions'. *Spatial Economic Analysis* 16(1): 47–72.

Piore, Michael J., and Charles F. Sabel. 1984. *The Second Industrial Divide: Possibilities for Prosperity*. New York: Basic Books.

Rodríguez-Pose, Andrés. 2015. 'Leveraging Research, Science and Innovation to Strengthen Social and Regional Cohesion'. Policy Paper by the Research, Innovation, and Science Policy Experts (RISE), European Commission, http://doi.org/10.2777/237283.

Rodriguez-Pose, Andrés, and Riccardo Crescenzi. 2008a. 'Research and Development, Spillovers, Innovation Systems, and the Genesis of Regional Growth in Europe'. *Regional Studies* 42(1): 51–67. https://doi.org/10.1080/00343400701654186.

———. 2008b. 'Mountains in a Flat World: Why Proximity Still Matters for the Location of Economic Activity'. *Cambridge Journal of Regions, Economy and Society* 1(3): 371–88.

Rosenberg, Nathan. 1974. 'Science, Invention and Economic Growth'. *The Economic Journal* 84(3): 90–108. https://doi.org/10.2307/2230485.

Sassen, Saskia. 1991. *The Global City*. New York: Princeton University Press.

Saxenian, Annalee. 1996. *Regional Advantage: Industrial Adaptation in Silicon Valley and Route 128*. Cambridge, MA: Harvard University Press.

Storper, Michael. 1995. 'The Resurgence of Regional Economies, Ten Years Later the Region as a Nexus of Untraded Interdependencies'. *European Urban and Regional Studies* 2(3): 191–221. https://doi.org/10.1177/096977649500200301.

———. 2013. *Keys to the City: How Economics, Institutions, Social Interaction, and Politics Shape Development*. New York: Princeton University Press.

Storper, Michael, and Anthony J. Venables. 2004. 'Buzz: Face-to-face Contact and the Urban Economy'. *Journal of Economy and Geography* 4(4): 351–70. https://doi.org/10.1093/jnlecg/lbh027.

Teece, David, and Gary P. Pisano. 1994. 'The Dynamic Capabilities of Firms: An Introduction'. *Industrial and Corporate Change* 3(3): 537–55. https://doi.org/10.1093/icc/3.3.537-a.

Tola, Alessio, and Maria Vittoria Contini. 2015. 'From the Diffusion of Innovation to Tech Parks, Business Incubators as a Model of Economic Development: The Case of "Sardegna Ricerche"'. *Procedia – Social and Behavioral Sciences* 176: 494–503. https://doi.org/10.1016/j.sbspro.2015.01.502.

Van den Broek Jos, Roel Rutten and Paul S. Benneworth. 2018. 'Innovation and SMEs in Interreg Policy: Too Early to Move beyond Bike Lanes? Policy Studies'. *Policy Studies* 41(1): 1–22. https://doi.org/10.1080/01442872.2018.1539225.

von Hippel, Eric. 1994. '"Sticky Information" and the Locus of Problem Solving: Implications for Innovation'. *Management Science* 40(4): 429–39.

# Conclusion and Outlook

Uwe Müller

The introduction as well as the chapters in this volume were completed when the effects of the Covid crisis were not yet foreseeable. Even at this point in time (July 2023), all we know is that the Covid crisis has caused a period of economic stagnation in all European countries. National measures such as mobility restrictions were reinforced on a global level by border closures and disrupted supply chains. They caused companies, for example in the automotive industry, to limit production or even stop it for a certain period of time. As a result, significant economic downturns happened in 2020, which continue to affect growth prospects in Europe today. Nevertheless, fiscal policy measures have kept the labour market largely stable. The expansionary monetary policy of the European Central Bank during the Covid crisis also helped to decrease risks. However, three years after the outbreak of the pandemic, important macroeconomic variables are still below pre-crisis levels in some countries, indicating scarring effects. The medium- and long-term structural consequences of the Covid crisis are therefore not yet clear. This unclarity also applies to the question of the differences in the consequences in the individual regions of Europe.

Recently, an interim balance of the effects of the Covid pandemic and forecasts for emerging from the crisis for the eight East-Central and South-Eastern European economies that joined the European Union between 2004 and 2013 have been published (Mátyás 2022). The interim balance as well as the forecasts appear relatively optimistic. They are based on analyses of almost all sectors of the economy as well as on comparisons with the effects of the 2008/12 financial crisis. Although the question 'Can the eight economies avoid the so-called middle income trap?' is supposed to be the focus of the analyses (Mátyás 2022, v), the phenomenon of the middle-income trap itself is not examined. Most authors start from the view presented in the introduction to this volume: they assume that the middle-income trap is first and foremost an empiric threshold, that is, the inability of economies to approach the level of the most advanced economies. In other words, growing beyond a certain level of economic welfare is exceedingly difficult. This 'level' is measured according to neo-classical growth theory in terms of the amount of capital and labour and the development of GDP (per capita). Factors related to knowledge-based production capacities, such as human capital, investment in research, and development or number of patents, are also considered and quite critically evaluated but without mentioning their particular importance in overcoming the middle-income trap. As a consequence, most authors currently see no evidence that the convergence of the Eastern European states to the level of the Western European economies has stopped. Therefore, the authors conclude that there is no danger of a middle-income trap in the region.

However, the contributions to our book show that a mere snapshot of a growing economy does not yet allow an assessment on whether an economy can fall into a middle-income trap or not. We consider an approach predominantly based on GDP-figures to be insufficient and conclude that the analysed countries in Central and Eastern Europe need a structural change strengthening the knowledge-based sectors of industry and services. Previous attempts to initiate such a structural change in Central and Eastern Europe that are analysed in the contributions to the book as well as previous examples of successfully overcoming the middle-income trap, such as in South Korea, show that it is hardly possible to carry out such a structural change without political support. This political support should ideally be provided through an interplay of regional, national and European political institutions. Some governments, such as in Hungary and in Poland, however, have moved in the opposite direction and discredited European integration. Moreover, the economic nationalist course of these two states has so far not been very successful. The impact of the European Union is also quite ambivalent. On the one hand, institutions of the European Union support numerous activities in the fields of education as well as research and development. On the other, structures of division of labour have developed in the integrated European internal market, which assign the function of producer of raw materials, basic materials and selected industrial semi-finished goods to the less developed (and newly joined) economies of Central and Eastern Europe.

To what extent have the Covid crisis and the economic policy responses to it changed this situation? And what influence could Russia's invasion of Ukraine and the war that has continued since then have on the efforts of Central and Eastern European economies to avoid the middle-income trap?

First of all, historical experience shows that pandemics have a generally negative impact on the economy in three ways: large-scale decline in labour supply due to high death rates, low demand for investment and increased desire to save as a precautionary motive (Jordà, Singh and Taylor 2020). In the case of the Covid pandemic, death rates were relatively low and the decline in investment was only a short-term phenomenon, at least for our study area. A greater problem was in fact the increase and persistence of insecurity, the consequent reluctance to consume and the urge to save more for precautionary purposes.

Furthermore, in the case of the Covid pandemic, disrupted supply chains have played a greater role compared to previous pandemics (Meier and Pinto 2020). Globalisation and economic entanglements had already reached a much higher level in 2020 than was the case with all pandemics in history. Both the pandemic and the war in Eastern Europe have led not only to the disruption of supply chains, some of which had existed for decades, but they have also paved the way for the emergence of alternative trade relations. Overall, these processes have also provided an occasion for actors from politics and business to question many global linkages. In this situation fundamental changes in the international division of labour may occur. There is a high probability that, for political reasons and in order to strengthen reliability and speed, intra-European supply chains will gain in importance.

This situation raised the possibility that at least some manufacturing activity that European multinationals had previously outsourced to Asian countries (typically China) could be brought (back) to Europe. As a consequence of 'reshoring', the Central and Eastern European members of the EU as well as other South-Eastern European economies that are not (yet) members could take over functions in the division of labour that were previously filled by non-European economies. They could also benefit from the (re)relocation of strategically important industries to Europe.

Whether the Central and Eastern European countries can take advantage of this situation to escape the middle-income trap depends, first, on the extent of the re-spatialisation of supply chains. However, the majority of the Central and Eastern European EU-members are already major suppliers of Western European firms (Pellényi 2020). So, it does seem likely that they will be the targets for such reshoring activities.

Even more important, however, is the problem of the capacities of the Central and Eastern European economies to bring high-income knowledge-based industries into the new European division of labour. In this respect, there are some reasons to be sceptical about the large-scale relocation of industrial jobs to the region. Pellényi (2020) discusses the advantages and disadvantages of the Central and Eastern European countries of the EU (Czechia, Hungary, Poland, Romania, Slovakia and Slovenia) as participants in global supply chains. Their membership in the European Union, geographical closeness to the main European markets and producers, relatively skilled workforce and light regulation make them attractive as assembly locations. Low innovation activity and relative lack of high-skilled workers, however, prevent the region from upgrading into higher value-added activities. Darvas (2020) also casts doubt on the extent to which the Central and Eastern European countries can benefit from reshoring. Using international trade data during the first wave of the pandemic, Darvas (2020) finds that trade volumes declined even more between members of the Eastern part of Europe and Western Europe than they did between Western Europe and China. He also raises the issues of quality upgrading as well as lack of necessary innovation activities and higher education spending that could facilitate this in Central and Eastern Europe.

Third, in a survey of leading companies, Maqui and Morris (2021) report that those firms for which supply chains are important do not foresee major changes in their current arrangements. In particular, the majority of the survey companies did not plan on making their supply chains more diverse or more localized. All these indicate that major reshoring is unlikely to benefit the Eastern countries in the EU, at least in the short run. So, it remains to be seen whether changes in the geopolitical situation will alter the situation.

Last but not least, the political and economic framework conditions also play an important role. Mátyás (2022) presents the conditions for a recovery after the Covid pandemic rather positively. Unfortunately, however, these conditions have deteriorated in at least two respects. First, Russia's invasion of Ukraine and the EU's subsequent political and economic responses have led to an energy crisis and high inflation. This results in the risk of a deep recession. Furthermore, the need to push ahead with industrial structural change (including an ecological turnaround) is taking a back seat among actors from business and politics.

Second, Mátyás is mistaken in one essential point. He assumes 'that the natural rate of interest remains low for the foreseeable future' (Mátyás 2022, 39). After the financial crisis of 2008/9, the zero-interest rate policy of the European Central Bank (ECB) made this assumption plausible. However, this policy led to pent-up inflation. Since July 2022, the ECB raised key interest rates several times and will most likely continue to do so. This measure is intended to curb significant increase in inflation. In addition to the increase in energy and food prices as a result of the war in Ukraine, the historically low-key interest rates now take their revenge.

Under these conditions, it is still completely unclear whether the Central and Eastern European states can avoid the middle-income trap. A look back at the economic history of the region shows various attempts to catch up with Western European income levels. Time and again, internal structural deficits and global economic conditions have prevented successful convergence to varying degrees in each case. This applies to the phase of the formation of mostly still agrarian economies after the First World War under the conditions of economic nationalism and the Great Depression. Between 1945 and 1990, it was above all the economic order of 'socialist planned economy' that initially facilitated a surge in industrialisation. But since 1970 at the latest, it was incapable of transforming the Fordist growth model into a more innovation-driven growth strategy. After 1990, a market economy order could be installed. This new economic order and the admission to the European Union created good conditions for a catching-up process. However, it was initially the transformation shock of the 1990s and the focus on individual FDIs that made it difficult for the economies as a whole to catch up in the medium term (Berend 1996).

The contributions to this book have highlighted various opportunities as well as some problems of overcoming the middle-income trap in Central and Eastern Europe. In view of the new global political situation, it has become even more important for the whole 'Western world' that the Central and Eastern European economies can continue their trend towards convergence.

**Uwe Müller** earned a PhD in economic history at the Humboldt University in Berlin. He has done research and taught at the Humboldt University, the European University Viadrina in Frankfurt (Oder) and the Saarland University in Saarbrücken. Since 2011 he is a senior researcher at the GWZO Leibniz Institute for the History and Culture of Eastern Europe. His research interests include the economic history of Eastern Europe from the middle of the nineteenth century to the present day with a special focus on the integration of this region in the European and world economy.

### References

Berend, Ivan T. 1996. *Central and Eastern Europe, 1944–1993: Detour from the Periphery to the Periphery*. Cambridge: Cambridge University Press.
Darvas, Zsolt. 2020. 'Relocating Production from China to Central Europe? Not so fast!' *Eastern Focus* 4: 16–23.
Jordà, Òscar, Sanjay R. Singh and Alan M. Taylor. 2020. *Longer-Run Economic Consequences of Pandemics* (NBER Working Papers No. 26934). Cambridge, MA: National Bureau of Economic Research.
Maqui, Eduardo, and Richard Morris. 2021. *The Long-Term Effects of the Pandemic: Insights from a Survey of Leading Companies*. Vol. 8 Economic Bulletin Boxes. Frankfurt am Main: European Central Bank.
Mátyás, László. 2022. *Emerging European Economies after the Pandemic: Stuck in the Middle-Income Trap?* Cham: Springer.

Meier, Matthias, and Eugenio Pinto. 2020. *Covid-19 Supply Chain Disruptions* (CRC TR 224 Discussion Paper Series No. crctr224_2020_239). Bonn: University of Bonn and University of Mannheim.

Pellényi, Gabor. 2020. *The Role of Central and Eastern Europe in Global Value Chains: Evidence from Occupation-Level Employment Data* (Economic Brief No. 062). Brussels: European Commission.

# Index

11 Bit Studios, 49

AGH University in Krakow, 130–31, 134
agriculture, 41–42, 46–47, 193
Albania, 57, 83, 183
Arrighi, Giovanni, 204, 208–9, 218
Asia, 2, 13, 98–106, 183, 214, 283. *See also* East Asia
Asseco, 123–24, 129–36
association agreement, 2
austerity, 237–38
Austria, 110, 182, 196, 198–99
autarky, 10, 170–73
Azerbaijan, 181–82

Baltic states, 1, 11, 14, 97, 100–101, 174–77, 183, 191, 194–95, 215, 236–38
bankruptcy enforcement, 68, 76–82, 85
Belarus, 182, 194
Belgium, 4, 196
Big Bang, 56–57, 232–33, 238. *See also* shock therapy
BPH Bank, 132
brain drain, 26, 143, 161, 273
Bratislava, 263
Brexit, 3, 26, 231, 240–41, 249–50
Brussels, 241–42, 246
Budapest, 187, 248–49
Budapest-Gyor corridor, 187, 193
Bulgaria, 9, 16, 57, 63, 83, 97–98, 100, 107, 110, 143–44, 148–162, 183, 191, 193–94, 232–36, 238, 242, 271

call centre, 154
capital, 2, 7, 10, 12, 26, 30, 35, 48, 61–64, 75, 97, 110–112, 122–27, 131–32, 135–36, 145, 147, 156, 170, 173, 180, 193, 196, 206, 208, 210–211, 218–21, 223, 225, 255, 257–63, 265, 273, 282
stock, 2, 33, 35, 47, 104

capitalism, 101, 103, 122–23, 127–28, 136, 204–205, 208–209, 256–58
catch-up growth, 171, 174–77, 180, 199–200, 237–41
catching-up, 1, 4, 9–10, 25, 28, 42, 174, 177, 204–19, 222–25, 285
CD Project Group, 48
China, 3, 100–103, 283–84
cohesion, 17, 48, 213, 234, 237, 240, 267
policy, 2, 14, 204–14, 216–17, 224–25, 254–57, 266–69, 271–75
Cold War, 28, 235, 243
Comarch, 123–24, 129–32, 134–37
COMECON, 185. *See also* Council for Mutual Economic Assistance (CMEA)
Commonwealth of Independent States (CIS), 58, 63, 83–84, 85n5, 182–185
communism, 1, 10, 26–28, 30, 33, 36, 40, 47, 231
COMP Rzeszów, 129, 133
company(ies), 46, 103, 113–14, 116–17, 126, 150, 155, 158–59, 262. *See also* Asseco; Comarch
competition, 13, 40, 56, 85, 186, 214, 225
enhancing/enhancement policy(ies), 55, 64–68, 76–83
global, 123, 208–09, 214, 223
international, 3
office policy(ies), 82
policy, 137, 272
transition policy(ies), 77, 79–80
convergence, 2–3, 26, 83, 104, 169–71, 173–74, 177, 180, 186, 198, 200, 208–11, 212–13, 215–16, 218–20, 225, 236, 266–67, 272, 282, 284–85
cooperation, 131, 241–43, 247–49, 267
Copenhagen criteria, 232–36, 248
corporate financial discipline, 63–66, 75–76, 84–85

Council for Mutual Economic Assistance (CMEA), 10. *See also* COMECON
Covid, 231, 248, 281–85. *See also* pandemic
Cracow University of Technology, 134
Croatia, 106, 111–12, 191, 194
Cyprus, 25, 234
Czechia (Czech Republic), 6–7, 10, 12, 15, 25, 28–29, 42–43, 47, 57, 87n29, 102–103, 106–107, 110, 122, 125–26, 128, 180–82, 188, 194, 196, 199, 204, 208, 212, 215, 218, 220–24, 232, 234, 238, 242, 244, 283
Czechoslovakia, 12, 33–35, 42, 47, 87n29, 103

democracy, 1, 13, 15, 17, 97, 240, 242, 247–49
democratization, 240
Denmark, 196
dependency
approach, 208–11, 225
economic, 206
ESIF, 205–06, 208–210, 216, 218, 222, 224–25
FDI, 205–06, 216, 218, 222–25
region's, 205
theory, 208
dependent market economy (DME), 13, 99, 103–105, 113, 117–18, 122–23, 127, 205, 208, 225
development
model, 2, 98, 122
strategy, 15, 108
direct sales, 11, 58, 64, 72–73, 84, 89n56

East Asia, 11, 98, 101–102, 200, 204
Eastern Bloc, 11, 27, 172, 185–86
Eastward enlargement, 233–35, 243
economic
complexity index, 183–85
development, 3, 9, 11, 17, 25–27, 37, 42, 61–62, 143, 169, 196, 254, 256–60, 264, 273
geography, 6, 174, 193–94, 267
nationalism, 1–2, 15, 208, 218, 225, 240, 282, 285
stagnation, 170–71, 177, 200, 281

economy
centrally planned, 28, 32, 40, 170–73, 185–87
command, 27–28, 169, 171, 182, 193, 199
dual, 13–15, 206, 221–24
knowledge, 14–16, 112, 161, 257–66, 268, 273–74
socialist planned, 1, 10, 285
education, 2, 4, 16, 27, 40–46, 58, 114, 128, 144, 146–148, 151, 157, 161, 177, 179, 198, 200, 219–20, 223, 265, 269, 282, 284
Eichengreen, Barry, 7, 177
enterprise investors, 131–32
enterprise restructuring, 55–57, 62–65, 69–74, 82
Estonia, 7, 25, 57, 106, 182, 188, 194, 196, 199, 233, 236–39, 242, 271
EU funds, 109, 133, 137, 205, 248
euro area, 14, 84. *See also* eurozone
Europe
South-Eastern, 11, 234, 281, 283
Southern, 3, 5, 14, 204, 209, 212, 215, 232, 234–38, 243–44, 248
Western, 1–2, 8, 11, 13, 16–17, 41, 84, 131, 152, 162–63, 170–71, 174, 182–83, 195–96, 204–06, 215, 224, 232, 246, 255, 259, 282, 284
European
Bank for Reconstruction and Development (EBRD), 13, 54–56, 63–64, 68, 82, 98–100, 104–105, 199
Central Bank (ECB), 236, 281, 284
Commission (EC), 25, 177, 204, 232, 234, 237, 248, 256, 266, 268
Semester, 101, 248
Structural and Investment Fund (ESIF), 205–206, 208, 210–16, 220–21, 223–24
Union (EU), 2–6, 8–11, 13–15, 17, 25–26, 42, 47, 55–56, 60, 84, 97, 100, 104, 107–108, 110–11, 133–34, 137, 143, 145–46, 148, 170, 174, 182–83, 199, 204–05, 208–12, 214, 216, 218–19, 223–25, 231–44, 246–50, 254–56,

263, 266–68, 272, 274, 281–83, 284, 285
Europeanization, 232, 236
European Structural and Investment Funds (ESIF), 205–206, 208–210, 216, 218, 222, 224–25
eurozone, 174, 194, 199, 215, 231–32, 235–38, 241, 243–47, 249. *See also* euro area
export, 7, 10, 13, 97–101, 103–107, 109, 111, 113–114, 117–18, 171, 177, 180, 182–83, 186, 198, 205, 212, 214, 248
export-led growth, 97, 99, 174, 208, 243
extended workbenches, 13–14, 30, 48

Fidesz, 216, 221–22, 247
financial crisis. *See* global financial crisis
Finland, 106, 196
First World War, 285
foreign company, 13, 48
foreign direct investment (FDI), 2–3, 7–12, 17, 26, 55, 58, 63, 100, 107–108, 170, 173, 180, 182, 205–06, 216, 218, 222–25, 237–38, 240, 243, 254, 285. *See also* growth model: FDI
Formula Systems, 130, 132
France, 4, 7, 27, 103, 106, 113, 131, 198, 235, 243, 248, 249, 263

Germany, 4, 7, 27, 30, 42–43, 101, 103–04, 106–107, 110, 113–14, 128–29, 131, 144, 150–52, 158–59, 182, 196, 199, 212, 215, 233–35, 237, 241–44, 246–49
global
  economic crisis, 204, 208–09, 211–16, 221–23
  financial crisis, 171, 174, 177
  value chains, 102, 135, 169–170, 181–82, 199–200, 212, 216, 222–23
globalization, 3, 209, 240, 257, 283
governance, 57, 60–61, 63, 69, 72, 74–75, 82, 84–85, 104, 129, 169, 206, 210, 215–16, 225, 232, 236, 241, 242, 274
gradual approach, 56–57
Great Britain, 196, 235
Great depression, 285

Greece, 3, 5, 102, 196, 212, 234–35, 244, 270
Gross Domestic Product (GDP), 4, 7, 9–10, 12, 25–29, 33–39, 42, 46–48, 56–59, 62, 68–70, 72, 75–78, 81–83, 99–105, 110, 128, 171, 174–79, 183, 215, 232–33, 235–36, 267, 272, 282
growth model, 12, 54, 170–71, 180, 199–200, 237, 285
  FDI, 4, 6–7, 10, 12–13, 99, 117
  export-led, 99, 103, 174

health, 16, 105, 116–117, 219–20
higher education, 146, 150–51, 284
human capital, 2, 4, 8–9, 12, 15–17, 27, 37, 40–43, 46–47, 60, 171, 198, 219–220, 264–66, 269–272, 282
Hungary, 2, 4, 10, 12, 15, 25, 28–29, 33–35, 42–43, 47, 57, 103, 106–107, 110, 122, 126, 128, 172, 182, 187–88, 199, 204, 208, 212, 215–16, 218, 220–24, 232, 234, 236, 238, 240, 242, 244, 246–49, 282–83

Iceland, 196
International Computers Limited (ICL), 133
illiberalism, 15, 17, 247–49
immobility, 150, 160
implementation gap, 56, 83, 156
import substitution, 1
industrialization, 1, 15, 36, 122–23, 134–35, 237, 257–58, 285
  de-, 10, 30, 35–36, 100–103, 187
  re-, 206, 209, 212, 214–15
industry, 4, 10, 13, 15, 26, 30, 32–33, 35, 40–42, 47–49, 107–108, 112, 123, 125–26, 134–35, 137, 170, 193, 235, 258–60, 263–65, 271, 282
  automotive, 99, 106, 109, 112–18, 258, 260, 281
  IT, 13, 123, 125, 134–35, 137, 138n1
inequality, 3, 41, 48, 58, 169–171, 173, 180, 194–200, 210, 254–55, 263, 266
infrastructure, 2, 14, 18n1, 30, 104, 109–111, 134–137, 146, 152, 162,

193–194, 210, 212–15, 219–20, 224, 256, 261, 270
innovation, 4, 6, 8, 10, 16, 49, 60, 98, 105, 107, 109–111, 118, 122–26, 128–29, 133–37, 145, 150, 152, 156, 162, 172, 194, 212, 215–16, 220, 222–24, 255, 258–59, 261, 264–74, 284–85
institutional development, 54–59, 72, 75–78, 82–85, 179–80, 205
institutions, 13, 26–27, 54, 57–62, 66, 68–70, 72, 74–75, 77, 82–85, 98, 111, 128, 130, 136, 161–62, 169–74, 199, 216, 224, 240, 261, 282
integration, 2–3, 10, 15, 18, 26, 72–75, 111, 123–124, 126, 133, 135, 137, 143, 156, 169, 172–173, 177, 180–81, 183, 187, 199, 204–206, 208–210, 212, 215–216, 218–19, 224, 234, 249, 254, 256, 282
intentional unpredictability, 146
internationalisation, 154, 169–70, 173–174, 177, 180–83, 186
Ireland, 106, 110–111, 196, 212, 214, 234–35, 237, 270
Italy, 5, 27, 103, 196, 199, 212–15, 234–35, 254–55, 260, 265

Kazakhstan, 182–183
knowledge-based
 accumulation model, 273
 companies, 6, 30
 economy(ies), 15, 40, 171, 267
 industries, XI, 14, 16, 283
 production, 40, 48, 282
Krakow, 131–34
Kraków Technology Park, 134
Kresy (Eastern Territories of Poland), 41–42, 46–47

Latin America, 11, 56, 98, 100–103
Latvia, 25, 57, 100, 106, 111, 189, 195–196, 233, 236, 238–39, 242
Lee, Jong-Wha, 8–9, 42–43
liberal, 56, 58, 75, 105, 107, 112, 127, 209, 240–43, 246, 248–49. *See also* neoliberalism

liberalization
 price, 68, 81, 85
 wage, 11, 67–68, 76–81, 85, 87n31
life course decisions, 143–144, 148–51, 160
Lithuania, 25, 57, 182, 189, 194–95, 233, 234, 236, 238–39, 242

macroregion, 36–39
Malta, 25, 234
management and employee's ownership (MEBO), 64, 72–73, 84, 88n40
manufacturing sector, 11, 108, 122, 258–61
middle-income trap, 4, 6–12, 14–17, 48–49, 57, 97, 100, 102–105, 108, 110–13, 117–18, 122–23, 162, 170–71, 177, 179, 196, 198, 200, 204–05, 208, 212, 220, 223–25, 237–38, 255–57, 273, 281–85
migration, 46, 143–47, 150, 155–56, 161, 169–70, 180–82, 193, 235, 241–42, 246, 249
 emigration, 6, 16, 26, 106, 143–49, 152, 156–58, 160–62
 return, 16, 143–47, 157 (*see also* returnee)
mobility, 40–41, 144, 150, 157–58, 160, 219, 263, 265, 281
modernization, 27, 40–41, 171, 208–209, 219–20, 236, 259
Moldova, 57, 115
monopoly, 68, 82–83, 171
Montenegro, 100
multinational corporations (MNCs), 15, 99–100, 107–108, 112–13, 122, 127, 130, 136, 180, 205, 210, 214, 218, 220–21, 224, 263, 283

NASDAQ (National Association of Securities Dealers Automated Quotations Stock Market), 130
neoliberalism, 11–12, 97, 105, 111, 122, 137, 209, 212, 214, 216, 218, 221, 225
North Macedonia, 83
NUTS1 (Nomenclature of Territorial Units for Statistics), 36, 37

NUTS2 (Nomenclature of Territorial Units for Statistics), 36, 39

operational Restructure, 64–66, 70–71, 73–75, 84–85
Oracle, 109–110, 126, 133–34
Orbán, Viktor, 242–44, 246–47
ordoliberal, 244
Organization for Economic Co-operation and Development (OECD), 102, 104, 128, 170, 195, 199

pandemic, 25, 48, 281–82. *See also* Covid
patents, 4–6, 60, 262, 282
path dependence, 181
periphery, 231, 238–244, 248–49
  core-, 205–206, 208–210, 224–25, 246–48
  rural, 3
  semi-, 204, 209, 212, 216
Piątkowski, Marcin, 7, 27, 40–43
Playway, 49
Poland, 2, 4, 6–7, 9–13, 15, 25–43, 46–49, 57, 97, 100, 106–107, 110, 112, 122, 124–32, 134–35, 137, 146–47, 160, 172, 182, 190, 196, 204, 208, 212, 215–16, 220–24, 233–34, 236, 238, 240, 242–44, 246–49, 282–83
populism, 17, 56, 179, 240, 246
Portugal, 3, 5, 114, 212–13, 234, 255
privatization, 11, 30, 57–58, 62–66, 72–74, 84, 87n28, 87nn39–40, 127.
productivity, 3–4, 8, 10–11, 13, 32, 36–37, 39–42, 48, 55–62, 66, 69, 72–78, 81–85, 88n43, 98, 100–101, 104–08, 173, 177, 179–80, 186–88
Prokom, 130–31, 133, 136
pro-market policies/reforms, 55–56, 58–59, 83, 170

regional
  disparities, 12, 171, 179, 194, 196, 199, 255
  income, 27, 170
  inequality, 3, 266
  policy, 266, 268, 272

regionalization, 257, 264
remittance, 146, 181–83
research and development (R&D), 8, 106–113, 118, 128, 133–34, 137, 223–24, 261, 267–72
returnee, 143–57, 161–62
Romania, 12–13, 15–16, 57, 63, 83, 97, 99–100, 103–113, 117–18, 183, 232, 234–38, 242, 244, 283
Russia (Russian Federation), 42, 98, 104, 181–183, 194, 247–48, 282, 284
Rzeszów, 133, 138n5

Schröder, Gerhard, 233, 235, 243
second-class members, 14, 236
Second World War, 10, 29, 47, 243, 257, 259–60
Serbia, 104
shock therapy, 56, 86n11, 285. *See also* Big Bang
Slovakia (Slovak Republic), 10, 14, 25, 47, 57, 100, 107, 114, 122, 125, 128, 181–82, 189, 191, 196–99, 204, 208, 212, 215, 218, 220, 222–24, 233, 236, 238–39, 242, 244, 283
Slovenia, 6, 14, 25, 57, 97, 103, 190–91, 193, 196, 232, 236–38, 271, 283
smart specialization S3, 268, 272–73
social
  capital, 147, 156, 196
  costs, 56, 58, 62, 66, 193–94
  disparities, 12
  inequality, 3, 41
  Insurance Institution (ZUS), 130, 136
  networks, 147, 155–59, 262
  policy, 7, 10, 17
  return, 145
socialism, 10, 28, 193–94, 249
Softbank, 130, 133
South Korea, 11, 98, 102–103, 282
sovereignty, 137, 238, 240, 242
Spain, 5, 114, 195, 212, 234, 255
standard of living, 1–2, 28, 171, 193–94, 199, 238–39
start-up, 111, 152–153, 255, 269
state aid, 107–111
state ownership, 26, 62, 64, 69, 84

structural change, 2–3, 10, 12, 14–15, 101, 111, 196, 282, 284
structural policy(-ies), 4
supervision, 174, 242
supply chains, 4, 100, 114, 183, 248, 281, 283–85
sustainability, 143–44, 150, 157–60, 219

Taiwan, 11, 98
target earners, 144–45
tax privileges, 16
Techland, 48–49
technological backwardness, 173
Telekomunikacja Polska SA (TPSA), 130–32
transformation, 1, 3–4, 6, 11–12, 25, 27, 30, 35, 41, 47, 97, 99, 103, 105, 128, 143, 173, 187, 198, 231, 236, 238, 241, 249, 258, 263, 267–68, 285
transition, 2, 30, 40, 47–48, 54–64, 66–72, 75–85, 101, 112, 146–47, 152, 160, 169–74, 180, 182, 186–87, 193–94, 196, 199, 232–33, 237, 256–58, 266, 273
    policies, 54–59, 62–64, 68–69, 72–85
transnational social networks, 156–60

Trump, Donald, 3
Turkmenistan, 57, 181–82

Ukraine, 11, 57, 100–101, 181–82, 247–48, 282, 284
unemployment, 3, 25, 55, 58, 66, 174, 196, 215, 232–33, 266
United States, 3, 8, 98, 158, 259

value chains, 10, 102, 122–25, 129, 133–35, 169–70, 174, 177, 181–86, 196, 199, 212, 216, 222–23
Visegrád, 1, 11, 13, 97, 103, 126, 128, 237, 241, 246–47
vouchers, 11, 64–66, 70, 84

Warsaw, 36, 39, 248, 255, 263
Warsaw Stock Exchange, 13, 127–28, 131–32, 136
Washington consensus, 240
Weimar Triangle, 243
World Bank, 13, 54, 97–98, 100–102
World Trade Organization, 170

Yugoslavia, 172–73, 183

Milton Keynes UK
Ingram Content Group UK Ltd.
UKHW020603161123
432678UK00002B/28